MW01114369

Democracies in Development

Politics and Reform in Latin America

J. Mark Payne
Daniel Zovatto G.
Fernando Carrillo Flórez
Andrés Allamand Zavala

Published by the Inter-American Development Bank and the
International Institute for Democracy and Electoral Assistance
Distributed by The Johns Hopkins University Press

Washington, D.C.
2002

Produced by the IDB Publications Section.

To order this book, contact:
IDB Bookstore
Tel: 1-877-PUBS IDB/(202) 623-1753
Fax: (202) 623-1709
E-mail: idb-books@iadb.org
www.iadb.org/pub

The views and opinions expressed in this publication are those of the authors and do not necessarily reflect the official positions of the Inter-American Development Bank or the International Institute for Democracy and Electoral Assistance.

Cataloging-in-Publication data provided by the
Inter-American Development Bank
Felipe Herrera Library

Payne, J. Mark.

Democracies in development : politics and reform in Latin America / J. Mark Payne ...
[et al.].

    p. cm. Includes bibliographical references.
    ISBN: 1931003319

    1. Elections—Latin America. 2. Latin America—Politics and government—1980- .
3. Latin America—Economic conditions—1982- . I. Inter-American Development Bank.
II. International Institute for Democracy and Electoral Assistance. III. Title.

324 P397--dc21   2002108625

Acknowledgments

Assembling this book depended on contributions from many different individuals. The project was made possible by the solid support of Edmundo Jarquín, Chief of the State, Governance and Civil Society Division of the IDB's Sustainable Development Department, and Bengt Säve-Söderbergh, Secretary-General of the International Institute for Democracy and Electoral Assistance. Without their strong commitment to this project in intellectual and logistical terms, it could not have gone forward.

The theoretical and conceptual discussions in each chapter drew on insights and analysis in the published works of numerous scholars. Given their studies' particular importance to the conceptual frameworks and theoretical ideas presented in various chapters, we owe special gratitude to the following scholars: Manuel Alcántara, John Carey, Fernando Cepeda, Rodolfo Cerdas, Larry Diamond, Scott Mainwaring, Dieter Nohlen, Pippa Norris, Guillermo O'Donnell, Marc F. Plattner, Juan Rial, Dani Rodrik, Andreas Schedler, Timothy R. Scully, Amartya Kumar Sen and Matthew Soberg Shugart.

We also thank Manuel Alcántara, Humberto de la Calle, Fernando Cepeda, Flavia Freidenberg, Dieter Nohlen, Guillermo O'Donnell, Juan Rial, Daniel Sabsay and Michael Shifter for the valuable comments they provided on various chapters.

We are also grateful for contributions made by the following experts in assembling and checking the information on institutional rules and structures for particular countries: Laura Velásquez, Delia Matilde Ferreira Rubio and Daniel Sabsay (Argentina); René Mayorga (Bolivia); David Fleischer and Torquato Jardim (Brazil); Rolando Franco, Pedro Ignacio Mujica B. and Juan Ignacio García (Chile); Gabriel de Vega and Augusto Hernández Becerra (Colombia); Rubén Hernández (Costa Rica); José Ángel Aquino (Dominican Republic); Medardo Oleas (Ecuador); Francisco Bertrand and Félix Ulloa (El Salvador); José M. Serna de la Garza (Mexico); Rosa Marina Zelaya (Nicaragua); Ermitas Pérez (Panama); Jorge Silvero Salgueiro (Paraguay); Ximena Zavala and Jorge Valladares (Peru); Liliana Cella and Juan Rial (Uruguay); Mercedes de Freitas and José Enrique Molina (Venezuela); and Ronny Rodríguez (Central American countries).

We are also indebted to Marcelo Varela and Ileana Aguilar at International IDEA and Stephanie Hogan, Claudio Galan, Sean Reagan and Elisa Vannini at the IDB for their valuable research assistance.

Foreword

Recent efforts by the countries of Eastern Europe and the developing world to invigorate the functioning of markets and find a niche in an increasingly global economy have highlighted the indispensable role played by state-supported institutions. Sustainable and equitable development clearly requires confidence and predictability in the legal system and public policy; a sound regulatory framework; the protection of property rights; ongoing investment in the skills and health of the labor force and in economic infrastructure; transparent, honest and efficient government; and effective mechanisms for social and environmental protection and poverty alleviation.

Establishing these market-support institutions in turn requires consolidating democracy. Well-entrenched political freedoms and civil rights, effective and respected representative institutions, and independent and impartial judicial institutions are essential to creating the broader institutional framework needed to promote savings, investment and steady economic expansion.

Over the past 25 years, democratic freedoms and competitive electoral processes have taken hold as never before in Latin America and the Caribbean. This trend has brought invaluable benefits in terms of protecting human rights and providing opportunities for citizens to organize and become more involved in public decision-making. However, the ongoing struggle of the region's democracies to establish legitimate representative institutions, put in place more participatory and consensual decision-making processes, consolidate the rule of law, and control corruption has underscored the long-term and difficult nature of building democracy.

This book examines how different rules and institutional features of democratic systems affect their functioning as well as prospects for their consolidation. It systematically reviews and analyzes Latin America's experience with democratic reform over the past two decades in order to identify prevailing trends and to glean some tentative and contingent lessons about the types of reforms that may or may not hold promise for strengthening democracy. This book will stimulate debate about the possible paths for reform available to enhance democracy and, in the process, continue to promote the well being of citizens in the region.

Enrique V. Iglesias
President
Inter-American Development Bank

Bengt Säve-Söderbergh
Secretary-General
International IDEA

Contents

Introduction

The past two decades in Latin America witnessed the departure of authoritarian regimes in country after country. Today, democracy has failed to take hold in only one country in the region—Cuba. Given Latin America's turbulent political history, the spread of democracy is an extraordinary development that has brought tremendous benefits to citizens, including the guarantee of fundamental political freedoms, civil liberties and human rights.

As the new millennium begins, however, the celebration of universal democracy has been replaced by a more sober perspective focusing on the serious social, economic and political challenges confronting the countries of the region. Despite profound economic policy reforms along the lines of the liberal "Washington consensus," economic growth across the region over the past decade was relatively slow and remained volatile. The high levels of poverty and inequality in most countries declined little, if at all. Progress in alleviating other significant social problems such as unemployment, crime and corruption was also minimal. Despite their importance to the region's development prospects, investments to upgrade the quality and efficiency of health care, education and infrastructure were insufficient.

In light of this experience, as well as that in other developing regions, there is growing consensus that modernizing the state and consolidating the broader institutional framework at the foundation of a market-centered economy are essential to accelerate the pace of social and economic progress. But what has often been neglected in development analysis and activities is the centrality of political factors, and more specifically, the quality of democratic politics. Contrary to previous lines of thinking, the task of building a legitimate, representative and effective democratic system is not something that can be put off, or even worse subverted, along the road to development. In fact, a well-functioning democracy appears to be indispensable to strengthening institutions and implementing efficient and sustainable public policies.

Political factors are rarely considered in a systematic fashion by multilateral and bilateral agencies as they develop lending programs or in the design of particular policy reforms. There is deficient understanding of how variations in democratic political institutions affect the ability of societies to implement sound and sustainable development policies. In keeping with this relative neglect of politics, there has been little examination of the frequent and sometimes far-reaching changes in the rules of democratic politics that have taken place in the region over the past two decades. This collective oversight is even more notable when contrasted with the intense study and debate over the economic reforms adopted during the period.

However, a growing recognition of the importance of democratic political institutions as ends in themselves, as well as to the successful implementation of policy reforms and long-term development, has recently led to more concerted international cooperation aimed at strengthening them. The Quebec Summit of the Americas (April 2001) emphasized the importance of strengthening democracy, while the adoption of the Inter-American Democratic Charter in Lima, Peru (September 2001) affirmed respect for core democratic values as a condition for membership in hemispheric organizations.

This book aims to raise the level of attention to and understanding of the importance of politics, and more specifically of the way in which democratic politics is structured and operates, to Latin America's development potential. With respect to distinct institutional dimensions of democratic systems, the book examines the various prevailing arrangements as well as the changes that have been adopted over the past two decades. The goals are to underline the effects that different rules can have on the operation of democratic systems, identify major regional trends regarding democratic reform, and provide a preliminary assessment of these reforms in terms of their potential to enhance the governability of democratic systems in the region.

The book does not pretend to offer prescriptions or recipes regarding the types of reforms that are desirable in the region as a whole or in particular countries. Rather, its purpose is to highlight many of the key issues, provide a map of the reform options available, and contribute conceptual tools and information to the debate about democratic reform. The book is envisioned as a starting point for the examination of the topic that can be expanded and updated in the future.

Since the book aims to contribute to the debate over political reform, its structure and language are designed to be accessible and appealing to practitioners, policymakers, representatives of civil society, the media, and the development assistance community. The goal is not to break new theoretical ground or to test hypotheses. Instead, the book is novel in that it marks the first time that a common conceptual framework has been used to describe and analyze the different institutional arrangements across Latin America. Conceptual and theoretical tools brought together from the literature on democratic institutions provide the basis for reflecting on the implications for democratic governability of the institutional rules and reform trends found across the region.

The book covers 18 Latin American countries over the period that begins with the arrival of the region's "third wave" of democracy in 1978 and ends at the close of the 20th century (Table 1). The specific period examined for each country begins either in 1978 or at the point of the first reasonably free and fair democratic elections following that year. The definition of this transition point in some countries is a matter of controversy. The reason for setting such a dividing line for each country is to allow for a common conceptually-based starting point, and to ensure that the democratic reforms considered are those that were adopted in a basically democratic context. The cutoff date for the analysis of political reforms and electoral outcomes is December 31, 2000. More recent events that seem particularly relevant to the analysis are mentioned in footnotes.

The focus of the book is on the institutional arrangements and reforms at the national level. Thus, even though the period has been marked by profound political reforms at the subnational level in most countries in the region, their treatment is beyond the scope of this book.

Table 1. Transition to Democracy		
Country	**Transition year or start year of study**	**Years of democracy since start year of study**
Argentina	1983	17
Bolivia	1982	18
Brazil	1985	15
Chile	1990	10
Colombia[1]	1978	22
Costa Rica[1]	1978	22
Dominican Rep.	1978	22
Ecuador	1979	21
El Salvador	1984	16
Guatemala	1985	15
Honduras	1982	18
Mexico[2]	1982	18
Nicaragua	1990	10
Panama	1989	11
Paraguay	1989	11
Peru	1980	20
Uruguay	1985	15
Venezuela[1]	1979	21

[1] Colombia, Costa Rica and Venezuela elected their leaders through reasonably free and competitive electoral processes well before 1978, the start year of the overall study. Thus, for these countries the start year is when the first president elected during the period from 1978–2000 took office.

[2] Since Mexico underwent a long-term process of political liberalization and democratization during the period, we do not pin down a particular transition year. Rather, political institutional change in Mexico is examined beginning in 1982, the year when the first elected president of the 1978–2000 period took office.

Chapter One introduces the main theme of the book: the mechanisms through which the quality of democratic politics affects development. This chapter also highlights the particular relevance of democratic political reform to Latin America's development prospects. Chapter Two examines the level of citizen support for democracy and its component institutions in the region as a whole, as well as in individual countries. Chapter Three studies the level and evolution of electoral participation, also at both individual country and regional levels. The chapter focuses in particular on how the level of electoral participation compares with other world regions, as well as on the extent to which electoral participation trends have been effected by parallel trends in citizen confidence in democracy.

Each of the next seven chapters focuses on a different institutional dimension of presidential democracy. First, they delineate the types of possible arrangements and define the relevant concepts. Second, they discuss from a theoretical perspective the possible effects of different institutional choices on the governability of democracy. Third, they examine current arrangements in countries of the region and identify the main regional reform trends over the period of the study. The chapters conclude with a partial and preliminary assessment of the reasonableness of the reforms in relation to the theoretical ideas elaborated earlier in the chapter, as well as their apparent impact in practical terms.

Following this structure, Chapter Four focuses on the different systems used for electing the president, as well as the timing of presidential and legislative elections, the length of the president's mandate, and whether the president can be reelected. Chapter Five examines the different systems used in the region for electing legislative representatives. Chapter Six focuses on the structure and degree of institutionalization of political party systems. Chapter Seven studies two important issues related to the functioning of political parties: 1) the rules and practices relating to how parties select candidates for public office, particularly the presidency, as well as their internal leadership positions; and 2) the rules and enforcement mechanisms related to the financing of electoral campaigns and the everyday activities of political parties. Chapter Eight analyzes the constitutional rules defining the formal balance of power between the executive and legislature, as well as the extra-constitutional, partisan-based factors shaping the capabilities of the two branches. Chapter Nine examines the authority and institutional origins and designs of three of the main types of horizontal accountability agencies: supreme audit institutions, attorney general/public prosecutor office, and the office of the human rights ombudsman. Chapter Ten focuses on the variety of different mechanisms established to facilitate more direct participation of citizens in the national decision-making process.

The final chapter summarizes the major political reform trends across the region. It examines the implications of these trends for democratic governability, and identifies the key issues emerging from the analysis of this experience.

Appendix 1 features a table for each country that describes the prevailing rules and structures pertaining to the institutional dimensions considered in each chapter of the book. This provides a reference for the reader who wants to view the institutions in a particular country without having to read all of the individual tables presenting such information in each chapter.

Appendix 2 provides tables for each country regarding the level of electoral participation for each election from the beginning of the study period through the year 2000.

Appendix 3, which is contained in the CD-ROM that accompanies this book, features tables for each country that show the percentage of the vote obtained by the political parties for presidential and legislative elections, as well as the distribution of legislative seats by party.

The theoretical and conceptual components of each chapter are built in large part from a review of the significant literature on the particular institutional dimension being considered. Some of the chapters also draw on empirical information provided in such works as a starting point for analyzing prevailing institutional arrangements and the reforms that have been adopted.

The bulk of the information on institutions and reforms considered in Chapters Four through Ten is derived from extensive consultations with experts from the countries of the region, as well as from primary and secondary research carried out by the authors. This research covered the various constitutions, statutes, electoral laws, political party laws and other supplementary laws in force at different points of time during the period studied.

The information on electoral participation, as well as the votes by party for presidential and legislative elections, were drawn from the electoral management body for each country, the International Institute for Democracy and Electoral Assistance (International IDEA, 1997), the *Enciclopedia Electoral* (Nohlen, 1993), as well as other national statistical publications.

The indices and survey data on the strength of institutions, the quality of democracy, and citizen attitudes in Chapter One are derived from the Latinobarómetro, World Economic Forum (2000), Transparency International (2001), Freedom House (2001), and Kaufmann, Kraay, and Zoido-Lobatón (2001). The discussion of citizen attitudes towards democracy in Chapter Two is based mainly on the region-wide Latinobarómetro, but also on a survey carried out in a more limited group of countries by the Consorcio Ibero-americano de Empresas de Investigación de Mercado y Asesoramiento (CIMA), with coordination from the Gallup Institute of Argentina.

The effort to obtain, assimilate and ensure the accuracy of a detailed and comprehensive set of data on institutions and electoral outcomes in the region was a difficult one. Though much greater attention has been given to institutional variables in recent years, the lack of reliable information in part reflects the historic scholarly neglect of such factors. In addition, the legal source for a given set of institutional arrangements, such as mechanisms of direct democracy or audit agencies, is not necessarily the national constitution, but may be more specific laws. Given the detailed knowledge required to understand how particular institutions are structured, and how they have been reformed, local expertise is essential. The unavailability or unreliability of particular types of information—such as electoral registration or votes by party for a given election—may also reflect the relatively weak capacity, and in some cases, still limited transparency, of some national political institutions. As a consequence, even if one relies exclusively on a single official source, it is common to find conflicting information. The problem, of course, is multiplied when one is forced to rely on various sources that are secondary in nature.

The specific wording of laws is also quite different from how they are enforced or applied in practice. Constitutions and political laws are inherently ripe with ambiguity, and the entities established to interpret them vary considerably in their degree of political independence and capacity. Thus, while the rules governing a particular institutional area may be correctly described in the book, the practical implications of such rules may be mis-interpreted, given the leeway possible in their actual application. The book simplifies this problem somewhat by concerning itself with the formal and literal reading of the rules and laws. Nevertheless, it also attempts to take into account as much as possible the diver-gences between rules and their practical application.

Taken together, the various factors that affected the gathering of information for this study reiterate the importance of considering this book to be an ongoing project that will evolve based on feedback from readers and additional research and collective reflection.

CHAPTER ONE

Politics Matters for Development

As the new millennium begins, the Latin American and Caribbean region finds itself in a dramatically different position politically than a little over two decades before. Though not without faults or immune from threat, democracy is the form of government practiced throughout the region, except in Cuba. In every other country, the rules of the political game emanate mainly from democratic constitutions, and public officials are elected through competitive elections. Considering the limited reach of democracy in the mid-1970s and the region's turbulent political history, this is a remarkable development.

In the mid-1970s, leaders were selected through free, fair and competitive electoral processes in only three countries: Costa Rica, Colombia and Venezuela. But by the end of that decade, political transitions in the Dominican Republic and Ecuador marked the start of a democratic trend—later baptized the "third wave" by Samuel Huntington—throughout the region. The trend was given renewed energy and a more global breadth beginning around 1990 as a result of the surprising and relatively peaceful collapse of Communist regimes in Eastern Europe, and democratization processes in several countries in Africa and Asia.

Benefiting from the lost prestige for alternative forms of government and a friendlier global and regional context, the new democracies survived despite multiple obstacles. For instance, few of the democratizing countries had extensive prior experience in competitive politics. Many had to face the conflictive issue of widespread human rights offenses that had been committed by the previous regime; manage and subdue violent internal conflicts; or implement the terms of peace agreements in order to establish a basis for peaceful co-existence between formerly warring parties. Nearly all of the new democracies had to cope with severe economic traumas stemming from large levels of public indebtedness and the sudden cutoff of foreign capital flows to the region. Despite these inhospitable circumstances, the region's embrace of democracy held fast, surviving through instances of slippage of democratic norms and rebelliousness by the military.

The ascendance of democracy has brought invaluable benefits in terms of the protection of human rights, the scope of individual political freedoms, and the breadth of opportunities for citizen involvement in public decision-making. Whatever flaws can be found in the region's democracies, it is a tremendous advance that public officials and the government in these countries are expected to serve the citizens and to be accountable to them.

Rebuffing a widely held myth that authoritarian government was superior in stabilizing and reforming economies, the region's democracies have succeeded in implementing socially disruptive and controversial economic transformations. Fiscal prudence and monetary discipline put the brakes on decades of high inflation. More far-reaching reforms—such as those which opened protected economies to foreign trade and investment, privatized state-owned enterprises, modernized social security systems, and liberalized labor markets—were also adopted to varying degrees in many of the countries of the region. The fiscal adjustment and the adoption of profound economic reforms enabled countries to emerge from the stranglehold of debt and to return, at least temporarily, to the path of positive economic growth.

Despite these significant accomplishments, there is still reason for disappointment with respect to both the results and processes of democratic governance in the region. The liberal reforms emphasizing fiscal responsibility and market liberalization contributed to an overall average annual growth rate of 3.2 percent in Latin America in the 1990s (ECLAC, 2001).[1] However, when the increase in the region's population is factored in, this growth rate equated to an annual per capita average of 1.5 percent.[2] Coming after a period of negative growth during the 1980s, the economic advances of the 1990s brought only a small net gain over the 20-year period between 1980 and 2000 (Table 1.1).

In fact, in eight of the 18 countries in this study, the average citizen was worse off in 2000 than in 1980. While 20 years of development doubled or even tripled the average income of citizens in certain East Asian countries, it brought an average gain of only 8 percent in the average Latin American country. This poor long-term performance resulted in part from the continued volatility of the region's economies and their vulnerability to international price fluctuations and financial crises in other emerging markets. The prospects for economic gain by the region in the first two years of the 21st century are also not very promising.

The relatively slow pace of economic expansion has not been sufficient to significantly reduce the high level of poverty in the region. The Inter-American Development Bank estimates that the percentage of the poor (those living on less than $2 per day) declined only slightly from about 43 percent in 1990 to 39 percent in 1999. Persistently high income inequality, which worsened over the period, prevented economic growth from having a larger impact on reducing the rate of poverty (Székely, 2001). Without higher levels of economic growth, little hope can be offered to the estimated 220 million people of Latin America who live in poverty, or to the high percentage of people who are underemployed or unemployed.

---

[1] For the 18 countries in this study, the average was 3.7 percent.
[2] The figure was about 1.7 percent for the 18 countries in this study.

Table 1.1. Economic Growth, 1980–2000

	2000/1980 GDP per capita	Avg. annual % growth 1980–2000	1990/1980 GDP per capita	Avg. annual % growth 1980–1990	2000/1990 GDP per capita	Avg. annual % growth 1990–2000
Argentina	1.06	0.30	0.81	−2.14	1.32	2.80
Bolivia	0.95	−0.26	0.83	−1.88	1.15	1.38
Brazil	1.08	0.40	0.96	−0.41	1.13	1.22
Chile	1.78	2.92	1.15	1.38	1.55	4.48
Colombia	1.24	1.07	1.17	1.62	1.05	0.53
Costa Rica	1.13	0.59	0.94	−0.67	1.20	1.87
Dominican Rep.	1.51	2.08	1.02	0.17	1.48	4.02
Ecuador	0.88	−0.62	0.92	−0.86	0.96	−0.38
El Salvador	1.07	0.32	0.86	−1.46	1.23	2.13
Guatemala	0.98	−0.12	0.85	−1.61	1.15	1.39
Honduras	0.95	−0.25	0.92	−0.79	1.03	0.29
Mexico	1.16	0.76	0.98	−0.25	1.19	1.78
Nicaragua	0.69	−1.86	0.66	−4.10	1.04	0.43
Panama	1.22	1.01	0.93	−0.68	1.31	2.73
Paraguay	0.91	−0.47	1.00	−0.05	0.91	−0.89
Peru	0.90	−0.54	0.72	−3.30	1.25	2.30
Uruguay	1.16	0.74	0.94	−0.59	1.23	2.09
Venezuela	0.74	−1.52	0.72	−3.23	1.02	0.22
Latin American avg. (by country)	1.08	0.37	0.91	−0.95	1.18	1.66
Latin American avg. (weighted by size of economy)	1.12	0.56	0.94	−0.62	1.19	1.75
Latin American avg. (weighted by population)	1.10	0.47	0.94	−0.60	1.17	1.55
United States	1.54	2.17	1.25	2.22	1.23	2.12
France[1]	1.35	1.51	1.20	1.85	1.12	1.17
Spain[1]	1.49	2.01	1.19	1.73	1.26	2.31
Korea	3.34	6.22	2.04	7.38	1.64	5.07
Thailand	2.45	4.58	1.78	5.94	1.37	3.23
Indonesia	1.75	2.84	1.40	3.44	1.25	2.23
Singapore	2.50	4.68	1.58	4.68	1.58	4.69
China	4.97	8.35	2.09	7.67	2.37	9.03

[1] For France and Spain, the period covered by this table is 1978–98.
Sources: Figures calculated by the authors based on ECLAC (2001) for Latin America and on IMF (2001) for the other countries.

The Importance of Democratic Political Institutions to Development

When investment, employment and output did not materialize to the extent expected during Latin America's reform process, it signaled that dynamic market economies could not be created solely by changes in the macroeconomic framework. Similarly, the complex task of transforming the economies of former Communist states plainly demonstrated the importance of the fundamental institutional underpinnings to market economies. Satisfying the key requirements for development—such as sound public financial systems, competitive markets, legal predictability, property rights protection, effective investment in infrastructure, and steady advances in the skills and productivity of the workforce—depends upon broad and deep *institutional* reforms. Though the scope of the state's activities was in many cases reduced, the need for effectiveness and neutrality in the performance of its remaining functions became evident. Rules governing competition and transactions in diverse markets, including those for labor, capital, goods and services, had to be put in place at the same time that the regulatory agencies and courts required to enforce and adjudicate them had to be strengthened and made more independent. Tax systems had to be overhauled, and collection agencies strengthened. At the same time, the state had to manage the use of its available resources to ensure the efficient provision of infrastructure, as well as the delivery of equitable education and health services of reasonable quality.

However, by their very nature, these institutional reforms—referred to as "second generation" reforms by some observers[3]—are considerably more complex to implement than the typical macroeconomic measures adopted in response to the public financial crises of the 1980s and early 1990s (Naím, 1995; Graham and Naím, 1998). Raising taxes, reducing state subsidies, eliminating price controls, lowering public sector wages, and reducing trade tariffs could be accomplished in some cases by executive decree and in others by legislative approval of a single bill. On the other hand, enhancing the management of public sector institutions, creating a more independent and effective judiciary, and establishing regulatory frameworks usually involves coordination and agreement among a wide array of public institutions and societal actors, as well as a series of legislative and bureaucratic actions over a long period. In addition, realizing the benefits of institutional reform is contingent upon simultaneous changes in diverse organizations and areas of law.

Clearly, much is at stake for society in the creation of regulatory frameworks, the redesign of service delivery systems, and the restructuring of public sector institutions. Such changes inevitably entail taking on powerful interests while giving privileges to certain social groups or interests to the disadvantage of others. If the benefits of institutional change end up being overly concentrated on relatively narrow interests, then larger societal groups

---

[3] The use of the term "second generation" is a matter of controversy. Some experts disagree with the implied message that the focus on institutional reform should succeed in time or is in some sense secondary to the neo-liberal or market-oriented economic reforms. Some also object to much of the neo-liberal approach ("Washington consensus") and thus do not want to adopt a terminology that associates support for institutional reforms with endorsement of that economic policy agenda.

such as consumers, workers and entrepreneurs will suffer. For instance, administrative reforms of the public sector—like enhancing governmental transparency, controlling corruption, or establishing a professional civil service—require incumbent politicians to relinquish instruments of power and open up their conduct and decisions to more intense public scrutiny.

Thus, it is clear that *politics matter* in the process of creating, implementing and sustaining sound institutions and adopting public policies that work to the benefit of all citizens. More precisely, however, it is the *quality of democracy* that matters. Not only is the exercise of democratic political and civil rights intrinsically valuable in expanding the range of possibilities and choices open to citizens, it is also instrumentally valuable for identifying and conceptualizing citizen needs and building the policies and institutions that will most effectively address them (Sen, 1999). Thus, contrary to a line of thinking prevalent in the past, the task of building a legitimate, representative and effective democratic system is not something that can be put on hold until there is an adequate level of development. Rather, given its indispensability to strengthening institutions and implementing efficient and sustainable public policies, a well-functioning democracy appears to be indispensable for equitable and sustainable development.

As Dani Rodrik (2000) points out, "market" institutions are necessarily "embedded" in a set of non-market "political" institutions. Efficient market institutions would appear to require democratic political institutions that can ensure both that fair and efficient rules are created, and that these rules are even-handedly and consistently enforced and adjudicated. Suitable and efficient market institutions must be well-adapted to the particular social, economic, historical and cultural conditions and needs of a given country. Given the impossibility of universal blueprints, the creation and maintenance of institutions depends on broad and effective citizen participation through well-developed representative institutions. In light of this reasoning, democratic political institutions can be viewed as "meta-institutions" underlying the larger universe of institutions supporting a market economy. As stated in IDB (2000), "politics exercises its greatest impact on development through its effect on institutions. The logic is clear: if politics matter for institutions, and institutions matter for development, politics must matter for development."

Thus, the effective practice of democracy would appear to be at the basis of the creation of an effective public sector and the establishment of a legal framework propitious for social and economic development. The adoption of effective, fair and sustainable public policies, the efficient and fair allocation of public resources, and the effective delivery of public services depend on the existence of representative institutions that allow the preferences and interests of citizens to be taken into account. Public policies need to be adopted and implemented in a way that fully considers the views of diverse civil society organizations, without falling capture to any particular group or narrow set of interests. This requires that citizens and civil society organizations have opportunities to express their preferences and influence decision-making, and that representative institutions have the capacity to effectively aggregate these preferences into consensual policies with broad bases of social support. Public decisions adopted in this manner will not only be efficient (responsive to the preferences and needs of society), but they also are more likely to enjoy legitimacy and social compliance, and to be sustainable over time.

Democratic Governability as the Basis for Efficient Institutions

"Democratic governability" is an elusive term, often loosely defined in practice, that has been used to attempt to capture this broad notion of a democracy that is generally seen as stable, legitimate and efficient. It has been defined narrowly by some political scientists as pertaining to the ability of the executive to work in reasonable harmony with the legislature to address the country's social and economic problems. But the concept has also been applied more broadly to the capacity of a democratic political system to absorb and process societal demands, adopt decisions in the broader public interest, and manage social conflict.

In this book the term "democratic governability" will be used to refer to *democratic systems where decisions necessary to resolve social problems can be enacted, implemented and sustained because they are arrived at through institutionalized democratic procedures that fully consider the views and interests of relevant political and social actors.*

Latin America's relatively low and volatile economic growth rate and unyielding levels of poverty and social inequality appear to be attributable in great part to continued institutional deficiencies. However, at their root, these institutional weaknesses reflect and are exacerbated by problems of democratic governability. Without changes in the rules and conduct of democracy, it is doubtful that major improvements can be made in the quality of institutions or, by extension, in the pace of economic and social progress.

Some signs of democratic dysfunction are highly visible. News headlines across the region report executives accused of wide-scale corruption or of bribing legislators to back their initiatives; election processes and results being questioned by opposition political forces and international observers; irregular or premature successions of presidential power because of mass protest, military action or impeachment; and ongoing struggles by the state to preserve the rule of law against unofficial arbiters such as drug traffickers, organized crime groups, and guerrilla or paramilitary forces. Other problems of democratic governability, while more subtle, still are significant in impeding progress toward establishing the institutional bases and political conditions for equitable and sustainable social and economic development.

Public opinion surveys and other data suggest that instead of becoming more deeply rooted and legitimized, democratic institutions are losing credibility and weakening in many countries in the region. As will be shown in Chapter Two, not only do citizens in many countries appear to have little confidence in such key political institutions as political parties, congress, the public administration and the judiciary; they also give democratic governments low marks in terms of their ability to improve living standards, reduce poverty, deliver services, control crime and reduce corruption.

Democracy with Underdeveloped Institutions

In parallel with these sentiments, the ratings of Freedom House suggest that on average political freedoms and civil liberties have tended to erode once countries have made the transition to democracy. Clearly, the advent of democracy in country after country in the region has brought marked improvements in political freedoms, due process and freedom of association when compared to the situation under the previous authoritarian regimes. Figure 1.1 shows this transition from authoritarianism to democracy through the 1980s and early 1990s, and the consequent advance in democratic values.

Figure 1.2 indicates, however, that once the transition to competitive politics has been made, the practice of such freedoms and rights diminishes over time rather than strengthening and being consolidated. The figure plots the average score in each year for political rights and civil liberties only in those countries that are already deemed to have completed the transition to democracy (see Table 1 in the Introduction). For example, in 1978 only Costa Rica, Colombia, the Dominican Republic and Venezuela are included in the regional average, while by 1985 all but four of the countries—Chile, Nicaragua, Panama and Paraguay—are included. Thus, the decline in the regional average in this figure reflects the tendency for political rights and civil liberties scores to decline once countries complete the transition to democracy.

In particular, Freedom House scores for civil liberties (measuring such institution-related factors as equality under the law, due process, and property rights) have been relatively low and have eroded over time. The 2000 average of the political rights and civil lib-

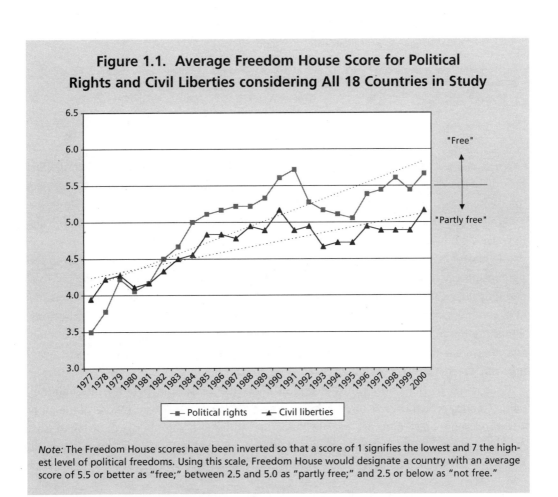

Figure 1.1. Average Freedom House Score for Political Rights and Civil Liberties considering All 18 Countries in Study

Legend: —■— Political rights   —▲— Civil liberties

Note: The Freedom House scores have been inverted so that a score of 1 signifies the lowest and 7 the highest level of political freedoms. Using this scale, Freedom House would designate a country with an average score of 5.5 or better as "free;" between 2.5 and 5.0 as "partly free;" and 2.5 or below as "not free."

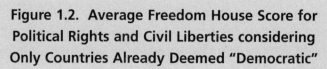

Figure 1.2. Average Freedom House Score for Political Rights and Civil Liberties considering Only Countries Already Deemed "Democratic"

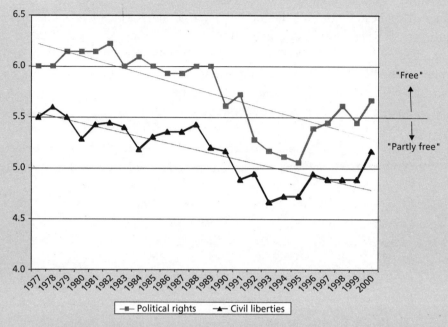

Note: The Freedom House scores have been inverted so that a score of 1 signifies the lowest and 7 the highest level of political freedoms. Using this scale, Freedom House would designate a country with an average score of 5.5 or better as "free;" between 2.5 and 5.0 as "partly free;" and 2.5 or below as "not free."

erties scores across the 18 countries in this study would place the region on average just outside of the Freedom House category of "free" and put it into the in-between category of "partly free."

The deficient performance of democratic institutions has impeded progress in putting in place the broader rubric of institutions that is the cornerstone of a competitive and dynamic market economy. Institutional weakness is tangibly evident in the many corruption scandals involving governmental officials, the deficiencies in the quality of public services, and long delays in processing cases in the court system. However, cross-national measures of government quality also point to the relative weakness of Latin American institutions. While caution must be taken in making international comparisons based on such subjective measures—since standards can vary systematically between countries—such measures can nevertheless be useful for pointing to general tendencies.

According to the Corruption Perception Index (2001) of Transparency International, Latin America is characterized by levels of corruption that greatly exceed those of the more advanced economies, and also exceed those prevailing in a sample of countries in East Asia, Central and Eastern Europe, and the Middle East and North Africa (Figure 1.3). Latin America also falls behind these same regions with respect to an indicator of the rule of law

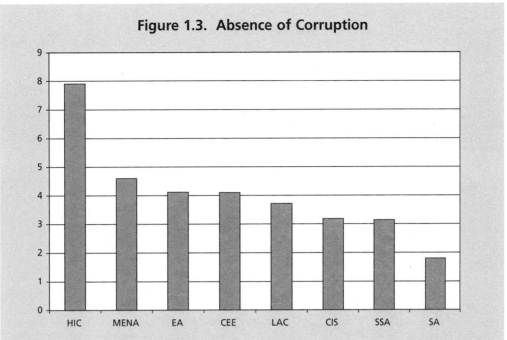

Figure 1.3. Absence of Corruption

Note: HIC = High-income countries; MENA = Middle East and North Africa; EA = East Asia; CEE = Central and Eastern Europe; LAC = the 18 Latin American countries in this study; CIS = the former Soviet Republics; SSA = Sub-Saharan Africa; SA = South Asia.
Source: Transparency International (2001).

developed by researchers at the World Bank (Figure 1.4) (Kaufmann, Kraay and Zoido-Lobatón, 2001).[4]

According to measures published by the World Economic Forum (2000) a sample of countries from the Latin American region also lags behind a sample of the high-income countries as well as Central and Eastern Europe and East Asia with respect to the independence of the civil service and the independence and integrity of the judiciary (Figures 1.5 and 1.6).

By contrast, the advances over the past two decades in the region as a whole with respect to democratic freedoms are reflected in Figure 1.7, which compares the average of the scores for Latin American countries for political rights and civil liberties with averages for other regions. Despite the fact that such rights (particularly civil liberties) have not been consolidated in many Latin American countries, the region ties for second place with Central and Eastern Europe. The region's average score, nevertheless, places it in the category of "partly free," just below the score that would be needed for it to be regarded as "free" according to the Freedom House criterion.

---

[4] The index value is an aggregate of numerous indicators available from a variety of different sources. The individual measures are based on polls of experts who rate countries (on a global or regional basis) and on cross-country surveys of firms or citizens carried out by international and nongovernmental organizations. The aggregate indicators for each dimension were estimated by means of a statistical procedure (unobserved components model) that expresses the available measures for each country as a linear function of the unobserved common component of governance, plus a disturbance term capturing perception errors and/or sampling variation in each indicator. See Kaufmann, Kraay and Zoido-Lobatón (1999a and 1999b).

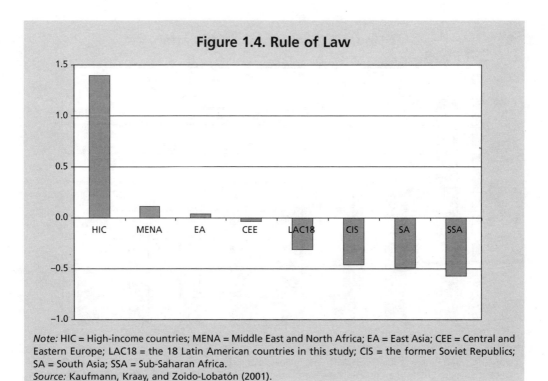

Figure 1.4. Rule of Law

Note: HIC = High-income countries; MENA = Middle East and North Africa; EA = East Asia; CEE = Central and Eastern Europe; LAC18 = the 18 Latin American countries in this study; CIS = the former Soviet Republics; SA = South Asia; SSA = Sub-Saharan Africa.
Source: Kaufmann, Kraay, and Zoido-Lobatón (2001).

Thus, if problems of democratic governability are responsible in large part for the region's institutional deficiencies and mediocre development performance, then it is critical to identify their causes and to work on overcoming them.

Variations in Presidentialism Affect Democratic Performance

During the 1970s and 1980s, a great deal of the academic discussion about the reasons for previous collapses of democratic systems centered on the type of regime that was prevalent in the region (Linz and Stepan, 1978; Linz, 1990; Di Palma, 1990; Linz and Valenzuela, 1994). Some argued that presidentialism, with its popularly elected head of government and fixed terms of office, contributed to problems of governability that could have been avoided, or at least managed better, in a parliamentary system. With separate bases of legitimacy and a pre-determined election calendar for the president and legislators, critics contended that presidential regimes were more vulnerable to policy stalemate between the executive and legislature and less flexible in coping with governance crises. Critics argued that the risk of gridlock and mounting polarization and instability was especially pronounced in the multi-party contexts typical of Latin American countries (Mainwaring, 1993; Lijphart, 1994).

By contrast, the prevailing viewpoint was that parliamentary systems, in which the government is elected by a legislative majority and must maintain this support, provide built-in incentives for cooperation between the executive and the legislature and for the forma-

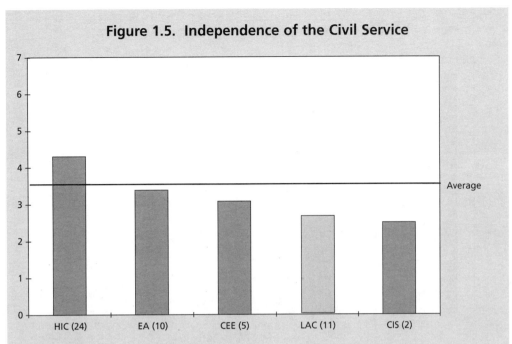

Figure 1.5. Independence of the Civil Service

Note: Based on the statement: The civil service is independent from political pressure. 1 = strongly disagree; 7 = strongly agree. The numbers in parentheses represent the number of countries included in the average. Thus, particularly in the case of the CIS countries, the average is not very representative of the region as a whole. The other regions were excluded because measures were available for only one or at most two countries. HIC = High-income countries; EA = East Asia; CEE = Central and Eastern Europe; LAC = 11 of the 18 Latin American countries examined in this study; CIS = the former Soviet Republics.
Source: World Economic Forum (2000).

tion of inter-party governing coalitions. Parties in the governing coalition gain cabinet positions and a share of power, while parties that withdraw their support risk bringing on new elections in which they may lose seats and influence. Thus, it was argued that governing coalitions tend to be more durable and inter-party bargaining and agreement is facilitated. Parliamentary systems were believed to be more flexible in coping with situations of divided or minority government. If the government loses legislative or popular support, new elections can be called, potentially producing a new balance of power in the legislature and the formation of a new government with a fresh basis of legitimacy.

Despite the prevailing scholarly pessimism about the prospects for stable presidential democracy in Latin America, none of the new democracies formally adopted a fully parliamentary or semi-presidential form of government. However, constitutions in a few countries have incorporated semi-presidential or semi-parliamentary mechanisms, and in some instances such mechanisms have been used in practice. Moreover, the issue of changing to either a parliamentary or semi-presidential system remains alive in at least a couple of countries in the region.

Fortunately, the pessimistic scholarly assessment of presidentialism was not completely borne out by the region's democratic experience over the past two decades. Despite significant difficulties and occasional deviations from constitutional dictates, the democracies held on, the armed forces mostly stayed in the barracks, and successions of power were generally

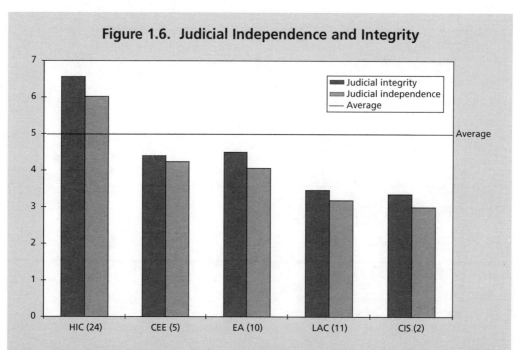

Figure 1.6. Judicial Independence and Integrity

Legend:
- Judicial integrity
- Judicial independence
- Average

Note: Based on the statement: The judiciary is independent of the government; the judiciary rarely accepts irregular payments. 1 = strongly disagree; 7 = strongly agree. The numbers in parentheses represent the number of countries included in the average. Thus, particularly in the case of the CIS countries, the average is not very representative of the region as a whole. The other regions were excluded because measures were available for only one or at most two countries. HIC = High-income countries; EA = East Asia; CEE = Central and Eastern Europe; LAC = 11 of the 18 Latin American countries in this study; CIS = the former Soviet Republics.
Source: World Economic Forum (2000).

determined by competitive elections. A more balanced appraisal of presidentialism gained attention that called into question the notion that this regime type is inevitably more prone to instability or governability problems (Shugart and Carey, 1992; Sartori, 1994; Mainwaring, 1990; Mainwaring and Shugart, 1997; Nohlen, 1998; Lanzaro, 2001; Chasquetti, 2001).

As these more agnostic observers pointed out, what may be as important to the governability and stability of democratic systems are the particular institutional variations within each type of regime and the broader social and political contexts in which they operate (Mainwaring and Shugart, 1997; Nohlen and Fernández, 1998). Notwithstanding the election of the president apart from the legislature, presidential systems are not cut out of the same mold. For one, they vary significantly in terms of the powers granted to the chief executive with respect to lawmaking and control over the tenure of members of the cabinet (see Chapter Eight). In addition, they vary in terms of the formal powers of the legislature to control and monitor the executive branch. As a consequence, in some systems the president has the potential to dominate the legislative process, while in others he may be relegated to playing a more subsidiary role. While some Latin American systems adhere to the "pure" presidentialist ideal by giving the president exclusive powers of appointment and dismissal, in others the legislature can remove cabinet officials. These differences in the allocation of constitutional power as well as the configuration of partisan forces mean that

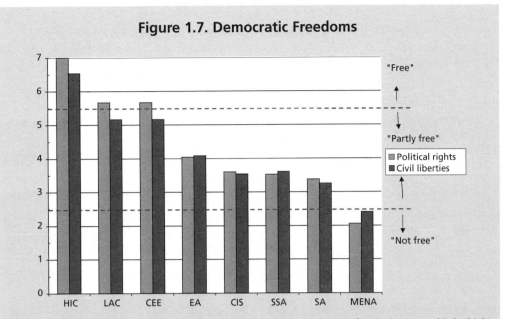

Figure 1.7. Democratic Freedoms

Note: The Freedom House scores have been inverted so that a score of 1 signifies the lowest and 7 the highest level of political freedoms. Using this scale, Freedom House would designate a country with an average score of 5.5 or better as "free;" between 2.5 and 5.0 as "partly free;" and 2.5 or below as "not free." HIC = High-income countries; LAC = the 18 Latin American countries in this study; CEE = Central and Eastern Europe; EA = East Asia; CIS = the former Soviet Republics; SSA = Sub-Saharan Africa; SA = South Asia; MENA = Middle East and North Africa.

the capacity of the legislature to monitor and control the executive and to participate fully in the policy-making process is far from uniform across presidential systems.

In addition, while public officials are in all cases elected, the nature of election procedures—such as the share of votes required for winning the presidency, the allocation of legislative seats, and the degree of concurrence between presidential and legislative elections—differs significantly across presidential systems (see Chapters Four and Five). Election rules have far-reaching effects, ranging from their impact on the popular legitimacy and authority enjoyed by public officials to their impact on the number of political parties represented in the congress and the incentives for individual legislators to respond to the needs and demands of their constituents.

Though not directly linked to the constitutional or legal make-up of the system, the structure of the political party system is another element whose varied forms can profoundly affect the dynamics of presidential democracy (see Chapter Six). The number of parties represented in the legislature, the stability of inter-party competition, and the depth of parties' roots in society can affect the quality of political representation, prospects for effective executive oversight by the congress, and the likelihood of reasonable cooperation between the executive and the legislature.

Aside from the general structure of the party system, the internal organization of political parties, including the openness and competitiveness of procedures for selecting candidates for public office and party officials, can profoundly affect the quality of political representation and leadership and the strength and credibility of representative institutions. Similarly the framework of laws and enforcement mechanisms surrounding the financing of electoral campaigns and party activities can also exert an important influence on the equity of political representation and the vulnerability of the political system to corruption (see Chapter Seven).

Included in the Madisonian constitutional design is a judicial branch whose responsibility is to interpret the constitution and enact laws, and to check and balance the authority of the executive and the legislature. However, while most presidential systems have followed this design by putting in place supreme courts or constitutional tribunals, the nature of the role of the judiciary varies greatly. The degree to which the judiciary can assert itself as an independent branch and interpret and enforce the law and the constitution in a non-partisan manner is greatly affected not only by different legal traditions and administrative structures, but also by the rules governing the nomination, selection, tenure and dismissal of judges.

Aside from the checks and balances implicit in the existence of the three main branches, presidential systems have developed additional appointed branches to monitor and control the elected branches. Examples are supreme audit institutions, attorney general and public prosecutor offices, and ombudsman offices (see Chapter Nine). Depending on how their directors are appointed and dismissed, their budgetary and administrative autonomy, and the extent of the authority granted them, these offices can help to ensure that governmental officials adhere to the law and do not abuse the public trust, and that citizen rights are protected.

To varying degrees, democracies have also incorporated mechanisms for more direct citizen participation such as referenda, plebiscites, citizen initiatives, and the recall of elected officials. If well designed and used, such mechanisms can complement the traditional "representative" structure of democracy, thereby increasing the responsiveness of government to its citizens (see Chapter Ten).

It must be recognized, however, that political institutions are not the only factors that affect the performance of democratic systems. A host of noninstitutional factors—including the level of social and economic development, the intensity of ethnic, religious and socioeconomic divisions, the proclivity of citizens toward association and cooperation, the independence and plurality of the news media, and international political and economic pressures—shape the operation of all democratic systems, regardless of their particular constitutional structure.

The quality of political leadership is also important. Regardless of the structure of incentives provided by formal institutions, individual politicians still have room to influence the performance of the political system. Daring and capable political leadership, in fact, is necessary to bring about sound political and institutional reforms. Because of different political leadership and the collective learning of political actors, the same formal institutional structure may produce crisis in one historical context and stability and effective governance in another.

To a great extent, the socio-structural factors specified above are inherited and cannot easily be changed in a short span of time. By contrast, despite being embedded to some extent in this larger context, political institutions can be changed relatively swiftly. Thus, to improve the governability of democracy, the reform of political institutions is at least one crucial place to start.

Political Reform and Development

The specific configuration of institutions within the broad rubric of presidentialism can help account for why some systems operate relatively smoothly while others are constantly in a state of crisis. The relevance of the formal political institutions of democratic governance has clearly been recognized by political actors and citizen groups in Latin America. Alongside the profound economic reforms adopted in much of the region, the last two decades have also witnessed a ferment of constitutional reform and other modifications to democratic rules. Each of the 18 countries examined in this study has reformed or replaced the constitution that it brought into the period. Nearly all of the countries have reformed laws governing elections and political parties.

The motivation behind such reforms varies considerably from case to case. Such reforms rarely, if ever, contradict the interests of the largest political parties. In fact, they are often motivated by the desire to further the advantages and privileges of those parties and the social groups supporting them. The achievement of a more governable and stable democratic system, while often in the background, is only in some instances the central goal. Even in cases where this objective has been the predominant goal of reformers, broad consensus about the reforms needed has been rare. Thus, given the force of pragmatic and political considerations and the indeterminacy of, and lack of consensus about, the effects of reform, the process of political change is even more prone than economic reform to missteps.

Much attention has been paid to examining the *economic reforms* adopted by countries in the region over the past two decades. Such considerations have generated a lively and impassioned debate about the adequacy and appropriateness of the "neo-liberal" thrust of much of the economic reforms. By contrast, however, few attempts have been made to study in a systematic and a broadly comparative manner the *political reforms* of the period, or to assess the extent to which they hold the possibility for reducing the problems of governability plaguing the region's young democracies. What have been the main regional reform trends with respect to the institutional dimensions highlighted above? What have been and are likely to be the effects of these changes on the functioning of democracy? What do these reform experiences suggest about the types of political reforms that will be most needed in the near future? The chapters that follow provide at least partial and contingent answers to these questions.

Bibliography

Chasquetti, Daniel. 2001. Democracia, multipartidismo y coaliciones en América Latina: evaluando la difícil combinación. In Jorge Lanzaro (ed.), *Tipos de presidencialismo y coaliciones políticas en América Latina*. Buenos Aires: Consejo Latinoamericano de Ciencias Sociales.

Di Palma, Giuseppe. 1990. *To Craft Democracies: An Essay on Democratic Transitions*. Berkeley, CA: University of California Press.

Economic Commission for Latin America and the Caribbean (ECLAC). 2001. *Current Conditions and Outlook: Economic Survey of Latin America and the Caribbean, 2000–2001*. New York: United Nations.

Freedom House. 2001. *Freedom in the World: The Annual Survey of Political Rights and Civil Liberties, 2000–2001*. New York: Freedom House.

Graham, Carol, and Moisés Naím. 1998. The Political Economy of Institutional Reform in Latin America. In Nancy Birdsall, Carol Graham, and Richard H. Sabot (eds.), *Beyond Tradeoffs: Market Reforms and Equitable Growth in Latin America*. Washington, DC: Brookings Institution Press.

Hodess, Robin, Jessie Banfield, and Toby Wolfe (eds.). 2001. *Global Corruption Report 2001*. Berlin: Transparency International.

Inter-American Development Bank. 2000. *Development Beyond Economics: Economic and Social Progress in Latin America*. Washington, DC: IDB.

International Monetary Fund. 2001. *International Financial Statistics Yearbook*. Washington, DC: IMF.

Kaufmann, Daniel, Art Kraay, and Pablo Zoido-Lobatón. 1999a. *Aggregating Governance Indicators*. Washington, DC: World Bank.

———. 1999b. *Governance Matters*. Washington, DC: World Bank.

———. 2001. *Governance Matters II: Updated Indicators for 2000/01*. Washington, DC: World Bank.

Lanzaro, Jorge. 2001. Tipos de presidencialismo y modos de gobierno en América Latina. In Jorge Lanzaro (ed.), *Tipos de presidencialismo y coaliciones políticas en América Latina*. Buenos Aires: Consejo Latinoamericano de Ciencias Sociales.

Lijphart, Arend. 1994. Presidential and Majoritarian Democracy: Theoretical Observations. In Juan J. Linz and Arturo Valenzuela (eds.), *The Failure of Presidential Democracy*. Baltimore: The Johns Hopkins University Press.

Linz, Juan J. 1990. The Perils of Presidentialism. *Journal of Democracy* 1(4). Fall.

Linz, Juan J., and Alfred Stepan (eds.). 1978. *The Breakdown of Democratic Regimes*. Baltimore: The Johns Hopkins University Press.

Linz, Juan J., and Arturo Valenzuela (eds.). 1994. *The Failure of Presidential Democracy*. Baltimore: The Johns Hopkins University Press.

Mainwaring, Scott. 1990. Presidentialism in Latin America. *Latin American Research Review* 1(25). Latin American Studies Association.

————. 1993. Presidentialism, Multipartism and Democracy: The Difficult Combination. *Comparative Political Studies* 2(26).

Mainwaring, Scott and Matthew Soberg Shugart. 1997. Presidentialism and the Party System. In Scott Mainwaring and Matthew Soberg Shugart (eds.), *Presidentialism and Democracy in Latin America*. New York: Cambridge University Press.

Naím, Moisés. 1995. *Latin America's Journey to the Market: From Macroeconomic Shocks to Institutional Therapy*. San Francisco: ICS Press.

Nohlen, Dieter. 1998. *Sistemas electorales y partidos políticos*. Mexico City: Fondo de Cultura Económica.

Nohlen, Dieter, and Mario Fernández Baeza (eds.). 1998. *El presidencialismo renovado: Instituciones y cambio político en América Latina*. Caracas: Editorial Nueva Sociedad.

Rodrik, Dani. 2000. Institutions for High-Quality Growth: What They Are and How to Acquire Them. *Studies in Comparative Development* 35(3). Fall.

Sartori, Giovanni. 1994. Neither Presidentialism nor Parliamentarism. In Juan J. Linz and Arturo Valenzuela (eds.), *The Failure of Presidential Democracy*. Baltimore: The Johns Hopkins University Press.

Sen, Amartya Kumar. 1999. *Development as Freedom*. New York: Knopf.

Shugart, Matthew Soberg, and John M. Carey. 1992. *Presidents and Assemblies: Constitutional Design and Electoral Dynamics*. Cambridge: Cambridge University Press.

Shugart, Matthew Soberg, and Scott Mainwaring. 1997. Presidentialism and Democracy in Latin America: Rethinking the Terms of the Debate. In Scott Mainwaring and Matthew Soberg Shugart (eds.), *Presidentialism and Democracy in Latin America*. New York: Cambridge University Press.

Székely, Miguel. 2001. *The 1990s in Latin America: Another Decade of Persistent Inequality, but with Somewhat Lower Poverty*. Research Department Working Paper Series no. 454, Inter-American Development Bank, Washington, DC.

World Economic Forum. 2000. *The Global Competitiveness Report 2000*. New York: Oxford University Press.

CHAPTER TWO

Gauging Public Support
for Democracy

The experience of the past two decades, along with historical trends over time, suggests that the democratic wave that has swept through Latin America could be reversed. While no countries in the region have abandoned elections or permanently shut down democratic institutions, in several instances extra-constitutional maneuvers have been used to retain, usurp or augment power. Given the tremendous challenges posed by economic volatility, high levels of poverty and inequality, and organized crime and violence, democracy remains under stress in many countries. The consolidation of democracy rests on public support that is built over time. Expanding the legitimacy of democratic systems, in turn, hinges significantly (though not exclusively) on the performance of the democratic regime.

This chapter examines attitudes towards democracy in Latin American countries in the second half of the 1990s. The primary emphasis is on comparing levels of support for democracy as a system of government and for its institutions across the countries of the region. But, to broaden the perspective, the findings for Latin America are also compared to those of other world regions. Given the absence of cross-national comparative data, it is not possible to systematically study the evolution over time of public attitudes towards democratic systems over the whole period of the study. However, the results of an annual public opinion survey conducted five times since 1995 in 17 Latin American countries show recent trends and allow for assessing the variability from year to year of public attitudes in particular countries (Latinobarómetro, 1996–2001).

One reason to assess public attitudes towards democracy and the institutions comprising it is to examine progress toward legitimizing and consolidating democratic systems. Two decades after the onset of Latin America's "third wave" of democratization, how solid are the region's democracies? To what extent can they be expected to withstand current and future pressures and threats?

Public confidence in politicians and democratic political institutions affects the functioning of these agents and institutions and, therefore, the performance of the democratic system. A certain minimum level of public trust in politicians and institutions is necessary to enable the government to make the tough decisions necessary to manage the economy and implement public policies, especially during a crisis. In addition, if there is little public trust in politicians and the democratic system, one would expect that few citizens would actively participate in politics. As will be discussed further in the next chapter, low levels of citizen involvement and interest would likely undermine the accountability of elected officials to citizens and could potentially create biases in representation, spurring further disenchantment. Similarly, if citizens do not trust political parties, those parties will be less able to perform their key functions of articulating and aggregating citizen preferences. A weakening of political parties would tend to promote an increasingly personalistic and particularistic form of representation in which the broader public interest is lost in a cacophony of narrow and regionally concentrated demands.

Support for democracy can be assessed at several different levels, starting from a more diffuse basis of evaluation to a more specific one.[1] The first level considered here refers to support for the core *regime principles*. Survey questions addressing this matter gauge the extent to which citizens agree with such democratic values as freedom, participation, tolerance and compromise, or whether they agree that democracy is the best form of government.

The second level of evaluation concerns *regime performance*, meaning support for how democratic or authoritarian regimes function in practice. In cross-national surveys, this is usually measured by citizens' responses to a question asking them to rate their degree of "satisfaction with the functioning of democracy" (or "satisfaction with the way democracy works"). This measure is more ambiguous than that for the previous dimension, however, since alternative interpretations are possible. Some respondents may still center their attention on democracy as a value, while others will primarily consider the performance of the incumbent government or a series of previous governments.

A third level of evaluation relates to support for *regime institutions* such as the government, legislature, executive, political parties, public administration, judiciary, police and the military. Survey items focusing on institutions gauge confidence in the institution broadly considered, rather than in particular individuals associated with it. This level of evaluation allows for a deeper and more differentiated consideration of regime performance, separating somewhat the matter of incumbent government performance from that of the more permanent "institutional" elements of the regime.

A fourth level of evaluation, not emphasized here, is that of support for *political authorities*, usually meaning trust in political leaders as players in the political system. The cross-national survey for Latin America used in this chapter—Latinobarómetro—has not specifically addressed this matter, so it will be left out of the empirical discussion.

Reasons for Discontent with Democracy

Democratic transitions in the late 1970s in Ecuador, the Dominican Republic and Peru launched a region-wide trend that culminated with the transitions in Panama, Paraguay,

---

[1] The classification of levels of support for democracy is from Norris (1999) and Klingemann (1999).

Chile and Nicaragua around 1990. Despite the fact that the transition process in some cases was accompanied by great uncertainty and left areas of social conflict unresolved, citizens generally embraced the advent of democracy and felt a renewed sense of optimism and confidence in their country's political future.

Citizens and political parties reactivated quickly and democratic institutions resumed or initiated the performance of their basic functions, filling the void left by departing military officers or other civilian incumbents. In the countries where there was little previous experience with democratic governance, the transition process was inevitably more difficult, since it entailed not only the creation of democratic institutions and procedures but also the formation of a new institutional culture that had to be internalized by participants. Where democratic institutions had already functioned, but had ceased to operate during military rule, establishing the basic rule of law and democratic practices was typically more rapid and less complicated.

The predominant public attitude during the first years of democracy was to give the recently restored or created institutions some breathing room to assume their responsibilities and fulfill their roles. As might have been expected, the democratic honeymoon period in most cases did not last very long. Citizen demands grew, social conflicts reactivated, and in most cases public disappointment in the performance of democratic governments escalated.

Part of the growing disenchantment can be attributed to the always-negative correspondence between idealized expectations of democracy and actual performance in the context of difficult political and economic circumstances. But several more specific factors rooted in either regional or global circumstances can also be identified.

First, the socioeconomic context confronting most governments during the period under study contributed to the erosion of the initial reservoir of public faith in democratic institutions. The cutoff of foreign lending, public financial crises, and skyrocketing inflation signaled that the previous statist and protectionist models of development were no longer viable. Faced with large macroeconomic imbalances and financing constraints, democratic governments were forced to adopt fiscal adjustment and other austerity policies and, in some cases, reduce the scope of the state and its role in the economy. While the aim of these policies was to promote long-term growth, they exacerbated the immediate economic difficulties, especially for the poor, and heightened social tensions. Regardless of what were the real causes of these economic problems, democratic governments and institutions absorbed the blame for the painful remedies adopted to surmount the economic crisis. And Latin America's fledgling democracies were not alone in dealing with such problems. Severe economic distress and the need for structural adjustment and economic transformation also prompted public disillusionment with many of the emerging democracies in Central and Eastern Europe, Africa, and, later, in Asia.

A second reason for growing disenchantment with democracy was because politicians and political institutions in many countries performed poorly. Citizens reacted negatively to the inability of governments to make sound and effective decisions either on their own or in the face of recalcitrant legislative opposition; to the poor and deteriorating quality of public services; and to the dishonest and corrupt conduct of politicians, as well as their remoteness from constituents. Though such problems may not have been worse than under previous regimes, they were certainly more exposed and intensely reported by the media.

Public dissatisfaction also was a result of ongoing deficiencies in the fulfillment of democratic values. As was shown in Chapter One (in Figure 1.7), the region's average scores in 2000 according to Freedom House for political rights and civil liberties placed it in the category "partly free" rather than "free." Nine of the 18 Latin American countries in the study were rated as "free," while the other half were "partly free," this latter rating due to deficiencies in guaranteeing civil rights or in the scope for free expression and political organization.[2]

Trends in political support for democracy across the world—including the more established democracies—suggest that other, more global, phenomena might also have contributed to growing citizen disenchantment with democratic institutions. Recent studies by Norris (1999) and Dalton (1999) showed a mixed trend in established democracies with respect to the different dimensions of support for democracy. Support for the ideal of democracy remains quite strong, and the level of satisfaction with the performance of democratic regimes undulates across time and place without exhibiting any clear trend. But available survey data from the 1950s and 1960s onward shows a significant, though not severe, decline in trust in political authorities as well as in political institutions such as parties and legislatures.

Among the factors that might underlie disenchantment with politicians and institutions in established as well as emerging democracies is the change in the modalities of political representation that resulted from the end of the Cold War, the ascendance of television and other forms of mass communication, and the globalization of politics. As a consequence, traditional social class and ideological bases for citizens' political identity and for the cohesion of political parties have been undermined. Thus, citizens and parties have to some degree lost their bearings, while at the same time new issues have emerged— such as the environment, human rights and crime—which traditional structures of representation are struggling to incorporate (Inglehart, 1990 and 1997). The growing importance of television news and advertising has also enhanced the personalization of the links between public officials and citizens, undermining the salience and importance of political parties as intermediary institutions. The decline in citizen identification with particular political parties and the loss in confidence in representative institutions in established democracies possibly stem from this unsettling of the historic lines of social division, and from the changes in the modalities of electoral competition and representation.

Another factor that transcends global regions is the loss of power of national governments (states)—from above because of the globalization of politics and economic policy, and from below because of processes of decentralization. Along with the greater penetration of international economic forces, the creation of transnational governmental and trading bodies and agreements such as the European Union, the World Trade Organization, Mercosur, and the North American Free Trade Association is shifting economic and other powers away from nations and towards external actors or forces. In addition, decentraliza-

---

[2] The countries rated as "free" were Argentina, Bolivia, Chile, Costa Rica, the Dominican Republic, El Salvador, Mexico, Panama and Uruguay. Those rated as "partly free" were Brazil, Colombia, Ecuador, Guatemala, Honduras, Nicaragua, Paraguay, Peru and Venezuela.

Democracies in Development

tion in many countries has weakened the authority and responsibilities of national governments. While this "outsourcing" of what used to be national governmental responsibilities may in the end be beneficial for citizens, public perceptions of the efficacy of national governments and institutions may, at least in the short term, be negatively affected.

Measuring Support for Democracy

The examination of the different dimensions of support for democratic regimes is based primarily on data from Latinobarómetro, a public opinion survey that has been conducted in 17 Latin American countries since 1995. The concentration of most of the analysis on this single source is due to the fact that it is the only one available that covers such a large number of countries using the same set of questions and a similar methodology. The surveys are limited to urban populations and based on a sample of roughly 1,000 respondents per country. Data from five completed surveys (1996, 1997, 1998, 1999/2000, 2001) are examined in order to compare attitudes toward democracy across the region and, in some cases, to make comparisons between Latin America and Europe and the United States. Information for these cross-regional comparisons comes from the Eurobarometer, Central and Eastern Eurobarometer, and the World Values Survey.[3]

Support for Democratic Ideals

Until the 2001 survey, responses to Latinobarómetro reflected a fairly high level of support for democracy, understood as a set of ideals and a form of government. On average, about 61 percent of citizens interviewed in the 1996 through 1999/2000 surveys endorsed the view that "democracy is preferable to all other forms of government" (Table 2.1). Only about 18 percent thought that an authoritarian form of government might sometimes be preferable, and about 16 percent were indifferent between authoritarian and democratic regimes.

The 2001 survey revealed a dramatic drop in the share of respondents unequivocally embracing democracy as their preferred system of government. Less than half (48 percent) of the respondents expressed a clear preference for democracy. Despite this collapse in support for democracy, the percentage of those surveyed expressing a preference for authoritarianism under some circumstances barely changed (20 percent instead of 18 percent). Preference for democracy appears instead to have lost favor to apathy and indifference: the share of respondents who said that the form of government makes no difference, or that they do not know, increased from 16 percent to 21 percent and from about 3.5 percent to 9 percent, respectively. Another reflection of growing indifference was that about 50 percent of respondents agreed with the statement that it would not matter to them if the military assumed power. Only 44 percent of respondents disagreed with that statement.

The extent of the decline in support for democracy in the region overall in the 2001 survey was influenced by the dramatic fall in a handful of countries (Table 2.2). Though democ-

---

[3] Eurobarometer 45 (1996); Eurobarometer 24 (1986); Central and Eastern Eurobarometer 8 (May 1998); Eurobarometer 53 (October 2000); World Values Survey (1990–93 and 1995–97).

Table 2.1. Support for Democracy in Latin America, 1996–2001
(In percent)

	1996	1997	1998	1999/2000	2001
Democracy is preferable	61	63	60	60	48
Authoritarian government is sometimes preferable	17	18	20	18	20
Indifferent between authoritarianism and democracy	17	14	16	17	21
Do not know	4	3	3	4	9
No response	2	2	1	1	3
Total	100	100	100	100	100

Note: Percentages represent averages across countries.

racy was supported by an average of 62 percent of respondents in El Salvador in surveys from 1996 to 2000, that support fell to 27.3 percent in the 2001 survey. Sharp declines in support were also observed in Panama (69.9 percent to 34.3 percent), Colombia (58.4 percent to 36.3 percent), and Nicaragua (63.6 percent to 42.7 percent). Argentina, Brazil, Ecuador, Guatemala and Paraguay also witnessed a 10 percent or more drop in those affirming a preference for democracy.

By contrast, support for democracy held fairly steady in Uruguay (80.5 percent), Costa Rica (71.4 percent), Peru (62.1 percent), Venezuela (58.1 percent), and Honduras (56.6 percent).

Thus, the results of the 2001 survey sharply reduced the number of countries in which democracy could be viewed as enjoying solid public support. The percentage of respondents unequivocally backing democracy was lowest in El Salvador (27.3 percent), Brazil (30.2 percent), Panama (34.3 percent), Guatemala (34.4 percent) and Paraguay (35.9 percent). The most indifference about the military assuming power was found in Ecuador, Paraguay, Colombia and Venezuela, where 70 percent, 66 percent, 64 percent, and 62 percent, respectively, agreed with the statement that such a development would not bother them.

It is possible that sustained public dissatisfaction with living conditions and the performance of democratic governments has begun to erode faith in the more abstract notion of democracy as a set of ideals and a system of government. Or it could be that the economic difficulties and uncertainties in much of the region contributed to making the 2001 survey atypical and not illustrative of a new trend in public opinion. Given its importance to the future of democratic governance in the region, this matter requires close examination in the years ahead.

According to the 2001 survey, the largest percentage of respondents who at least in some circumstances would favor authoritarianism is found in Paraguay (41.2 percent), fol-

Table 2.2. Support for Democracy as a System of Government in Latin America, 1996–2000 and 2001
(In percent)

	Democracy preferable		Authoritarian sometimes preferable		Indifferent between authoritarian and democratic		Do not know		No response	
	Avg. 1996–2000	2001	Avg. 1996–2000	2001	Avg. 1996–2000	2001	Avg. 1996–2000	2001	Avg. 1996–2000	2001
Argentina	72.3	56.8	15.2	21.2	10.1	17.6	1.8	3.6	0.6	0.8
Bolivia	62.4	54.6	17.4	17.1	14.7	17.2	4.2	8.4	1.3	2.7
Brazil	46.5	30.2	21.1	18.0	24.8	30.8	6.4	17.6	1.2	3.4
Chile	56.2	47.8	17.3	20.7	23.9	25.0	1.8	4.1	0.7	2.4
Colombia	58.4	36.3	18.8	16.4	17.9	21.8	4.0	23.6	0.9	1.9
Costa Rica	78.7	71.4	10.7	8.2	6.3	12.5	2.3	6.6	2.0	1.3
Ecuador	51.0	40.5	17.9	23.8	24.4	25.8	4.8	7.3	2.0	2.6
El Salvador	61.8	27.3	11.8	10.7	19.9	37.0	3.6	17.9	2.9	7.2
Guatemala	49.2	34.4	24.3	20.1	18.4	22.2	4.6	16.3	3.5	7.1
Honduras	56.5	56.6	15.5	9.7	19.2	20.7	7.2	9.0	1.6	4.0
Mexico	50.2	44.5	29.0	37.4	17.7	14.0	2.3	2.6	0.8	1.5
Nicaragua	63.6	42.7	13.0	22.1	17.9	25.9	3.9	5.2	1.6	4.2
Panama	69.9	34.3	11.7	23.2	14.2	29.6	2.8	8.6	1.4	4.3
Paraguay	51.4	35.9	34.9	41.2	11.8	18.5	1.6	4.2	0.5	0.2
Peru	62.4	62.1	13.6	11.6	14.3	13.2	7.3	9.7	2.4	3.4
Uruguay	83.1	80.5	8.6	9.7	5.9	7.4	2.1	2.3	0.4	0.2
Venezuela	62.0	58.1	21.3	20.3	12.9	17.1	2.5	3.6	1.4	1.0
LAC	60.9	47.9	17.8	19.5	16.1	21.0	3.7	8.9	1.5	2.8

lowed by Mexico (37.4 percent), Ecuador (23.8 percent), and Panama (23.2 percent). The least sympathy for authoritarianism is found in Costa Rica (8.2 percent), Uruguay (9.7 percent) and Honduras (9.7 percent).

The level of support for democracy in Europe provides one basis for comparison with that observed in Latin America. Data from the 1990 Eurobarometer, which included 12 Western European countries, showed that about 96 percent of respondents viewed democracy as preferable to all other forms of government. Less than 2 percent thought that authoritarianism at times might be preferable.

In summary, the 2001 survey data indicate that the fairly robust support for democracy present since the beginning of the study period is showing some signs of slippage. While there remains little support for authoritarian alternatives, there is considerable indifference and apathy with respect to the form of government. As the contrast between the survey results for Latin America and Europe clearly shows, in many Latin American countries the reservoir of support is not so deep that democracy can be expected to consistently withstand potential stresses and threats in the future.

Satisfaction with Democracy

Public sentiment about democracy as an ideal and as a form of government is distinct from the matter of whether citizens are satisfied with how the democratic system is working in practice. Satisfaction varies more extensively over time and is more sensitive to changes in economic conditions. For instance, support for the ideal of democracy barely wavered in Western European countries during the 1970s, but given spiraling inflation and growing unemployment, satisfaction with democratic performance declined considerably in many countries.

While the two factors are not directly related, several scholars have concluded that sustained, effective democratic performance and, particularly, success in addressing social and economic problems, contribute to broad and fundamental support for the legitimacy of democracy (Lipset, 1993; Diamond, Linz and Lipset, 1989; McAllister, 1999). Thus, satisfaction over the long term with governmental performance may be a precondition for consolidating support for democratic regimes, because it allows for a reservoir of intrinsic support to be built. The regime, in turn, can draw on that support in the event of temporary crises. Clearly, however, the legitimacy of democratic regimes is also derived from many other factors, including the political culture, the performance of the regime in providing valued political goods such as order, human rights and political freedom, and perceptions of feasible alternative regimes.

The influence of social and economic issues on the performance of democratic regimes is likely to be particularly important in Latin America, where income levels are relatively low, poverty is widespread (40 percent of the population lives below the poverty line), and trust in politicians and political institutions is particularly low (Lagos, 2001). Thus, the findings of the 2001 Latinobarómetro that only 6 percent of Latin Americans feel the economic situation in their country is good, and only 15 percent think that it has improved in the last year, do not auger well for further legitimization of democracy. Similarly, it is troublesome that only about 6 percent think that the level of poverty has been reduced in the past five years, and that between 85 percent and 93 percent believe that crime, income inequality, corruption and drug addiction are getting worse rather than staying the same or improving.

Given the relatively poor assessments of the performance of democratic regimes, it is not so surprising that from 1996–2000, an average of just 35 percent of respondents (across the 17 countries for all four years of the survey) reported that they were satisfied with the functioning of democracy. Worse, however, is that the 2001 survey revealed an even lower degree of satisfaction with democracy: only one out of every four citizens. It is at least some consolation that this decline in satisfaction did not translate into as dramatic an increase in the expressed level of dissatisfaction (from 62.5 percent to 65.5 percent) as might have been expected.[4] As in the case of support for the principles of democracy, much of the withdrawn affirmative responses turned into indifference rather than outright negative assessments.

The data for 1996–2000 showed Latin America with a similar level of satisfaction with democracy as Central and Eastern Europe (1998), where democracy was a still more recent development (Figure 2.1). But the 2001 Latin American average was considerably below the average level of support for democracy of 35 percent reported in the May 1998 Central and Eastern Eurobarometer for a group of 10 countries.[5] The average level of dissatisfaction with democracy for that region was 60 percent.

As might be expected, in the more established democracies and advanced economies of Western Europe, the level of satisfaction with democracy is considerably higher. Public satisfaction with democracy there, as sampled in the 2000 Eurobarometer, presents almost the mirror image of levels of support in Central and Eastern Europe and Latin America from 1996–2000. An average of 62 percent of respondents sampled in Western Europe said they are satisfied with democracy, while just 35 percent are dissatisfied. None of the 16 Western European countries surveyed had a level of satisfaction with democracy below the *average* level for Latin America from 1996 to 2000.

The individual country responses back up the fact that perceptions of the efficacy of democracy do not necessarily go hand in hand with beliefs in its legitimacy. Many countries where an ample majority supports democracy as a form of government are nonetheless characterized by a low level of satisfaction with the performance of the regime. On average, about 37 percent of the people who responded to the 2001 Latinobarómetro survey can be labeled "dissatisfied democrats." They prefer democracy as a system of government, but are displeased with how their governments or institutions are performing. By contrast, just 19 percent of respondents are "satisfied democrats," believing both in the ideal of democracy and that their democratic systems are performing reasonably well. The question is how well can beliefs in the legitimacy of democracy hold up in the face of dissatisfaction with the performance of the regime if it persists over time.

Given the impact on perceptions of the effectiveness of democratic regimes in terms of economic performance and satisfying basic needs, it is understandable that this measure is much more sensitive to changes than the level of support for democracy (Table 2.3).

Respondents' degree of satisfaction with democracy has varied considerably over the five years of the study across Latin America as a whole, as well as at the level of individual countries. The average across countries of respondents reporting to be either "very satisfied" or "fairly satisfied" with democracy was only about 27 percent in 1996, then climbed to near 40 percent in 1997, only to fall back down to just under 25 percent in 2001. At the country level, variation in levels of satisfaction with democracy has been particularly pronounced in Central America (except Costa Rica), Mexico and Venezuela. In El Salvador, for instance, satisfaction with democracy climbed from 26 percent to 48 percent from 1996 to

---

[4] The percentage of those characterized as satisfied includes both those who responded that they are "very satisfied" and those who responded that they are "fairly satisfied." Those characterized as dissatisfied include respondents who said that they are "not very satisfied" and those that said they are "not at all satisfied."

[5] The countries were Poland, Romania, Estonia, Slovenia, Lithuania, the Czech Republic, Hungary, Slovakia, Latvia and Bulgaria.

Table 2.3. Satisfaction with Democracy (Very Satisfied and Fairly Satisfied) *(In percent)*

	1996	1997	1998	1999/2000	2001	Avg. 1996–2001
Uruguay	51	65	68	70	55	62
Costa Rica	51	68	54	61	51	57
Venezuela	30	36	35	55	41	39
Argentina	34	42	49	46	21	38
Honduras	19	49		44	32	36
Panama	28	39	34	47	21	34
Guatemala	17	40	57	36	16	33
Chile	28	37	32	35	25	31
El Salvador	26	48		27	20	31
Nicaragua	24	51		16	24	29
Mexico	12	45	21	37	27	28
Ecuador	33	31	34	23	15	27
Bolivia	25	33	34	22	19	27
Colombia	16	36	24	27	9	22
Brazil	21	23	25	19	21	22
Peru	28	21	18	24	16	21
Paraguay	21	15	24	12	10	17
LAC average	27	40	36	35	25	32

Figure 2.1. Satisfaction with Democracy in Latin America compared with Central and Eastern Europe and Western Europe *(In percent)*

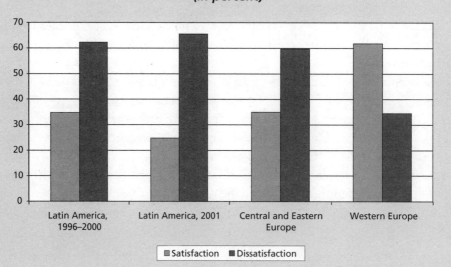

Sources: Latinobarómetro 1996, 1997, 1998, 1999/2000, 2001; Central and Eastern Eurobarometer 8, May 1998; Eurobarometer 53, October 2000.

Democracies in Development

1997, but then fell down to 21 percent by 2001. In Guatemala, satisfaction rose from 17 percent in 1996 to 57 percent by 1998, but then collapsed to 16 percent in 2001. Substantial shifts in public satisfaction with democracy might be more expected in these countries, as well as in Mexico, given that democratic transition is ongoing or recent, and that democracy is weakly institutionalized. But as evidenced by Venezuela, other more longstanding democracies have not been immune from considerable variation in citizen satisfaction with democracy.

Five-year averages across the region show a wide variation in the level of satisfaction with the functioning of democracy. On the positive side are Uruguay (62 percent) and Costa Rica (57 percent), which stand out clearly from the rest of the region. In Venezuela and Argentina, which are next in rank, about 18 percent fewer respondents on average than in Costa Rica expressed satisfaction with democracy. By contrast, the same percentage difference encompasses 10 countries at the lower end of the scale, from Paraguay (17 percent) to 6th ranked Panama (34 percent).

In the most recent survey, satisfaction with democracy plunged dramatically in Argentina (46 percent to 21 percent), Panama (47 percent to 21 percent), and Guatemala (36 percent to 16 percent), and hit new lows in Colombia (8.5 percent) and Paraguay (10.3 percent).

Thus, while support for the principles of democracy has been fairly strong, especially in the first four years of the Latinobarómetro survey, there has been far less satisfaction with its actual operation and performance. Clearly, broad sectors of the population feel that democratic systems, which they support in principle, are not meeting their expectations.

Confidence in Institutions

Given the wide range of factors that may affect citizen satisfaction with democracy—including external factors often outside the control of democratic officials or institutions—a more direct assessment of public perceptions of democratic systems may be derived from measuring confidence in democratic institutions. Such a measure can help determine whether dissatisfaction stems from poor macro-level outcomes of government or from perceptions that the core processes and institutions of democracy are not functioning up to par.

One institution that enjoys considerable prestige in Latin America is the Catholic Church (Table 2.4). In the 1996–2001 Latinobarómetro surveys, around 75 percent of respondents consistently said that they had "much" or "some" confidence in the church. Given that this institution's private role likely plays a central role in people's perceptions while its public role is not always that visible, such a high rating is not that surprising.

Citizens also place a fairly high level of confidence in television (47 percent), though that figure is considerably lower than the level of confidence in the Catholic Church. The prestige and visibility of television relative to that of other democratic institutions reflects the modern mode of politics, in which image is at least as important as substance. To be successful, politicians must work on developing an appealing persona on television, often at great expense. Television personalities, in turn, often play an important role in focusing and moving the political debate and agenda, shaping the images of politicians, and filtering the news reported to the public.

Table 2.4. Confidence in Institutions in Latin America
(In percent)

	1996	1997	1998	1999/2000	2001	1996–2001
Church	76	75	79	77	72	76
Television	51	46	46	42	49	47
Armed forces	45	47	42	45	39	44
Presidency	28	39	38	39	35	36
Judiciary	33	37	32	34	32	34
Police	30	36	32	35	33	33
Public administration	30				28	29
Congress	27	36	27	27	23	28
Political parties	21	28	22	20	19	22

Note: Average percentage across 17 countries.

The third highest level of public confidence is in the armed forces, which on average over the five survey years had a 44 percent confidence rating. This support, however, varies substantially across countries. In El Salvador, Guatemala, Nicaragua and Argentina, confidence in the armed forces is scarcely greater than confidence in the principal representative institutions. By contrast, in Ecuador, Brazil and Venezuela, confidence in the armed forces is more than double the level of trust in these fundamental democratic institutions. Across the region, this positive image of the armed forces does not translate into a high level of support for military authoritarianism, as shown in Tables 2.1 and 2.2.

The presidency (or executive) is next in line in terms of public confidence, with an average rating of 36 percent. Across time and between countries, however, it is also the institution that by far exhibits the highest degree of variability. Rather than judging an institution with any kind of permanence, respondents in this instance seem to evaluate the executive on the basis of their feelings toward the incumbent president and the government as a whole. As is well known, the popularity of presidents changes like the wind according to perceptions of governmental performance and the integrity and competence of the president and his cabinet. Given the advantages of presidents in terms of being able to represent the nation as a whole and appear decisive, it is not surprising that, on average, the presidency would enjoy greater respect than the more diffuse representative institutions.

Just below the presidency in terms of public trust are the judiciary and the police, which on average enjoy the confidence of between 33 and 34 percent of the citizens sampled. Considering the data from individual countries, it is clear that these institutions are rated in comparable fashion.

The institutions in which citizens place the least confidence are the public administration and two of the principal institutions of representative democracy: the legislature and political parties. Only 23 percent of respondents place "much" or "some" confidence in political parties, making them less esteemed even than congress or the public administration, whose confidence ratings are 28 percent and 29 percent, respectively.

This ordering in the degree of citizen confidence in institutions is consistent with that revealed in a regional survey conducted by a different organization in the middle of 2001.[6] This survey reported that 71 percent of respondents had confidence in the Catholic church, 51 percent in the armed forces, 26 percent in the justice system, 19 percent in the congress, and 14 percent in political parties.

The average level of confidence in democratic political institutions in Latin America is considerably below that in Western Europe, even considering the decline in confidence in the latter region over the past two decades. Relative to Latin America, legislatures in Western Europe enjoy the confidence of 20 percent more respondents, judicial systems 32 percent more, and governments 10 percent more (Table 2.5).

Hidden behind Latin America's regional averages, there is a considerable variation in levels of confidence in the principal institutions of representative democracy (Table 2.5). Confidence in the legislature ranges from a high of around 43 percent and 42 percent in Uruguay and Chile, respectively, to a low of 17 percent in Ecuador and 22 percent to 24 percent in Brazil, Colombia, Bolivia, Guatemala and Argentina. Very low levels of confidence in political parties extend across a broader group of countries, including Ecuador (13 percent), Bolivia (16 percent), Colombia (17 percent), and Brazil, Guatemala and Argentina (18 percent). Only in Uruguay (37 percent) do political parties continue to hold the respect of what might be viewed as a significant share of the citizenry. The widest range in confidence across countries is observed in the case of the judiciary. This institution enjoys a substantial degree of trust in Uruguay (52 percent) and Costa Rica (44 percent), but is not trusted very highly in Peru (21 percent), Argentina (22 percent), Ecuador (24 percent), or Bolivia (25 percent). Faith in public administration is highest in Chile (44 percent) and Uruguay (43 percent), and lowest in Colombia (20 percent), Argentina (21 percent), and Bolivia (22 percent).

The lack of esteem for congress and political parties is further illustrated by responses to a question in the 2001 Latinobarómetro survey about a hypothetical closure of these institutions. Overall, 35 percent of respondents in the region said that they would approve, while 54 percent said that they would disapprove. But in Colombia, Ecuador, Mexico and Paraguay the percentage that said that they would approve (51 percent, 71 percent, 46 percent, and 56 percent, respectively) exceeded the percent that said they would disapprove.

In summary, dissatisfaction with democracy does not appear to be simply a reflection of bad economic times or unhappiness with the more visible and concrete outputs of democratic governance. Rather, given the lack of confidence expressed in particular institutions, democratic dissatisfaction seems to be rooted in a more basic disappointment in the operation of the fundamental processes, actors and organizations of the democratic system. Though a certain level of cynicism is common in every democratic system, the perception that politicians and political parties are primarily concerned about gaining and keeping power and enriching themselves, rather than pursuing the public interest, appears to be pervasive in many Latin American countries. Of course, it is difficult to separate out these sentiments, since it is certainly the case that peoples' views of democratic institu-

---

[6] The survey covered 13 of the 18 countries included in this study. It was conducted by the Consorcio Iberoamericano de Empresas de Investigación de Mercado y Asesoramiento (CIMA), with coordination from the Instituto Gallup de Argentina.

Table 2.5. Confidence in Democratic Political Institutions
(In percent)

	Congress	Parties	Judiciary	Public admin.	Presidency	Democratic institutions (average)
Uruguay	43	37	52	43	46	44
Chile	42	27	38	44	56	41
El Salvador	35	28	35	29	35	32
Costa Rica	30	23	44	27	33	31
Honduras	33	24	35	25	39	31
Venezuela	28	20	36	25	41	30
Panama	25	23	31	34	35	30
Mexico	30	27	28	27	34	29
Paraguay	29	24	31	27	35	29
Brazil	22	18	40	29	31	28
Nicaragua	28	23	30	32	26	28
Guatemala	24	18	27	29	29	25
Peru	27	20	21	27	33	25
Colombia	23	17	34	20	26	24
Argentina	24	18	22	21	29	23
Bolivia	23	16	25	22	28	23
Ecuador	17	13	24	26	28	22
Latin America	28.1	21.9	32.4	28.7	34.5	29.1
Western Europe	48.5		65.2		46.5	

Sources: For Latin American countries, Latinobarómetro (1996, 1997, 1998, 1999/2000, 2001); for Western Europe, data on congress and government, Eurobarometer 45 (1996) Table 7.13, and data on the judiciary, Eurobarometer 24 (1986).
Note: Average percentage over 1996–2001.

tions are colored by governmental performance in delivering public goods and managing the economy.

Levels of Interpersonal Trust

There has been renewed attention by scholars in recent years to the importance of trust and social capital for the effective functioning of representative governments and for social and economic development (Putnam, 1993; Fukuyama, 1995; and Boix and Posner, 1998). The efficient operation of markets, governmental institutions and other forms of social relations requires an environment in which mutually beneficial transactions can be carried out between individuals and groups on a regular basis, without undue reliance on outside enforcement. Greater trust between individuals would be expected to foster greater cooperation in the pursuit of social ends, and encourage civic association and community participation. High levels of interpersonal trust might facilitate more effective citizen engagement in community politics and social and economic activities, as well as greater cooperation within bureaucratic and representative institutions, thus enabling them to be more effective in the pursuit of the public good.

Responses to the Latinobarómetro surveys provide support for the notion that there is a link between interpersonal trust and the proclivity to participate in politics. Respondents who said that they trust others are 27 percent more likely than those who distrust others to also report that they participate in their communities, and 23 percent more likely to report that they talk about politics with friends.

The relationship between trust and the effectiveness of political institutions is bi-directional. Given the great reach of the government and the lower density and intensity of social relations in modern communities, political institutions may be expected to play an important role in shaping the more diffuse and fragile trust that can develop.[7] For trust to develop in the modern age, rules of conduct must be enforced consistently and impartially. Without the consistent and structured social interactions that might have existed naturally in the past, the development of social trust would appear to be more closely dependent on reliable institutions that gain the trust of citizens. Thus, while high levels of interpersonal trust ease the problems of governing (as well as the costs of exchange in economic markets), steady work in building trust in governmental institutions may help foster trust in society.

One of the more prominent characteristics of Latin America's political culture is the low level of interpersonal trust. Responses to the Latinobarómetro surveys over the past five years (Table 2.6) show that from an already low level of about 21 percent, the percent of respondents saying that they could trust most people fell to a still lower level of 15 percent in 1999/2000 and 17 percent in 2001. Only in Mexico and Uruguay do more than 30 percent of respondents say that they can trust other people most of the time. In more than half of the countries surveyed, the level of interpersonal trust is below 20 percent. In Brazil, it has been below 5 percent over the last four years of the survey.

Data from the World Values Survey (1990–93) reveal considerably higher levels of interpersonal trust in most countries of Western Europe, as well as in the United States, Canada and Japan. On average, about 47 percent of respondents in Western European countries say that they can trust others, while 51 percent, 53 percent and 42 percent say so in the United States, Canada and Japan, respectively (Figure 2.2).

The low level of interpersonal trust in Latin America coexists with a more broadly critical view of citizens in their countries. For example, just 32 percent of Latin Americans believe that the citizens of their own country are very or fairly honest; only 36 percent believe that other citizens are aware of their duties and obligations; and 77 percent think that their fellow citizens either never or seldom comply with the law. These values and attitudes contribute to the weak associative inclinations of Latin American societies, particularly low levels of participation in neighborhood councils, parent-teacher organiza-

---

[7] See Newton (1999) for a discussion of the impact of modernization and social change on the development and maintenance of social trust.

Table 2.6. Interpersonal Trust in Latin America
(In percent)

	1996	1997	1998	1999/2000	2001
One can trust in the majority of people	21	22	21	15	17
One can never be sufficiently careful in relations with others	76	75	76	83	80
No response	3	3	3	2	3

tions, and other civil society organizations. This property of the political culture encourages the development of a social and political order in which people relate separately to the political sphere instead of doing so through social networks and associations that have the capacity for greater influence on public decision-making and governmental conduct.

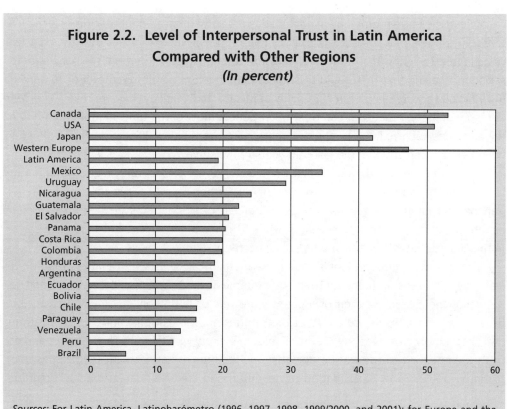

Figure 2.2. Level of Interpersonal Trust in Latin America Compared with Other Regions
(In percent)

Sources: For Latin America, Latinobarómetro (1996, 1997, 1998, 1999/2000, and 2001); for Europe and the United States, World Values Survey (1990–93).
Note: Average percentage over 1996–2001.

Democracies in Development

Conclusions

The positive news from the examination of public attitudes is that most Latin Americans appear to support democracy as their form of government, at least relative to the perceived alternatives. Citizens may express more confidence in the military as an institution than congress or political parties, but they do not support the armed forces assuming power. Democracy is supported in part because citizens believe that they should have a right to select their leaders and influence the making of public policy. It is also supported because citizens believe that, while less than perfect, it is better than all feasible alternative regimes.

Whether based on principle or more pragmatic considerations, support for democracy as a form of government was fairly strong in most Latin American countries until the 2001 Latinobarómetro survey. The responses to this recent survey are cause for concern, since a continued decline in legitimacy across the region impedes the consolidation, and even threatens the survival, of democratic regimes. Support for democracy has shown particular vulnerability in a few countries (Brazil, Colombia, Ecuador, El Salvador, Guatemala and Paraguay). At the same time, it may be strengthening in others, such as Mexico.

Despite general support for the idea of democracy and the rejection of authoritarian alternatives, most citizens are disenchanted with the performance of their democratic systems. Governments and the larger processes of democracy have not met their expectations with respect to the delivery of goods and solving social problems, nor in terms of the processes through which public functions are carried out. In spite of the relatively generalized nature of the disenchantment, the political consequences have been distinctive in different countries. Polls in some countries suggest a kind of nostalgia for strong leadership, which has helped bring to power by electoral means leaders (at the national and subnational levels) who had previously attempted to access power through coup d'états, who had been generals in the military, or who had previously participated in more restrictive, if not oppressive, regimes. In other cases, the disenchantment has propelled to power political "outsiders" who either had weak or no ties to established political parties, or were previous leaders of such parties who had now distanced themselves from such associations. In both cases, the political discourse acquired a clear anti-party orientation and the tendency towards a more personalistic form of representation was reinforced.

The end result is that in some countries, the political party system has been seriously weakened, and the credibility of congress, other democratic institutions and politicians individually and as a class of actors in the political system has eroded. This has led, in some cases, to the practical disappearance of longstanding and important political parties, and has made it more difficult for traditional representative institutions to effectively carry out their critical functions. A consequence of this development is that democratic competition tends to become more uncertain and fraught with tension, representation more personalistic, and accountability between politicians and constituents looser. In some cases, the loss in credibility of elected officials, political parties and the legislature has clearly weakened the capacity of government to effectively respond to economic and social problems, given the fragility of public trust in the integrity and reasonableness of whatever actions that are initiated. The weakened reputation of political parties and legislatures also tends to move such systems more firmly into the category of "delegative" democracies, in which the executive predominates in decision-making, with only weak oversight over the exercise of its powers (O'Donnell, 1994).

The relatively low level of confidence in and satisfaction with democratic institutions and politicians impede progress toward the consolidation of democracy. Broadening the group of citizens who strongly support democracy for reasons of principle rather than just for instrumental reasons (i.e., "democracy is better than visible alternatives") depends on improving perceptions of the performance of democracy. When democracy is supported only instrumentally, it is more vulnerable to sabotage by leaders who offer efficient solutions to the country's problems in exchange for reduced checks on their power.

Possibly associated with this lack of confidence in institutions is also a relatively low level of trust between individuals in society. This lack of interpersonal trust may impede the willingness of citizens to participate in their communities and in the political system, and is probably associated with widespread problems of crime and corruption and the difficulties in fighting them.

As will be discussed in the following chapter, disenchantment with the functioning of democratic institutions and with the conduct of politicians can eventually affect the inclination of citizens to become involved in political activity and, in particular, to vote. In turn, this decline in participation may then contribute to a further deterioration in the responsiveness and accountability of politicians and, as a consequence, lead to further disenchantment.

To enhance the functioning of democracy and further its consolidation, it is important that attention be given to building confidence in democratic processes and institutions. This means that elected leaders should govern by consensus and allow representative institutions to build their capacity and credibility. Of course, building the credibility of democratic institutions is a long-term task that in some cases may entail relatively profound reforms. Strengthening public administration and delivering public services more efficiently can help build support for democracy.

Bibliography

Boix, Carles, and David Posner. 1998. The Origins and Political Consequences of Social Capital. *British Journal of Political Science* 28.

Central and Eastern Eurobarometer. 1998. *Status of the European Union, October-November, 1996*. Ann Arbor, MI: Inter-University Consortium for Political and Social Research.

Consorcio Iberoamericano de Empresas de Investigación de Mercado y Asesoramiento (CIMA). 2001. Public opinion survey in cooperation with the Instituto Gallup de Argentina.

Diamond, Larry, Juan Linz, and Seymour Martin Lipset (eds.). 1989. *Democracy in Developing Countries*. London: Amantine.

Eurobarometer 26. 1986. *Political Cleavages in the European Community*. Brussels: INRA.

Eurobarometer 45. 1996. *European Union Rights, Sun Exposure, Work Safety, and Privacy Issues*. Brussels: INRA.

Eurobarometer 53. 2000. *Racism, Information Society, General Services, and Food Labeling*. Brussels: INRA.

Freedom House. 2000. *Freedom in the World: The Annual Survey of Political Rights and Civil Liberties, 1999–2000*. New York: Freedom House.

Fukuyama, Francis. 1995. *Trust: The Social Virtues and the Creation of Prosperity*. New York: Free Press.

Inglehart, Ronald F. 1990. *Culture Shift in Advanced Industrial Society*. Princeton: Princeton University Press.

———. 1997. *Modernization and Postmodernization: Cultural Economic and Political Change in 43 Societies*. Princeton: Princeton University Press.

———. 2000. *World Values Survey (1990–93 and 1995–97)*. Ann Arbor, MI: Inter-University Consortium for Political and Social Research.

Lagos, Marta. How People View Democracy: Between Stability and Crisis in Latin America. *Journal of Democracy* 12(1).

Latinobarómetro. 1996–2001. *Latinobarómetro: Opinión pública Latinoamericana*. Santiago, Chile.

Lipset, Seymour Martin. 1993. The Centrality of Political Culture. In Larry Diamond and Marc F. Plattner (eds.), *The Global Resurgence of Democracy*. Baltimore: The Johns Hopkins University Press.

McAllister, Ian. The Economic Performance of Governments. 1999. In Pippa Norris (ed.), *Critical Citizens: Global Support for Democratic Governance*. New York: Oxford University Press.

Newton, Kenneth. 1999. Social and Political Trust in Established Democracies. In Pippa Norris (ed.), *Critical Citizens: Global Support for Democratic Governance*. New York: Oxford University Press.

Norris, Pippa (ed.). 1999. *Critical Citizens: Global Support for Democratic Governance*. New York: Oxford University Press.

O'Donnell, Guillermo. 1994. Delegative Democracy. *Journal of Democracy* 5(1). January.

Putnam, Robert D. 1993. *Making Democracy Work*. Princeton: Princeton University Press.

CHAPTER THREE

Trends in Electoral Participation

Electoral participation is central to the functioning of democratic systems: people otherwise scarcely involved in a nation's political life nonetheless express their preferences among competing candidates on Election Day.

Democratic political participation is a much broader concept than voting, which is a more formal and episodic form of citizen participation. Political participation connotes ongoing involvement in the formulation, approval or implementation of public policies—a level of commitment and engagement in public affairs that rarely attracts more than a quarter of the adult population (CAPEL, 1989). In contrast, of the various forms of citizen participation—including involvement in political campaigns or party meetings, membership in community organizations, joining protests, or communicating with legislative representatives—voting is the only one in which more than 50 percent of the citizenry of democratic countries usually take part.

Since quantitative and comparative data are available for electoral participation but are more uneven and sparse for the broader notion of political participation, the evaluation of trends and levels in the region in this chapter will examine only the former. There is evidence that suggests, however, that voters are more likely than non-voters to be interested in politics and to participate more regularly in other forms of political activity (Putnam, 2000). One factor that will not be measured directly, but which clearly affects the quality of political participation, is the degree to which citizens acquire information about politics through newspapers, television and other media. Thus, from a conceptual standpoint, political participation should be measured in at least two dimensions: the *level* of participation, meaning the number of citizens that vote or otherwise participate to some degree in the political system; and the *intensity* of participation, meaning the extent to which citizens engage in the more demanding forms of participation and acquire information about politics (IDB, 2000).

Of course, when one refers to electoral participation and its value for democracy, implicit assumptions are being made about the nature of the voting process. It is assumed that elections are held in a context in which democratic freedoms are fully protected, and that the voting process is fair and honest. Considerable progress has been made across Latin America during the period of this study in terms of improving the fairness and credibility of elections. Electoral management bodies now exist in every country of the region, and in many countries these entities have taken on a more permanent character and assumed a growing number of functions. As a consequence, only in relatively few cases over the past decade have the procedures followed on Election Day or the tabulation of votes been perceived as fraudulent by objective observers.

Despite this important accomplishment, developing more permanent professional and managerial capacity in these electoral bodies could further enhance the electoral process. That would enable them to maintain accurate voter registration lists and effectively enforce regulations with respect to electoral and party financing and access to the media. The fairness of elections depends on more than simply guaranteeing an unbiased expression and counting of voter preferences. The broader issue of electoral fairness entails ensuring relatively equal access to campaign resources for candidates, a politically independent media, and transparency in the origin and use of campaign donations (see Chapter Seven). Efforts have been made across the region in these areas but, just as in some of the more established democracies, serious problems remain. As a consequence, citizens in some countries remain skeptical about the integrity and fairness of the electoral process.[1]

Importance of Electoral Participation

The extent to which citizens exercise their right (or duty) to vote clearly affects the degree to which elections perform the functions expected of them in a modern democracy. Among the functions commonly mentioned are: 1) legitimizing governmental authority; 2) forming governments; 3) recruiting political leaders; 4) fostering public discussion and debate about issues; and 5) facilitating the development and exercise of citizenship (Heywood, 1997). While all of these functions are important, this chapter will focus on two that are central to the notion of democracy: 1) *providing citizens a means to signal their preferences with respect to public policies, and* 2) *providing citizens a means to hold public officials accountable for their performance.*

Democratic representation entails a kind of bargain between citizens and elected officials. Citizens confer authority (by voting) in exchange for promises by politicians to pursue a given package of policy goals, serve the public good, and respect the law and the constitution. Given the informality of this transaction, the infrequency of elections, and the deficient information possessed by citizens, this process never produces fully responsive or even always honest politicians. But the effectiveness of democracy can be traced in part to the quality of this two-way exchange (Lupia and McCubbins, 1998).

---

[1] See Figure 3.4 for survey information on public opinion regarding this issue.

The likelihood that elections will produce effective and accountable political representation hinges on a range of institutional factors, including the nature of the electoral and party systems (see Chapters Four, Five and Six), the capacity of the legislature (see Chapter Eight), and the independence and effectiveness of agencies of horizontal accountability (see Chapter Nine). However, it can be argued that at the foundation of "good" government is a well-informed and highly participatory citizenry.

The fewer the number of citizens who participate individually and as members of civil society organizations, the more probable it is that the public's needs and demands will be ignored, and that public officials will give in to the natural inclination to pursue private interests at the expense of the public good. There are two broad dangers from low levels of electoral participation. First, they often result from relatively low participation by certain groups of citizens, such as the poor, the less educated, women, the young or the old, or people of particular ethnic backgrounds or geographical regions. If certain groups of citizens tend not to participate, it is likely that public policies will be biased against them. A vicious circle may arise in which under-participating groups are ignored in decision-making, thus further alienating them from the political system and reinforcing the bias in public policies. The second danger of low levels of political participation is that it means that the actions of public officials will be less subject to public scrutiny, thus increasing the possibility that unresponsive or corrupt behavior will fail to be noticed and consequently punished at the polls (IDB, 2000). Societies with low levels of political participation and knowledge will be less able to foresee and signal to public officials the policies that will lead to good performance, and less determined to press for implementation of those policies.

A low or declining level of electoral participation may not only hinder efficient democratic representation, it also may reflect a lack of confidence in democratic institutions, which could delay consolidation of the democratic regime or even threaten its stability.

Low electoral participation is of particular concern in societies where the transition to democracy is recent and a broad foundation of democratic values and practices is lacking. If large numbers of people do not vote, it is difficult to build a democratic culture and strengthen the legitimacy and functional capacity of democratic institutions such as the legislature and the judiciary. In sum, low levels of electoral participation can set off a deteriorating cycle in which disappointment in the performance of politicians breeds further distrust and political alienation, in turn further reducing participation and the incentives for better performance. Disenchantment with democratic actors and institutions can open the doors of power to leaders and movements more willing to rule unconstitutionally.

Factors Affecting Electoral Participation

The question of why citizens participate actively in civic affairs in some countries or regions and not in others has been studied extensively.[2] While it is not the intention of this chapter

---

[2] See Almond and Verba (1965), Nie and Verba (1975), Verba, Nie and Kim (1971), Powell (1980), Powell (1986), LeDuc, Niemi and Norris (1996), International IDEA (1997), and Jackman (1987).

to review this literature or to explain voter turnout levels in the region, it is useful to briefly consider the main forces that are expected to influence levels of electoral participation. Though these factors have been found to shape turnout to some degree, a large portion of the variance remains unexplained in most studies.

Factors that have been fairly stable over time and could help explain comparative levels of electoral participation (though not sudden shifts in turnout) include political culture (that is, the level of interpersonal trust and civic cooperation); educational levels of the population; the level of economic development; the extent of the linkages between political parties and salient cleavage groups in society; and the degree of ethnolinguistic homogeneity (Powell, 1980).

Clearly, citizens would be more likely to vote in large numbers in societies where people place greater trust in others and are therefore more inclined to join civic organizations. More years of education and higher incomes would be expected to enhance citizens' political awareness as well as their capacity to participate in politics. However, given the minimal educational and resource demands of voting, income and education might have a greater effect on the intensity of political participation than on the level of electoral participation per se.

It would also be expected that when parties represent important lines of cleavage in society—such as religion or social class—the electoral outcomes take on a more readily identifiable significance and parties can more easily mobilize their more poorly informed and less interested supporters. Finally, greater ethnolinguistic diversity would likely reduce electoral participation, since the sense of national community is weaker and linguistic or cultural barriers may impede political activity and voting by those from minority groups.

An additional factor that is structural in nature pertains to legislation in place regarding the process of registering to vote and voting itself. First, more citizens would be expected to participate when voting is obligatory rather than purely voluntary. In fact, studies of relatively established democracies suggest that compulsory voting laws result in somewhat higher levels of turnout (Powell, 1980; Jackman, 1987). The degree to which legal requirements make a difference, however, depends on the severity of the penalty and the likelihood of being caught and punished. If the penalty is minimal or rarely enforced, then the law will likely have little effect. Such conditions would be more likely to prevail in democracies such as those in Latin America, where the rule of law is less well established.

Second, the number of citizens who vote may be affected by whether election registration is automatic, mandatory or voluntary. If it is an obligation of the state to maintain updated lists of registered voters or periodically canvas citizens to create or update lists, then registration itself should not impose a significant obstacle to voting. One would also expect mandatory registration to encourage more citizens to register and vote. But if it is up to citizens to apply to the authorities to get on the registration lists, then a larger number may not become registered and therefore not vote.

In Latin America, registration and voting in most countries is currently mandatory, although this requirement is hotly debated. Advocates of penalties for non-voting view voting as a public duty and believe that such legislation can increase electoral participation above what it would otherwise be. Critics of legal mandates believe that voting is a right,

Table 3.1. Compulsory Registration and Voting

	Registration			Voting	
	Compulsory	Automatic	Voluntary	Compulsory	Voluntary
Argentina	X			X[1]	
Bolivia	X			X	
Brazil		X		X[2]	
Chile			X	X[3]	
Colombia			X		X
Costa Rica			X	X	
Dominican Rep.	X			X	
Ecuador		X		X[4]	
El Salvador	X			X	
Guatemala	X			X	
Honduras	X			X	
Mexico	X			X	
Nicaragua	X				X
Panama	X			X	
Paraguay	X			X	
Peru			X	X[5]	
Uruguay	X			X	
Venezuela	X			X	

[1] Voting is mandatory up to the age of 70.
[2] Voting is mandatory for those 18 to 70 who are literate, and optional for those who are 16–17 years old, over 70, or illiterate.
[3] Voting is mandatory only for citizens who are registered to vote.
[4] Voting is mandatory for those who are literate and 65 or younger.
[5] Voting is mandatory up to age 70 for citizens who are literate.

and that including votes of citizens who participate only for fear of being penalized may spoil the election process.

In Brazil, Costa Rica and Ecuador, voter registration is automatic, while in 12 other countries it is compulsory (Table 3.1). Registration is voluntary in only three countries: Chile, Colombia and Peru. Voting is compulsory in 16 of the 18 countries in this study. In Chile, voting is compulsory only for those who are registered to vote, and in Colombia and Nicaragua, voting is not mandatory. Colombia, then, is the only country where both registration and voting are fully voluntary.

Given that in some countries electoral turnout varies considerably from one election to the next, it is evident that more than just structural factors play a role in electoral participation. Factors that might cause episodic or more persistent upward and downward movements in turnout include changes in 1) the political regime; 2) the popularity of the candidates or the perceived importance of the issues at stake in a given election; 3) the level of confidence in democratic political institutions and practices (including the perceived integrity of electoral processes) or in the degree of respect for politicians; or 4) in the degree of institutionalization of political parties.

For example, turnout might be unusually high in the elections that mark the transition to democracy, since such changes in regime are often characterized by considerable citizen mobilization and enthusiasm for the exercise of new democratic freedoms. When this extraordinary period wanes and the populace experiences the realities of governing in complex circumstances, turnout might decline in subsequent elections. Aside from this initial possible decline, electoral participation may oscillate in response to circumstantial factors, such as the attractiveness of particular candidates, the competitiveness of the electoral contest, or the perceived seriousness of the issues at stake.

More systemic and enduring trends in electoral participation may be caused by the degree of faith that citizens have in their political leaders and their trust in representative and other governmental institutions. Thus, to some extent, long-term trends in electoral participation may reflect changes in public perceptions of the operation and performance of the democratic system. However, low turnout in one country relative to the regional average does not necessarily indicate a lack of confidence in democratic institutions. Rather, low turnout could be due to more constant structural features of the society, such as those discussed above.

Voter Turnout in Latin America

How does the level of electoral participation in Latin America compare with that of other regions of the world? The average percentage of the eligible population that turned out to vote in elections over 1990–95 in the 18 Latin American countries in this study was 62.5 percent. Figure 3.1 shows that this turnout is less than that in Central and Eastern Europe, the high-income countries, or East Asia, where more than 70 percent of the voting age population generally turns out to vote. Average turnout among the countries of the former Soviet Union is roughly comparable to that of this sample of Latin American countries. Lower turnout was reported in the three remaining regions: South Asia, the Middle East and North Africa, and Sub-Saharan Africa.[3]

Average turnout for the region, however, masks a large degree of variation between countries. Table 3.2 shows the average percentage of registered voters and of the voting age population who participated in Latin American presidential elections from 1978–2000. For legislative elections, the percentage of registered voters who participated is shown.[4] The average turnout in presidential elections measured as a share of registered voters ranges from a low of around 45 to 55 percent in Colombia, El Salvador and Guatemala to a high of around 90 percent in Chile and Uruguay. Electoral participation in legislative elections is somewhat lower in most countries.

---

[3] The relative positions of the regions with respect to electoral participation do not change substantially if one restricts the sample of countries to only those whose political systems are reasonably democratic, as measured by the indicators of Freedom House.

[4] Turnout in legislative elections measured as a percentage of the voting age population is shown in Appendix 2.

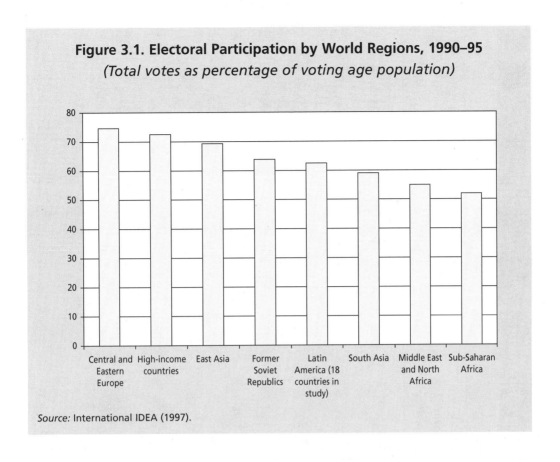

Figure 3.1. Electoral Participation by World Regions, 1990–95
(Total votes as percentage of voting age population)

Source: International IDEA (1997).

When the more meaningful measure of voting as a share of the voting age population is considered, there are a few countries for which the turnout figure changes significantly. Given the optional nature of voter registration in Chile, turnout as a share of the voting age population is 10 percent less than turnout that is measured as a share of the number of registered electors. Turnout is also considerably lower in terms of voting age population in Peru, Bolivia, Paraguay, Guatemala and, to a somewhat lesser extent, the Dominican Republic, Venezuela and Ecuador. In these countries, there are a fairly large number of citizens who are not registered to vote. When voting age population is used as the denominator instead of the number of registered voters, the regional ranking of Chile, Peru and Bolivia goes down by more than two places, while that of Costa Rica goes up by three places.

When just the 1990s are considered (Figure 3.2), most countries are clustered in the range between 68 and 80 percent of registered voters participating in elections. However, in four countries—Colombia, El Salvador, Guatemala and Venezuela—turnout is 60 percent or below. In the 1990s, turnout has averaged above 80 percent in Uruguay, Chile, Argentina, Nicaragua and Brazil. Turnout has generally been at this level in Costa Rica as well, except for 1998, when it dipped to close to 70 percent. El Salvador and Guatemala had the lowest level of electoral participation, with fewer than 45 percent of registered voters exercising their right to vote.

Table 3.2. Electoral Participation in Latin America, 1978–2000

Country	Presidential elections			Legislative elections	
	Elections included	Turnout (% of registered voters)	Turnout (% of voting age population)	Elections included	Turnout (% of registered voters)
Chile	1989, 93, 97	92.0	80.3	1989, 93, 99	92.0
Uruguay	1984, 89, 94, 99	89.8	95.6	1984, 89, 94, 99	90.0
Argentina	1983, 89, 95, 01	83.6	81.9	1983, 85, 87, 89, 91, 93, 95, 97, 99	83.0
Brazil	1989, 94, 98	82.9	76.0	1986, 90, 94, 98	85.3
Nicaragua	1990, 96	81.3	75.9	1990, 96	81.7
Peru	1980, 85, 90, 95, 00	80.9	67.8	1980, 85, 90, 95, 00	73.4
Costa Rica	1978, 82, 86, 90, 94, 98	79.6	79.8	1978, 82, 86, 90, 94, 98	79.1
Panama	1989, 94, 99	75.6	71.1	1994, 99	74.0
Honduras	1981, 85, 89, 93, 97	74.7	70.9	1981, 85, 89, 93, 97	72.3
Bolivia	1980, 85, 89, 93, 97	74.7	58.0	1980, 85, 89, 93, 97	74.7
Dominican Rep.	1978, 82, 86, 90, 94, 96, 00	73.2	61.2	1978, 82, 86, 90, 94, 98	67.0
Venezuela	1978, 83, 88, 93, 98, 00	72.9	61.8	1978, 83, 88, 93, 98, 00	71.0
Ecuador	1978, 84, 88, 92, 96, 98	72.7	61.7	1979, 84, 86, 88, 90, 92, 94, 96, 98	69.4
Paraguay	1989, 93, 98	68.0	54.2	1989, 93, 98	65.5
Mexico	1982, 88, 94, 00	66.5	58.3	1982, 85, 88, 91, 94, 97, 00	65.0
Guatemala	1985, 90, 95, 99	56.6	41.4	1985, 90, 95, 99	49.0
El Salvador	1989, 94, 99	47.7	41.9	1988, 91, 94, 97, 00	50.2
Colombia	1978, 82, 86, 90, 94, 98	44.1	39.3	1978, 82, 86, 90, 91, 94, 98	41.1
LAC average		73.2	65.5		71.2

Figure 3.2. Average Turnout in Presidential Elections, 1990s
(Total votes as percentage of registered voters)

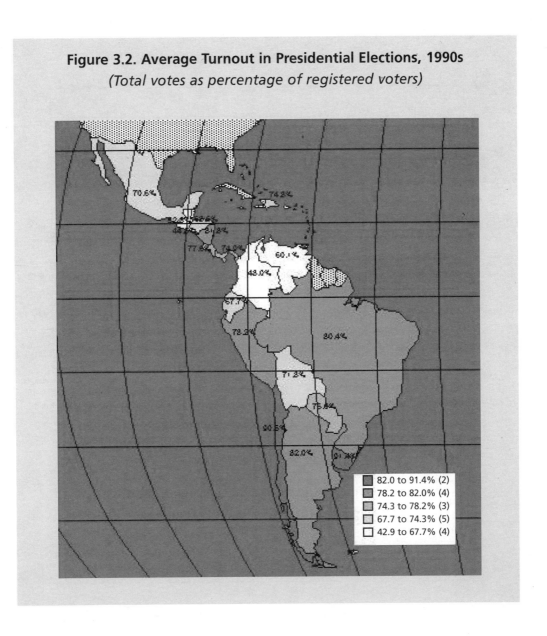

Legend:
- 82.0 to 91.4% (2)
- 78.2 to 82.0% (4)
- 74.3 to 78.2% (3)
- 67.7 to 74.3% (5)
- 42.9 to 67.7% (4)

It is readily seen, then, that registration and voting laws alone cannot account for the varying levels of electoral participation in Latin America. Even though voting is compulsory in all countries except Colombia and Nicaragua, there is still a large range in voter turnout. Despite the presence of such laws, in several countries as much as 40 percent of registered voters still do not vote. Though not compelled by law, more citizens in Nicaragua turn out to vote than in all but three of the countries where voting is mandatory.

Two factors associated with the level of electoral participation are the degree to which political rights and civil liberties are protected, and the perceived integrity of the electoral process. As shown in Figure 3.3, countries across the world where democratic freedoms are more highly respected have higher rates of turnout. Even when other control factors such as income levels, literacy rates and the degree of ethnolinguistic fragmentation are consid-

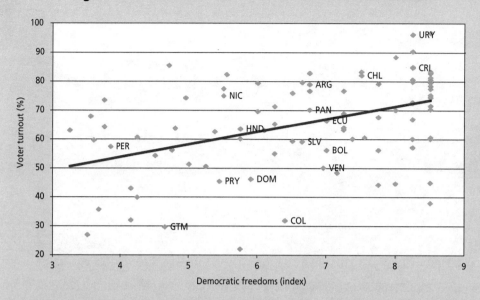

Figure 3.3. Turnout vs. the Democratic Freedom Index

Note: This figure plots for each country the average percentage of the eligible population that voted in elections from 1990–95, the average of Freedom House ratings for political rights and civil liberties (rescaled from 1 to 10), and the democracy indicator provided by Jaggers and Gurr (1995) in the Polity III database.

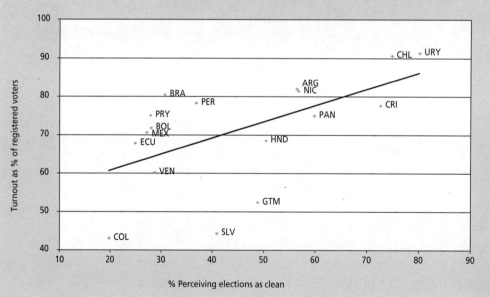

Figure 3.4. Turnout in Presidential Elections vs. the Perceived Integrity of Electoral Processes

Note: The percentage perceiving elections as "clean" is an average of the responses from each country to the 1999/2000 Latinobarómetro surveys.

ered, the influence of the scope and depth of democratic freedoms remains robust.[5] Thus, the extent of political freedom and competition, and perhaps the depth of respect for democratic principles, appear to motivate electoral participation.

Data from the 18 Latin American countries in this study clearly show that electoral participation in presidential elections (as a percent of registered voters) is associated with the perceived integrity of the electoral process (Figure 3.4). Despite efforts across the region to reduce or eliminate fraud in the election process, citizens in a number of countries are not convinced that such processes are sufficiently clean and fair. The association with electoral participation suggests that if steps could be taken to increase public confidence in elections, turnout might increase.

Trends in Electoral Participation

How has the level of electoral turnout in Latin America evolved over the past two decades? Is there a clear and persistent upward or downward trend in electoral participation? Figure 3.5 plots the average turnout for 18 Latin American countries in presidential and legislative elections from 1978–2000. Given that elections occur only every four or five years in most countries, the turnout value for one election is included in the computation of the regional average for a period of four years; the year before the election actually took place; the year of the election; and two years following the election. In this way the figure computed for the average regional turnout is not distorted by the differences in the particular set of countries included in each year's average.

Figure 3.6 shows the trend in average turnout in a somewhat more rigorous manner. It first estimates a linear trend line for each country that plots "predicted" values for each year of the study. These predicted values are derived from the actual values using a statistical procedure. A regional average for each year was computed on the basis of these predicted values.

Figures 3.5 and 3.6 show a clear but not precipitous declining trend in electoral turnout. However, some caution must be exercised in interpreting these figures, since the trend line potentially captures two types of developments. On the one hand, the trend line reflects the average of the changes *within* countries across time. If this were the only phenomenon at work, a downward trend would unambiguously point to a decline in turnout in most countries of the region. But on the other hand, the lines show the effects on the regional average of the gradual inclusion in the study sample of new countries in which elec-

---

[5] The index of democratic freedoms remains statistically significant when any combination of per capita GDP, the literacy rate, and an index of ethnolinguistic diversity are included as variables in the regression analysis. When all of the variables are considered, ethnolinguistic diversity and GDP per capita are not statistically significant, while the literacy rate and the index of democratic freedoms are. The association between the index of democratic freedom and the turnout level is more statistically significant when the least free countries (those with an index rating less than 3) are excluded from the analysis. This finding is consistent with the hypothesis that greater political freedoms encourage participation. In the case of highly restrictive authoritarian regimes, one might expect citizens to participate in large numbers despite the absence of real competition and open political debate, since abstention is more likely to result in harsh penalties and voting may be more directly coerced.

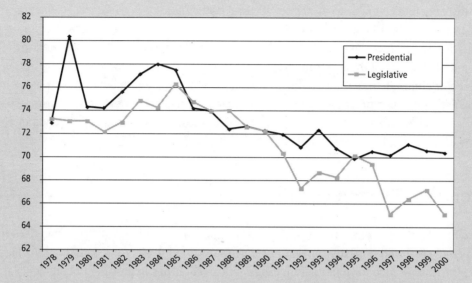

**Figure 3.5. Evolution of Electoral Turnout
in Latin America, 1978–2000**
(Percent of registered voters)

Note: The computation of the regional average for a given year includes turnout figures for countries considered at that time to be "democratic." The elections included are the same as those in Table 3.2.

tions were previously not held, or where democracy was insufficiently established to be included in the study.

Starting with 1985, when 14 of the 18 countries are considered "democratic" and are included in the computation of the regional average, Figure 3.5 shows that the average turnout in presidential elections fell by about 7 percent—from 77 to 70 percent. Turnout in legislative elections declined by a somewhat more sharp 11 percent—from 76 to 65 percent. Whatever its interpretation, this aggregate trend, while significant, is not yet a cause for serious alarm. Supporting this benign assessment is the fact that average turnout as a share of registered voters for presidential elections has remained fairly steady since 1991, hovering between 70 and 72 percent.

Figure 3.6 plots the average of the estimated (predicted) turnout values (computed as a percent of registered voters) for each country. It shows a trend that is similar in terms of its overall direction and magnitude.[6] The average of the estimated values declined from about 78 percent in 1985 to about 71 percent in 2000.

According to the reasoning above, the downward trend that appears in the figures may not reflect a general decline in turnout in most countries of the region. Rather, the decline in the regional average could have resulted from the gradual inclusion after 1985 of four ad-

---

[6] For each country, a best-fit linear regression line is computed from the actual turnout values. On the basis of the equation describing this best-fit line, estimated values are computed for each year, even those in which elections were not actually held. This trend is more stable than the actual trend since a linear fit is assumed, when the actual turnout values may not follow such a pattern.

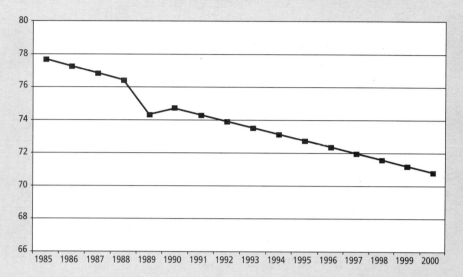

Figure 3.6. Trend in Electoral Turnout in Presidential Elections, 1985-2000

(Average annual percentage based on predicted values)

Note: For each country, a least squared regression procedure was used to estimate a best-fit trend line from the actual turnout values. The regional average plotted in the figure is computed on the basis of the individual country estimates for each year.

ditional countries characterized by lower levels of turnout than the 14 countries included previously. In that case, turnout might be fairly constant across time in most countries. The only change would have been in the composition of the sample. A more careful analysis, however, shows that the downward trend does indeed reflect a decline in turnout in countries of the region. The average turnout of the four countries added to the sample after 1985 is, if anything, larger than the 14 countries previously included. Thus, the average decline in turnout could actually be slightly over 7 percent.

How much of this decline is due to the post-transition election effect discussed earlier? It might be expected that turnout would be unusually high in the inaugural election of a democratic system. Most countries in the study experienced a transition from authoritarian to democratic systems during the period under consideration. Therefore, the aggregate decline could be a product of these individual country descents from an unusually high initial turnout figure. However, this possibility is only weakly supported by the data. On average, only 1 percent separates the rate of electoral participation in inaugural presidential elections from that of the succeeding election. Thus, the decline cannot be attributable solely to this effect.

As always, however, the aggregate trend line conceals widely diverging patterns in different countries across the region. Individual countries do not show a neat conformity to the aggregate trend of gradual decline. Some show unambiguous declines or increases in turnout, while others show relative stability and unpredictable upward and downward movements (Figure 3.7 and Table 3.3; see also Appendix 1).

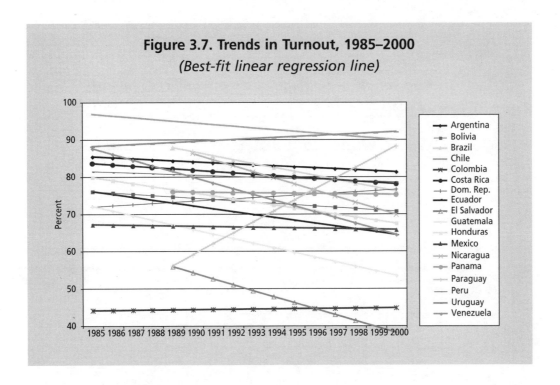

Figure 3.7. Trends in Turnout, 1985–2000
(Best-fit linear regression line)

Legend: Argentina, Bolivia, Brazil, Chile, Colombia, Costa Rica, Dom. Rep., Ecuador, El Salvador, Guatemala, Honduras, Mexico, Nicaragua, Panama, Paraguay, Peru, Uruguay, Venezuela

Turnout has clearly fallen during the period in Venezuela, Ecuador, El Salvador, Honduras, Guatemala and Brazil. Of these, the first three show the sharpest drops. In Venezuela, turnout as a share of registered voters went from about 87 percent in 1978 to about 56 percent in 2000. In Ecuador, turnout fell from 81 percent in 1979 to 64 percent in 1998. In El Salvador, turnout dropped from 55 percent in 1989 to 39 percent in 2000. Given the complexities of the ballot in legislative elections in Brazil, there was an extraordinarily large proportion (around 30 percent) of blank or invalid votes cast until the 1998 election. With an improved voting system, 15 percent more ballots in legislative elections were validly cast for a party or candidate in the 1998 election. Thus, this increase could be seen as offsetting the decrease in votes cast as a share of registered voters.

Aside from these six countries where the turnout trend is unambiguously downwards, there are two additional cases where there is a visible, but provisional, negative trend. Turnout in Costa Rica was stable at around 80 percent until the most recent two elections (1998 and 2002), when it fell to around 70 percent. Turnout in Nicaragua fell 10 percent between 1990 and 1996, but remained stable in the most recent election (November 2001). Relatively minor negative trends in electoral turnout have also occurred in Argentina, Bolivia and Chile. In the Chilean case, turnout fell slightly from an extraordinarily high initial level of over 94 percent in 1990 to about 90 percent in 1999. In Argentina, turnout fell from 86 percent to 82 percent from 1983 to 1999. Similarly, turnout in Bolivia declined from about 74 percent in 1980 to about 71 percent in 1997.

Only in three countries was there an increasing trend, but in no case was it very profound. In Paraguay, turnout as a share of registered voters rose dramatically from 54 percent in 1989 to about 81 percent in 1998. But given that the number of voters who went to the polls actually decreased between 1989 and 1993, the apparent increase between the first two elections

Table 3.3. Trends in Turnout in Presidential Elections, 1978–2000

Country	Avg. turnout (% of registered voters)	Slope of trend line	Description of trend
El Salvador	47.76	−1.61	Clear, sharp negative trend
Venezuela	72.85	−1.54	Clear, sharp negative trend
Guatemala	56.57	−1.24	Clear, sharp negative trend
Brazil	82.93	−1.07	Clear, sharp negative trend
Honduras	74.71	−0.82	Relatively clear negative trend
Ecuador	72.67	−0.77	Relatively clear negative trend
Nicaragua	81.31	−1.64	Only two elections, but 10% drop from 1st to 2nd
Chile	92.00	−0.46	Relatively small negative trend from very high initial level
Costa Rica	79.61		Drops in most recent two elections
Bolivia	74.69	−0.35	Clear, relatively small negative trend
Argentina	83.58	−0.28	Clear, relatively small negative trend
Uruguay	89.81	0.26	Relatively small positive trend
Dominican Rep.	73.29	0.31	Ambiguous, slight upward trend
Paraguay	68.01	2.92	Upward trend between most recent elections
Colombia	44.12		No clear trend
Mexico	66.54		No clear trend
Panama	75.56		No clear trend
Peru	80.86		Ambiguous; if data correct recent election reversed negative trend

Note: Only those elections that took place during the "democratic" period for each country (as defined in Table 1 in the Introduction) are included in the computation of the average for the period and of the slope.

in the democratic period was due to the inflated voter registry used in the 1989 election. As a consequence, turnout as a proportion of registered voters was underestimated for the 1989 election (Riquelme and Riquelme, 1997). Nonetheless, there was a real increase in absolute and relative turnout between the 1993 and 1998 elections, since turnout as a share of the voting age population reached close to 60 percent after having been in the 50 percent range. In the Dominican Republic, turnout appears to have fallen from 1978 to 1990, but to have then risen again in the subsequent three presidential elections to a level above that of 1978.[7] Turnout also rose slightly in Uruguay from an already impressive 88 percent in 1984 to about 92 percent in 1999.

---

[7] The dramatic fall in participation in the 1998 legislative elections can probably be attributed to the fact that beginning in that year, elections for the president were not held concurrently.

In the remaining four countries in the study, no clear trend can be discerned. In Mexico and Colombia, turnout has moved up and down erratically with no clear trend in either direction. In Panama, it has been relatively constant over three elections. In Peru, a declining trend that started after the second post-transition election of 1985 was reversed in 2000, as turnout rose from about 74 percent in 1995 to around 83 percent in 2000. The turnout figure for 2000 is suspect, however, since the results of this election were heavily disputed by the opposition and by international observers. In addition, another factor, particularly in the 1995 legislative and 2000 second round presidential election, was a large share of invalid or null votes in the total. Though voters went to the polls in similar numbers, an unusually large percentage (31 percent in the 1995 legislative elections) either did not specify a preference or spoiled their ballots.

Thus, taking all the countries into account—even those where the trend is not very significant or long-term—we find that turnout has declined in 11 countries and risen in three countries. In the remaining four countries, no clear trend can be discerned.

Conclusions

Focusing narrowly on the question of electoral participation, this chapter does not permit more far-reaching conclusions about the effectiveness or equity of democratic delegation and representation in Latin America. Although the level of electoral participation may be related to the level and intensity of participation conceived in more general terms, the two factors do not necessarily go together. What can be said is that on average about 62 percent of eligible citizens vote in major national elections. Whether this is considered to be high, moderate or low turnout depends, of course, on the basis for comparison. That is, turnout relative to what other countries or sets of countries and what periods of time?

In absolute terms, the regular abstention of almost 40 percent of the eligible population from taking part in a process so fundamental to the working of democratic systems would appear to suggest a substantial deficiency in Latin American democracies. However, given that a far lower proportion of citizens vote in some stable and apparently successful democracies, such as the United States (50 percent) and Switzerland (45 percent), this fact by itself may not be cause for serious concern. Relative to other regions, Latin American turnout is roughly in the middle of the pack: below the countries of Western and Central Europe, but above the poorer and less democratic regions of Sub-Saharan Africa, the Middle East and North Africa and South Asia. If the participation levels of the more established democracies are taken as the standard, then Latin American systems clearly could benefit from higher levels of voting.

More extensive and intensive political participation might enhance the fairness of representation, improve the efficiency of government, and reduce corruption. The level of voter turnout likely corresponds to some degree to measures of this broader notion of political participation. To the extent that this is true, we would expect higher turnout figures to be related to these other positive outcomes. The analysis of avail-

Figure 3.8. Electoral Turnout vs. Government Performance

a. Turnout vs. the Absence of Corruption

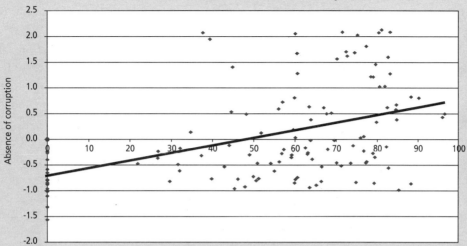

Electoral participation (% of voting age population)

b. Turnout vs. Government Effectiveness

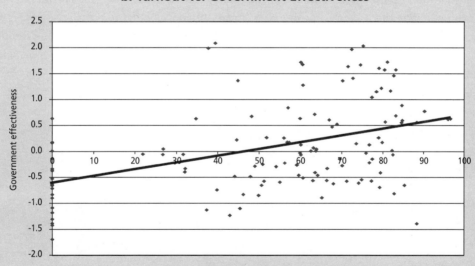

Electoral turnout (% of voting age population)

Sources: Data on the absence of corruption and government effectiveness from Kaufmann, Kraay and Zoido-Lobatón (1999a and 1999b); electoral participation data from International IDEA (1997).
Note: The turnout of countries scoring an average of 2.5 or below in terms of (an inverted scale) of Freedom House's ratings of political rights and civil liberties (categorized "not free") is considered to be zero in Figures 3.8a and 3.8b. It is assumed that in cases of minimal democratic freedom, turnout is not valuable from the standpoint of controlling leaders. If anything, a high level of turnout in such cases may reflect a higher coercive capability on the part of the political leadership.

able cross-national data suggests that turnout is associated at least to some extent with the absence of corruption and better governmental performance (Figure 3.8a and 3.8b). If the level of respect for democratic freedoms as well as political knowledge (or inquisitiveness) of citizens are also taken into account, this relationship becomes stronger (Adserà, Boix and Payne, 2000).

Electoral participation varies considerably from one country to the next in Latin America. In seven countries, turnout as a share of registered voters has been close to or above 80 percent. In three countries, less than 60 percent of registered citizens vote on average, while in the remaining eight countries turnout has ranged on average from about 65 to 80 percent.

Though the level of electoral participation across the region has declined modestly since the mid-1980s, it appears to have stabilized more recently. On the whole, turnout appears to have declined in 11 countries. Of these, the decline was significant in six countries and especially sharp in three others. Only in three countries has the trend been at least modestly positive. In the rest, there has either been little change or an ambiguous pattern of change.

Thus, in the region as a whole, the trends in turnout do not point to either a clear crisis of representation or to a growing legitimization of democracy. While the trend in the regional average does not indicate serious troubles, the sharp decline in several countries (particularly Ecuador, Venezuela and El Salvador) does appear to reflect increased disenchantment with democratic politics. The legitimacy crisis has in some cases resulted in political instability, the ascent to power of political outsiders, the virtual collapse of the political party system, or significant constitutional changes. Thus, such a pattern extended into the future could entail problems for the institutionalization of democracy for a significant portion of the region.

Bibliography

Adserà, Alícia, Carles Boix, and Mark Payne. 2000. *Are You Being Served? Political Accountability and Quality of Government*. Research Department Working Paper Series No. 438, Inter-American Development Bank, Washington, DC.

Almond, Gabriel, and Sidney Verba. 1965. *The Civic Culture*. Boston: Little, Brown.

————— (eds.). 1980. *The Civic Culture Revisited*. Boston: Little, Brown.

Centro Interamericano de Asesoría y Promoción Electoral, programa especializado del Instituto Interamericano de Derechos Humanos. 1989. In *Diccionario electoral*. San José: CAPEL.

Heywood, Andrew. 1997. *Politics*. London: Macmillan Press.

Inter-American Development Bank. 2000. *Development Beyond Economics: Economic and Social Progress in Latin America*. Washington, DC: IDB.

International IDEA. 1997. *Voter Turnout from 1945 to 1997: A Global Report on Political Participation*. Stockholm: International IDEA.

Jackman, Robert. 1987. Political Institutions and Voter Turnout in the Industrial Democracies. *American Political Science Review* 81 (June).

Jaggers, Keith, and Ted Robert Gurr. 1995. Tracking Democracy's Third Wave with the Polity III Data. *Journal of Peace Research* 32(4).

Kaufmann, Daniel, Aart Kraay, and Pablo Zoido-Lobatón. 1999. *Aggregating Governance Indicators*. Washington, DC: World Bank.

—————. 1999. *Governance Matters*. Washington, DC: World Bank.

Latinobarómetro. 1996–2001. *Latinobarómetro: Opinión pública Latinoamericana*. Santiago, Chile.

LeDuc, Lawrence, Richard G. Niemi, and Pippa Norris (eds.). 1996. *Comparing Democracies: Elections and Voting in Global Perspective*. London: Sage.

Lupia, Arthur, and Mathew D. McCubbins. 1998. *The Democratic Dilemma: Can Citizens Learn What They Need to Know?* Cambridge: Cambridge University Press.

Milbrath, Lester W. 1997. *Political Participation: How and Why Do People Get Involved in Politics*. Chicago: Rand McNally.

Nie, Norman, and Sidney Verba. 1975. Political Participation. In Fred I. Greenstein and Nelson W. Polsby (eds.), *Handbook of Political Science*. Reading, PA: Addison Wesley.

Powell, G. Bingham, Jr. 1980. Voting Turnout in Thirty Democracies: Partisan, Legal and Socio-Economic Influences. In Richard Rose (ed.), *Electoral Participation: A Comparative Analysis*. London: Sage.

—————. 1986. American Voter Turnout in Comparative Perspective. *American Political Science Review* 80 (March).

Putnam, Robert D. 2000. *Bowling Alone: The Collapse and Revival of American Community*. New York: Simon & Schuster.

Riquelme, Marcial A., and Jorge G. Riquelme. 1997. Political Parties. In Peter Lambert and Andrew Nickson (eds.). *The Transition to Democracy in Paraguay*. New York: St. Martin's Press.

Verba, Sidney, Norman H. Nie, and Jae-On Kim. 1971. *The Modes of Democratic Participation: A Cross-National Comparison*. Beverly Hills: Sage.

CHAPTER FOUR

The Effect of Presidential Election Systems on Democratic Governability

A key feature of presidential democracies is that the head of the government and the members of the legislature are separately elected by citizens. With one partial exception, this basic criterion has been fulfilled during the entire period of this study by all 18 of the Latin American countries being reviewed.[1]

The division in presidential regimes of the selection, basis of authority and governing responsibilities of the two branches of government implies a greater probability of conflict between them than is the case in parliamentary regimes. Whether this inherent tension in presidential regimes can be effectively managed depends in part on the methods used for electing the chief executive and the legislators.

The electoral processes for the two branches are clearly not independent if they are held at the same time. Inevitably, the direct election of the head of government in a winner-take-all formula affects voter choices and party strategies in the legislative elections. Given that in a presidential race there can be only one winner, voters are constrained to choose among individual candidates who have a viable chance of winning. Smaller parties with little chance of winning by themselves have an incentive to band together and nominate a single candidate. Thus, when elections for the two branches are held on the same day, fewer parties are likely to receive significant shares of the vote in legislative elections. This is because many voters will follow the "coattails" of their preferred presidential candidate by voting for legislative candidates or lists from the same party (Shugart and Carey, 1992).

---

[1] In Bolivia, the first-round presidential election and the legislative election are separate. But in the usual event that no candidate obtains a majority in the first round, the congress chooses the president from the two candidates with the most votes. Before the 1994 constitutional reform, the congress decided among the top three vote-getters from the first round.

There are many effects of electoral systems on democratic governability. First, the legitimacy accorded an incumbent president is shaped by the apparent scope of victory, which is influenced by the election method used. Second, the interaction between the methods used for electing presidents and legislators affects the extent of party system fragmentation and the proportion of the congressional seats controlled by the chief executive's party. Both of these factors affect the ability of presidents to obtain support in the legislature for their policy initiatives. Through its effect on the number of parties able to obtain representation in the legislature, the electoral system also influences the fairness of political representation.

This chapter will examine the influence of the system used for electing the president on the operation of democracy. The subsequent chapter will examine the influence of rules governing the election of legislators. Given the interactions between the two electoral processes, this chapter will by necessity also consider the matter of their timing and, in general terms, how the effects of presidential election systems may vary depending on the different methods chosen for electing legislative representatives.

Two related factors that will also be examined in this chapter are the length of the mandate (term of office) of the chief executive and the matter of whether or not presidents can be reelected. Shorter terms of office for presidents allow more frequent turnover and validation of popular support, and thus may alleviate the problem of "rigidity" associated with presidential regimes (see Chapter Eight). If a president loses all popular support and is rendered ineffective, there is less time to endure before someone else can be elected with a fresh mandate. At the same time, however, short terms limit the scope of the honeymoon period when the president is likely to be most effective in implementing major policy reforms.

Reelection encourages presidents to be accountable to citizens, since success in the next election depends on accomplishments and on maintaining the public trust. In addition, the possibility of reelection allows presidents to preserve congressional support later into their terms of office. Without the possibility of reelection, presidents have less to offer supporters and fewer tools with which to punish party defectors. Considering the political history of many Latin American countries, however, bans on reelection have been deemed necessary to prevent elected presidents from using or abusing the power and resources of their position to perpetuate themselves in office. Without adequate horizontal and vertical checks on presidential authority, such constitutional limits may be necessary to prevent the emergence of such "democratic dictatorships."

Systems for Electing Presidents

In general, presidents are elected by *plurality* or by *majority* (sometimes called a *runoff* or, borrowing from the French, *ballotage*). In plurality systems, the candidate with the most votes wins. In majority systems, a candidate must obtain one vote more than 50 percent of the votes if a winner is to be declared in the first round. If no candidate reaches this threshold, then a second round is held between the top two finishers from the first round. Following the pioneering approach taken by Costa Rica in its 1949 constitution, several Latin

American countries have adopted a threshold below a majority (40 percent in Costa Rica) for a candidate to be declared the winner in the first round. In this chapter, such a system is referred to as *runoff with a reduced threshold*.

Another matter is whether the president is elected *directly* or *indirectly*. Does the popular vote directly determine the winner of the presidential contest, or do voters elect representatives who, in turn, vote for the president? Prior to the adoption of the 1994 constitution in Argentina, voters elected delegates to an electoral college that was responsible for choosing the president.[2] In Bolivia, the congress is responsible for selecting the president if, as is common, no candidate obtains a majority in the first round. The first president elected in the post-authoritarian period in Brazil in the 1980s was chosen by the congress. These instances notwithstanding, however, all of the other Latin American countries in this study have elected their presidents through direct popular vote.

Other key issues related to presidential elections are their timing relative to legislative elections, and whether the votes for the two branches of government are linked together on the ballot. When the presidential elections occur on the same day as the parliamentary elections they are *concurrent*. Their degree of *concurrence* or *simultaneity* is even greater when the elections are not only on the same day but the elector is limited to one vote that signifies his preference for both the presidential candidate and a legislative candidate or list from the same party. When the elector is able to vote for a presidential candidate of one party and a legislative candidate or list of another party (called *voto cruzado* in Spanish), then the link between the elections is somewhat weaker.

At the same time, the simultaneity can be *complete* or *partial*. It is complete when the elections for president and the legislature are always held on the same day. It is partial when a portion of the legislative body is elected at a different point in time during the term of a sitting president. In Argentina, for example, half of the lower house and one-third of the senate are elected two years into the four-year presidential term. The extent of simultaneity is even less complete when varying term lengths for the presidency and legislature mean that elections are only rarely held at the same time. For instance, presidential and congressional elections in Chile coincide only every 12 years, since the presidential term is six years long, the term of deputies four years, and the term of senators eight years (half elected every four years).

With respect to reelection, there are a variety of different rules. The most restrictive case is that which forbids a president from being reelected at any point after having served one term of office. An intermediate case is one that allows reelection, but only after the passing of a period of at least one presidential term. The less restrictive case allows at least one consecutive term of office, that is, one-time reelection. Some systems that allow immediate reelection allow yet another term after the passing of at least the period of one presidential term.

---

[2] This was similar to the system still used in the United States, where an electoral college composed of slates of delegates from each of the 50 states elects the president. The candidate winning a plurality of the vote is generally awarded all of the delegates from the state. The candidate who obtains the vote of the majority of the delegates in the electoral college becomes president. It is extremely rare and in many cases illegal for delegates to vote against the candidate who won the plurality of the vote in their state. But as seen in the U.S. presidential election in 2000, the winner-take-all, state-by-state selection of delegates makes it possible for a candidate to win a plurality of the vote at the national level but not be selected as president.

How Plurality, Majority and Reduced Threshold Systems Affect Governability

The manner in which presidents are elected has *direct* and *indirect* effects. The direct effect has to do with the level of popular legitimacy obtained by the elected president as a consequence of the margin of the electoral victory. For example, a president who receives 60 percent of the votes in the first round, with a large advantage over all competitors, initiates his mandate with greater popular legitimacy and political backing than one who reaches power with a fairly small percentage of the vote (such as 30 percent). If the president is elected on the basis of a small percentage of the overall vote, then this could make it difficult for him to govern effectively and could lead to stalemate.

Whether the election is decided by plurality, majority or some lower threshold does not *directly* affect the share of the votes received by the candidate placing first in the first round. Rather, the margin of the result in the first round is related to the number of parties and candidates participating, as well as to circumstantial factors (such as party strategies affecting the number of candidates competing and the popular appeal of individual candidates). The runoff system is designed to amplify the apparent mandate of the elected president by requiring a second round if no candidate receives a sufficient proportion of the votes in the first round. The second round guarantees that the president is ultimately elected with a majority of the vote, regardless of how small a share of the vote that candidate received in the first round.

Thus, with respect to the question of the *mandate* or *popular legitimacy* of the elected president, the direct effects of a runoff system would appear to be beneficial, at least in cases in which the leading candidate in the first round typically receives one-third of the vote or less. However, a second round majority vote is unlikely to provide a mandate equivalent to that bestowed on a president who won on the basis of a majority, or even somewhat less than a majority, in the first round. In the runoff, many people who vote for the winning candidate do so only because they see him or her as the lesser of two evils. The "manufactured" majority in the second round may alleviate, but often does not solve, the problem of legitimacy for minority presidents. Nevertheless, considering only the direct effects, it would appear that the majority runoff system provides advantages for governability without any clear costs.

The adoption of a majority runoff system, however, is also likely to produce *indirect* effects that may result in presidents being elected with a weaker mandate, and with less legislative support than would have been the case if there were a plurality system. As mentioned above, if the elections are simultaneous, the presidential contest tends to narrow the field of parties competing for legislative seats.

The extent of this effect depends on the system used for electing the president and the closeness of the link on the ballot between the elections for the two branches. In plurality systems in which the candidate with the most votes in the first and only round wins, there is an incentive for parties (especially small and medium-sized ones) to seek alliances or organize coalitions before the election and for voters to focus their choices among those candidates/parties with a viable chance of winning. Given coattail effects, if the number of candidates/parties contending for the presidency is constrained, then this is also likely to limit the number of parties and party coalitions gaining seats in the legislature. By contrast, in majority runoff systems there are weaker incentives for parties to coalesce before the first round election, since there are potentially two winners and the contest is unlikely to decide who will become president. Even relatively small parties have an incentive to put forth a presidential candidate, since this will enhance their chance of winning legislative seats, and since a strong finish will enhance their bargaining position with respect to one of the two candidates in the runoff. In addition, voters are more free to express their true preference in the first round, since they will have a second opportunity to choose among the two most viable candidates (Shugart and Carey, 1992; Shugart, 1995; Jones, 1996).

Thus, a majority runoff formula encourages a larger number of parties to compete in the presidential race and obtain seats in the legislature than would be the case under a plurality system. Over time, therefore, the movement from a plurality to a majority runoff system could end up worsening the problem of democratic governability by lowering the share of the first round vote typically received by the eventual victor, and by reducing the partisan congressional support for the president.

Of course, for the presidential election to limit the number of parties competing and obtaining seats in the legislative contest, the two elections must be held on the same day. Other things being equal, concurrent elections are likely to result in fewer parties being represented in the congress than would be the case if they were held separately. In addition, concurrent elections lead to the direct effect of providing a larger share of the seats for the president's party. But when presidents are elected by plurality, the constraining effects on the number of parties competing and obtaining seats should be greater than in the case of majority runoff systems. The constraining effects of a single round presidential race on the legislative contest should be even greater when the elector is restricted to a single vote for the two branches. In that case, the coattail effects are perfect and the share of the vote for parties in the legislature exactly mirrors the share of votes received by the presidential candidates for these parties.

Runoff systems with a reduced threshold such as 40 or 45 percent act a little more like a plurality system in constraining the number of presidential candidates competing and the number of parties gaining legislative seats. Given the greater possibility that a candidate will be elected in the first round, parties still have some incentive to coalesce prior to the election and voters have to be more strategic. But if no candidate obtains this lower threshold in the first round, the runoff provides the benefit of expanding the elected president's mandate.

Holding constant the rules for electing the congress, Table 4.1 shows the expected effects of the timing of the elections for the two branches and the type of presidential election system. A plurality system combined with concurrent presidential and legislative elections is expected to lead to the greatest degree of concentration of the party system. The most fragmented party system would be expected to arise in the context of a majority runoff system with non-concurrent elections.

The theoretical expectation that plurality or runoff-with-reduced-threshold systems are more inclined to promote governability and stability may not always hold in practice. For example, if party systems are ideologically polarized and fragmented, parties may be disin-

Table 4.1. Tendency toward Concentration of the Party System according to Different Presidential Election Systems		
	Concurrent	Not concurrent
Plurality	1	3
Runoff with reduced threshold	2	4
Majority runoff	4	6

Note: A score of one means the most concentrated outcome, six the least concentrated.

clined to coalesce prior to the first round. Thus, a presidential candidate representing an extreme segment of a polarized political spectrum may be elected with a small share of the vote, but attempt to govern as a majority president. The election by majority in the second round would impede the election of the candidate who is furthest from the political center. In addition, in a fragmented system in which the winner of the first round typically obtains 30 percent of the vote or less, a runoff may be necessary to provide the president-elect with some basic level of legitimacy.

Mid-term Legislative Elections and Governability

Countries with mid-term elections are set apart, since they combine concurrent elections with another non-concurrent legislative election. If a plurality system is used, the concurrent presidential/legislative election should restrain the proliferation of parties. However, the non-concurrent legislative election may provide opportunities for small parties to compete more effectively and gain representation.

The efficiency of governmental policymaking may also be impeded for two additional reasons. First, the holding of an election that is not linked to the presidential outcome logically increases the probability that the president's party will lack a majority in the congress. In fact, experience with such elections suggests that the opposition parties often gain ground as voters take the opportunity to protest the performance of the incumbent government. Second, the honeymoon period for elected governments is likely to be shortened, since in the period leading up to the elections the legislative blocs of the opposition parties and even the governing party are more likely to refrain from supporting controversial legislative initiatives. The positive side of mid-term elections, however, is that they provide another opportunity for voters to hold the executive as well as their legislative representatives accountable for their performance.

Latin American Presidential Election Systems

Of the 18 countries in this study, five (Honduras, Mexico, Panama, Paraguay and Venezuela) elect presidents by a plurality system. Nine countries employ a majority runoff system

(Table 4.2). In one of these, Bolivia, the second round takes place in the congress. The other four countries (Argentina, Costa Rica, Nicaragua and Ecuador) set a lower threshold for a candidate to be elected in the first round. In Argentina, the winner of the first round becomes president if he or she has obtained either 45 percent of the valid votes, or 40 percent of the valid votes and at least a 10 percent advantage over the nearest competitor. In Costa Rica, the threshold is 40 percent, a level sufficiently low to have allowed for first round victories for every elected president since the adoption of the 1949 constitution (although a second round became necessary for the first time in the 2002 election).

As a result of a 1999 constitutional reform, Nicaragua now has a threshold of 40 percent, or 35 percent and at least a 5 percent advantage over the nearest competitor. In Ecuador, an absolute majority or at least 45 percent of the vote and an advantage of 10 percent or more over the second place finisher is required. This threshold represents only a slight deviation from a pure majority runoff system.

Six countries changed the formula used for electing presidents during the period under study. Colombia, the Dominican Republic and Uruguay changed from a plurality to a majority runoff system, and Argentina and Nicaragua changed from a plurality system to a runoff with a reduced threshold. Nicaragua changed its system from plurality to a runoff with a threshold of 45 percent in 1995, then reduced the threshold further in 1999. The only country that changed in the reverse direction was Ecuador, which went from a majority runoff system to majority with a (slightly) reduced threshold. The second reform in Nicaragua also had the effect of moving the system away from a majority system to one that is closer to a plurality system.

Three additional reforms were made to systems for electing the president, but of a different nature. Argentina and Brazil replaced their indirect systems with direct ones. Bolivia changed its second round (decided in congress) such that only the top two finishers, rather than the top three, are eligible for election. Overall, during the period there was a clear trend away from the plurality system towards a runoff system.

Tables 4.3 and 4.4 examine the extent to which theoretical expectations regarding the effects of the different systems for presidential elections are consistent with electoral outcomes in Latin America. Table 4.3 shows that, in fact, plurality and runoff-with-reduced-threshold systems are associated with fewer significant candidates running for office and fewer parties being elected to seats in the legislature. Table 4.4 shows that in plurality and runoff-with-reduced-threshold systems, the winner of the first round averaged very close to 50 percent of the vote, while in majority runoff systems, the winner typically received barely above 41 percent of the vote. In some countries, the winner averaged only about 30 percent of the vote.

The data in these tables, however, do not rigorously test the hypotheses related to the effects of presidential election systems. The reason is that the influence can clearly go in both directions. Countries where many parties typically compete and present presidential candidates are precisely the ones that are most likely to adopt a majority runoff system. Thus, a more valid test would require examining the change over time in the numerous instances when the system either changed in one direction or another or stayed the same. Then, if the expected change with respect to the number of candidates competing and parties receiving seats in fact occurred, one might have good grounds for upholding the

Table 4.2. Systems Used for Electing the President

Country	Majority runoff	Runoff reduced threshold	Plurality	Year of change	Description of the change
Argentina		X		1994	From plurality to runoff with a reduced threshold (45%, or 40% and 10% advantage over the nearest competitor); also from indirect to direct
Bolivia	X[1]			1990	Instead of choosing among top three finishers in first round, the congress chooses only among the top two in the runoff
Brazil	X			1988	From indirect to direct
Chile	X				
Colombia	X			1991	From plurality to majority runoff
Costa Rica		X[2]			
Dominican Republic	X			1994	From plurality to majority runoff
Ecuador		X		1998	From majority runoff to runoff with a reduced threshold (50% + 1 or 45% and a 10% advantage over the nearest competitor)
El Salvador	X				
Guatemala	X				
Honduras			X		
Mexico			X		
Nicaragua		X		1995 1999	From plurality to runoff with a reduced threshold of 45%; the threshold was then lowered further to 40%, or 35% with a 5% advantage over the nearest competitor
Panama			X		
Paraguay			X		
Peru	X[3]				
Uruguay	X			1997	From plurality to majority runoff
Venezuela			X		
Total	9	4	5		

[1] If no candidate obtains an absolute majority, the legislature selects a president among the candidates finishing first and second in the first round election.

[2] The threshold is 40 percent of the votes.

[3] Absolute majority was adopted as the rule for election in the 1979 constitution, but a separate article provided that it would not apply to the 1980 election. Rather, only 33 percent of the vote was needed for that election. If this figure was not reached, the congress was to decide among the two finishers. As it turned out, Fernando Beláunde Terry received 45 percent of the vote and became president.

Table 4.3. Fragmentation of Party Systems according to Type of Presidential Election System

Country	Effective number of presidential candidates (first round)	Effective number of parties (lower house seats)
Plurality		
Argentina (1983, 1989)	2.64	2.70
Colombia (1978, 1982, 1986, 1990)	2.48	2.33
Dominican Rep. (1978, 1982, 1986, 1990, 1994)	3.45	2.43
Honduras (1981, 1985, 1989, 1993, 1997)	2.15	2.10
Mexico (1982, 1988, 1994, 2000)	2.50	2.29
Nicaragua (1990)	2.14	2.05
Panama (1989, 1994, 1999)	2.78	3.77
Paraguay (1989, 1993, 1998)	2.18	2.20
Uruguay (1984, 1989, 1994)	3.23	3.18
Venezuela (1978, 1983, 1988, 1993, 1998, 2000)	2.73	3.62
Average of country averages	2.63	2.67
Average for all elections	2.67	2.72
Reduced threshold		
Argentina (1995, 1999)	2.88	2.64
Costa Rica (1978, 1982, 1986, 1990, 1994, 1998)	2.17	2.32
Ecuador (1998)[1]	4.10	5.73
Nicaragua (1996)	2.47	2.79
Peru (1980)	3.23	2.46
Average of country averages	2.97	3.19
Average for all elections	2.60	2.74
Majority runoff		
Bolivia[2] (1980, 1985, 1989, 1993, 1997)	5.01	4.40
Brazil (1982, 1986, 1989, 1994, 1998)	3.62	6.70
Chile (1989, 1993, 1999)[3]	2.36	5.04
Colombia (1994, 1998)	2.79	2.95
Dominican Rep. (1996, 2000)	2.87	2.32
Ecuador (1978, 1984, 1988, 1992, 1996)	5.15	5.69
El Salvador (1984, 1989, 1994, 1999)	2.81	3.11
Guatemala (1985, 1990, 1995, 1999)	4.33	3.19
Peru (1985, 1990, 1995, 2000)	2.80	3.76
Uruguay (1999)	3.30	3.07
Venezuela (2000)	3.38	3.44
Average of country averages	3.50	4.02
Average for all elections	3.72	4.37

Note: The format for this table is based on Shugart and Carey (1992, Table 10.2), but different data are used.
[1] Ecuador's system requiring 50 percent + 1 or 45 percent and a 10 percent advantage over the next finisher is close in practical terms to a majority runoff system. So its placement in this table is somewhat debatable.
[2] In Bolivia, the congress selects the president if no candidate obtains a majority in the first round.
[3] In Chile, a computation of the effective number of parties based on coalitions rather than individual parties would result in a much lower measure of fragmentation in the lower house.

Table 4.4. Average Percent of the Vote Obtained in the First Round by the First and Second Place Candidates

	1st Place	2nd Place
Plurality		
Argentina (1983, 1989)	49.60	36.34
Colombia (1978, 1982, 1986, 1990)	51.01	37.00
Dominican Rep. (1978, 1982, 1986, 1990, 1994)	43.43	39.10
Honduras (1981, 1985, 1989, 1993, 1997)	51.94	43.20
Mexico (1982, 1988, 1994, 2000)	54.65	27.76
Nicaragua (1990)	54.70	40.80
Panama (1989, 1994, 1999)	49.77	31.77
Paraguay (1989, 1993, 1998)	57.62	32.60
Uruguay (1984, 1989, 1994)	37.48	32.17
Venezuela (1978, 1983, 1988, 1993, 1998, 2000)	48.79	33.30
Average for all elections	49.48	35.43
Reduced threshold		
Argentina (1995, 1999)	49.15	33.66
Costa Rica (1978, 1982, 1986, 1990, 1994, 1998)	51.62	43.79
Ecuador (1998)	34.92	26.61
Nicaragua (1996)	51.00	37.80
Peru (1980)	46.49	28.19
Average for all elections	49.13	38.42
Majority runoff		
Bolivia[1] (1980, 1985, 1989, 1993, 1997)	31.01	23.00
Brazil (1989, 1994, 1998)	45.94	25.31
Chile[2] (1989, 1993, 1999)	53.70	33.77
Colombia (1994, 1998)	40.39	40.02
Dominican Rep. (1996, 2000)	45.39	31.77
Ecuador (1978, 1984, 1988, 1992, 1996)	27.99	23.42
El Salvador (1984, 1989, 1994, 1999)	49.55	30.08
Guatemala (1985, 1990, 1995, 1999)	37.13	24.15
Peru (1985, 1990, 1995, 2000)	50.28	29.19
Uruguay (1999)	40.11	32.78
Average for all elections	41.01	27.86

Note: The format for this table is based on Shugart and Carey (1992, Table 10.2), but different data are used.
[1] In Bolivia, the congress selects the president if no candidate obtains a majority in the first round.
[2] The binominal election system for the legislature, along with the societal cleavage for and against Pinochet, has encouraged the maintenance of party coalitions on the center-left and center-right, each of which presents a single candidate for the presidency.

hypothesis. However, given the relatively short life of the region's democracies, along with the brief period that has passed since most of the reforms, it is not possible to conduct such a test with the countries studied here.

Simultaneity of Elections

In 11 of the 18 countries studied here, presidential and legislative elections are held simultaneously (Table 4.5). Of these, Brazil represents only a slight deviation, with one-third or two-thirds of the senate being elected on an alternating basis in a given presidential/legislative election. In this case, elections for the two branches are nonetheless always held on the same day. In Argentina and Mexico, the elections are partially simultaneous. In Argentina, elections for half of the lower house and one-third of the upper house are held simultaneously with the presidential election, while the other half of the lower house and another third of the upper house are elected midway through the presidential term. In Mexico, the term of deputies in the lower house is three years, so elections for the whole body are elected simultaneously with the presidential election, as well as at the mid-way point of the six-year presidential term. In the remaining five countries (Chile, Colombia, the Dominican Republic, El Salvador and Venezuela), presidential and legislative elections rarely or never occur on the same day. Colombia is unusual among these five because the elections for the two branches occur in the same year on four-year cycles, but the legislative elections are held two and a half months prior to the first round of the presidential elections.

The six countries where the timing of elections has been changed during the period under study do not represent a clear trend in the region with respect to the coincidence of elections for the two branches. Chile, the Dominican Republic, and Venezuela shifted from systems with either fully or partially simultaneous (Chile) elections to ones with non-coterminous cycles. Brazil is the only case of a shift fully in the opposite direction, from having elections that were not concurrent toward concurrent elections. With the elimination of the mid-term election for legislators representing individual provinces, Ecuador transformed its system from partially simultaneous to simultaneous. In Argentina, there was a slight move toward greater simultaneity. The reduction of the presidential term from six to four years and the reduction of the mandate of the senators from nine to six years maintained the partially simultaneous nature of the electoral system, but reduced from two to one the number of mid-term elections.

Length of the Presidential Term

The length of the mandates of presidents in the region vary between four and six years (Table 4.6). In eight countries (Argentina, Brazil, Colombia, Costa Rica, the Dominican Republic, Ecuador, Guatemala and Honduras), the president has four-year terms; in seven, five-year terms (Bolivia, El Salvador, Nicaragua, Panama, Paraguay, Peru and Uruguay); and in three, six-year terms (Chile, Mexico and Venezuela).

Table 4.5. Simultaneity of Presidential and Parliamentary Elections

Country	Simulta-neous	Partially simulta-neous	Separate	Year of change	Description and direction of change
Argentina		X[1]		1994	Reduction of the presidential mandate from six to four years and that of senators from nine to six years, maintaining system as partially simultaneous, but with one rather than two midterm elections.
Bolivia	X				
Brazil	X[2]			1994	Reduction of the presidential mandate from five to four years transformed the system from separate to simultaneous.
Chile			X[3]	1993	Reduction of the presidential mandate from eight to six years transformed the system from partially simultaneous to separate.
Colombia			X[4]		
Costa Rica	X				
Dominican Rep.			X	1994	In 1994, the decision to cut the disputed mandate of President Joaquín Balaguer from four to two years while maintaining the elected congress in place for four years transformed the system from simultaneous to separate.

Seven countries changed the length of the presidential term during the period of the study. Five countries reduced the term of office and two increased it. Some of the term reductions, however, are open to interpretation. Brazil and Argentina reduced the presidential term from five and six years, respectively, to four years, but at the same time they established the possibility of an immediate reelection. This permits a president to potentially remain in office for eight consecutive years. Chile reduced its presidential term from a single (but long) eight-year term to a somewhat more modest six years. Guatemala reduced its presidential term from five to four years, and Nicaragua from six to five years. Bolivia increased the term of presidents from four to five years, and Venezuela from five to six years. As a result of these seven changes, the average length of the presidential mandate in the region was reduced from exactly 5 years to 4.7 years.

Country	Simultaneous	Partially simultaneous	Separate	Year of change	Description and direction of change
Ecuador	X			1998	Elimination of the mid-term elections for provincial deputies transformed the system from partially simultaneous to simultaneous.
El Salvador			X		
Guatemala	X				
Honduras	X				
Mexico		X[5]			
Nicaragua	X				
Panama	X				
Paraguay	X				
Peru	X				
Uruguay	X				
Venezuela			X[6]	1999	
Total	11	2	5		

[1] Half of the lower house and one-third of the upper house is elected simultaneously with the president.
[2] The system is considered simultaneous, since the lower house and one-third or two-thirds of the senate on an alternating basis are elected at the same time as the president, without any mid-term elections.
[3] The system is considered separate, since only every 12 years is the president elected at the same time as the whole lower house and half the upper house.
[4] Since 1978, congressional elections have been held two to three months prior to the presidential election but in the same year.
[5] The system is considered as partially simultaneous because, although the presidential elections always coincide with elections for the lower and upper house, the full lower house is renewed in the middle of the president's term.
[6] In 1998, a temporary reform moved up the legislative elections to one month before the presidential elections. Under the current (1999) constitution, the system is considered separate, since only every 30 years is the president elected at the same time as the national assembly.

Reelection of Presidents

Rules concerning the reelection of presidents vary considerably across the region (Table 4.7). Argentina, Brazil, Peru and Venezuela permit immediate reelection, while Bolivia, Chile, the Dominican Republic, Ecuador, El Salvador, Nicaragua, Panama and Uruguay allow reelection after the passage of at least one presidential term. The remaining six countries (Colombia, Costa Rica, Guatemala, Honduras, Mexico and Paraguay) prohibit reelection at any time. In other words, two-thirds of the countries studied (12 of 18) allow a president to be reelected at some point, either immediately or after one presidential term.

Nine countries changed their rules with respect to presidential reelection during the period studied. Argentina, Brazil, Peru and Venezuela moved from a system that allowed

Table 4.6. Term Length of Presidents

Country	Current term length	Previous term length	Year of change
Argentina	4	6	1994
Brazil	4	5	1994
Colombia	4	4	
Costa Rica	4	4	
Dominican Rep.	4	4	
Ecuador	4	4	
Guatemala	4	5	1993
Honduras	4	4	
Bolivia	5	4	1994
El Salvador	5	5	
Nicaragua	5	6	1994
Panama	5	5	
Paraguay	5	5	
Peru	5	5	
Uruguay	5	5	
Chile	6	8	1993
Mexico	6	6	
Venezuela	6	5	1999
Total	4.7	5.0	

reelection after the passage of at least one presidential period, to one that allows immediate reelection. Ecuador lifted its restriction somewhat by shifting from prohibiting reelection to allowing it after one presidential term. The three countries that allowed an immediate reelection at the beginning of the period no longer do. Paraguay now prohibits reelection at any point in time, while the Dominican Republic and Nicaragua allow reelection only after one presidential term has passed. Colombia also took a more restrictive approach, shifting from allowing reelection after a presidential period to a full prohibition of reelection.

Thus, there is not a clear tendency of reform in the region in terms of presidential reelection. Overall, five out of the nine changes were in favor of allowing presidential reelection, while four either prohibited it altogether or prevented immediate reelection.

Conclusions

The governability of presidential systems depends in part on the election of presidents who enjoy substantial popular legitimacy and can depend on a sizeable portion of the congress to work collaboratively to enact legislation. The system chosen for electing the president, along with the simultaneity of presidential and legislative elections, are two factors that can affect the likelihood of such conditions being met.

Table 4.7. Reelection of the President

Country	Immediate	Not immediate	Prohibited	Year of change	Nature of change	Effect of change
Argentina	X			1994	Not immediate to immediate	Less restrictive
Bolivia		X				
Brazil	X			1997	Not immediate to immediate	Less restrictive
Chile		X				
Colombia			X	1991	Not immediate to prohibited	More restrictive
Costa Rica			X[1]			
Dominican Rep.		X		1994	From immediate to not immediate	More restrictive
Ecuador		X		1996	From prohibited to not immediate	Less restrictive
El Salvador		X				
Guatemala			X			
Honduras			X			
Mexico			X			
Nicaragua		X		1995	From immediate to not immediate	More restrictive
Panama		X[2]				
Paraguay			X	1992	From immediate to prohibited	More restrictive
Peru	X			1993	From not immediate to immediate	Less restrictive
Uruguay		X				
Venezuela	X[3]			1998	From not immediate to immediate	Less restrictive
Total	4	8	6	9		

[1] Non-immediate reelection was allowed until a 1969 referendum (see Carey, 1997).
[2] Two presidential terms (10 years) must elapse before the president can seek office for a second time.
[3] Under previous rules, the president could not be reelected until two presidential periods had passed.

Over the period of this study, many countries have reformed their systems for electing the president, the timing of presidential and legislative elections, the length of the presidential term, and reelection. The clearest trend has been the shift from plurality to majority runoff or runoff-with-reduced-threshold systems. Five countries moved in this direction, while only one (Ecuador) moved very slightly in the opposite direction. Abandoning the plurality formula was generally motivated either by a desire to amplify the mandate of the winner or by partisan power strategies (such as preventing a third minority party from obtaining the presidency).

If one accepts prevailing academic theory, this change would appear under at least some circumstances to work against democratic governability. The undesirable outcome is expected to result from the tendency of a majority system to encourage more presidential candidates and increase the number of political parties gaining seats in the congress. Thus, instead of broadening the mandate of the elected president, such a system may in fact undermine it.

The actual impact of majority runoff systems is difficult to judge in a rigorous manner. In most cases, too little time has passed since the reform to assess the potential long-term impact on party system fragmentation. In terms of the immediate effect of enhancing the mandate of the elected president, it would appear that those expectations have not been fulfilled in most cases.

The failure to boost the popular legitimacy of the president may be due to the first round vote being perceived to more validly reflect true voter preferences. It is difficult to turn a 25 percent vote into a mandate for governing, even with a second round majority vote. In fact, a particular legitimacy problem emerges when the candidate who is ultimately elected in the second round is not the one that won in the first round. Among the 23 instances in which runoff elections were held over the period of this study, there were nine when the winner of the first round failed to become president. If one puts aside the two cases in Bolivia, where the second round decision was by congress, seven cases remain: President Jaime Roldós Aguilera, Ecuador, 1979; President León Febres Cordero, Ecuador, 1984; President Abdalá Bucaram Ortiz, Ecuador, 1996; President Alberto Fujimori, Peru, 1990; President Jorge Serrano Elías, Guatemala, 1993; President Andrés Pastrana, Colombia, 1998; and President Jorge Batlle Ibáñez, Uruguay, 1999. Most of these presidencies were characterized by highly conflictive relationships with the legislature and policy ineffectiveness. Impeachment was threatened or attempted in four instances. Bucaram was ousted by the legislature for "mental incapacity." Fujimori and Serrano used self-coups to head off impeachment threats and difficult relations with the legislature. Fujimori succeeded, while Serrano's bid ended in the president's resignation. Roldós' relations with congress were already strained when he was killed in a plane crash two years into his five-year term, while Febres Cordero faced impeachment attempts.

Aside from the problem of conflictive mandates, the real capacity of presidents to govern may not be strengthened by runoffs because the second round tends to encourage the formation of loose electoral coalitions between each of the two candidates and some minority parties, rather than result in more durable governing coalitions. Though the president's institutional authority based on parties and the congress may not increase by the second round, the majority election may give him an inflated sense of mandate and encourage attempts to circumvent or undermine democratic institutions.[3]

---

[3] This problem can be cited particularly in the case of Bucaram.

Democracies in Development

In terms of the timing of presidential and legislative elections, three countries moved towards separate elections, another shifted from separate to simultaneous elections, and another from partially simultaneous to simultaneous elections. Again, these changes are too recent for their effects to be clearly ascertained. But it is interesting to note that the two countries (Brazil and Ecuador) that moved toward making elections fully simultaneous are among those with the highest degree of party system fragmentation. Certainly the harmonization of the election cycles in Brazil has eased the problem of governing from what it would have been had President Fernando Henrique Cardoso faced mid-term congressional elections, as did his predecessors.

Mid-term elections, whether in systems with or without coterminous cycles, clearly contributed to difficulties in governing. The experience in each of these cases shows that such elections can weaken the policymaking effectiveness of the executive by altering the balance of partisan power mid-way through the term, and by shifting congressional attention from the policy agenda to electoral strategizing and campaigning.

There was no clear trend with respect to restrictions on the reelection of presidents. Five countries changed their systems in a direction favoring reelection (with one requiring an intervening presidential term), while four banned immediate reelection (two banned reelection altogether). Reelection was introduced in Argentina, Brazil and Peru at least partly as a consequence of popularity built through success in taming hyperinflation and restoring economic growth. Even during the second terms of President Alberto Fujimori in Peru and President Carlos Menem in Argentina, reelection remained an issue, since each of these presidents or his supporters contended that the first term did not count under the new or reformed constitution. President Fujimori was controversially elected to a third term in 2000, while President Menem did not pursue a further extension of his mandate. In several other countries, including Costa Rica, the Dominican Republic, Guatemala, Ecuador and Panama, bids to lift the prohibition on immediate reelection failed.

Again, it is hard to assess the impact of the reforms in this area. The restrictions on reelection imposed in the Dominican Republic, Nicaragua and Paraguay appear to be aimed at blocking the possibility that a strong leader could once again dominate politics over a long period of time, as was the case in the respective countries with Joaquín Balaguer, Anastasio Somoza (or Daniel Ortega), and Alfredo Stroessner. In such circumstances, the reforms mark a positive departure from the past style of politics and may be needed to ensure ongoing plurality in the division of national political power.

Countries where constitutions were amended to permit reelection point to the double-edged nature of the issue. Preventing the reelection of a popular president may stop in midstream a form of leadership that could make long-term contributions to the development of the country and also create problems of legitimacy for the president's successor. However, reelection also reinforces the tendency inherent in presidentialism toward personalistic leadership, and it undermines the development of a more pluralistic and institutionalized mode of exercising political authority. Although there have been a few successful presidencies that resulted from immediate or non-immediate reelection, the balance in general is not positive.

Bibliography

Carey, John M. 1997. Strong Candidates for a Limited Office: Presidentialism and Political Parties in Costa Rica. In Scott Mainwaring and Matthew Soberg Shugart (eds.), *Presidentialism and Democracy in Latin America*. New York: Cambridge University Press.

Jones, Mark P. 1996. *Electoral Laws and the Survival of Presidential Democracies*. Notre Dame: University of Notre Dame Press.

Mainwaring, Scott, and Matthew Soberg Shugart (eds.). 1997. *Presidentialism and Democracy in Latin America*. New York: Cambridge University Press.

Shugart, Matthew Soberg. 1995. The Electoral Cycle and Institutional Sources of Divided Presidential Government. *American Political Science Review* 89(2). June.

Shugart, Matthew Soberg, and John M. Carey. 1992. *Presidents and Assemblies: Constitutional Design and Electoral Dynamics*. Cambridge: Cambridge University Press.

CHAPTER FIVE

Legislative Electoral Systems and Democratic Governability

The design of systems for electing legislative representatives affects democratic governability. This chapter examines the functions that electoral systems should ideally perform in a democratic system, and classifies electoral systems in Latin America in terms of how well they fulfill those theoretical functions. It also assesses the extent to which electoral reforms in the region over the past two decades might alleviate governability problems related to the electoral systems.

"Electoral system" is defined here as the rules that determine the form and manner in which voters select the candidates and political parties of their preference, as well as the manner in which these votes shape the apportionment of seats (for parliamentary elections) and governmental offices (for presidential, gubernatorial and mayoral elections) between contending political forces (Nohlen, 1998, p. 35).

The effect of electoral systems on the governability of democratic systems is mainly exerted through their impact on the structure and functioning of the political party system, rather than directly. Even this effect is far from being fully predictable, since in exerting these effects, electoral systems interact with a host of other factors, including the depth and diversity of existing social, political and economic cleavages, the nature of the political regime, and the political culture, as well as other more contingent factors (International IDEA, 1997). Electoral systems set in place an important array of incentives that shape the behavior of electors and other political actors that influence both the structure of the party system and the orientation and conduct of elected officials. Even within the parameters of a given set of electoral rules, however, widely different behavior and outcomes can result because of differences in other aspects of the social and political setting.

Aside from structuring incentives, electoral systems exert a direct effect on how the election translates into a given allocation of power and authority. In somewhat different language, we can distinguish between the *mechanical* and *psychological* effects of electoral rules.

Mechanical effects relate to the practical impact of the method of allocating seats in terms of determining whether parties obtain representation and to what extent their share of the seats equates with their share of the votes. For instance, majoritarian first-past-the-post systems, where one legislator is elected by a simple plurality in each district, have the direct effect of under-representing minority parties. Even if such parties were to receive as much as 10 or 20 percent of the vote nationally, they would be unlikely to gain a single seat in the parliament if their support and that for other parties were distributed relatively evenly across the country.

Psychological effects result from the reactions over time of the electorate and political actors to the constraints and opportunities presented by the electoral rules. As pointed out in the previous chapter, rational voters are unlikely to continue voting for a party or candidate with no realistic chance of winning. Thus, in the plurality system, where only the candidate with the most votes obtains a seat, electors may choose to eschew their true preference for a minority party and vote instead for the best alternative among the larger parties. At the same time, rather than repeatedly being under-represented in the legislature, minority parties may choose to coalesce in order to enhance their chances of winning seats. Thus, over time, psychological effects are likely to reinforce the purely mechanical effects of the electoral system on the party system (Nohlen, 1998a).

Key Functions of Electoral Systems: Representativeness, Effectiveness and Participation

Electoral systems can be differentiated according to their intrinsic characteristics, which are expected to have consequences for the operation of democratic systems. Whether a given set of characteristics promotes or hinders democratic governability depends on the context. An electoral system may be workable and legitimate in one country but not functional in another. Nevertheless, the general direction of change likely to be induced by a given reform in a particular country can be predicted with some degree of confidence. By understanding the incentives arising from electoral systems, clearer hypotheses can be formulated about the effects that given reforms will have on the operation of democracy in specific contexts.

One way to distinguish between electoral systems is in terms of the extent to which they perform three functions: *representativeness*, *effectiveness*, and *participation* (Nohlen, 1999; Nohlen 1998b).

An electoral system that is optimally representative is one in which political groups obtain legislative seats in nearly exact proportion to their share of the vote. In such a system, all votes count the same and no political groups competing for elected office are over-represented or under-represented (that is, receive a share of seats larger or smaller than their share of the vote). In assessing the *representativeness* of the electoral system, we are adopting a fairly restrictive definition of the term. For other purposes, the term has been reasonably applied to the matter of whether the full heterogeneity of the social fabric is adequately represented in the political process. However, whether minority or other previously excluded groups have a proportionate voice in the political system involves many factors (equity of political participation, level of voter turnout, capacity of groups to organize, etc.) that are not necessarily related to the electoral rules per se. Judging the representativeness of an electoral system involves considering only whether those groups that form political parties or movements and enter electoral competition obtain representation in accordance with the proportion of the votes they receive.

An electoral system that fosters *effectiveness* is one that produces sufficient concentration of power in the legislature to make it possible for diverse societal preferences to be aggregated and resolved into acts of government. If a large number of parties obtain representation, then it is less likely that the governing party will enjoy reliable support in the legislature, and more difficult for legislators to reach agreements in order to enact necessary reforms. In a presidential system, the problem of governing in the context of a fragmented legislature is particularly difficult. Since the tenure of legislators does not depend on the success or failure of the government in adopting its legislative program (and since the presidency is a winner-take-all office that each party aims to occupy), there are weaker incentives than in parliamentary systems for parties to form and maintain coalitions.

The function of *participation*, which could also be called the *intensity of participation* (or *identifiability*), alludes to a different matter than the previous functions. While representation and effectiveness involve the way that the aggregate preferences of electors are translated into legislative seats, participation refers to how the form of voting affects the strength of the connection between the constituent and his or her representative. For example, in a plurality system in which a single representative is elected in each district, the relationship is close and direct. Citizens can choose the individual candidate who they think will best represent them and can reward or punish the incumbent based on performance in office. This means that candidates and elected representatives are rewarded when they focus their attention on gaining and holding onto the support of constituents.

At the other end of the scale, in proportional representation systems with closed and blocked party lists, the connection between the elector and representative is looser and more distant. In such systems, the party (either the party leaders or party members in a convention) puts together an ordered list of candidates for each district. Citizens cast a vote for the party list of their choice (thereby affecting the share of seats won by the party) but have no role in deciding which individual candidates are elected. Candidates and incumbents do not have a strong incentive to cultivate relations with their constituents, and electors are discouraged from learning the identities of individual candidates or tracking the conduct of those who get elected (Carey and Shugart, 1995). Legislators enhance their reelection chances by winning the favor of party leaders and thus earning a high position on the party list. Thus, while in such a system the electors can potentially hold the party accountable through their legislative votes, it is not realistically possible for them to hold legislators individually accountable.

Based on the above reasoning, it would seem at first glance that the best way to improve electoral systems in the region would be by simply maximizing the position of the system on the scale of the three functions. However, it is not possible for electoral systems to satisfy the different demands at the same time and in an absolute manner. Attempts to optimize performance with respect to one function almost inevitably worsen performance with respect to another (Nohlen, 1998b).

For example, enhancing the representativeness of the system (by making the translation of votes into seats more proportional) can lower effectiveness by increasing the number of parties that obtain representation in the legislature. In such a context, it is more likely that presidents will lack legislative support, and that the development of expeditious responses to collective problems may be impeded.

At the same time, reforms aimed at enhancing participation may reduce effectiveness by undermining party discipline and thereby inhibiting the executive-legislative cooperation needed to enact legislation. In addition, if efforts to enhance participation dilute the meaning of party labels and the programmatic focus of campaigns, then electors may lose the ability to hold representatives accountable for their decisions and positions on national policy issues. Instead of selling their constituents a package of policies and issue positions (or deeds in support of the public interest), legislative candidates will emphasize their personal qualities and the exchange of particularistic favors for electoral support (Carey and Shugart, 1995; Shugart and Wattenberg, 2001).

Theoretical Bases for Classifying Electoral Systems

Thinking in terms of the three functions and the tradeoffs between them is useful for evaluating and distinguishing between the different electoral systems. The most basic and well-known classification of electoral systems differentiates between majoritarian and proportional systems. Majoritarian systems are those that award the seats in each district to the candidate(s) with the most votes. As a consequence, such systems tend to systematically favor the larger parties and make it difficult for small parties to gain representation. As the name indicates, this system is designed to favor the formation of majorities. The classic examples of the majority system are those of the United States and Great Britain, where in each district one seat is awarded to the candidate with the most votes (first-past-the-post).

Proportional systems are those in which seats are awarded by reference to the percentage of the vote obtained by political parties. The logic behind the system is to favor the election of a legislature that reflects the political heterogeneity of the electorate. The classic proportional systems are the "pure" forms, such as those in Israel and the Netherlands, where there is effectively one electoral district (the whole nation) whose vote totals determine the allocation of all of the parliamentary seats, and those that elect a large number of legislators in each electoral district. In such systems, the share of the seats obtained almost exactly mirrors the share of the votes each party receives.

Within these two broad types there are many variations. The prototypical majoritarian systems are the *first-past-the-post* or *plurality systems*, where the candidate with the most votes wins; and the *majority-runoff systems*, where an absolute majority of the votes is required. However, other forms are possible and are used in Latin America. Under the system called *majority with representation of the minority*, the party with the most votes obtains most of the seats in the district, but the party finishing second also receives one representative. Another variation of the majoritarian system involves multiple seats being awarded in each district in order of the candidates who receive the most votes. In such systems, electors

Table 5.1. Simple Classification of Electoral Systems

	Representativeness	Effectiveness	Participation
Majoritarian	–	+	+
Proportional	+	–	–

choose one or more candidates listed under different party labels, but the votes accrue and seats are awarded only on an individual basis.

Proportional systems can be more complex, since the size of the electoral districts and the type of mathematical formulas used, as well as other features, together affect how the voting result translates into a given allocation of legislative seats. Taking their more classic types as the standard (first-past-the-post and proportional representation with party lists in large multi-member districts), we can evaluate majoritarian and proportional systems according to the functions that electoral systems should ideally perform (Table 5.1).

While majoritarian systems favor effectiveness and participation, they under-represent smaller parties and work to the advantage of larger parties. Proportional systems, on the other hand, favor equitable representation but may result in a more cumbersome and inefficient decision-making process and weaker links between representatives and constituents.

Though this dichotomous classification is valuable from the standpoint of simplicity, it is imprecise in its ability to distinguish electoral systems in terms of the degree to which they fulfill the expected functions, and their theoretical effects on democratic governability. In addition, this classification scheme is not very practical when it comes to distinguishing between the electoral systems found in Latin America. With respect to systems for electing members of the lower house, none of the 18 countries in the study use the classical forms of a majoritarian system (first-past-the-post or majority-runoff). Fifteen countries use a form of proportional representation for electing deputies to the legislative assembly, but there are huge differences between them. Of these 15, Bolivia and Venezuela use a personalized proportional representation system.

Of the three non-proportional cases, Ecuador (as of 1998) uses a system that in terms of the decision formula is majoritarian, but in which more than one legislator per district is elected. That is, the candidates from all parties are put in descending order of the votes received and seats are awarded from the top of the list until each seat is filled. Mexico uses a "mixed" or "segmented" system in which three-fifths of the seats are elected by plurality in single member districts, and two-fifths are elected by proportional representation. Chile's system, labeled *binominal* in Spanish, is more difficult to classify within these two broad systems. Parties (or coalitions) present lists of candidates in two member districts. Electors vote for one candidate, but the votes accrue to the party (or party coalition). Each of the two parties with the most votes wins a seat unless the first party doubles the votes of the second. In this case, the first party obtains both seats. The effect is a particular form of majoritarianism that favors the largest parties, and particularly the second largest party (or coalition).

Sharper distinctions in terms of the degree of true proportionality associated with proportional representation systems can contribute to a more analytically useful classification scheme. Three characteristics of proportional representation systems exert the greatest influence on the degree to which the share of seats closely reflects the distribution of the vote: the size of the districts, the mathematical formula used to allocate seats, and the presence and size of legal thresholds required for parties to obtain representation.

The size of the districts, or more precisely the number of legislators elected in each district, is generally the most important variable. Taking as fixed the particular formula used for translating votes into seats, as the number of seats available for distribution increases, the more proportional will be the assignment of seats and the greater the possibility that parties receiving a small share of the vote can obtain representation.[1] There are systems that despite being defined in the constitution as proportional have a significant number of districts that elect only one or two legislators. Obviously, when only one seat is being decided, the system operates as a majoritarian one (the most voted party wins). When two seats are being elected, the system operates like the Chilean binominal system.

The decision about where to divide systems in terms of district magnitude is inevitably somewhat arbitrary. One expert considers districts of five seats or less to be small, between six and 10, medium, and over 10, large (Nohlen, 1998, p. 58). These dividing lines seem reasonable when considering election outcomes at the district level. But given the fact that most proportional representation systems are characterized by a fairly large number of districts with widely varying sizes (some having a national district layered upon these territorial districts), the matter of summarizing the system as a whole in terms of district size is more complicated.

One way of summarizing the size of electoral districts across the country is to consider the share of the seats in the legislature that are elected in districts of a given size.[2] Systems in which more than half of the legislative body is elected in districts with five seats or less are considered to be "proportional representation with small district" systems. "Proportional representation with large district" systems are those in which more than half the seats in the legislature are elected from districts with 10 or more representatives. Systems that fall between these two extremes are considered "proportional representation with medium-sized district" systems.

Table 5.2 shows the classification of 13 of the 15 Latin American proportional representation systems, as well as data related to their district size. Though Bolivia and Venezuela are proportional representation systems, the personal nature of the voting in these cases warrants the creation of a different electoral system category. Using the criteria established in the previous paragraph, there are three large district proportional representation systems, nine medium-sized systems, and just one small one.

---

[1] The effect of district magnitude on the proportionality of the translation of votes into seats is conditioned by the number of parties and the distribution of the vote among them. Thus, a given average district magnitude might result in fairly proportional outcomes in a country with only a few significant parties, but produce a highly disproportional outcome in a country with a large number of significant parties.

[2] Another approach is to use the average, but this measure has some limitations. It requires that the frequency distribution of the magnitudes of the country's districts approximate a normal distribution (meaning that it is bell-shaped or fairly symmetric about the mean). But this is rarely the case.

Democracies in Development

Table 5.2. Classifying Proportional Representation Systems according to District Size

	District size classification	Average district magnitude	Share of districts with 5 seats or less (%)	Share of seats elected from districts with 5 seats or less (%)	Size of individual districts
Argentina	Medium	5.4	83.3	49.60	35, 12, 10, 9, 5(2), 4(5), 3(8), 2(5)
Brazil	Large	19.0	0.0	0.00	70, 53, 46, 39, 31, 30, 25, 22, 18, 17(2), 16, 12, 10(2), 9, 8(11)
Colombia	Medium	4.9	72.7	45.96	18, 17, 13, 7(3), 6(3), 5(5), 4(4), 3(3), 2(12)
Costa Rica	Medium	8.1	42.8	24.56	21,10, 6(2), 5(2), 4
Dominican Rep.	Medium	5.0	83.3	46.97	44, 14, 8, 7, 6, 5(2), 4(4), 3(6), 2(13)
El Salvador[1]	Medium	5.6	80.0	50.00	20 (national), 16, 6, 5(2), 4(2), 3(8)
Guatemala[1]	Medium	4.7	66.7	36.00	22 (national),12, 10, 8, 7, 6(2), 5, 4, 3(6), 2(5), 1(3)
Honduras	Medium	7.1	44.4	18.00	23, 20, 9(3), 8, 7(3), 6, 5, 4(2), 3(2), 2, 1(2)
Nicaragua[1]	Medium	5.0	72.2	36.67	20 (national), 19, 6(3), 4(1), 3(6), 2(5), 1
Panama	Small	1.8	97.5	91.55	6(1), 5(2), 4(3), 3, 2(7), 1(26)
Paraguay	Medium	4.4	72.2	38.75	17, 13, 6(2), 5, 4(2), 3(2), 2(4), 1(4)
Peru[2]	Large	120.0	0.0	0.00	100(1)
Uruguay[3]	Large	99.0	0.0	0.00	44, 13, 4, 3(6), 2(10)

[1] El Salvador, Guatemala and Nicaragua have a national district that coexists with numerous regional districts of varying size. In Guatemala and Nicaragua, electors vote twice—once for a party list in their departmental constituency, and once for a party list for the national district. In El Salvador, electors select a party, and that vote counts as their choice of party list for the regional constituency and the national constituency. For the purposes of assessing the aggregate magnitude of districts, the national constituency is treated for each of these countries as if it were another large regional constituency.

[2] For the 2001 election, Peru returned to a multi-member district system consisting of 25 districts and an average district magnitude of 4.8. So the current system is a medium-sized district system.

[3] The Uruguayan election system is divided into 19 districts of varying size, as can be seen from the last column. But even though the electors vote for party lists in the districts, the formula for allocating seats is applied to the aggregate (national) vote percentages, and the distribution of seats within districts is required to accommodate to the national seat distribution resulting from this calculation. Thus, in effect the Uruguayan system functions in a manner similar to a single national district system.

Electoral Formulas

The degree to which proportional systems produce proportional outcomes is also affected by the mathematical formula used to transform votes into seats. Though there are a wide variety of specific variations in the formulas used, in general most use either a divisor (highest average) system or a quota system.

The most well known divisor system—the D'Hondt system—is also the most common in Latin America. In this system, a series of divisors (1, 2, 3, etc.) is applied to the votes received by each party. Seats are assigned to parties in the order of the size of the quotients resulting from these divisions.

The most common quota system is the Hare (or simple quota) system, which entails dividing the total valid votes in the district by the number of seats in contention. Parties then receive the number of seats corresponding to the number of times the district quotient goes into the valid votes received by the party. But since seats usually remain unallocated after this operation, a second process must be used to assign the remaining seats. The typical approach is to award the remaining seats to the parties with the largest remainders resulting from dividing the party's valid votes by the quotient.

The possibility of gaining a seat through remainders, which in some cases entails obtaining a vote percentage well below the single Hare quota, tends especially to encourage party system fragmentation and the proliferation of small parties contending for seats. These parties (or more accurately, electoral vehicles) have little hope of obtaining significant representation at the national level, aiming instead only to elect a single individual or group of individuals to the congress. This phenomenon has been particularly evident recently in Colombia and Venezuela. A way to impede this tendency would be to adopt the rule that only parties that obtain seats through Hare quotas are eligible to compete for seats on the basis of remainders. Or, as in Costa Rica, a second round of seat allocation can be carried out on the basis of a sub-quotient (in this case, half of the Hare quotient) before considering the remainders.

Of these two types, the Hare quota and largest remainder system is the most impartial between large and small parties, and tends to yield closely proportional results. The D'Hondt formula tends to be the least proportional, even relative to other divisor systems, and systematically favors the larger parties. In the hypothetical case shown in Table 5.3, the Hare formula results in at least one seat going to each party while the D'Hondt formula shuts out the smallest party and over-represents the two largest parties.

Of the 13 proportional representation list systems in Latin America, seven use some form of the Hare and greatest remainder system and six use a form of the D'Hondt system.

The usefulness of the classification of proportional representation systems can be examined by studying a measure of the disproportionality of the translation of votes into seats. Does the classification of the systems in terms of district size, in fact, parallel the measure of proportionality of electoral outcomes? Does consideration of the type of electoral formula enhance the match between the electoral system attributes and the measurement of outcomes?

All of the different indices of proportionality entail calculating in some manner the deviations between the vote and seat percentages obtained by each political party and sum-

Table 5.3. Application of D'Hondt and Hare Formulas in a Hypothetical Six-member District with Four Parties

Seats allocated using D'Hondt divisors

Party	Votes (v)	Votes/1	Votes/2	Votes/3	Total seats	Seats (%)
A	41,000	41,000 (1)	20,500 (3)	13,667 (6)	3	50.00
B	29,000	29,000 (2)	14,500 (5)	9,667	2	33.33
C	17,000	17,000 (4)	8,500		1	16.67
D	13,000	13,000			0	0.00
Total	100,000				6	100.00

Note: The numbers in parentheses indicate the order in which the six seats are allocated to the parties.

Seats allocated using Hare and largest remainder system
Hare quota = 100,000 [votes]/6 [seats] = 16,667

Party	Votes (v)	Hare quotas	Full quota seats	Remaining seats	Total seats	Seats (%)
A	41,000	41,000/16,667=2.**45**	2	0	2	33.33
B	29,000	29,000/16,667=1.**73**	1	1	2	33.33
C·	17,000	17,000/16,667=1.**02**	1	0	1	16.67
D	13,000	13,000/16,667=0.**78**	0	1	1	16.67
Total	100,000	6.00	4	2	6	100.00

Note: The bolded decimal portion of numbers serves as the basis for the distribution of seats left after seats are distributed on the basis of quotas.

ming across the results for each party contesting seats in the election. In the "least-squares index" used here,[3] the larger the value of the index, the greater the degree of disproportionality (lower the proportionality) of the relationship between vote shares and seat shares.[4]

Table 5.4 examines the extent to which the classification of small, medium and large district proportional representation systems in Latin America align with the observed disproportionality of those systems.

---

[3] In the least-squares index, the vote/seat share differences for each party are squared and then added; this total is divided by 2; and then the square root of this value is taken. Low numbers indicate low disproportionality (or high proportionality), while high numbers indicate the opposite (Lijphart, 1994).

[4] Considering index values for other countries in the world helps to gauge the meaning of the values for Latin American countries. Lijphart (1994) cites the following index values for the last electoral system in use in the period prior to 1990: Australia 10.24, Austria 1.43, Canada 11.33, France 11.84, Germany .67, Italy 1.12, Netherlands 1.32, Norway 4.84, Sweden 1.67, United Kingdom 2.94, and the United States 5.41.

Table 5.4. Classification of Proportional Representation Systems vs. Measurement of Disproportionality

	District size classification	Average district magnitude	Formula for lower house	Least-squares index
Peru[1]	Large	120.0	D'Hondt	1.54
Uruguay	Large	99.0	D'Hondt	0.60
Brazil	Large	19.0	Hare	2.65
Costa Rica[2]	Medium	8.1	Hare	6.57
Honduras	Medium	7.1	Hare	2.92
El Salvador	Medium	5.6	Hare	4.58
Argentina	Medium	5.4	D'Hondt	4.91
Nicaragua	Medium	5.0	Hare	2.26
Dominican Rep.	Medium	5.0	D'Hondt	5.04
Colombia	Medium	4.9	Hare	3.47
Guatemala	Medium	4.7	D'Hondt	11.71
Paraguay	Medium	4.4	D'Hondt	5.47
Panama	Small	1.8	Hare	12.52

Note: The least-squared index of disproportionality in this table is for the most recent election.
[1] For the 2001 election, Peru returned to a multi-member district system consisting of 25 districts and an average district magnitude of 4.8. So the new system is a medium-sized district system.
[2] The least-squares index for the most recent election in Costa Rica was considerably higher than the 4.76 average score registered over the study period. Costa Rica uses a Hare quotient, 50 percent sub-quotient, and greatest remainder system, which tend to exclude small parties to a greater extent than a pure Hare and largest remainder system.

As can be seen, subdividing proportional representation systems according to the proportion of legislative seats elected in a given sized district does appear to make some sense. The large district systems—Peru, Uruguay and Brazil—are characterized by a relatively small degree of deviation from proportionality, while the small district system in Panama is characterized by a relatively large deviation. The index of disproportionality generally hovers in the middle of these two extremes for the medium-sized districts. Nevertheless, the relationship between district size and the index is clearly imperfect, and there are some striking outliers.

The nature of the electoral formula appears to account for at least part of the large variation in disproportionality among the medium-sized districts. The two medium-sized district systems with the lowest index of disproportionality—Honduras and Nicaragua—each use the Hare formula. Guatemala, which exhibits by far the greatest degree of disproportionality among the medium-sized district systems, uses the D'Hondt method.

At the same time, however, it is clear that electoral system characteristics do not by themselves determine the proportionality of electoral outcomes. This is because other fac-

Democracies in Development

tors—such as the number of parties competing in the election[5] as well as the system used for electing the president and the relative timing of presidential and legislative elections—can have significant effects on the actual functioning of the system. In general, the smaller the number of significant parties, the smaller the district magnitude that is required to produce a reasonably proportional outcome.

For example, it is likely that the wide variation between Guatemala and the cases of Honduras and Nicaragua is due in great part to the differences in the degree to which their party systems are fragmented. According to the "effective number of parties" measure, Guatemala had about five or six significant parties competing for votes during the period, while Nicaragua[6] had about two and a half and Honduras barely more than two. Thus, while the characteristics of electoral systems affect party systems, there is an important inertial component that is a legacy of past political divisions and history. As a consequence, at the same time that their development is shaped in part by electoral rules, party systems also mediate the influence of such rules in shaping political outcomes.

Legal Thresholds

Another factor that can affect the proportionality of seat allocation is whether there is a legally required threshold in terms of vote percentage or other criterion before parties can obtain representation. The purpose of a threshold is to limit the fragmentation of the party system and enhance effectiveness. However, few countries in Latin America have adopted a legal barrier to representation: the only one of the 13 (party list) proportional representation systems with a threshold is Argentina, where at the district level a party must receive votes equivalent to 3 percent of the citizenry eligible to vote. In addition, Bolivia and Mexico have thresholds of 3 percent and 2 percent, respectively, applied at the national level. Other countries have practical thresholds that result from the combined effects of the mathematical formula, the district magnitude, and the number of parties competing.

Other Electoral Systems

Proportional Representation with Preference Vote and Personalized (or Combined) Systems

Another relevant variation of proportional representation relates to the form in which voters manifest their preferences. In most of the proportional representation systems discussed in the preceding section, the elector is constrained to select among competing party lists. In Peru, Brazil and Panama, however, the voter can specify a preference for individual

---

[5] This is particularly evident from the index values cited in footnote 4 for the United States and the United Kingdom. Even though these countries use a single member district system that heavily discriminates against minority parties, their indices of disproportionality are fairly low. There is little inequity in the allocation of seats because in each case there are two parties that share most of the votes. It could be argued that the electoral system helped over time to create the two party system, but this type of indirect effect is not captured by the index.

[6] This result for the effective number of parties in Nicaragua is based on counting the many different parties participating in the center-right coalition as just one party.

candidate(s) within the list. In Peru, voters can select up to two candidates from a party list while in Brazil they can select one. In Panama, voters are given as many preference votes as there are seats to fill. Seats are awarded according to the percentage of the votes obtained by each party, but within the party seats are awarded according to the number of votes received by the candidates. Since in these systems votes still accrue to the party list, they remain as variants within the proportional representation list sub-categories.

Following the example of Germany, however, some countries have adopted a version of proportional representation that combines the election of individual candidates by plurality and the election of party lists by proportional representation. These systems are typically called "personalized" or "combined" proportional representation systems. All of the legislative seats are still allocated according to the principal of proportionality. That is, the totality of the seats to be awarded at the regional or national level are awarded in accordance with the result of applying the electoral formula to the party list vote. The seats won through plurality are subtracted from the seats allocated through proportionality. The election of a share of the legislators on an individual basis in single member districts (or small multi-member districts) is expected to strengthen the link between electors and their representatives. As mentioned above, Venezuela and Bolivia adopted this system in the early 1990s for the election of representatives to the lower house.

Segmented (or Mixed) Systems

Another arrangement is one in which both allocation formulas—proportional and majoritarian—coexist within the same system. In Mexico's segmented system, the elector has two votes. One is used to select an individual candidate in a single member district, and the other to select a party list in a multi-member constituency circumscribing the former in which seats are allocated through a proportional formula. The difference between a segmented and a personalized proportional representation system is that in the former there is no link between the two parts of the system to guarantee a more or less proportional result. The principle of proportionality is built into part of the system, but not the system as a whole.[7]

Classification of Latin American Electoral Systems

The discussion above finds that the electoral systems used for the lower and upper houses in Latin America can be placed within one of nine different categories. Table 5.5 lists those categories and evaluates each in theoretical terms according to the three functions that

---

[7] In reality, various and frequently changing rules have connected the two parts of the system in Mexico. For instance, when the system was adopted in 1977, a party that had won more than 60 percent of the single member district seats was not eligible to receive any of the seats awarded through proportional representation. A rule adopted subsequently guaranteed an absolute majority in the lower house to any party obtaining 35 percent of the deputies elected through plurality and 35 percent of the national vote. Currently, the deviation between the percentage of the total number of deputies a party is awarded and its national vote percentage is not allowed to exceed 8 percent.

Democracies in Development

Table 5.5. Evaluating Types of Electoral Systems in Terms of Functions

Type of electoral system	Representation	Effectiveness	Participation
Proportional representation in large districts	++	—	—
Proportional representation in medium-sized districts	+	–	–
Proportional representation in small districts	– +	+	–
Personalized proportional representation	+	–	+
Segmented system	+	–	+
Majoritarian in multi-member districts	–	–	+ –
Binominal	–	+	++
Plurality with representation of the minority	–	++	++
Plurality	—	++	++

Note: The ++ designation indicates that the function is highly fulfilled; + means fulfilled; + – and – + mean partially fulfilled; – means not very well fulfilled; and — means fulfilled only minimally.

electoral systems should ideally perform. The systems are listed roughly in order from the most classically proportional systems to the most classically majoritarian systems.

The evaluations in terms of functions obviously depend on additional features of the systems. A key issue already mentioned is whether the elector is limited to voting for a party list or is given the option of expressing a preference for an individual candidate or candidates on the list. In the first case, voters essentially can only express a choice for a party, which nominates and orders the candidates in the list and determines the particular individuals that become elected. This type of list is called "closed" (only those candidates on a party list can be selected) and "blocked" (the elector votes only for the party and thus cannot alter the order of candidates on the list). In the second case, voters can choose both the party and the particular individual or individuals they would like to have represent them. These lists are called "unblocked." Lists are said to be "open" when voters can add names to the list, or in the case of multiple votes, can vote for candidates that figure on different lists.

Proportional representation systems with closed and blocked lists score low in terms of participation, since the link between constituents and their individual representatives is weak. However, systems with closed and unblocked lists or with open lists promote greater ties between voters and representatives, even though the larger the number of representatives elected in the district the more diluted and narrow is the link. First, with multiple seats at stake it is more difficult for the elector to become informed about all of the contending candidates and to track the performance of incumbents. Second, representatives (candidates) are encouraged to build support (close relations) with only a portion of the constituency. Third, voters generally have only one vote and, therefore, can only hold one of the individuals representing them accountable.

At the same time, the unblocking of party lists may also have a negative impact on effectiveness. With a preference vote, the main preoccupation of candidates is to distinguish themselves from other individuals on their party's list and cultivate personal relations with a portion of the constituents. Thus, party leaders tend to lose the ability to discipline their legislative cohorts and parties lose the ability to articulate and defend common programmatic objectives. As a consequence, effectiveness is likely to be reduced (Shugart, 1999; Carey and Shugart, 1995)

In providing a general rating to each type of electoral system, such particularities of the systems are ignored. When the specific Latin American electoral systems are evaluated, these more specific traits will be more fully considered.

Proportional representation list systems score well in terms of the representativeness dimension and poorly in terms of effectiveness and participation. While smaller district size tends to reduce the score in terms of representation, it is expected to improve effectiveness and, to a lesser extent, enhance participation. Smaller districts mean that fewer parties are likely to obtain representation, making majority governments more probable and facilitating inter-party bargaining in the legislature. At the same time, even with closed and blocked party lists, if only one, two or three legislators are elected per district, then, at least to some extent, electors can potentially vote on the basis of their sentiments toward individual candidates.

Personalized proportional representation (or combined) systems attempt to enhance the intensity of participation without reducing representativeness. The fact that a proportional formula is used to allocate all of the seats means that these systems can be highly proportional, thus representative. At the same time, the election of a large share of the legislature through single member (or small) districts by plurality tends to foster a stronger link between representatives and voters. As with other proportional representation systems, however, these systems still run the risk of fostering a disperse party system, which makes governing more difficult.

Segmented systems are similar to personalized proportional representation in terms of promoting stronger links between representatives and constituents while holding on to the value of proportionality in the electoral system. However, proportionality in segmented systems is an element but not a universal principle of the system. That is, segmented systems help guarantee representation for minority parties, but they do not guarantee that the overall allocation of the seats will match the share of the votes that parties receive. Instead, it is likely that the larger parties, which are able to win seats across the country in the single member districts, will receive a disproportionate share of the seats. Thus, segmented systems are similar to personalized proportional representation with respect to the participation dimension, somewhat inferior in terms of representativeness, and somewhat better in terms of effectiveness.

Majoritarian in multi-member district systems are difficult to fully characterize without knowledge of the average magnitude of districts and the number of political parties. Since seats are awarded to the most voted candidates—rather than to parties according to the percentages of votes they receive—the system is not proportional and may even be more disproportional than first-past-the-post systems. At the same time, such systems are likely to weaken party cohesiveness and engender a more personalized and particularistic relationship between representatives and constituents than is the case in first-past-the-post systems.

For example, in a five-member district with six parties contesting, each party would present at least five candidates. Since the seats are awarded to the candidates with the most votes, each candidate would aim to differentiate himself from all of the others, including those in his own party, and appeal to a portion of the electorate. If electors vote along party lines, such systems could result in a more disproportional outcome than is the case in first-past-the-post (single member district) systems. All five seats could go to the plurality party if electors typically selected five candidates from the same party. But given the fact that such systems tend to go hand in hand with weak parties, vote splitting may be fairly common. In that case, the allocation of seats between parties would not necessarily be highly disproportional. Nevertheless, party weakness (low discipline and low programmatic content), combined with the continued possibility of party system fragmentation, is likely to entail low effectiveness. With party labels meaning little and a multitude of candidates (at least 30 in this example) running for office, it is likely to be difficult for voters to become acquainted with the offerings of individual candidates or to evaluate the performance of incumbents. Thus, in terms of the dimension of participation, such systems would also be expected to perform relatively poorly.

Binominal systems clearly favor the two largest political forces at the expense of smaller parties. Thus, they promote a two party (or party block) system that may be good for effectiveness but bad for representativeness. On the other hand, with two member districts and, at least in the Chilean case, voting for individuals rather than party lists, the links between electors and representatives can be relatively tight.

Plurality with representation of the minority and *plurality systems* are relatively similar in how they fulfill the main electoral system functions. The former may be somewhat better in terms of representativeness, since there is a guarantee that the first minority will be represented in each district. Nonetheless, both systems favor the large parties at the expense of small parties, and both promote the concentration of seats in the parliament, thus facilitating effectiveness. In addition, both systems facilitate the building of relatively close links between representatives and constituents. Of course, these links are stronger in the single member district plurality system, since only one candidate is elected and, in contrast with some plurality with representation of the minority systems, electors select individual candidates instead of party lists.

Tables 5.6 and 5.7 show the systems that are used in the lower and upper houses of Latin America, including information on district size, the electoral formula, and the form of the ballot. With respect to the lower houses, there are three systems of proportional representation in large districts, nine systems of proportional representation in medium-sized districts, one system of proportional representation in small districts, two personalized proportional representation systems, one mixed system, one binominal system, and one majoritarian in multi-member district system. In terms of the upper houses, there are three systems of proportional representation in large districts, one plurality system, three plural-

Table 5.6. Electoral Systems Used in the Lower House

Country	Type of system	Average district magnitude	Electoral formula	Ballot form
Argentina	Proportional representation in medium-sized districts	5.4	D'Hondt	Closed and blocked lists
Bolivia	Personalized proportional representation	14.4	D'Hondt	Candidate in single member districts and closed and blocked lists
Brazil	Proportional representation in large districts	19.0	Hare and largest average[1]	Closed and unblocked lists
Chile	Binominal	2.0	First two finishers unless first doubles vote of second	One vote for candidate
Colombia[2]	Proportional representation in medium-sized districts	4.9	Hare and largest remainder	Closed and blocked lists
Costa Rica[3]	Proportional representation in medium-sized districts	8.1	Hare quotient, 50% subquotient and greatest remainder	Closed and blocked lists
Dominican Rep.	Proportional representation in medium-sized districts	5.0	D'Hondt	Closed and blocked lists
Ecuador	Majoritarian in multi-member districts	5.5	Plurality	Open lists
El Salvador	Proportional representation in medium-sized districts	5.6	Hare and largest remainder	Closed and blocked lists
Guatemala	Proportional representation in medium-sized districts	4.7	D'Hondt	Closed and blocked lists
Honduras	Proportional representation in medium-sized districts	7.1	Hare and largest remainder	Closed and blocked lists
Mexico[4]	Segmented		Plurality; corrected electoral quotient	Candidate in single member district and closed and blocked lists

Table 5.6. *(continued)*

Country	Type of system	Average district magnitude	Electoral formula	Ballot form
Nicaragua[5]	Proportional representation in medium-sized districts	5.0	Hare and remainder quotient (4)	Closed and blocked lists
Panama	Proportional representation in small districts	1.8	Single member districts: plurality; multi-member districts: Hare	Closed and unblocked lists
Paraguay	Proportional representation in medium-sized districts	4.4	D'Hondt	Closed and blocked lists
Peru[6]	Proportional representation in large district	120.0	D'Hondt	Closed and unblocked lists (two preference votes)
Uruguay[7]	Proportional representation in large district		D'Hondt	Closed and blocked lists
Venezuela[8]	Personalized proportional	6.1	D'Hondt	Candidate in single member district and closed and blocked lists

[1] "Hare and largest average" means that the valid votes are divided by the mandates already obtained plus one. This system tends to favor small parties to a greater extent than the largest remainder method.

[2] In Colombia, the electoral law allows multiple factions to present lists under the same party label, over which the parties do not exert control. The proportional representation seat allocation procedure is applied in each district to factional lists instead of party lists. Thus, though the factional lists are closed and blocked, in effect the system can be considered to operate with unblocked party lists. However, in this case the elector can choose between factional lists within the party instead of between individual candidates within a given party list.

[3] In Costa Rica, the Hare and largest remainder plus sub-quotient formula means that parties that obtain at least half the electoral quotient are eligible to receive seats through remainders.

[4] The Mexican corrected quota system takes away the votes of those parties that do not reach the national threshold of 2 percent from the calculation of the electoral quotient. A second quotient is calculated in which the remaining effective votes (total votes less those used already to allocate seats) are divided by the remaining seats. Following both procedures, the remaining seats are allocated to the parties with the greatest remainders, but only those already receiving seats are eligible.

[5] In Nicaragua, the Hare and remainder quotient formula means that the remainders for each party are summed across all of the districts and divided by the number of remaining seats to determine the quotient for the allocation of remaining seats. In the national district, the remaining seats are allocated under a quota calculated as the mean of four regional quotas.

[6] For the 2001 election, Peru returned to a multi-member district system consisting of 25 districts and an average district magnitude of 4.8. So the new system is proportional representation in medium-sized districts.

[7] The Uruguayan election system is divided into 19 districts of varying size. However, even though the electors vote for party lists in the districts, the formula for allocating seats is applied to the aggregate (national) vote percentages, and the distribution of seats within districts is required to accommodate to the national seat distribution resulting from this calculation. Thus, in effect the Uruguayan system functions in a manner similar to a system of proportional representation in a single national district.

[8] In Venezuela, since the state vote totals are used to proportionally award the total seats contested in each state, the average district magnitude is calculated by dividing the size of the chamber by the number of state districts. But the system is really more proportional than this district magnitude would indicate, since additional seats (up to five) are available to parties that are under-represented, as determined by their national vote totals relative to the national electoral quotient.

Table 5.7. Electoral Systems Used in the Upper House

Country	Type of system	Average district magnitude	Electoral formula	Ballot form
Argentina	Plurality with representation of minority	3	Plurality/Minority	Closed and blocked lists
Bolivia	Plurality with representation of minority	3	Plurality/Minority	Closed and blocked lists
Brazil[1]	Plurality in single member and two member districts	1 and 2	Plurality	Open lists
Chile	Binominal	2	D'Hondt	One vote for a candidate
Colombia[2]	Proportional representation in large (national) districts	100	Hare and greatest remainder	Closed and blocked lists
Dominican Rep.	Plurality	1	Plurality	Vote for candidate
Mexico	Segmented: plurality with representation of minority, and proportional representation in large (national) district	3 and 32	Plurality/Corrected Hare with greatest remainder	Closed and blocked lists
Paraguay	Proportional representation in large (national) districts	45	D'Hondt	Closed and blocked lists
Uruguay[3]	Proportional representation in large (national) districts	30	D'Hondt	Closed and blocked sub-party lists

[1] When two-thirds of the senate is up for election and two senators are being elected per state, then electors have two votes for specific candidates who can be from different parties.

[2] In Colombia, the electoral law allows multiple factions to present lists under the same party label, over which the parties do not exert much control. The proportional representation seat allocation procedure is applied to factional lists instead of party lists. Thus, though the factional lists are closed and blocked, in effect the system can be considered to operate with unblocked party lists. However, in this case the elector can choose a factional list within the party instead of a particular candidate.

[3] As in Colombia, in Uruguay voters choose between closed and blocked sub-party lists. Unlike in Colombia, the proportional representation formula is applied to the total votes of the party in order to determine the inter-party allocation of seats. Then sub-party list votes determine the allocation of seats within parties.

ity with representation of the minority systems, one mixed system, and one binominal system.

In terms of the ballot structure, 10 countries use closed and blocked party lists in the lower house: Argentina, Colombia, Costa Rica, the Dominican Republic, El Salvador, Guatemala, Honduras, Nicaragua, Paraguay and Uruguay. In addition, in the personalized proportional representation systems (Bolivia and Venezuela) and the mixed case (Mexico), closed and blocked lists are used for the proportional representation component of the system. Among the proportional representation systems, preference votes are permitted in three countries (Brazil, Panama and Peru). Personalized voting is also used in the binominal Chilean system and the multi-member majoritarian system in Ecuador.

Closed and blocked lists are used for the upper houses in five countries (Argentina, Bolivia, Colombia, Paraguay and Uruguay). In Mexico, the proportional representation component uses closed and blocked lists, while the plurality component uses a personalized voting system. In the Dominican Republic and Brazil, voters opt for individual candidates.

Evaluation of Latin American Election Systems in Terms of Functions

The next step is to evaluate the specific electoral systems used in Latin America in terms of the three functions: representativeness, effectiveness and participation. It is important to emphasize that the evaluations at this point are theoretical—focused on the properties of the electoral systems—and not based on the actual functioning of the political system in the specific countries. Table 5.8 evaluates the electoral system used for the lower house in each country.

Given the prevalence of proportional representation with closed and blocked party lists, Latin American electoral systems for the lower house tend to serve the function of representativeness to the detriment of effectiveness and participation. Even though most countries use medium-sized districts, they generally provide opportunities for smaller parties to obtain representation. This would be expected to result frequently in governments that lack majorities in the legislature, and in a fairly high degree of party system fragmentation. Of the three wholly or partially majoritarian systems, only Chile's is expected to really concentrate legislative power and promote the election of majority governments. The segmented Mexican system may also tend to concentrate representation. The plurality portion of the system, the requirement for parties to present candidates in at least 200 single member districts in order to field lists in the regional proportional representation constituencies, and the 2 percent threshold may also limit the ability of small parties to compete effectively. However, in Ecuador, the tendency of multiple member districts with multiple votes to promote and reflect weak parties would lead one to expect difficulties in governing, even in the unlikely event that the majoritarian aspect of the system reduced the number of parties. Concentration of party representation might also be favored in Panama, where districts tend to be quite small, and in Guatemala, where the combination of relatively small districts and the D'Hondt formula raises the hurdle for small parties.

Because of the prevalence of closed and blocked lists and multi-member districts, Latin American systems also score relatively low in terms of participation. The electoral systems promote a kind of party-centered representation that inhibits electors from holding legislators individually accountable for their positions on issues or their conduct in office. In this type of system, accountability of individual politicians, if it can be achieved, rests on the existence of democratic internal party structures in which candidates and party leaders are se-

Table 5.8. Theoretical Evaluations of Electoral Systems for the Lower House in Terms of Functions

	Type of system	Representa-tiveness	Effective-ness	Partici-pation
Argentina	Proportional representation in medium-sized districts	+	–	–
Bolivia	Personalized proportional representation	++	–	+
Brazil[1]	Proportional representation in large districts	++	—	–
Chile	Binominal	–	++	+
Colombia[2]	Proportional representation in medium-sized districts	+	–	–
Costa Rica	Proportional representation in medium-sized districts	+	–	–
Dominican Rep.	Proportional representation in medium-sized districts	+	–	–
Ecuador[3]	Majoritarian in multi-member districts	–	–	–
El Salvador	Proportional representation in medium-sized districts	+	–	–
Guatemala[4]	Proportional representation in medium-sized districts	+ –	– +	–
Honduras	Proportional representation in medium-sized districts	+	–	–
Mexico	Segmented	+ –	–	+
Nicaragua	Proportional representation in medium-sized districts	+	–	–
Panama	Proportional representation in small districts	–	+	– +
Paraguay	Proportional representation in medium-sized districts	+	–	–
Peru	Proportional representation in large districts	++	—	–

lected through a fair and competitive process. As will be shown in Chapter Seven, however, the internal democratization of political parties is in the beginning stages in most countries of the region.

The personalized proportional representation systems in Bolivia and Venezuela, the segmented system in Mexico, the binominal system in Chile, and possibly the small district proportional representation system in Panama are the only exceptions in terms of the relatively low emphasis placed on the function of participation in lower house systems. But even in Bolivia, Venezuela and Mexico, the selection of candidates for the plurality contests

Table 5.8. *(continued)*

	Type of system	Representa-tiveness	Effective-ness	Partici-pation
Uruguay	Proportional representation in large districts	++	—	–
Venezuela	Personalized proportional representation	+	–	+

Note: The designation of ++ indicates that the function is highly fulfilled; + means fulfilled; + – and – + mean partially fulfilled; – means not very well fulfilled; and — means fulfilled only minimally.

[1] Even though voters have the choice to vote for an individual candidate, Brazil's system in terms of the function of participation was still rated –, since a large number of legislators are elected in each district and, therefore, the links between representatives and constituents are still likely to be weak.

[2] Even though multiple faction lists can be presented under the same party label in Colombia, these faction lists are still closed and blocked. Along with the still fairly large districts, this fact leads to a score of – for participation. Though the electoral system would be expected to produce a relatively fragmented legislature, until fairly recently, two main parties have gained most of the legislative seats. But this is misleading, since the two parties are highly factionalized and these factions often act quite independently of each other.

[3] The Ecuadorian system poses some particular difficulties for classification, as noted in the text. If parties were relatively well institutionalized, it might be expected that electors would vote only for those candidates listed under the party they prefer. Then this system would likely concentrate the distribution of seats toward large parties. But if parties are weakly institutionalized, or electors do not identify with particular parties, then multiple votes in multiple member districts could produce a fair amount of fragmentation. Even if parties were somewhat cohesive when the system was introduced, this cohesion would likely erode over time. Thus, the – score on representativeness comes from the fact that the system does not guarantee any kind of proportionality with respect to party labels or programs. The – score on effectiveness is based on the fact that party system fragmentation still may occur and the system is likely to weaken the cohesiveness of parties. The – + score on participation is based on the fact that an average of 5.5 seats are elected in each district. It is not possible for constituents to familiarize themselves with the policy positions of all of the contending candidates from the diverse parties and to follow the actions of those who wind up being elected, especially when the system tends to dilute the meaning of party labels, which might otherwise help to simplify this task.

[4] The + – score for representation for Guatemala is based on the fact that the district magnitude is relatively low (4.7) and that the D'Hondt system is used to allocate seats.

is still fairly highly centralized. Features designed to promote participation in the systems of Brazil, Ecuador and Peru do not seem to fulfill this objective, at least as defined here. The possibility of personalized voting in such large-district (large number of seats per district) systems does not allow a close link to be built between constituents and their representatives. This was especially true in Peru from 1993 to 2000, when there was a single national district for electing the 120 members of the National Assembly.

Different types of majoritarian systems are the norm for the upper houses in nine of the 18 countries in the study (Table 5.9). Just three of these nine bicameral systems elect their senators through proportional representation, and all use a single national district. Included in this group are Colombia, Paraguay and Uruguay. Of the majoritarian systems, Argentina and Bolivia elect senators by plurality with representation of the minority; Brazil alternates between plurality in single member districts and plurality in two member districts; Chile's system is binominal; and the Dominican Republic uses plurality in single member districts. As is the case for the lower house, the Mexican system is segmented. Three-fourths of the members of the Mexican senate are elected through the plurality with

Table 5.9. Theoretical Evaluations of Electoral Systems for the Upper House in Terms of Functions

Country	System type	Representa-tiveness	Effective-ness	Partici-pation
Argentina	Plurality with representation of minority	−	++	+
Bolivia	Plurality with representation of minority	−	++	+
Brazil	Plurality in single member and two member districts	−	++	++
Chile	Binominal	−	++	+
Colombia	Proportional representation in large (national) districts	++	—	—
Dominican Rep.	Plurality	−	+	++
Mexico	Segmented: Plurality with representation of minority and proportional representation in large (national) districts	+	− +	+
Paraguay	Proportional representation in large (national) districts	++	—	—
Uruguay	Proportional representation in large (national) districts	++	—	—

Note: The designation of ++ indicates that the function is highly fulfilled; + means fulfilled; + − and − + mean partially fulfilled; − means not very well fulfilled; and — means fulfilled only minimally.

representation of the minority system, and one-quarter by proportional representation in a national district.

The majoritarian systems generally receive low marks for representation but reasonably high marks for effectiveness and participation. Similar to the analysis of the lower house systems, the proportional representation in large national district systems for the upper house are expected to do well at representing the diverse political forces in society, but less well at producing effective governments and building personal links between representatives and constituents. As with its lower house system, Mexico's segmented upper house system is again a compromise between the principles of proportionality and majoritarianism. The Mexican system is scored with a "+−" for representation, since the proportional representation part of the system should allow smaller parties to be represented, though not proportionately. It is scored "+−" for effectiveness, since the election of three-quarters of the members through the plurality with representation of minority system should still tend to give the large parties a substantial share of the seats. Finally, the system is rated a "+" for participation, since the plurality component allows constituents to get to know their senators reasonably well.

The next step is to examine whether the theoretical expectations related to the properties of Latin America's electoral systems correspond to any significant degree with their actual functioning. Do electoral systems that appear to be designed to favor representation produce reasonably proportional results? Do electoral systems that appear in design to favor a concentration of political forces and effectiveness actually do so? In this analysis, it will not be possible to compare theoretical expectations in respect to participation with an outcome measure. Though in theory it may be possible through public surveys or interviews of legislators to test the closeness of the relationship between constituents and their representatives, comparable data on this matter do not exist at the present time.

Figure 5.1 shows the degree of correspondence between the theoretical representation scores given for each country and the measurement of the degree of disproportionality from the most recent election results.

Now that the electoral formula, along with the district magnitude, has been factored into the scoring for the proportional representation list systems, the least squares index of disproportionality corresponds more closely to theoretical expectations for the systems. The five systems that do not use proportional representation are included in the figure and appear to conform reasonably well with expectations. Where the systems have been scored "++" in terms of representation, the index of disproportionality is quite small, as we would expect. The systems ranked low in terms of the function of representation (scored "–") generally have high indices of disproportionality. The systems expected to more moderately favor representation (+) generally fall between these two extremes with respect to the disproportionality measure.

Clearly, however, the theoretical properties of electoral systems do not fully predict electoral outcomes. There remains a considerable range in proportionality for each of the possible theoretical scores for representativeness. Guatemala, Honduras, Nicaragua and Paraguay are outliers. Guatemala has more disproportionality in outcomes than would be expected, and Honduras, Nicaragua and Paraguay have less. Costa Rica's index reflects somewhat greater disproportionality than would be expected for a system in which the average district magnitude is 8.[8] In part, these discrepancies are due to the fact that the measurements are taken only from the most recent elections. For instance, the average disproportionality index over the period for Costa Rica is considerably less (4.76 instead of 6.57), while that for Paraguay is much greater (5.47 instead of 2.28). Thus, anomalous characteristics of the most recent election, such as the formation of an alliance in Paraguay between two of the three major parties (the Partido Liberal Radical Auténtico and the Encuentro Nacional), may distort the value of the index.

But as pointed out above, it is also likely that the differences in the nature of their party systems contribute importantly to the differences in the disproportionality of outcomes between the cases. While the Honduran party system has been dominated by two political parties and the Nicaraguan system has thus far been characterized by relatively few significant parties or party coalitions, in Guatemala several parties have seriously contended for

---

[8] Given that the average figure for Costa Rica is more typical, the other factor that may account for the higher disproportionality is the use of the Hare sub-quotient on top of the normal quotient. As a consequence, it is more difficult for small parties to earn seats through remainders, and larger parties tend to be favored more than with the simple Hare system.

Figure 5.1. Theoretical Representation Scores vs. Index of Disproportionality (Lower House)

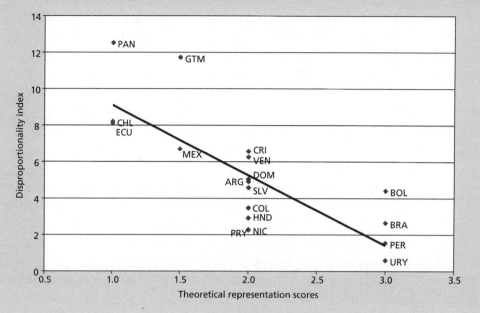

Note: The representation scores have been converted into numbers: ++ = 3, + = 2, + – = 1.5, and – = 1.

political office. These circumstances may explain why the results in Honduras and Nicaragua have been more proportional and, in Guatemala, less proportional than would be expected purely on the basis of their electoral system properties.

The two-way and imperfect nature of the relationship between electoral system attributes and party system characteristics is even more clearly evident when we compare the theoretical expectations for effectiveness with a measure of the effective number of political parties (Laakso and Taagepera, 1979).[9] The index of the effective number of parties measures the number of parties obtaining seats in the legislature weighted by the proportion of seats they obtain.

We have already seen that a more fragmented party system contributes to higher disproportionality by making it more difficult for a given electoral system (formula, district size, etc.) to fairly allocate seats among parties. More proportional systems are expected to allow more parties to be represented and to encourage more parties to compete for office.

---

[9] The index for the effective number of parties is computed by taking the inverse of the sum of the square of all parties' seat (or vote) shares. If there are three parties competing that receive close to an equal share of the vote, then the result for the index would be close to 3. But if two of the three parties receive about 45 percent of the seats (or votes) each, and the third party receives only 10 percent, then the result would be about 2.4. The index attempts to capture the fact that despite also having three parties, the latter system functions closer to a two-party system, while the former functions more purely like a three-party system.

However, if this happens, a more proportional electoral system could paradoxically lead to an increase in the disproportionality of electoral outcomes (or a smaller decrease than expected) because of the greater number of parties that would be contending for the seats available.

Similarly, the properties of the electoral system do not exclusively determine the number of significant political parties competing for or holding political office. This is because the electoral system is clearly not the only factor affecting the nature of the party system. The structure of today's party systems is as much a product of long-term historical events and social and political divisions as it is of the current properties of the electoral system. In fact, one can view electoral systems themselves as a product of this political history and of the evolution of the party system structure. Electoral systems do not emerge in a vacuum or from purely philosophical discussions. Rather, they are created typically by leading politicians in order to promote the interests of their political movements or parties. In addition, as shown in the previous chapter, the system for electing the president and the degree of concurrence between the presidential and legislative elections also influences the structure of the party system.

Thus, while highly proportional electoral systems create incentives for party system fragmentation, countries with such systems do not necessarily have a larger number of significant parties than countries with less proportional systems. Nevertheless, if a given country implements an electoral system reform that promotes greater proportionality, the expected trend is one of new party formation and more small parties obtaining representation in the parliament. A trend in the opposite direction could occur, but would not be expected.

Table 5.10 and Figure 5.2 show that some countries match expectations fairly well. Brazil, which has an electoral system that favors representativeness and disfavors effectiveness, has a highly fragmented party system. With an electoral system that is not very proportional, a fairly large number of parties compete for seats in Guatemala, but few parties obtain significant representation.

There are, however, some countries whose party systems appear to diverge from expectations. Honduras, Costa Rica and Uruguay, whose electoral systems would be expected to foster a relatively large number of effective parties, have had fairly concentrated party systems (as measured by the effective number of parties index). But there are signs that at least in Costa Rica, this may be in the process of changing. Given the factionalized nature of the parties in Uruguay, it may not be correct to view this as a deviant case. While three major parties typically dominate, the parties themselves are composed of numerous factions that compete internally for the party's seat share.

Among the countries that scored "−" in terms of effectiveness, there is a very large range of outcomes, from a low of nearly two significant parties for Honduras and Paraguay to a high of more than five for Bolivia and Ecuador. Chile also has more political parties than would be expected to be associated with a binominal system. However, when party alliances rather than individual political parties are considered, it is clear that Chile is not a deviant case. Thus, the electoral system appears to have had its intended effect of promoting government effectiveness by encouraging the formation and durability of two large alliances of the center-left and the center-right.

Table 5.10. Theoretical Expectations Compared with Outcome Measures: Lower House

Country	Representa-tiveness	Dispropor-tionality index	Effec-tiveness	Effective number of parties (votes)	Effective number of parties (seats)
Argentina	+	4.91	–	3.54	2.66
Bolivia	++	4.41	–	5.56	5.36
Brazil	++	2.65	—	8.33	7.99
Chile[1]	–	(8.20)	++	6.93 (2.39)	5.02 (2.01)
Colombia	+	3.47	–	3.32	2.96
Costa Rica[2]	+	6.57	–	3.07	2.32
Dominican Rep.	+	5.04	–	2.80	2.43
Ecuador	–	8.10	–	6.05	5.73
El Salvador	+	4.58	–	3.70	3.15
Guatemala	+ –	11.72	+ –	4.86	2.35
Honduras	+	2.92	–	2.26	2.10
Mexico	+ –	6.70	–	3.10	2.86
Nicaragua	+	2.26	–	2.93	2.79
Panama	–	12.52	+	7.16	3.26
Paraguay	+	2.28	–	2.41	2.20
Peru	++	1.54	—	3.65	3.44
Uruguay	++	0.60	—	3.21	3.16
Venezuela	+	6.25	–	5.71	4.74

[1] The figures in parentheses are the values of the indices if calculated on the basis of party alliances rather than on the basis of individual parties.
[2] The least-squares index for the most recent election in Costa Rica was considerably higher than the 4.76 average score registered over the study period.

Given the influence of other country-specific factors, the effect of electoral system properties on political outcomes may be obscured in cross-national comparisons of the type performed above. A preferred way to examine the impact of electoral systems would be to analyze the effects over time of reforms in specific countries. In this manner, the structural and historical factors that mediate between electoral system factors and political outcomes are better controlled. Thus, the next section examines the electoral system reforms of the past few decades, and ventures a preliminary attempt to determine whether the reforms had their expected effects on political representation outcomes. Such analysis is complicated in many cases, however, by the brief time period in which a reformed system has been in force, as well as by mostly exogenous political events, such as the delegitimization of political parties, which are likely to have a greater impact on outcomes than changes to the electoral system.

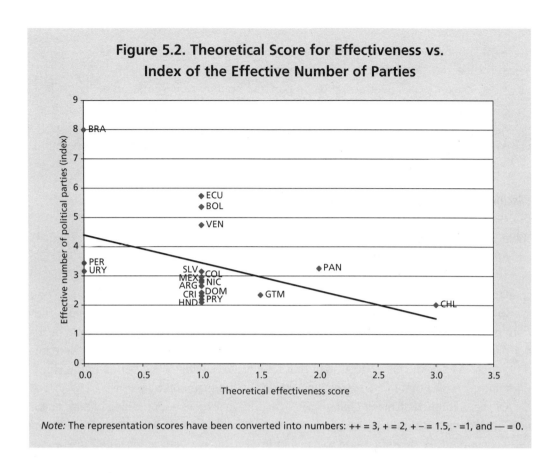

Figure 5.2. Theoretical Score for Effectiveness vs. Index of the Effective Number of Parties

Note: The representation scores have been converted into numbers: ++ = 3, + = 2, + − = 1.5, - =1, and — = 0.

Evolution of Latin American Electoral Systems

In examining the electoral system reforms adopted during the period of this study—which begins when a country is considered to have made the transition to democracy or, if democratic before 1978, the year of the inauguration of the first president to serve a full term after 1978—it is clear that many reforms were implemented even after the transitions to democratic government were completed. To gain a sense of their meaning from the standpoint of democratic governability, these reforms are examined in terms of their expected effects on the functions of representativeness, effectiveness, and participation. Many of the reforms are fairly subtle in nature, involving a slight adjustment of the electoral formula or a small change in the size of electoral districts. They would not be expected to have a significant impact on representation outcomes. Left out from this examination are many reforms that could be quite significant for the functioning of democracy, such as the creation of an independent electoral commission or the provision of public financing for political parties. The changes that are noted are the following:

- The type of electoral system, e.g., from proportional representation list system to a personalized proportional representation system

- The number of legislative seats and the magnitude of electoral districts
- The electoral formula, e.g., from Hare to D'Hondt
- The existence of legal thresholds for parties to obtain representation
- The relative timing of presidential, legislative and local elections
- The degree of linkage on the ballot between presidential and legislative elections
- The type of voting choice (whether for strictly party list, candidate preference, multiple candidate preferences, etc.).

Electoral Reforms that Affect the Lower House

Table 5.11 shows the reforms to systems for electing representatives to the lower house. Only three of the 18 countries did not change their legislative electoral system during the period of the study. In five countries (Bolivia, Ecuador, Peru, Uruguay and Venezuela), changes were made in the type of electoral system. All except Ecuador changed from one type of proportional representation system to another. Even in Ecuador, the change was not from proportional representation to a traditional plurality system, but to a multiple member plurality system. It is worth noting, however, that in Chile and Mexico there were important changes to the electoral system that took place outside of the period of the study. Chile moved to the binominal system and Mexico to the segmented system.

Of the systems that made changes, Bolivia and Venezuela adopted personalized proportional representation in place of a proportional representation list system in medium-sized constituencies. In Peru, there was a shift from a proportional representation list system in medium-sized districts to a "pure" proportional representation system in a national district (in both cases with preference votes).[10] And finally, in Uruguay a unique type of proportional representation list system in which parties could present multiple faction lists in each district was replaced by a more traditional proportional representation list system.

Aside from a change in the type of electoral system, some countries changed the timing of presidential and legislative elections. As shown in Chapter Four (see Table 4.5), Chile, the Dominican Republic and Venezuela shifted from systems with either fully or partially simultaneous elections to one with non-coterminous cycles. Brazil and Ecuador moved in the opposite direction, while Argentina moved slightly toward greater simultaneity.

Another important reform was the separation of the ballot for elections of legislators from that for other offices such as the presidency or the upper house. Such reforms were adopted in the Dominican Republic, Guatemala, Honduras, Panama, Paraguay and Uruguay.

The other types of changes noted in Table 5.11 mainly relate to the territorial distribution of legislative seats, the size of the chamber and the magnitude of electoral districts, and the type of electoral formula.

Though there has not been a pronounced shift in the region toward more emphasis on the three functions, there has been some movement in the direction of more emphasis on representation and participation and less on effectiveness. There have been changes in favor of representation in the Dominican Republic, El Salvador, Guatemala, Honduras, Mexico, Nicaragua, Panama and Peru. However, in a few of these cases the change was fairly

---

[10] With the 2001 election, Peru returned again to a multi-member district system consisting of 25 districts.

Table 5.11. Lower House Electoral System Changes

Country	Year	Nature of change	Expected effect
Argentina	1994	Only one mid-term election instead of two because of shortening of presidential term from six to four years.[1]	Effectiveness +
Bolivia	1986	Seat allocation formula changed from D'Hondt to double quotient.[2]	Representation — Effectiveness +
	1991	Seat allocation formula changed from double quotient to Saint-Lague divisor system.	Representation + Effectiveness –
	1994	Changed system from proportional representation list to personalized proportional representation (about half of deputies elected through plurality in single member districts); plurality vote separate from vote for president, vice-president and senate; threshold of 3% introduced at national level.	Participation +
Brazil		No changes.	
Chile[3]		No changes.	
Colombia	1992	Reduction in the size of districts by creating new districts and reducing the size of the congress.[4]	Representation — Effectiveness +
		Creation of special districts for indigenous groups.	Representation +
Costa Rica		No changes.	
Dominican Republic	1985	Restoration of simultaneous vote (voting for president and congressmen with the same vote).	Effectiveness + Participation –
	1990	Separation of two votes, one for president and one for congressmen.	Effectiveness — Participation +
	1994	Presidential and congressional elections separated into different four-year cycles resulting in further separation of voting for president and congress.	Effectiveness — Participation +
	1997	Size of lower house increased from 120 to 149 deputies. Average district magnitude increased from 4 to 5.	Representation + Effectiveness —
Ecuador	1998	System changed from proportional representation list with small national district and regional multi-member constituencies to plurality in multi-member districts. Proportional representation list in 20 member national constituency maintained for 1998 election but to disappear in subsequent elections.	Representation – Effectiveness — Participation +?

Country	Year	Nature of change	Expected effect
Ecuador		All deputies elected simultaneously; previously, provincial deputies were elected every two years. Size of congress increased from 82 to 121 seats. For 1998 election, 20 national deputies instead of 12.	Effectiveness +
El Salvador	1988	Number of deputies increased from 60 to 84; creation of national constituency for election of 20 out of 84 deputies but still one vote for congress.	Representation +
Guatemala	1990	Number of deputies increased from 100 to 116 (district deputies went from 75 to 87 and national deputies from 25 to 29).	Representation +
	1994	Number of deputies reduced and fixed at 80 with 64 district deputies and 16 national deputies.	Representation — Effectiveness +
		Separate vote for national deputies (the vote for president previously entailed a vote for a party list for national district).	Participation +
	1998	Number of deputies increased to 113 with 91 members elected in departmental constituencies and 22 in national constituency.	Representation +
Honduras	1985	Number of deputies increased from 82 to 134. Average district magnitude increased from 4.56 to 7.44.	Representation + Effectiveness –
	1988	Decree established that congress composed of fixed number of 128 deputies. Remainders allocated at national level on the basis of national quotient.	
	1992	Separate vote for president and deputies to national congress. Separate boxes on the same ballot for president, congress and municipal councils.	Participation +
	1993	Requirement for fully separate ballots for president, congress and municipal councils, first used in 1997.	Participation +
Mexico[5]	1986	Number of proportional representation seats raised from 100 to 200; total size of chamber increased from 400 to 500; plurality winner assured majority in congress; change from two votes to one; PRI given access to seats won through proportional representation.	Representation +[6] Participation — Effectiveness +

Table 5.11. *(continued)*

Country	Year	Nature of change	Expected effect
Mexico	1989	Majority party limited to 70% of seats in lower house; electoral alliances prohibited; elector given two votes again, one for candidate in plurality and one for party list in proportional representation constituency.	Participation +
	1990	Any party receiving 35% of plurality of deputies and 35% of national vote to be guaranteed an absolute majority in the chamber; limit of 60% of seats or up to 315 if party obtains more than 60% of popular vote.	Representation —? Effectiveness +
	1993	35% rule eliminated.	Representation + Effectiveness –
	1996	Threshold for representation raised from 1.5% to 2%; no party can be awarded a percentage of total deputies 8% more than the percent of national vote it obtains. If this happens solely in plurality seats the rule does not apply.	Representation + Effectiveness +
	1996	Creation of five multiple member constituencies to replace national constituency.	
Nicaragua	1988	Eliminated second of three steps for assigning seats based on the sum of district residuals and a new quotient, but kept the third step of regional assignment of seats in order of greater to lesser valid votes.	Representation — Effectiveness +
	1992	Distribution formula for department level changed so that very small parties especially favored.	Representation + Effectiveness –
	1996	Electoral regions established in 1984 replaced by departmental districts of smaller population and with smaller number of deputies; creation of national constituency of 20 deputies.	Representation + Effectiveness –
Panama	1993	Eliminated the restriction introduced in 1988 that prevented parties from obtaining seats through residuals that had not previously obtained a seat. Remaining seats are allocated first to parties that have not obtained a seat but have received minimally a half quotient in order of votes received. Second, if seats remain, they are allocated to the candidates receiving	Representation + Participation +

Table 5.11. *(continued)*

Country	Year	Nature of change	Expected effect
		the most votes, counting each of the lists in which the candidate has postulated. The law eliminated the deduction of the half quotient as the previous means of assigning seats by residual. Eliminated the impediment against a party obtaining more than two-thirds of the seats in a district, as was the case since 1930. Separate ballots put in place for each office.	
Paraguay	1990	Separate ballots put in place for election of senators and deputies	Participation +
	1990	Change from one national constituency to 18 multiple member constituencies corresponding to the country's 17 administrative departments and the capital	Representation — Participation +
Peru	1993	Change from bicameral to unicameral system; basis of representation changed from 25 multiple member constituencies to one national constituency; size of lower house reduced from 180 to 120.	Representation + Participation –
	2000	Change back to use of 25 multiple member constituencies to elect 120 representatives to the unicameral legislature	Representation –
Uruguay	1996	For lower house, change from the double simultaneous vote system, in which parties can present multiple faction lists *(sub-lemas)* and the votes cumulate across faction lists, to the traditional proportional representation list system, where each party can only present one list in each district.	Effectiveness +
Venezuela	1990	Changed system from proportional representation list in medium-sized districts to personalized proportional representation; 35% of deputies elected by plurality (in single member districts) and 65% by proportional representation; vote for deputies separated from vote for senate; electors choose candidate in plurality districts, party lists for chamber deputies; and party list for senate.	Participation +
	1997	Some multiple member constituencies created for plurality portion of the chamber in the case	Participation +

| | | Table 5.11. (continued) | |

Country	Year	Nature of change	Expected effect
		of large municipalities that the constitution says should not be divided; half of deputies elected by plurality and half by proportional representation.	
		Temporarily, legislative elections moved up to one month before presidential elections.	Participation + Effectiveness −
		Change to unicameral system; 60% of deputies elected by plurality and 40% by proportional representation; separation of presidential elections from congressional elections as a result of lengthening of president's term from five to six years.	Participation + Effectiveness + −[7]

Note: Some of the information on electoral system reform for Central America and the Dominican Republic was found in Instituto Interamericano de Derechos Humanos (2000).

[1] Also in 1990, a new province was added (Tierra del Fuego), which increased the number of deputies in the lower house from 254 to 257. Though significant for the citizens of Tierra del Fuego, this is not expected to have a major impact on the three functions considered here.

[2] The double quotient requires that parties receive at least one quota (total valid votes/seats contested) before they can receive any seats through remainders.

[3] With the adoption of the 1980 constitution during the Pinochet regime, Chile changed its electoral system from one of proportional representation to the binominal system. This change is not mentioned in the table since it occurred outside of the period of the study, i.e., before the transition to democracy in Chile.

[4] See Archer and Shugart (1997) for the broader impact of the change in terms of clientelistic practices. On the one hand, smaller districts mean it is harder to win with a narrow base of support. But expansion of the number of districts means that there are some very under-populated districts where particularistic appeals can flourish.

[5] In Mexico, the segmented electoral system was adopted in 1977. This change is not mentioned in the table since it occurred outside of the period of the study.

[6] The increase in the size of the proportional representation part of the system would be expected to enhance representation of minority parties. But the fact that the PRI was given access to the seats won through proportional representation could have enhanced the share of seats won by the majority party.

[7] The elimination of the senate tends to promote greater effectiveness, since one potential point of opposition to the government has been eliminated. But the separation of the presidential and legislative elections tends to undermine effectiveness by increasing the chances that a different party or parties can control the legislature than which controls the presidency, and by also leading to an increase in the number of parties in the legislature. When presidential and congressional elections are held concurrently, legislative votes tend to be channeled toward the parties of the leading presidential candidates. This limits the number of parties that obtain representation and enhances the chances that the president's party will obtain a large share of the seats.

minimal. The only country whose system appears to have moved in the opposite direction is Paraguay.

Since greater emphasis on representation usually entails a larger number of parties in the legislature and less of a chance of majority governments, the changes in these countries have generally also entailed lower effectiveness. In a couple of cases, effectiveness has also been potentially sacrificed by the separation of the legislative vote from the presidential vote, either in terms of the separate timing of the elections (e.g., Chile, Dominican

Republic and Venezuela) or the separation of the ballots (e.g., Guatemala, for national list deputies, Honduras, and Bolivia for plurality deputies).

Though proportional representation with closed and blocked party lists remain the norm in the region, there has been a slight movement in favor of participation, giving more freedom to electors to choose the individual(s) who will represent them. The moves to personalized proportional representation in Bolivia and Venezuela represent the clearest advances in favor of participation. But the separation of ballots for the election of legislative deputies from ballots for the presidency and other offices (e.g., senators)[11] also gives electors greater discretion and weakens the dominance of party labels in the voter decision. Nevertheless, party leaders or organizations still tend to exercise great control in determining the particular individuals who are elected and reelected to the congress.

Table 5.12 shows the changes over time in the disproportionality of outcomes produced by the Latin American electoral systems for the lower house. Numbers in bold not in parentheses indicate elections held immediately following electoral reforms that were expected to have favored the function of representation. Thus, if outcomes match expectations, the values for the index of disproportionality should be smaller in this election than for the preceding elections. Numbers in bold within parentheses indicate elections held immediately after reforms that would have been expected to have the opposite effect. Thus, if outcomes match expectations, then these disproportionality index values should be larger than those for the preceding elections. For the cases in which theoretical expectations are fulfilled, the numbers are in italics.

As can be seen, there are 14 cases of reforms that might have been expected to affect the proportionality of electoral outcomes. Of these, 11 appear to have affected outcomes in the expected direction. But in only a few cases was the reform very dramatic or the change very pronounced. In all of the cases of significant reform and pronounced change, the direction of change with respect to proportionality was according to expectations.

Examining the regional average,[12] it is clear that there has not been a dramatic shift in terms of the function of representation over the period. On average, the Latin American systems continue to generate relatively proportional outcomes, thus neither discriminating very strongly against smaller parties nor unduly favoring large parties. Nor have there been many dramatic changes with respect to individual countries. This is to be expected, since, with the partial exception of Ecuador, no countries have abandoned a proportional system in favor of a majoritarian system or vice versa.[13] Peru experienced a fairly substantial increase in proportionality after 1993 as a consequence of the change from medium-sized, multi-member constituencies to a single national district.

---

[11] A significant trend has been the proliferation of elections for choosing representatives and leaders at the subnational level, and the increasing separation of these elections from national ones both with respect to their timing and the ballot structure. A systematic treatment of this matter, however, is beyond the scope of this chapter.

[12] The index values from elections over a four-year span are counted for each country.

[13] The Ecuadorian constitution specifies that the electoral system should ensure the proportional representation of minorities. The open list "personalized" form of voting approved in the 1997 referendum (Consulta Popular) appears to contradict this norm. For the 1998 election, a transitory law was adopted that partially reconciled these norms by including a national district in which the proportional and closed list system still operated. Twenty of 121 deputies were elected by proportional representation and 101 deputies by plurality in multi-member districts. It is unclear what system will be adopted for the next election scheduled for 2002.

Table 5.12. Evolution of Latin American Electoral Systems: Representation
(Index of disproportionality based on elections to the lower house)

Country	1978–79	1980–81	1982–83	1984–85	1986–87	1988–89	1990–91	1992–93	1994–95	1996–97	1998–99	2000
Argentina			4.85	5.60	5.51	7.04	5.65	6.42	7.75	3.75	4.91	
Bolivia		5.72		3.80		(6.94)	3.20	6.48	3.08	4.41		
Brazil			2.42		3.46		3.20		3.08		2.65	
Chile						7.02		5.59		8.20	3.47	
Colombia	3.23		1.43		3.26		2.99		(4.90)			
Costa Rica	5.47		3.18		3.25		4.59		5.50		6.57	
Dominican Rep.	3.46		5.57		5.64		4.95		4.83		5.04	
Ecuador	11.06			11.82		17.04		4.60		5.18	(8.10)	
El Salvador				10.45		4.87	3.88			4.70		4.58
Guatemala				11.41			11.03		(12.41)		11.72	
Honduras		0.93		1.34		2.70		2.13		2.92		
Mexico	1.42		7.39	6.43		3.53	2.52		7.45	6.70		
Nicaragua							1.79			2.26		
Panama									15.55		12.52	
Paraguay						8.23		5.91			2.28	
Peru		9.30		7.88			6.63		2.80			1.54
Uruguay				0.41		0.54			0.43		0.60	
Venezuela	4.22		4.97			4.02		3.85			5.42	6.25
Four-year average	5.06	4.79	5.41	5.40	5.21	5.46	4.86	5.73	5.62	5.26	4.94	

Table 5.13 shows the changes over time in the effective number of parties obtaining representation in the legislature. The regional average reveals a fairly substantial increase, from a 1988–89 value of 3.14 effective parties to 3.54 in 1998–99. But closer examination on a country-by-country basis makes clear that this regional trend was marked by large increases in relatively few countries. By far the most pronounced instances of party system fragmentation occurred in Brazil from 1986 to 1990, and in Venezuela from 1988 to 1993 and in 1998. In neither of these cases could the change be attributed to an electoral system reform, since in Brazil no significant reform occurred and in Venezuela the reform should not have strongly affected the proportionality of the system. There was also a large increase in the number of effective parties represented in the legislature in Peru from 1985 to 1990, but this was not sustained in 1995, despite a constitutional reform that emphasized greater proportionality. Less pronounced increases in the number of effective parties occurred in Bolivia, Ecuador, El Salvador and Mexico. In each of these cases, an electoral system reform favored the function of representativeness at the expense of effectiveness. But it is doubtful, at least in the case of Ecuador and Mexico, that electoral reform was the only or the main factor driving the increase in the number of effective parties.

How do Latin American election systems perform with respect to the dimension of effectiveness? To answer this question completely, of course, one would need to determine the number of effective parties that is compatible with a well-performing presidential democracy. But this depends on other factors such as the degree of ideological polarization between the parties and the disposition of political parties toward cooperation. In fact, in several countries of the region the problem of governing in the context of multi-party systems has been addressed by forming party alliances and coalitions (what might be called "presidentialism through coalitions," as will be examined further in Chapter Eight). Nevertheless, the possibilities for effective government would still seem to be complicated in numerous cases by the high degree of party system fragmentation reinforced by the proportional representation system.

Table 5.13 shows that in four countries (Bolivia, Brazil, Ecuador, and Venezuela) there are more than five parties with significant representation in the legislature. When there are three or more parties with significant representation, it is improbable that the president will be elected with a majority in the congress. Nine of the 18 countries in this study fall within that range. Aside from the ones already mentioned, this group includes Colombia, El Salvador, Guatemala, Panama, Peru and Uruguay.

As in Table 5.12, the figures in bold in Table 5.13 represent the index values for elections immediately following electoral reforms that would have been expected to have had an impact on the function of effectiveness. If the reform would have been expected to favor effectiveness (i.e., reduced party system fragmentation), the number is in parentheses. Theoretical expectations are confirmed if the value is smaller than for previous elections. The cases that match theoretical expectations are italicized, while those that do not are in bold without italics. Of the 14 cases of reform, only in seven does the effective number of parties change in the expected direction. The most profound reform of this type, in Peru, did not have the expected effect, at least in the initial election in which the new system was used.

Table 5.13. Effective Number of Parties according to Legislative Seats in the Lower House

	1978–79	1980–81	1982–83	1984–85	1986–87	1988–89	1990–91	1992–93	1994–95	1996–97	1998–99	2000
Argentina			2.23	2.37	2.58	2.85	3.16	2.87	2.87	2.49	2.56	
Bolivia		4.13		4.31		*(3.92)*		*4.29*		5.36		2.55
Brazil			2.39		2.83		8.68		8.15		7.13	
Chile						2.04		2.00		2.01		
Colombia	2.06		1.98		2.45		2.17/3.00		*(2.72)*		3.17	
Costa Rica	2.38		2.27		2.21		2.21		2.29		2.56	
Dominican Rep.	1.99		2.25		2.53		3.05		2.43		**2.32**	
Ecuador	3.94			6.15	7.56	4.17	6.55	6.61	5.44	5.11	*(5.73)*	
El Salvador				2.56		2.41	*3.01*		3.06	4.13	3.47	
Guatemala				2.98			*4.44*		3.47/(2.73)		**2.35**	
Honduras		2.17		2.12		2.00		2.03		2.18		
Mexico	1.77		1.72	1.85		*3.04*	2.21		2.29	2.86		2.55
Nicaragua							2.05			*2.79*		
Panama						3.72			4.33		3.26	
Paraguay						1.89		*(2.45)*			2.27	
Peru		2.46		2.31			5.83		*2.91*			3.97
Uruguay				2.92		3.33			3.30		3.07	
Venezuela	2.65		2.42			2.83		4.74			6.05	3.44
Four-year average	2.69		2.55	2.62	3.21	3.14	3.49	3.89	3.57	3.49	3.54	3.59

Table 5.14. Upper House Electoral System Changes

Country	Year	Nature of change	Expected effect
Argentina	1994	Change to direct election of senators—previously they were elected by provincial assemblies; term of senators shortened from nine to six years; number of senators elected in each district increased from two to three, with one seat for representation of the first minority.[1]	Participation + Representation +
Bolivia		No changes.	
Brazil		No changes.	
Chile		No changes.	
Colombia	1991	Substitution of regional districts for 100 member national district. Creation of special districts for indigenous peoples.	Representation + Participation – Representation +
Dominican Republic	1985	Restoration of simultaneous vote for president and congressmen.	Representation – Effectiveness + Participation –
	1990	Restoration of two votes, one for president and one for congressmen.	Representation + Effectiveness — Participation +
	1994	Presidential and congressional elections separated into different four-year cycles. Further separation of voting for president and congress.	Representation + Effectiveness — Participation +
	1994	Vote for senate candidates separated from vote for lower house lists.	Representation + Effectiveness —
Mexico	1993	Increased number of each state's senators from two to four, with one seat going to the first minority and three to the plurality party.	Representation + Participation –
	1996	Number of senators in each state reduced from four to three and a 32-member national constituency created. Senate system segmented so that three-quarters elected by plurality with representation of minority and one-quarter by proportional representation list in national constituency.	Representation + Participation — Effectiveness –
Paraguay	1990	Separate ballots put in place for election of senators and deputies.	Participation +
Peru	1993	Change from bicameral to unicameral system; senate previously elected in large (national) district.	Effectiveness +
Uruguay	1996	No change.	

		Table 5.14. *(continued)*	
Country	**Year**	**Nature of change**	**Expected effect**
Venezuela	1990	Vote for deputies separated from vote for senate; change so that electors choose candidate in plurality districts, party lists for chamber deputies, and party list for senate.	Participation + Effectiveness +
	1999	Change to unicameral system.	

¹The senate chamber increased from 46 to 48 due to the addition of Tierra del Fuego as a province in 1990.

Electoral Reforms that Affect the Upper House

Among the 11 countries with bicameral systems at the start of the study period, there have been relatively few changes affecting the representativeness of the electoral system for the upper house (Table 5.14). In Peru and Venezuela, there has been a shift to a unicameral system that in both cases could be seen to favor the function of effectiveness, since an important potential source of opposition to the executive's initiatives was eliminated (the upper house) and the problem of developing legislative compromises was eased.

Adoption of a national district in Colombia, a proportional representation component in Mexico, and a plurality with representation of the minority system in Argentina are all system changes that would be expected to enhance representativeness to some degree. The separation of the vote for senators from that for other offices in the Dominican Republic and Paraguay works in favor of participation, since voters have more freedom to select the particular candidates or parties they prefer. But this change—especially in the Dominican Republic, where not just the ballot structure but the timing relative to the presidential election was changed—could undermine effectiveness, since now there is a greater chance for the senate to be controlled by the political opposition. The move to direct election of senators in Argentina also clearly favors the participation dimension.

Conclusions

The dominant system used for electing representatives to the lower house (or the national assembly in the case of unicameral systems) is proportional representation with closed and blocked party lists. Medium-sized districts, averaging about five to six representatives per constituency, are also the norm. Five of the nine bicameral systems use a system whose effects are majoritarian, while one uses a mixed system (Mexico) and three use a pure proportional system. Thus, with respect to the lower house, the function of representativeness is favored by most Latin American electoral systems, but not to an extreme degree. Small parties have a chance to obtain representation, though usually not in full proportion to their electoral strength.

Given the predominance of proportional electoral systems in lower houses, effectiveness is relatively de-emphasized. In such systems, there is little assurance that presidents will obtain majorities in congress, and a fairly large number of parties can typically obtain significant representation. In the context of presidential systems, where the head of government and legislators have separate bases of legitimacy and their tenure is fixed in time, it could be difficult to establish a consensual basis for governing when political power is so fragmented.

The bicameral nature of nine of the political systems would be expected to further complicate effectiveness, since the executive must try to amass majorities in two chambers simultaneously. This problem may be mitigated to some extent in the case of plurality-type systems or when upper house elections are held simultaneously with those for the president. But effectiveness may be particularly compromised when the upper house is elected through a pure proportional representation system.

The predominance of closed and blocked party lists in both the lower and the upper houses tends to impede the development of close links between constituents and their representatives (participation). In many cases, constituents typically do not know who their representatives are, let alone know about their votes in the congress or their level of competence in performing their jobs. For their part, representatives have little incentive to appeal to their constituents on the basis of policy positions or serving their particular needs. This tendency is also reinforced by the relatively low proportion of legislators who seek or obtain reelection in many of the countries in the region (Cox and Morgenstern, 1998). Thus, incentives generally lead them to focus their attention on pleasing national or regional party leaders in order to obtain privileged positions in the party list for the next election, or to be favored as candidates for other elected or appointed political offices. Partly as a consequence of electoral system-based incentives, the legislature in most countries has failed to develop an assertive and independent role in policy-making or in overseeing the executive branch (as discussed further in Chapter Eight).

Theoretically, closed and blocked list proportional representation systems might be expected to foster the development of "strong" parties in one sense of the word. Legislators in such systems typically tend to follow the orders of their particular leaders, and thus parties can operate with some cohesion. But such systems do not help build parties that earn the loyalty and respect of citizens, and which represent clear sets of principles and programmatic orientations. The lack of accountability of individual legislators has likely contributed to the growing sense of disconnection between citizens and political parties, as well as the eroding legitimacy of politicians in general.

During the period of this study, most countries have implemented some kind of reform to rules governing the election of legislators. Only in five countries, however, did the reforms represent a change in the type of electoral system (as defined in this chapter). In all of these cases except Ecuador, the change was from one type of proportional representation system to another. Though there are few cases of electoral system reform that would be expected to profoundly affect proportionality, the reforms that have taken place have tended to favor the dimension of representativeness at the expense of effectiveness.

Thus, while the region began the study period with fairly fragmented party systems, electoral system reform would be likely to strengthen this tendency. The reforms, therefore, have not followed the conventional wisdom in academic writings that a more concentrated party system is necessary to make presidential democracy work more effectively.

There also have been different types of reforms aimed at enhancing the discretion of voters in choosing their representatives. The most profound reforms were the adoption of personalized proportional representation systems in Bolivia and Venezuela. It is difficult to assess the impact of these changes in terms of democratic governability. In Venezuela, it is clear that the reform neither caused nor prevented the breakdown of the traditional party system or the onset of the broader crisis of legitimacy of the nation's democratic system. This reform was probably implemented at a time when the discrediting of traditional leaders and institutions had already reached a crisis point. Others have criticized the reform as not going far enough in curtailing the power of central party leaders in selecting legislative candidates (Crisp, 1997; Kulisheck, 1997; Shugart, 1999).

Ecuador, Brazil and Peru have incorporated different forms of preference votes into their legislative election systems that might be expected to promote a stronger link between voters and representatives. But given the demands on them in terms of information and time, it is difficult for citizens to make an informed choice between the large number of contending parties and candidates in each district. In addition, the weakness of parties, which is likely to be reinforced under such a system, undermines the ability of electors by their votes to signal preferences to politicians with respect to important policy issues, and to hold legislators accountable on that basis.

Another type of reform adopted in several countries that has enhanced citizen discretion in choosing leaders is the separation of ballots for legislative offices from that for the presidency or other offices. When this has been done without separating the timing of presidential and legislative elections, it has likely enhanced the function of participation without significantly undermining effectiveness.

Clearly determining the appropriate design of an electoral system for a given country is fraught with difficulties. There are significant tradeoffs entailed in adopting reforms aimed at enhancing performance with respect to a given function, be it representativeness, effectiveness or participation. Adopting the combined system is one way to increase ties between citizens and legislators without sacrificing too much in terms of representation or effectiveness. This goal could also be advanced by the adoption of reforms that lie outside the scope of the narrow electoral system traits considered in this chapter. For instance, adopting primaries for selecting candidates and using democratic procedures to choose party leaders could also help to strengthen the credibility of parties and enhance the ties between voters and legislators. This matter is the focus of Chapter Seven.

In sum, while many electoral system reforms have been adopted in Latin America during the period of this study, they have generally been relatively conservative in their design and effects. The electoral reforms do not appear to have significantly alleviated the problems of governability, or to have raised the credibility of representative institutions in the region. Twenty years after the onset of the wave of democratic transitions in the region, the 18 countries in this study have, for the most part, retained their proportional electoral systems. Like that of other parts of the world, the Latin American experience shows the difficulty of changing an electoral system that is already in place.

Bibliography

Abente Brun, Diego. 1996. Paraguay: Transition from Caudillo Rule. In Jorge I. Domínguez and Abraham Lowenthal, *Constructing Democratic Governance: South America in the 1990s*. Baltimore: Johns Hopkins University Press.

Alcántara Sáez, Manuel. 1999. *Sistemas políticos de América Latina*, Vol. 1. Madrid: Tecnos.

Archer, Ronald P. 1995. Party Strength and Weakness in Colombia's Besieged Democracy. In Scott Mainwaring and Timothy R. Scully (eds.), *Building Democratic Institutions: Party Systems in Latin America*. Stanford, CA: Stanford University Press.

Archer, Ronald P., and Matthew Soberg Shugart. 1997. The Unrealized Potential of Presidential Dominance in Colombia. In Scott Mainwaring and Matthew Soberg Shugart (eds.), *Presidentialism and Democracy in Latin America*. New York: Cambridge University Press.

Caballero Carrizosa, Esteban. 1998. Elecciones y democracia en el Paraguay, 1989–1996. In Juan Rial and Daniel Zovatto G. (eds.), *Elecciones y democracia en América Latina 1992–1996: Urnas y desencanto político*. San José, Costa Rica: Instituto Interamericano de Derechos Humanos.

Carey, John M., and Matthew Soberg Shugart. 1995. Incentives to Cultivate a Personal Vote: A Rank Ordering of Electoral Formulas. *Electoral Studies* 14.

Conaghan, Catherine M. 1995. Politicians against Parties: Discord and Disconnection in Ecuador's Party System. In Scott Mainwaring and Timothy R. Scully (eds.), *Building Democratic Institutions: Party Systems in Latin America*. Stanford, CA: Stanford University Press.

Cox, Gary, and Scott Morgenstern. 1998. Reactive Assemblies and Proactive Presidents: A Typology of Latin American Presidents and Legislatures. Paper presented at the 21st International Congress of the Latin American Studies Association. Chicago, September 24–26.

Crisp, Brian F. 1997. Presidential Behavior in a System with Strong Parties: Venezuela, 1958–1995. In Scott Mainwaring and Matthew Soberg Shugart (eds.), *Presidentialism and Democracy in Latin America*. New York: Cambridge University Press.

De Riz, Liliana, and Eduardo Feldman. 1992. *Guía del parlamento argentino*. Buenos Aires: Fundación Friedrich Ebert.

Fleischer, David. 1998. Elecciones y sistema electoral en Brasil 1990–1997. In Juan Rial and Daniel Zovatto G. (eds.), *Elecciones y democracia en América Latina 1992–1996*. San José, Costa Rica: Instituto Interamericano de Derechos Humanos.

Grullón, Sandino. 1999. *Historia de las elecciones en la República Dominicana desde 1913 a 1998*. Santo Domingo, Dominican Republic: Oficina Nacional de Derecho de Autor.

Instituto Interamericano de Derechos Humanos. 2000. *Sistemas de elecciones parlamentarias y su relación con la gobernabilidad democrática en América Central y República Dominicana*. San José, Costa Rica: Instituto Interamericano de Derechos Humanos.

International IDEA. 1997. *The International IDEA Handbook of Electoral System Design*. Stockholm: International IDEA.

Izaguirre, Ramón. 2000. Análisis del caso de Honduras. In Instituto Interamericano de Derechos Humanos, *Sistema de elecciones parlamentarias y su relación con la gobernabilidad democrática en América Central y República Dominicana*. San José, Costa Rica: Instituto Interamericano de Derechos Humanos.

Kulisheck, Michael R. 1997. Electoral Laws and Politicians: The Behavioral Effects of Electoral Reform in Venezuela. Paper prepared for the annual meeting of the American Political Science Association, Washington, DC, 28–31 August.

Laakso, Markku, and Rein Taagepera. 1979. The Effective Number of Parties: A Measure with Application to Western Europe. *Comparative Political Studies* 12(1). April.

Lijphart, Arend. 1994. Presidential and Majoritarian Democracy: Theoretical Observations. In Juan J. Linz and Arturo Valenzuela (eds.), *The Failure of Presidential Democracy*. Baltimore: The Johns Hopkins University Press.

Marconi Nicolau, Jairo (ed.). 1998. *Dados eleitorais do Brasil (1982–1996)*. Rio de Janeiro: Revan.

Nohlen, Dieter. 1998a. *Sistemas electorales y partidos políticos*. Mexico City: Fondo de Cultura Económica.

———. 1998b. Sistemas electorales parlamentarios y presidenciales. In Dieter Nohlen, Sonia Picado, and Daniel Zovatto (eds.), *Tratado de derecho electoral de América Latina*. Mexico City: Fondo de Cultura Económica.

———. 1999. El distrito electoral. Paper presented at the International Seminar on Electoral Legislation and Organization, Lima, Peru, 9–11 February.

Nohlen, Dieter (ed.). 1993. *Enciclopedia Electoral Latinoamericana y del Caribe*. San José, Costa Rica: Instituto Interamericano de Derechos Humanos.

Shugart, Matthew Soberg. 1999. Efficiency and Reform: A New Index of Government Responsiveness and the Conjunction of Electoral and Economic Reforms. Mimeo.

Shugart, Matthew Soberg, and Martin P. Wattenberg (eds.). 2001. *Mixed-Member Electoral Systems: The Best of Both Worlds?* New York: Oxford University Press.

Urbina Mohs, Sandra. 2000. El sistema de elección de diputados en Costa Rica. In Instituto Interamericano de Derechos Humanos, *Sistema de elecciones parlamentarias y su relación con la gobernabilidad democrática en América Central y República Dominicana*. San José, Costa Rica: Instituto Interamericano de Derechos Humanos.

CHAPTER SIX

Party Systems and Democratic Governability

Political parties are indispensable to the working of democracy. Every democracy in the modern era has revolved around a party system in which at least two viable political parties compete freely for shares of political power. Parties are essential for recruiting and selecting candidates for political office, organizing the electoral process, structuring public political support around identifiable sets of policy programs, socioeconomic interests and values, aggregating citizen interests and preferences in the policymaking process, and forming governments and legislative policy agreements (Sartori, 1976; Lipset and Rokkan, 1967; La Palombara and Weiner, 1966).

At least three different characteristics of political party systems shape their impact on the governability of democracy: 1) their *level of institutionalization*; 2) their *degree of fragmentation*; and 3) their *degree of polarization*. Following Mainwaring and Scully (1995), party systems can be considered to be *institutionalized* when patterns of inter-party competition are relatively stable; parties have fairly stable and deep bases of societal support; parties and elections are viewed as legitimate and as the sole instruments for determining who governs; and party organizations are characterized by reasonably stable rules and structures.

The *degree of fragmentation* of party systems relates to the number of parties that regularly obtain a significant share of the votes and seats in the legislature. The *degree of polarization* relates to the extent of the differences between parties with respect to political ideology and their social bases of political support.

When party systems are institutionalized, parties are important actors in channeling and aggregating political demands.[1] Reasonably cohesive parties with steady bases of so-

---

[1] See Mainwaring and Scully (1995) for a more extensive analysis of the importance of party system institutionalization for the governability of democratic systems. The discussion of the link between party systems and democratic governability draws significantly on their framework of analysis.

cietal support and identifiable political programs facilitate the representation of citizen preferences and interests, and also enhance the possibility that citizens can hold elected officials accountable. Given the great costs entailed in ascertaining the policy positions and conduct of individual candidates and incumbents, the existence of such parties enables citizens through their vote to express preferences with respect to the broad political philosophy, set of values, and policy direction that they favor. Citizens' judgments of candidates will be based at least to some degree on the programs and performance of the party to which they are affiliated, rather than merely on the candidates' individual personalities and patrimonial links with voters. Likewise, in the context of more institutionalized party systems, politicians are at least somewhat dependent on parties for their positions and career advancement. Thus, not only are citizens better able to signal their preferences, but politicians are more constrained to adhere to the rules of the democratic game, adopt decisions that conform with the broad programmatic objectives of the party, and refrain from making populist and demagogic appeals to the masses.

Institutionalized party systems also tend to promote greater political stability and governmental effectiveness. When parties are institutionalized, societal actors come to accept that the most propitious way to influence policymaking is through electoral and legislative channels (Mainwaring and Scully, 1995). The articulation of the demands of citizens and civil society organizations through legitimate and established institutions lowers the risk that conflicts will intensify and overwhelm the political system.[2] Citizens and social groups trust that political parties and political leaders will act in their interests, and thus are more prepared to grant some degree of decision-making authority in times of crisis when difficult and controversial decisions must be made. There is an acceptance of the inevitability of compromise. Working through political parties and the legislature, no societal group or interest can obtain all of its demands, but few will be totally ignored either.

Similarly, in the context of an institutionalized party system, politics is more predictable. Election results do not dramatically change from one election to the next, with some parties vanishing and many others being born (Mainwaring and Scully, 1995). The rules of conduct and interaction are better known and accepted, and political actors know reasonably well how best to pursue their interests. By contrast, in less institutionalized settings, political actors are more worried about the future and more prone to follow narrow short-term interests, even when this entails potential long-term costs for themselves or for the polity as a whole. Such uncertainties about the future can also lead some political actors to work to undermine or dissolve the democratic system.

Finally, institutionalized party systems favor governability because they enhance the likelihood that the executive will obtain support in the legislature (Mainwaring and Shugart, 1997). When parties are weak and undisciplined, it is less likely that the president will be able to count on stable partisan support in the legislature. This is because in such systems presidents are more likely to be elected without relying on the backing of an established party, and so their victories will not necessarily translate into numerical

---

[2] As Arriagada (2001) points out, a strengthened civil society in the context of a weakening political party system can be a source of political instability. Thus the strengthening of civil society is valuable for improving democratic performance, but only if intermediary representative institutions, such as political parties, can adequately perform their roles.

strength for their party in the congress. In addition, even when the governing party does obtain a significant share of the seats, given the lack of party discipline, the support of co-partisans in the legislature is likely to be fragile. When the president is popular, legislators may find it in their interest to join the bandwagon and lend their support. But given the lack of importance of party affiliation, when the president's popularity fades there is little incentive for legislators to remain loyal to the president.

In a presidential system, there are inherent difficulties in sustaining governments supported by a coalition of diverse parties (see Chapter Eight). Given the independent bases of legitimacy and tenure of the executive and legislative branches, the government's coalition partners have less incentive than in parliamentary systems to adhere to the coalition. These impediments to coalition building in presidential systems are likely to be magnified further when parties are weakly institutionalized. In such contexts, parties are generally unable to act as a unit behind a defined leadership, and with their members bound to a given course of action. Often the support of individual legislators must be purchased through the promise of budgetary resources, legislative concessions or, sometimes, corruption. Given the limited degree of cohesion within parties, when coalitions do form they are likely to be more transitory.

The more traditional factors used to distinguish party systems—the *number of relevant parties* and the *degree of ideological polarization*—can also be expected to affect the governability of democratic systems.[3] The number of parties affects the likelihood that the president's party will control a majority of the seats in the legislature and the possibilities for building majority legislative support behind the executive's legislative program. The more fragmented the party system, the more likely it is that coalitions will be required, and the more difficult it will be to sustain them. Thus, while executive-legislative gridlock may be avoidable in the context of a fragmented party system, it is more likely in such a situation than when there are few parties. Governmental paralysis is a negative outcome by itself, but it also provides a justification for actions aimed at subverting or circumventing democratic institutions, and thus may contribute to the destabilization of the democratic system.

Polarized party systems, which tend to be more likely in multi-party contexts, also tend to generate greater difficulties for democratic governance than those characterized by low or moderate polarization. The formation of inter-party coalitions and the making of piecemeal agreements that smooth the working of the legislature are more difficult in polarized party systems. The likely dynamic of such systems is one in which polarization impairs the stability and performance of governments led by parties near the center of the political spectrum, which exacerbates the polarization of the system and endangers the stability of the regime (Sartori, 1976; Sani and Sartori, 1983).

The above reasoning implies that systems with relatively few significant parties and low or moderate levels of polarization are more conducive to stable and effective governance in democratic systems. This does not mean that the opposite conditions—such as where electoral laws aim to artificially concentrate the party system or discourage mobilization along ideological lines—are necessarily advantageous for democracy. Aside from effectiveness,

---

[3] Sartori (1976) developed the conventional classification of party systems centered on the number of parties and their degree of ideological polarization.

the health of democracy in the long run depends on the representativeness and legitimacy of democratic institutions.

It is also important to note that a given type of party system does not determine success or failure in democratic governance. Certainly the emerging democracies, with their (almost by definition) weakly institutionalized party systems, are not all doomed to failure. Party systems can evolve based on the conscious and unconscious behavior of the political elite and the influence of the broader social and economic context. Recent decades in Latin America have witnessed the unraveling of what had been fairly well institutionalized party systems, and the steady development of a few once weakly institutionalized systems. In some countries, the same structural features that appeared to contribute to democratic breakdown in the 1960s or 1970s now appear compatible with reasonably effective and stable democratic governance. Thus, institutionalized party systems, with moderate degrees of ideological polarization and a limited number of relevant parties, facilitate democratic governability. But these characteristics do not guarantee success, nor are they necessarily required for it.

Given the advent of television and other forms of mass communication, the weakening of traditional ideological cleavages, and the larger power of the state, the context for party system development is very different today than that which existed in Western Europe and North America when their current party systems emerged. As is apparent from the loosening of citizen attachments to parties across the globe, the party systems that develop in the new or reborn democracies will likely not have the same stability and depth of connection to society that they reached at one time in the more established democracies. Nevertheless, parties remain essential to the electoral process and the representation of interests and preferences in the legislature.

Assessing the Institutionalization of Party Systems in Latin America

The party systems that countries carried over into the past two decades were formed at different points in their respective histories. In some cases, the major parties entering the period were formed as far back as the 19th century on the classical liberal/conservative cleavage line that influenced party evolution in Western Europe. In other cases, the major parties entering the 1980s arose as recently as the latter half of the 20th century. In addition to the differences in the age of party systems, there are also considerable differences in terms of the extent of national experiences with democracy. In countries such as Colombia, Costa Rica and Venezuela, there had been decades of uninterrupted political competition prior to the 1980s. Among the "third wave" democracies in the region, there were some countries, such as Argentina, Chile and Uruguay, where the party system that took shape in the transition from authoritarianism was largely a continuation of that which had existed in prior periods of electoral competition. In others, such as Brazil, Mexico, Paraguay and most of the Central American countries, the transition entailed construction of new parties to compete against the party (or military faction) that headed the previously more restrictive regime.

The level of institutionalization of party systems is in great part a product of the countries' political histories. Party system institutionalization facilitates the governability of democratic systems, but in countries where democratization entails the construction of inter-party competition where this had scarcely existed before, a certain degree of de-institutionalization must occur before a democratic party system can be institutionalized. While such systems may be handicapped relative to those that can simply resurrect dormant party systems, the structuring of party politics is a necessary and sometimes lengthy process on the way toward the consolidation of democratic systems.

This section compares Latin American countries in terms of the different dimensions of the institutionalization of party systems, as well as through the use of an overall index of party system institutionalization that is an aggregation of these individual dimensions.[4] The dimensions to be examined are those that characterize an institutionalized party system, as defined earlier: 1) patterns of inter-party competition are relatively stable; 2) parties have fairly stable and deep roots in society; 3) parties and elections are viewed as legitimate and as the sole instruments for determining who governs; and 4) party organizations have reasonably stable rules and structures.

Stability of Patterns of Inter-Party Competition

The stability or regularity of patterns of inter-party competition can be measured through an index of electoral volatility.[5] The index measures the net change in the seat (and vote) shares of all parties from one election to the next. For example, assume that in a prior election Party A receives 60 percent of the seats and Party B receives 40 percent, while in the current election Party A receives 40 percent and Party B receives 60 percent. In this case, the volatility between these two elections is 20 percent. Party A loses 20 percent of the seats and Party B gains 20 percent for a net change of 20 percent. Volatility can result either from shifts in the vote (and seats) from a given group of parties to another, or from the appearance or disappearance of parties.

Table 6.1 shows the mean volatility measured in terms of lower chamber seats and vote percentages in presidential elections for the 18 countries covered in this study. The countries are listed in order of lowest to highest volatility based on average volatility according to both types of measures. The table shows that there is a huge range in the mean volatility among the countries of the region. Volatility has been minimal in Honduras, Costa Rica, Chile and Uruguay, but extremely large among the countries in the lower third of the table. With respect to lower chamber seats, there has been practically no change in the partisan breakdown from one election to the next in Chile and little change in Honduras. But in Peru and Guatemala, more than 40 percent of the seats have shifted on average between parties. Volatility percentages of close to 30 percent on average were registered in Ecuador, Brazil, Venezuela and Bolivia.

---

[4] This analysis follows the structure laid out by Mainwaring and Scully (1995) but updates their measures and adds others. The additional measures are derived from data from the Latinobarómetro survey, which were not available to these authors.

[5] Pedersen's index of electoral volatility is used here. This index is derived by adding the net change in the percentage of the seats (or votes) gained or lost by each party from one election to the next, then dividing by two.

Table 6.1. Electoral Volatility in Latin America

	Lower chamber seats			Presidential vote			Mean volatility (A) + (B) / 2
	Time span	No. of electoral periods	Mean volatility (A)	Time span	No. of electoral periods	Mean volatility (B)	
Honduras	1981–97	4	7.67	1981–97	4	6.23	6.95
Costa Rica	1978–98	5	13.68	1978–98	5	9.93	11.81
Chile	1989–97	2	1.67	1989–99	2	22.17	11.92
Uruguay	1984–99	3	11.78	1984–99	3	12.08	11.93
Nicaragua[1]	1990–96	1	15.59	1990–96	1	11.19	13.39
Argentina	1983–99	8	13.71	1983–99	3	22.37	18.04
Mexico	1979–00	7	14.93	1979–00	3	21.44	18.18
Paraguay	1989–98	2	16.04	1989–98	2	24.74	20.39
Dominican Rep.	1978–98	5	20.38	1978–00	6	21.21	20.80
Colombia	1978–98	6	14.56	1978–98	5	28.32	21.44
El Salvador	1985–00	5	20.76	1984–99	3	24.05	22.40
Panama[2]	1994–99	1	24.92	1994–99	1	22.99	23.96
Bolivia	1980–97	4	28.65	1980–97	4	34.29	31.47
Venezuela	1978–00	5	28.98	1978–00	5	37.04	33.01
Brazil	1982–98	4	31.94	1989–98	2	37.60	34.77
Ecuador	1979–98	8	29.55	1979–98	5	43.64	36.60
Guatemala	1985–99	4	43.56	1985–99	3	53.75	48.66
Peru	1980–00	4	49.58	1980–00	4	49.74	49.66
Total		79	22.06		61	27.66	24.86

Note: This table is a modification of Table 1.1 in Mainwaring and Scully (1995), focusing on the period of this study and updated through the year 2000.
[1] The figures for Nicaragua are debatable. The difficulty is in how to compare the share of the seats held by legislators elected under the Unión Nacional Opositora (UNO) coalition in 1990 with those elected in the Alianza Liberal coalition in 1996. The UNO coalition did not hold the allegiance of elected legislators for very long, but information was not available for the authors on the identity of the party to which individual legislators migrated. In the calculation of the volatility index, the number of seats won by UNO in 1990 is compared with the seats won in 1996 by all of the parties that formed part of this coalition.
[2] The 1989 election in Panama is excluded from the calculation given the questioned nature of the official initial results and the reversal of the electoral outcome.

The volatility of the vote in presidential elections yields roughly the same ordering of countries as that for legislative seats. With the recent surge in voting for the center-right candidate in Chile, a significantly greater figure was registered for volatility in presidential elections than for lower chamber seats. Ecuador and Colombia also have greater volatility when one considers voting in presidential elections.

In comparison with Western European democracies, at least half of the Latin American countries experienced very high electoral volatility. A study of all of the elections in 13 western European countries from 1885 to 1985 revealed that the highest single instance of volatility—that of Germany from 1919 to 1920—was 32.1 percent.[6] The highest mean volatility over the whole period—registered in France—was 15.2 percent. The average volatility over the period in several Latin American countries has exceeded the largest recorded value in this long period of European democratic history. And in terms of the period averages, more than two-thirds of the Latin American countries experienced more electoral volatility than the most volatile European democracy.

Measuring average electoral volatility over the period conceals considerable change in the party systems of a few countries. Prior to the 1990s, patterns of electoral competition in Venezuela were among the most stable in the region. But the collapse in the legitimacy of the major political parties and changes in the electoral system resulted in a surge in electoral volatility and the emergence of an extraordinarily large number of new parties and movements. Changes in the electoral system and growing fragmentation in the two main parties in Colombia have also resulted in a significant, albeit less dramatic, increase in volatility. By contrast, Brazil's party system evolved during the period from being extremely volatile to more moderate levels. This pattern of development reflects in part the fact that the democratic transition was marked by the emergence of new political forces to fill the many gaps left by the two-party system that had been imposed for much of the period of military rule. With little inheritance from the previous democratic period, the transition in Brazil entailed the creation of a new party system. The consecutive electoral victories of President Fernando Henrique Cardoso and his coalition of party-backers increased the stability of political competition in the second half of the 1990s.

Thus, patterns of inter-party competition over the period have been fairly stable in Honduras, Costa Rica, Chile, Uruguay and Nicaragua (at least in terms of broad party coalitions); moderately stable in Argentina, Mexico, Paraguay, the Dominican Republic, Colombia and El Salvador; and unstable in Peru, Guatemala, Ecuador, Brazil, Bolivia, Venezuela and Panama.

Stability and Depth of Party Roots in Society

The second dimension of party system institutionalization is the depth of the links between parties and citizens and organized groups. It would be expected that stronger ties between parties and society would contribute to more stable patterns of voting. That is, when a large share of voters feel close to a political party, it is less likely that there will be

---

[6] Bartolini and Mair (1990), as cited in Mainwaring and Scully (1995).

dramatic shifts in the partisan distribution of the vote from one election to the next. Nevertheless, the two dimensions do not necessarily go hand in hand, and they measure different aspects of the concept of party system institutionalization (Mainwaring and Scully, 1995).

The most direct way to measure how deeply parties penetrate society would be through cross-nationally comparable election surveys, which would make it possible to examine the stability of voters' party preferences, the depth of their attachment to parties, and the consistency of voting among given socioeconomic groups. But such comprehensive and comparable election surveys do not exist for the range of countries considered here. In lieu of such information, two alternative measures are developed based on citizen responses to the Latinobarómetro survey and long-term shifts in electoral outcomes.

One indication of the stability of their links to voters is the ability of parties to endure over long periods of electoral competition. If parties keep fading out of existence and new parties keep emerging, then it is doubtful that they have obtained the strong allegiance of citizens or have sunk roots in society. Table 6.2 compares the share of legislative seats controlled by the significant parties at the beginning of the study period to the share these same parties controlled following the most recent election. Parties are judged as "significant" if they gained 10 percent or more of the seats in the lower house in the first election of the study period. The last column shows the percentage decline over the period in the share of the seats controlled by these parties.

The table shows a tremendous variation across the region in the fate of the parties that were politically dominant at the beginning of the period. In Guatemala, Peru and Ecuador, the major parties experienced significant losses or practically disappeared. By the 2000 election, the stature of the two previously well-established parties in Venezuela had been severely eroded. By contrast, the level of electoral support for the major parties in Chile, Honduras, Uruguay and Costa Rica remained quite stable. The major parties also held onto their status reasonably well in Paraguay, Panama and Mexico, with a somewhat greater loss of support in Bolivia and Argentina.

To some extent, the varying lengths of the countries' recent democratic period may distort the comparison. But only Chile, Nicaragua, Panama and Paraguay have a significantly shorter period than the rest of the countries. Given the fact that in Chile the major parties actually gained seats, the passage of more time would probably not make a big difference in the measure of party system stability. But the interpretation of the cases of Nicaragua, Panama and Paraguay might be expected to change once they experience a comparable number of elections.

A second way to gauge the depth of public allegiance to parties is through public opinion surveys. The 1996 and 1997 rounds of the Latinobarómetro survey asked respondents whether they consider themselves to be close to any particular political party, and if so, how close. Table 6.3 shows the percentage of respondents who said that they feel "very close," "somewhat close," "merely a sympathizer," or "not close" to a political party. The countries are arranged in descending order according to a party identification score that is a weighted average of the percentages of respondents making the four possible responses ("very close" is weighted 1.0; "somewhat close," .67; "only sympathetic,".33; and "not close," 0.00).

Table 6.2. Share of Legislative Seats Controlled by Significant Parties at the Start and End of Study Period

Country	Significant parties at moment of transition (10% or more of seats)	Percent of seats at start of study period	First election year	Percent of seats after most recent election	Most recent election year	Percent decline
Chile	PDC, PPD, RN, UDI	78.34	1989	82.51	1997	-4.17
Honduras	PLH, PNH	95.50	1981	95.50	1997	0.00
Uruguay	PC, PN, FA/EP	97.97	1984	95.95	1999	2.06
Costa Rica[1]	PLN, Coalición Unidad/PUSC	91.23	1978	87.72	1998	3.85
Paraguay	ANR, PLRA	95.84	1989	90.00	1998	6.09
Panama	PRD, MOLIRENA, PDC, PPA	91.00	1989	84.50	1999	7.14
Mexico	PRI, PAN	100.00	1979	86.40	2000	13.60
Bolivia	AND, MIR, MNR, MNRI	80.76	1982	64.61	1997	20.00
Argentina[2]	UCR, PJ	94.49	1983	73.20	1997	22.53
Colombia	PCC, PLC	97.49	1978	69.56	1998	28.65
Dominican Rep.	PRD, PR/PRSC	100.00	1978	67.11	1998	32.89
El Salvador	ARENA, PDC, PCN	96.70	1985	57.20	2000	40.85
Brazil	PMDB, PFL	77.62	1986	36.64	1998	52.80
Venezuela	AD, COPEI	86.43	1978	22.42	2000	74.06
Ecuador	CFP, ID, PCE	78.26	1979	14.89	1998	80.97
Peru	AP, APRA	86.66	1980	7.50	2000	91.35
Guatemala	DCG, UCN, MLN, PDCN, PR	92.00	1985	1.80	1999	98.04

[1] The Partido Unidad Social Cristiana (PUSC) was formed in 1983 and was a regrouping of the United Coalition, the conservative alliance that presented candidates in 1978 and 1982. The Partido Republicano Calderonista (PRC), Partido Renovación Democrática (PRD), Partido Demócrata Cristiano (PDC) and Partido Unión Popular (PUP) were the parties that merged to form the PUSC. Given the continuity in bases of support and elites, the PUSC is considered as a successor to the United Coalition and not as a new party.
[2] The 1997 election in Argentina is the last one considered because information was not available on the breakdown of seats of the Alianza for 1999. To measure the decline, it is necessary to know the share of seats of the Unión Cívica Radical (UCR) in 1999.

Table 6.3. Extent that Citizens Feel "Close" to a Political Party
(Percent average for 1996 and 1997)

Country	Very close	Somewhat	Sympathizer	Not close	Party identification score
Uruguay	12.45	20.42	36.09	31.05	38.09
Paraguay	7.12	22.08	43.90	26.89	36.48
Nicaragua	14.66	9.44	46.34	29.57	36.39
Honduras	13.58	8.23	46.00	32.20	34.40
El Salvador	8.64	9.28	38.47	43.62	27.65
Costa Rica	7.32	6.29	36.80	49.60	23.77
Mexico	2.76	6.49	48.39	42.38	23.21
Ecuador	4.34	7.29	41.31	47.07	22.97
Panama	6.88	10.90	23.28	58.96	21.90
Guatemala	8.31	4.87	29.96	56.87	21.54
Bolivia	2.86	4.94	42.61	49.59	20.35
Colombia	3.68	7.54	29.63	59.16	18.58
Chile	2.50	9.04	28.10	60.38	17.89
Venezuela	4.85	5.73	27.49	61.94	17.83
Argentina	3.63	9.23	21.54	65.62	16.96
Peru	2.18	2.77	31.64	63.42	14.57
Brazil	2.75	4.88	24.40	67.98	14.13
Average	6.38	8.79	35.05	49.78	23.92

Note: The years 1996 and 1997 are used because this question was not asked in the subsequent three editions of the Latinobarómetro survey.

The strongest degree of identification with political parties is seen in Uruguay, Paraguay, Nicaragua and Honduras. While the relative closeness of citizens to parties in Paraguay likely reflects the historically intense rivalry between the Asociación Nacional Republicana (Partido Colorado) (ANR) and the Partido Liberal Radical Auténtico (PLRA), it also was likely reinforced by the patron-client ties developed by the Colorado party during the authoritarian period. In Nicaragua, the relatively high degree of polarization stemming from the experience of the leftist Sandinista regime and the civil war likely contributes to the substantial percentage of party identifiers in that country.

By contrast, a far smaller percentage of citizens identify with political parties in Brazil, Peru, Argentina, Venezuela, Chile and Colombia. The low level of party identification is surprising in Chile, since voting patterns are very stable and parties have been known historically to have a strong presence in society. But it is possible that, apart from the general trend of political detachment that appears to be affecting the region as a whole, the electoral system-imposed competition between two encompassing coalitions of the center-left and the center-right has weakened citizen attachment to individual parties.

Democracies in Development

Relative to Western European countries, a considerably smaller share of citizens feel close to parties in Latin America. While the average party identification score is about 23.9 percent in Latin America, the average for 12 Western European countries was 31.5 percent in 1989 (Eurobarometer, 1991). The levels for the first four countries (Uruguay, Paraguay, Nicaragua, Honduras) in Table 6.3 are quite close to that of the Western European countries with the highest degree of party identification. But only one of the 12 Western European countries had a score below 20 percent, while six Latin American countries did.

Thus, in terms of both measures, party roots in society appear to be reasonably deep in Uruguay, Honduras, Paraguay and Costa Rica. Support for parties has been very stable in Chile, but citizens do not appear to be strongly attached to individual parties. By contrast, parties do not seem to enjoy stable bases of societal support in Brazil, Peru or Venezuela. Ecuador's parties have not endured during the current democratic period, but some citizens feel at least a modest attachment to a particular political party. In Argentina, the Partido Justicialista (PJ) and to a somewhat lesser extent the Unión Cívica Radical (UCR) have sustained much of their support over the period, but very few citizens appear to feel a strong attachment to either of them.

Parties and Elections Accorded Legitimacy and Parties Perceived as Central to Determining Who Governs

The third dimension of party system institutionalization refers to the extent to which citizens and organized interests accord the electoral process and parties legitimacy and perceive parties and elections as the main route to government. Three measures based on questions in the Latinobarómetro surveys are used to compare countries: 1) respondents' degree of confidence in political parties; 2) respondents' perceptions of the integrity of electoral processes; and 3) respondents' perceptions of the importance of political parties to the progress of the country.

Table 6.4 shows the percentage of respondents in each year of the survey that expressed that they had "a lot" or "some" confidence in political parties. The countries are arranged in descending order of the average value of this percentage across the five years of the survey.

Based on this measure, parties appear to be accorded some legitimacy in Uruguay. But beyond this case, about 70 percent or more of respondents have little or no confidence in political parties. Parties are viewed somewhat more favorably in El Salvador, Mexico, Chile and Honduras, but confidence in parties is particularly low in Ecuador, Bolivia, Brazil and Colombia. In 2001, confidence in parties fell significantly in Guatemala, but also reached new lows in several other countries. However, there are no clear lines of demarcation separating one group of countries from another.

In addition to public confidence in political parties, this dimension also refers to the legitimacy of electoral processes. Table 6.5 shows the percentage of respondents who perceive that elections are conducted fairly. Again, the countries are arranged in descending order of the average of the 1996 through 2000 surveys in terms of the percentage of respondents perceiving that elections are clean. The table shows there is a very wide variation in the legitimacy accorded electoral processes. While 70 percent of respondents in

Table 6.4. Confidence in Political Parties
(In percent)

Country	1996	1997	1998	1999/2000	2001	1996–2001
Uruguay	31.66	44.83	34.58	35.67	38.10	36.97
El Salvador	24.63	45.35		23.98	17.00	27.74
Mexico	17.82	31.04	33.42	34.02	20.50	27.36
Chile	27.25	34.08	24.34	23.67	23.80	26.63
Paraguay	36.96	27.13	25.00	15.12	14.60	23.76
Honduras	22.65	39.56		17.95	14.20	23.59
Nicaragua	33.66	30.54		9.79	18.80	23.20
Panama	16.12	28.11	18.30	27.40	25.90	23.17
Costa Rica	15.29	25.72	28.90	23.68	19.70	22.66
Venezuela	11.33	20.83	15.41	23.25	29.60	20.08
Peru	18.50	20.59	16.65	18.83	23.40	19.59
Guatemala	21.78	23.80	19.40	17.40	9.20	18.32
Argentina	16.93	28.35	16.56	15.33	12.30	17.89
Brazil	16.94	17.98	19.70	13.40	20.00	17.60
Colombia	11.23	29.08	16.94	16.50	11.10	16.97
Bolivia	16.32	20.48	19.90	11.85	10.90	15.89
Ecuador	18.25	15.50	14.41	7.59	8.30	12.81
Average	21.02	28.41	21.68	19.73	18.67	21.90

Uruguay, Chile and Costa Rica perceive elections to be fair, only around 25 percent of respondents feel this way in Colombia, Ecuador, Mexico and Paraguay. Regardless of whether such perceptions reflect real deficiencies, they certainly impair the ability of representative institutions to assume their full roles in the democratic process, and may deprive governments and political parties of the legitimacy necessary to govern effectively.

The third measure related to this dimension assesses the extent to which political parties are viewed as central to the democratic political process. A question asked only in the 1997 Latinobarómetro survey asked respondents to pick from a list of governmental and nongovernmental institutions the ones that they thought were "indispensable to the progress of the country" (Table 6.6).

Again there is an extremely wide range across the region. More than half of respondents in Mexico, Uruguay, Honduras and Costa Rica believed political parties to be indispensable, while relatively few shared that view in Paraguay, Brazil, Ecuador and Peru. The high percentage of respondents mentioning political parties in Mexico likely owes in large part to the historically close relationship between the Partido Revolucionario Institucional (PRI) and the state, and its deep penetration into the organizational life of the country. With the defeat of the PRI in the most recent presidential election, public perceptions of political parties and their role in the polity might be expected to change in the future.

Table 6.5. Percentage of the Public that Perceives Elections as Clean

Country	1996	1997	1998	1999/2000	1996–00
Uruguay	83.39	80.77	77.71	78.63	80.13
Chile	74.22	73.41	71.04	80.47	74.78
Costa Rica	79.41	62.27	74.87	73.83	72.60
Panama	62.99	49.34	50.22	76.68	59.81
Nicaragua	74.32	52.11		43.89	56.77
Argentina	52.53	56.48	52.59	63.94	56.38
Honduras	42.80	56.54		51.91	50.42
Guatemala	38.42	38.51	48.09	70.34	48.84
El Salvador	42.50	40.54		39.91	40.99
Peru	53.76	28.56	23.92	41.23	36.87
Brazil	29.25	16.49	32.45	44.84	30.76
Venezuela	8.22	11.88	27.84	67.01	28.74
Bolivia	28.57	28.89	28.67	25.90	28.01
Paraguay	34.57	14.15	36.30	26.61	27.91
Mexico	14.32	41.35	29.30	23.81	27.20
Ecuador	37.59	18.86	23.70	19.80	24.99
Colombia	15.32	13.10	22.60	28.41	19.85
Average	45.42	40.19	42.81	50.42	44.80

Note: This question was not asked in the 2001 edition of the Latinobarómetro survey.

Strength of Party Organizations

The fourth dimension of party system institutionalization refers to the strength of party organizations. To what extent are political elites and legislators loyal to their parties? To what extent is the party label associated with a set of ideals and programmatic objectives and a diverse portfolio of leaders rather than a single personality? To what extent do party organizations have a presence at the local and national levels both during and between elections? How much money is available for parties to spend on their activities apart from what is exclusively devoted to particular electoral campaigns?

While this dimension may be the most critical to the concept of party system institutionalization, there is not sufficiently standardized information available to develop a reliable comparative measure. Thus, the qualitative evaluations in case studies in Mainwaring and Scully (1995) are used. Given the subjective nature of these assessments and the absence of most of Central America and the Dominican Republic from that study, this dimension will not be included in the summary index of party system institutionalization presented below.

Based on the case studies, which were completed around 1993, Mainwaring and Scully concluded that party organizations were reasonably strong in Uruguay, Costa Rica, Chile,

Table 6.6. Percentage of the Public that Considers Political Parties Indispensable to the Progress of the Country, 1997

Mexico	77.38
Uruguay	64.51
Honduras	61.23
Costa Rica	53.13
El Salvador	42.48
Venezuela	42.17
Nicaragua	41.12
Chile	40.17
Colombia	39.08
Panama	37.22
Argentina	34.78
Guatemala	30.50
Bolivia	30.40
Peru	29.98
Ecuador	27.33
Brazil	27.17
Paraguay	19.83
Average	41.09

Mexico, Paraguay and Venezuela. They contend that in these countries "political elites are loyal to their parties, and party discipline in the legislature is reasonably solid. Parties are well organized, and although they are centralized, they have a presence at the local and national levels." Since the leading parties in Mexico and Paraguay acquired their scope and cohesion in a non-democratic setting, the authors assert that party organizations may weaken as competition intensifies. In the period since the completion of this study, however, the position of the founding parties of Venezuelan democracy has eroded dramatically. Given that the parties taking their place are considerably less well institutionalized, the rating for Venezuela on this dimension now needs to be revised downwards.

Colombia and Argentina were categorized as intermediate cases. In Argentina, parties are fairly highly disciplined and legislators are generally loyal to their parties, but individual leaders have often dominated them to the detriment of their organizational development (McGuire, 1995). In Colombia, the electoral system weakened party control over candidate selection and has encouraged the proliferation of factions as well as numerous small unaffiliated electoral movements. Thus, while to some extent the major parties commanded the loyalties of political elites in the past, they are considerably less disciplined today and party organizations are more fragmented (Archer, 1995).

Democracies in Development

Table 6.7. Strength of Party Organizations	
Country	Rating for party organization strength
Chile	3.00
Costa Rica	3.00
Mexico	3.00
Paraguay	3.00
Uruguay	2.50
Argentina	2.00
Colombia	2.00
Venezuela	2.00
Peru	1.50
Bolivia	1.00
Brazil	1.00
Ecuador	1.00

Note: 3.0 = high; 2.5 = medium high; 2.0 = medium; 1.5 = medium low; 1.0 = low.

The Mainwaring and Scully study finds party organizations to be weakest in Bolivia, Brazil, Ecuador and Peru. In Brazil and Ecuador, in particular, it is common for politicians to change parties and for parties to exert little constraint on individual legislators in the congress (Conaghan 1995; Mainwaring, 1995). In Ecuador, 54 percent of the deputies elected in 1979 had abandoned their parties by the end of the congressional term (Arriagada, 2001). In each of these cases, personal appeals to voters are more important than politicians' partisan attachments. Though Peru might have been placed near the intermediate group at the beginning of the period, with the eclipse of the parties that led the democratic transition and the *autogolpe* of former President Alberto Fujimori, party organizations weakened considerably.

Table 6.7 presents the ratings of Mainwaring and Scully in terms of the dimension of party organization strength, with a modification in the case of Venezuela.

Index of Party System Institutionalization

The measures developed for the first three dimensions of party system institutionalization are aggregated into a single index in Table 6.9. Table 6.8 summarizes the criteria and values that went into the calculation of the aggregate index. For the reasons mentioned above, the dimension of party organization strength is left out of the index. The absence of this dimension is obviously a significant limitation of the index.

In the calculation of the index score for each country, the raw value for each measure within the three dimensions was first re-scaled from 1 to 3. The re-scaling was carried out

Democracies in Development

Table 6.8. Summary of Measures Used in Computation of Party System Institutionalization Index

Country	Criterion 1: Electoral volatility	Criterion 2: Party system stability (0 =highest; 100 =lowest)	Criterion 2: Party identification (1996, 1997)	Criterion 3: Confidence in parties (1996–2001)	Criterion 3: Legitimacy of electoral processes (1996–99)	Criterion 3: Parties indispensable to a country's progress (1997)
Argentina	18.04	22.53	16.96	17.89	56.38	34.78
Bolivia	31.47	20.00	20.35	15.89	28.01	30.40
Brazil	34.77	52.80	14.13	17.60	30.76	27.17
Chile	11.92	0.00	17.89	26.63	74.78	40.17
Colombia	21.44	28.65	18.58	16.97	19.85	39.08
Costa Rica	11.81	3.85	23.77	22.66	72.60	53.13
Dominican Rep.	20.80	32.89				
Ecuador	36.60	80.97	22.97	12.81	24.99	27.33
El Salvador	22.40	40.85	27.65	27.74	40.99	42.48
Guatemala	48.66	98.04	21.54	18.32	48.84	30.50
Honduras	6.95	0.00	34.40	23.59	50.42	61.23
Mexico	18.18	13.60	23.21	27.36	27.20	77.38
Nicaragua	13.39		36.39	23.20	56.77	41.12
Panama	35.75	7.14	21.90	23.17	59.81	37.22
Paraguay	20.39	6.09	36.48	23.76	27.91	19.83
Peru	49.66	91.35	14.57	19.59	36.87	29.98
Uruguay	11.93	2.06	38.09	36.97	80.13	64.51
Venezuela	33.01	74.06	17.83	20.08	28.74	42.17
Total	25.16	33.82	23.92	21.90	44.80	41.48

Table 6.9. Party System Institutionalization in Latin America

Country	Criterion 1: Electoral volatility	Criterion 2: Party system stability	Criterion 2: Party identification (1996, 1997)	Criterion 3: Confidence in parties (1996–2001)	Criterion 3: Legitimacy of electoral processes (1996–99)	Criterion 3: Parties indispensable to national progress (1997)	Institutionalization index
Uruguay	2.77	2.96	3.00	3.00	3.00	2.55	2.87
Honduras	3.00	3.00	2.69	1.89	2.01	2.44	2.65
Costa Rica	2.77	2.92	1.81	1.82	2.75	2.16	2.46
Chile	2.77	3.00	1.31	2.14	2.82	1.71	2.38
Mexico	2.47	2.72	1.76	2.20	1.24	3.00	2.29
Paraguay	2.37	2.88	2.86	1.91	1.27	1.00	2.21
El Salvador	2.28	2.17	2.13	2.24	1.70	1.79	2.11
Argentina	2.48	2.54	1.24	1.42	2.21	1.52	2.03
Nicaragua	2.70		2.86	1.86	2.22	1.74	2.02
Panama	1.65	2.85	1.65	1.86	2.33	1.60	1.94
Colombia	2.32	2.42	1.37	1.34	1.00	1.67	1.85
Bolivia	1.85	2.59	1.52	1.25	1.27	1.37	1.74
Venezuela	1.78	1.49	1.31	1.60	1.30	1.78	1.58
Brazil	1.70	1.92	1.00	1.40	1.36	1.26	1.50
Ecuador	1.61	1.35	1.74	1.00	1.17	1.26	1.43
Guatemala	1.05	1.00	1.62	1.46	1.96	1.37	1.32
Peru	1.00	1.14	1.04	1.56	1.56	1.35	1.19
Total	2.16	2.31	1.82	1.76	1.83	1.74	1.93

considering the party systems of Latin America only. Thus, the re-scaling is based on a range of variation that is not as broad as would be the case if a larger world sample were considered. The average of the re-scaled values of the measures within each of the dimensions was then calculated (Criterion 1 had only one measure; Criterion 2, two measures; Criterion 3, three measures). The index of party system institutionalization was computed as a simple average of the scores along each dimension of the concept, thus giving each dimension an equal weight.

According to the measures considered, the most institutionalized party systems are those in Uruguay, Honduras, Costa Rica and Chile. Peru, Guatemala, Ecuador, Brazil and Venezuela have weakly institutionalized systems. The index value for the Bolivian party system would also fall within the range of this latter group, except for the fact that it scores relatively high in terms of the longevity of its major political parties. Depending on where the dividing lines are drawn, one can say that the party systems of Mexico, Paraguay, El Salvador and Argentina are moderately institutionalized, while those of Nicaragua, Panama and Colombia are weakly to moderately institutionalized.

The measures for the three criteria rank the countries in a roughly similar fashion, but some variation is expected given that they relate to different aspects of the broader concept of institutionalization. For instance, given the recent opening up of political competition in Mexico and Paraguay, measures showing low electoral volatility and high party system stability are compatible with the finding that citizens remain skeptical about the integrity of the electoral process. Some deviations between the measures, however, are a little more puzzling. For instance, the level of identification with parties is lower than might be expected in Costa Rica and Chile, considering that the party system is institutionalized. In addition, the percentages of respondents viewing parties as critical to the country's progress is not as high as might be expected in Chile. As mentioned above, the two-way competition among party coalitions may be a factor in weakening the salience of parties in Chilean politics. Or, it could be that even aside from this factor, parties are weakening.

Assessing Party System Fragmentation and Polarization

Apart from its level of institutionalization, a party system's degree of fragmentation and polarization are also factors that affect the governability and stability of democratic systems.[7] The number of parties affects the likelihood that the party of the president will obtain a majority of seats in the legislature and provide sustained legislative support for the executive's policy proposals. A large number of parties also tends to be associated with a higher level of polarization.

Clearly, the relationship between multiple parties and polarization depends partly on the level of institutionalization of the party system. For instance, when parties are weak, one would expect that executive-legislative relations in a multi-party system would be more problematic and the possibilities for forming durable governmental coalitions more limited. On the other hand, it could be argued that, given their greater inflexibility, highly co-

---

[7] These two factors are the basis for the conventional classification of party systems developed by Sartori (1976).

Table 6.10. Effective Number of Parties (Based on Lower Chamber Seats)

	Time span	Number of elections	Effective number of parties: average of period	Most recent election
Honduras	1981–97	5	2.10	2.18
Paraguay	1989–98	3	2.20	2.27
Mexico	1979–00	8	2.29	2.55
Costa Rica	1978–98	6	2.32	2.56
Nicaragua[1]	1990–96	2	2.42	2.79
Dominican Rep.	1978–98	6	2.43	2.32
Colombia	1978–98	7	2.51	3.17
Argentina[2]	1983–99	9	2.68	2.56
El Salvador	1985–00	6	3.11	3.47
Uruguay	1984–99	4	3.16	3.07
Guatemala	1985–99	5	3.19	2.35
Peru	1980–00	5	3.50	3.97
Venezuela	1978–00	6	3.69	3.44
Panama	1989–99	3	3.77	3.26
Bolivia	1980–97	5	4.40	5.36
Chile[3]	1989–97	3	5.04	5.08
Ecuador	1979–98	9	5.70	5.73
Brazil	1986–98	4	6.70	7.13
Average			3.29	3.52

[1] The Unión Nacional Opositora (UNO) coalition in 1990 and the Alianza Liberal in 1996 are each treated as one party.
[2] The Alianza is treated as one party in 1997 and 1999.
[3] In Chile, the center-left and center-right party coalitions have been unusually durable, in large part because of the incentives stemming from the binominal electoral system. Thus, in this case the value for the effective number of parties that better reflects the functioning of the system might be that computed on the basis of party coalitions. If this is done, the average index value for the period would be 2.02 and the value for the most recent election, 2.01.

hesive parties commanding loyal followings in society might actually aggravate governance problems when there is a high level of ideological polarization.

Party System Fragmentation

The fragmentation of the party system is measured using the index of the effective number of parties introduced in Chapter Five.[8] Table 6.10 shows the average of that index for the full study period, as well as the value for the most recent election for each country. Focusing on

---

[8] See footnote 9 in Chapter Five for an explanation.

the figures for the most recent election, it is clear that the party systems in Latin America range from a few that are close to being two party systems, to four systems in which between five and seven parties typically obtain significant shares of the legislative seats.

Considering the outcomes of the most recent election, Honduras, Paraguay and the Dominican Republic have the most concentrated party systems. The party system in Honduras is the only one that remains close to a purely two-party system, with the Partido Liberal de Honduras (PLH) and the Partido Nacional (PN) gaining most of the legislative seats. In Paraguay, the two-party system consisting of the Asociación Nacional Republicana (Partido Colorado) (ANR) and the Partido Liberal Radical Auténtico (Partido Liberal) (PLRA) has been shaken somewhat by the emergence of the Encuentro Nacional (EN) in the more open and competitive elections of the 1990s. The party system in the Dominican Republic has gone from a two-party to at least a two-and-a-half party system with the Partido Revolucionario Social Cristiano (PRSC), Partido Revolucionario Dominicano (PRD), and the Partido de la Liberación Dominicana (PLD) fighting over shares of the legislative seats.

Mexico and Costa Rica also have relatively concentrated party systems with about 2.5 effective parties. In the 2000 elections in Mexico, the Partido Revolucionario Institucional (PRI) and the coalition led by the Partido Acción Nacional (PAN) each obtained a large share of the seats, while the coalition led by the Partido de la Revolución Democrática (PRD) obtained a smaller share. In Costa Rica in 1998, the Partido Liberación Nacional (PLN) and the Partido Unidad Social Cristiana (PUSC) won a large share of the seats, while several other small parties obtained a few seats each. But this situation has changed as a consequence of the election in 2002.

Nicaragua has a large number of parties vying for seats, but most of the seats have been captured by either the center-right party coalition (in 1996, the Alianza Liberal) or the Frente Sandinista de Liberación Nacional (FSLN). Guatemala is the only country where the party system has clearly become more concentrated during the study period. In the most recent election, the Frente Republicano Guatemalteco (FRG) and the Partido de Avanzada Nacional (PAN) obtained most of the seats, while several other parties shared the remaining 13 percent of the seats.

Colombia has traditionally had a party system dominated by the Partido Liberal and the Partido Conservador, which themselves were ridden with internal factions. In the past decade, however, the electoral system and the weakening of the two traditional parties have contributed to a proliferation of small parties and movements.[9] Nineteen parties obtained one seat or more in the most recent election. Thus, the effective number of parties measure has climbed from just over 2 to over 3. Until 1993, the Argentine party system was dominated by the Unión Cívica Radical (UCR) and the Partido Justicialista (PJ), with numerous regional parties and a few small national parties obtaining some representation. Since then, with the creation of the Frente Grande and then Alianza Frente Pais Solidario (FREPASO), Argentina has flirted with a three-party system. But the formation of the al-

---

[9] The electoral formula used in Colombia (Hare and largest remainder) encourages individuals to create new parties or movements so that they might obtain a seat through remainders. This means that the percentage of the vote that they obtain is greater than the percentage remaining to the larger parties after quotas have been deducted in the awarding of seats through the first part of the allocation procedure.

liance between the Unión Cívica Radical (UCR) and the Alianza Frente País Solidario (FREPASO) for the 1997 legislative and 1999 presidential and legislative election kept the score on the index down to its previous level of about 2.5.[10]

Beyond these eight countries, Latin America is characterized by systems with three or more parties. Clearly the most fragmented systems are those of Brazil, Ecuador, Chile and Bolivia. However, given the binominal nature of Chile's electoral system and the manner in which it pressures parties into two broad party coalitions, the Chilean political system may be thought to operate as if it has a two-party system. If one considers coalitions rather than parties in the Chilean case, the effective number of parties score is only slightly greater than 2.

More moderate levels of fragmentation with between three and four effective parties characterize the remaining countries. Party systems have splintered in the past two decades in Peru and more sharply in Venezuela. In both cases, the dispersion of the party system resulted in large part from the discrediting of the previously dominant parties and a proportional electoral system. The systems in Uruguay, El Salvador and Panama are typically characterized by three effective parties. With the basic three-way division of seats between the Partido Nacional (Blanco), Partido Colorado and Frente Amplio in Uruguay, this description is particularly apt.

In summary, the average Latin American system is a multi-party system with between three and four effective parties. Figure 6.1 shows that the average number of parties across Latin American political systems has grown significantly since the beginning of the study period.[11] The two-party systems in several countries at the beginning of the study period have largely given way to two-and-a-half or three-party systems. In part this expansion reflects the increase in pluralism and competition in countries where the process of democratic transition entailed the creation or strengthening of new or anti-authoritarian parties. Thus, part of the growth in the average reflects the expansion of democratic competition in such countries as Brazil, Mexico and Paraguay. Nevertheless, the data from each country individually in Table 5.13 shows that in only a few countries did the party system either become more concentrated (Guatemala) or remain the same over the period. And there are several countries—including Argentina, Bolivia, Colombia, Ecuador, Peru and Venezuela—where there was a clear increase in the number of effective parties.

Party System Polarization

Though clearly important to the functioning of democratic systems, the polarization of party systems in the region is more difficult to measure on a systematic basis. The best form of measurement would be opinion surveys at the levels of both the elite population and the general public. A survey question from the Latinobarómetro offers a means to assess the

---

[10] It may be more accurate to consider these to be separate parties. In that case the score on the index would be closer to 3.

[11] In the calculation of the average for each year, all lower chamber elections held within a four-year band of the year in consideration are included (one year before the election, the year of the election, and two years after the election). In this way the yearly regional average does not move randomly in relation to the unsynchronized electoral calendars of the countries in the region.

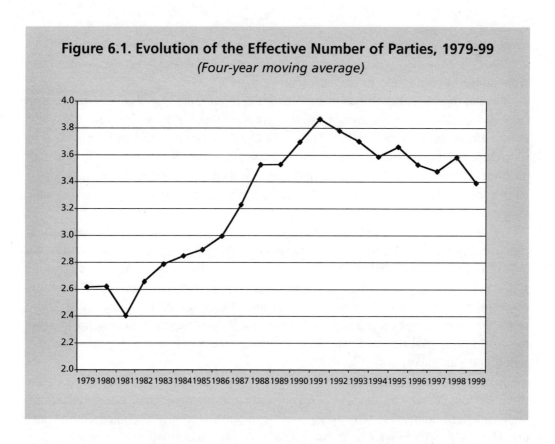

Figure 6.1. Evolution of the Effective Number of Parties, 1979-99
(Four-year moving average)

degree of polarization at the level of the general public. However, ideological dispersion at this level need not be reflected among party elites. One would expect some correspondence between the general public and elite levels, but this may not always be the case. Thus, lacking fully adequate survey data, the assessment of polarization will consider the Latinobarómetro responses as well as more impressionistic observations made in the country studies included in Mainwaring and Scully (1995).

Without considering objective measures, it seems clear that in most countries the degree of polarization along the traditional left-right ideological divide declined considerably at both the general public and elite levels between the 1960s and the 1990s. The fall of communism in Eastern Europe and the decline of the extreme left have tended to close this bridge across much of the world. However, there clearly remain bases for impassioned political differences along this traditional cleavage, as well as with respect to values, religion, ethnicity, etc. The outbreak of mass demonstrations and violent protest in several countries over the past decade and the continued guerrilla warfare in Colombia show that the potential for political conflict, if not readily apparent, always simmers below the surface when conditions are such that economic opportunities are limited, the middle class is relatively small, and there is widespread poverty and severe social inequality.

Nevertheless, the lessening of ideological polarization has clearly contributed to the durability of the current wave of democracy. Countries whose prior experiences with democracy had been disrupted by sharp political divisions and, at times, open subversion from the left and the right, are now benefiting from societal and elite attitudes that are more favorable to the functioning of democracy.

Table 6.11. Degree of Citizens' Self-placed Polarization on an Ideological Scale
(Average from 1996–99)

Country	Spread of left-right placements
Ecuador	3.05
Nicaragua	3.03
Venezuela	3.01
Costa Rica	2.92
Brazil	2.86
Panama	2.84
Guatemala	2.83
Honduras	2.80
El Salvador	2.66
Colombia	2.63
Mexico	2.63
Uruguay	2.60
Paraguay	2.45
Bolivia	2.37
Chile	2.28
Peru	2.26
Argentina	2.18
Average	2.66

In each year of the Latinobarómetro survey, respondents were asked to place themselves on an ideological scale from 0 to 10, with 0 referring to the furthest left and 10 to the furthest right. One way of assessing the degree of polarization in public attitudes is to calculate the standard deviation (or the spread) in the distribution of the responses to this question. Assuming a normal distribution,[12] if the mean response in a given country is 5, a standard deviation of 2 implies that about 68 percent of the responses are between 3 and 7. On the other hand, if the standard deviation is 3, a wider range, from 2 to 8, is required in order to include the same proportion of the responses. Thus, in the second case respondents' ideological placements reflect a much greater degree of polarization.

Table 6.11 shows the average for four survey years of the standard deviations of self-placement on the ideological scale. According to this measure, polarization of general public opinion is greatest in Ecuador, Nicaragua and Venezuela. Brazil is not too far behind, nor

---

[12] A normal distribution means that the distribution pattern of the responses is roughly symmetric about the mean and is shaped like a bell curve—meaning that the bulk of the responses is clustered fairly close to the mean, and gradually recedes as one moves further and further from the mean.

is Costa Rica, which is surprising given the dominance of the party system by two moderate parties close to the center of the ideological spectrum. According to this measure, at the level of the general public, Argentina, Peru and, surprisingly, Chile are among the least polarized.

Mainwaring and Scully (1995) classify the 12 (mostly South American) countries included within their study into four distinct categories of polarization: low, moderately low, moderately high, and high. Based on the findings of the book's country studies (completed in 1993), the party systems in Peru and Brazil are rated as highly polarized; in Mexico, Venezuela, Uruguay, Bolivia, Chile and Ecuador as moderately high; in Colombia and Argentina as moderately low; and in Paraguay and Costa Rica as low. A criterion that figured in this analysis and could also be used when considering the other Central American countries and the Dominican Republic is whether a party of the left is a significant player in the political system. While the meaning of left has certainly changed, such parties would appear to exist most clearly in Chile, El Salvador, Mexico, Nicaragua, Brazil and Uruguay.[13]

The survey-based ranking of polarization does not align in many cases with expert assessments of party system polarization. In particular, the survey measure shows a greater degree of polarization among Costa Rican citizens than among party elites, at least as judged by one country expert (Yashar, 1995). The reason for this discrepancy is unclear. It could be that the two party character of the system has produced moderation at the elite level that is not reflected fully in the broader general public, which clings to more idealistic viewpoints. In Venezuela, the political crisis and the election of President Hugo Chávez appears to have wrought growing polarization, which may be reflected somewhat in the public opinion data, though this dates to 1999.

The reverse relationship between the survey data and expert judgments occurs for Peru. Survey data indicate relatively little polarization in ideological self-placement among the masses, while the Mainwaring and Scully study identifies the party system as highly polarized (Cotler, 1995). In part, this could be a product of the different timing of the two measures. It is possible that during the 1990s, the degree of polarization in society and in the party system declined significantly. In fact, the party coalition cited as clearly on the left in the 1980s—the Izquierda Unida—had broken up by the early 1990s, and the left did not make any other strong showing throughout the decade.

The different timing of the measures may also be a factor in the case of Chile, as well as the restricted degree to which the left-right self-placement probed in the Latinobarómetro survey captures the full concept of political polarization. Given the continuity in economic policy between the Pinochet regime and the Concertación governments of the 1990s, Chilean parties certainly are considerably closer in terms of traditional connotations of left and right than they were previously and not so widely apart in absolute terms. But at least at the beginning of the 1990s, there remained a significant degree of polarization in the

---

[13] Recent studies by Alcántara and Freidenberg (2001 and forthcoming) measure party system polarization through a survey of party elites. The countries with the most polarized systems according to this analysis are El Salvador, Nicaragua, Chile, Guatemala and Mexico (Brazil and Panama were not included in this study). The study concludes that political party systems in the region are characterized by a "relatively high" degree of ideological polarization (at least in terms of the two parties at opposite ends of the left-right scale).

Chilean society and political system with respect to how the Pinochet regime was viewed, whether and to what extent justice should be sought for human rights victims, and how Pinochet personally and the legacy of his regime should be dealt with in the new democratic government.

In summary, without firm evidence the following three-way categorization of party polarization might tentatively be advanced:

- High to moderate polarization: Brazil, Ecuador, Nicaragua, Venezuela and El Salvador
- Moderate polarization: Uruguay, Guatemala, Bolivia, Peru, Panama, Chile, Mexico and Costa Rica
- Low polarization: the Dominican Republic, Honduras, Argentina, Colombia and Paraguay.

Conclusions

In keeping with the considerable differences in political histories across Latin America and, in particular, the extent of previous national experiences with democracy, the nature of party systems and how they have evolved varies greatly across the region. This chapter has found that party systems in some countries are reasonably well institutionalized, while in other systems few parties are able to hold on to citizen support, party organizations are weak, and representatives show little loyalty to the party through which they are elected.

In a few countries, including Peru, Ecuador, Venezuela and Colombia, party systems have clearly weakened. Colombia and Venezuela had relatively institutionalized party systems at the beginning of the study period, but by the end their party systems were much more fragmented with more diffuse bases of social support. Party systems in Peru and Ecuador had not reached such a high level of institutionalization, but the parties that did comprise the system at the beginning of the period were seriously weakened or replaced by the end of it. In contrast, the Argentine and Bolivian party systems appeared through the end of 2000 to have made some progress toward greater institutionalization over the course of the period. With the emergence of more vigorous and fair electoral competition, the party system in Mexico can also be viewed to have made some progress toward becoming institutionalized in democratic terms.

During the period of the study, the party systems in the region became more fragmented, with several two-party systems gradually becoming two-and-a-half or multi-party systems. The group of countries with three-and-a-half or more parties has expanded to include seven countries.

Several countries have party systems in which two or at most three parties dominate the political arena. In these countries—Honduras, Paraguay, Mexico, Costa Rica, Guatemala, Argentina, Chile (with its coalitions) and Colombia—it has been fairly common for presidents to be elected with majorities or near-majorities in the congress, or for presidents to build governing coalitions, though not always in a durable and effective manner. But in the remaining countries, and particularly those with four or more effective parties (Ecuador, Brazil, Bolivia and Peru), minority governments have been more common and governing through normal representative channels has in many instances been extremely difficult. Brazil has at least temporarily and partially managed some of these difficulties through a reasonably successful coalition backing the government of President Henrique Cardoso. But implementing reforms remains quite laborious and the basis for government continues to be fragile. At the same time, in Bolivia the second round election of presidents by the legislature has facilitated the formation of government coalitions where this might otherwise have been more difficult.

In Peru, President Alberto Fujimori overcame the difficulties of governing in the context of a fragmented congress by remaking the constitutional framework (with the backing of the military), which greatly amplified his power. The impact of the more fragmented party system in Venezuela initially worked to the benefit of a populist president, who has also succeeded in obtaining the acquiescence of other institutions that might serve as a check on his power. But in a different political context, such a high level of party system fragmentation could greatly complicate the achievement of stable and effective democratic governance.

Classifying Latin American party systems in terms of their degree of ideological polarization is more difficult. While differences between countries clearly exist, they are not as sharp as in the case of the other two-party system features. Polarization may be a factor for governability and political stability in Brazil, Ecuador, Nicaragua, Venezuela and El Salvador. Since most systems are less polarized than they were in the 1960s and 1970s, the impact that different degrees of polarization have on the performance of the democratic systems is less clear. In contexts of high levels of poverty, underdevelopment and extreme inequality, latent bases for political conflict may be as important as the visible level of polarization among political elites. The potential of underlying conditions to produce a more polarized political atmosphere in the context of an economic crisis is clear at least in the cases of Venezuela and Ecuador.

Bibliography

Alcántara Sáez, Manuel, and Flavia Freidenberg. Forthcoming. *Estructura y funcionamiento de los partidos políticos en América Latina.* Salamanca: Ediciones de la Universidad de Salamanca.

———. 2001. Los partidos políticos en América Latina. Website of Observatorio Electoral Latinoamericano.

Archer, Ronald P. 1995. Party Strength and Weakness in Colombia's Besieged Democracy. In Scott Mainwaring and Timothy R. Scully (eds.), *Building Democratic Institutions: Party Systems in Latin America.* Stanford, CA: Stanford University Press.

Arriagada Herrera, Genaro. 2001. Crisis de los sistema de partidos en América Latina. In *Democratización del estado: el desafío pendiente.* Lima: Asociación Civil Transparencia.

Bartolini, Stefano, and Peter Mair. 1990. *Identity, Competition, and Electoral Availability: The Stabilization of European Electorates, 1885–1985.* Cambridge: Cambridge University Press.

Conaghan, Catherine M. 1995. Politicians against Parties: Discord and Disconnection in Ecuador's Party System. In Scott Mainwaring and Timothy R. Scully (eds.), *Building Democratic Institutions: Party Systems in Latin America.* Stanford, CA: Stanford University Press.

Eurobarometer. 1991. *European Elections, 1989. Pre-Election Survey, March–April 1989.* Ann Arbor, MI: Inter-University Consortium for Political and Social Research.

Laakso, Markku, and Rein Taagepera. 1979. The Effective Number of Parties: A Measure with Application to Western Europe. *Comparative Political Studies* 12(1). April.

La Palombara, Joseph, and Myron Weiner (eds.). 1996. *Political Parties and Political Development.* Princeton: Princeton University Press.

Latinobarómetro. 1996–2001. *Latinobarómetro: Opinión pública Latinoamericana.* Santiago, Chile.

Lipset, Seymour Martin, and Stein Rokkan. 1967. *Party Systems and Voter Alignments.* New York: Free Press.

Mainwaring, Scott. 1995. Brazil: Weak Parties, Feckless Democracy. In Scott Mainwaring and Timothy R. Scully (eds.), *Building Democratic Institutions: Party Systems in Latin America.* Stanford, CA: Stanford University Press.

Mainwaring, Scott, and Timothy R. Scully (eds.). 1995. *Building Democratic Institutions: Party Systems in Latin America.* Stanford, CA: Stanford University Press.

Mainwaring, Scott, and Matthew Soberg Shugart (eds.). 1997. *Presidentialism and Democracy in Latin America.* New York: Cambridge University Press.

McGuire, James W. 1995. Political Parties and Democracy in Argentina. In Scott Mainwaring and Timothy R. Scully (eds.), *Building Democratic Institutions: Party Systems in Latin America.* Stanford, CA: Stanford University Press.

Pedersen, Mogens N. 1983. Changing Patterns of Electoral Volatility in European Party Systems, 1948–1977: Explorations in Explanations. In Hans Daalder and Peter Mair (eds.), *Western European Party Systems: Continuity and Change.* Beverly Hills: Sage.

Sani, Giacomo, and Giovanni Sartori. 1983. Polarization, Fragmentation and Competition in Western Democracies. In Hans Daalder and Peter Mair (eds.), *Western European Party Systems: Continuity and Change*. Beverly Hills: Sage.

Sartori, Giovanni. 1976. *Parties and Party Systems: A Framework for Analysis*. New York: Cambridge University Press.

Yashar, Deborah J. 1995. Civil War and Social Welfare: The Origins of Costa Rica's Competitive Party System. In Scott Mainwaring and Timothy R. Scully (eds.), *Building Democratic Institutions: Party Systems in Latin America*. Stanford, CA: Stanford University Press.

CHAPTER SEVEN

Internal Democratic Processes and Financing of Political Parties

The examination of Latin America's political party systems in the previous chapter shows them on the whole to be somewhat weakly institutionalized, moderately to highly fragmented, and moderately polarized. However, that analysis leaves out two critical dimensions: the internal processes by which party officials are selected and candidates are nominated, and the rules that regulate the financing of political parties and electoral campaigns.

The development and operation of political parties is affected, first, by the relationships that evolve within parties, particularly the interaction between the party chairperson, the leader of the party in the legislature, and the president. As important as this topic is, particularly with respect to the operation of presidential systems, it is not directly addressed in this chapter. Rather, it is the second component of this dimension that is the initial focus here: the processes by which party officials are selected and candidates are nominated for popularly elected offices.

Both of these issues are frequently blamed for the negative image of political parties among citizens. Perpetual conflict among party factions and individual politicians appears to be at odds with the kind of leadership that fosters economic and social development. At the same time, continued leadership of parties by bosses or groups of political cronies, especially when party activists and supporters are excluded from decision-making, undermines public respect for parties and participation in them. As a result, there is a growing demand for reforms to establish democratic procedures within political parties both to select party officials as well as candidates for public office.

How these two important issues are addressed is influenced by the dual private/public nature of political parties. While the strict internal organization of political parties—that is, their administration and the configuration of their leadership—could be conceived as a private matter, the nomination of candidates for political office is by nature public. It is in this latter area that there have been greater demands for transparency and participation.

These demands have resulted in the emergence of two prevalent mechanisms for selecting candidates for public office: party conventions and primaries. A third mechanism—the selection of candidates by the top party leadership—has become considerably less important, particularly with regard to the nomination of candidates for the presidency but also to a lesser extent in the nomination of candidates for other elected offices.

The first and more traditional mechanism—conventions—involves an assembly of representatives that has the power to elect the party officials as well as the candidates for public office. Although this mechanism has begun to be displaced by primaries, it continues to be important in the nomination processes of many parties in the region. The second and more recent mechanism is primaries which have been adopted as a means to open up the process of selecting candidates. Primary elections are understood as the process by which candidates for public office are chosen in a free, fair, competitive and direct fashion by secret vote either by party members (closed primaries) or by all citizens who wish to participate (open primaries).

There are four broad types of benefits from this move toward greater internal democracy within political parties. First, there is an expectation that such reforms will deepen democracy by extending it to the internal workings of the political parties. Politicians can hardly speak out with authority in the name of democracy if the origins of their leadership are tainted by non-democratic practices. Second, competition at the heart of political parties is expected to enhance mobility among party elites and strengthen the competence of party leadership. Third, it is expected that broader segments of society, or at least activists, will be encouraged to assume for themselves greater responsibilities in running political parties and thereby become more engaged in the democratic process and in strengthening one of its key institutions. Finally, internal party democracy is expected to lend added legitimacy to democratic processes by helping to offset negative practices such as political nepotism, *clientelismo* (patronage networks), and *caciquismo* (control of the party from the top by bosses), thereby also enhancing responsiveness to citizens.

The only factor that might work against these positive developments would be if internal democratization were to disrupt the internal harmony or the unified external image of the party. Moreover, adverse results for incumbent leaders, such as victories for outsider candidates, could initially cause instability and uncertainty, and thereby, in the short term, weaken individual political parties.

The Evolution of Internal Democratization of Parties

There were profound reforms of constitutions and laws governing political parties and elections during the final two decades of the 20th century. This was not only due to the transition in many countries from authoritarianism to democracy, but also to political reforms aimed at enhancing the quality of democratic representation.

These reforms initially sidestepped the issue of the internal democratization of political parties and the more difficult subject of party financing. However, party democratization was addressed more directly in the phase of reforms that began in the second half of the 1990s.

In fact, the trend in the 18 Latin American countries over the period of this study was toward higher levels of transparency, openness and participation in the selection of political party leaders as well as in the nomination of presidential candidates. As for the latter, in a growing number of countries, election procedures that were once conducted mainly by the highest-ranking party leaders or in internal party conventions are now carried out through various types of primary processes. The selection of candidates through primaries can serve to strengthen the elected president's legitimacy both within his own political party and among the broader citizenry.

Electing Party Officials and Candidates

As the internal democratization of political parties has unfolded, internal party officials have in many cases not been the persons chosen as candidates for political office. As a result, sometimes there are conflicts between them. Tables 7.1 and 7.2 show that these two

Table 7.1. Mechanisms for Electing Internal Authorities of Political Parties

Country	Regulated by the constitution or by electoral law	Constitution or electoral law refers back to political party statutes	Constitution and electoral law do not regulate or refer back to political party statutes
Argentina	No	No	✓
Brazil	No	Constitution Electoral law	
Bolivia	No	Electoral law	
Colombia	No	No	✓
Chile	No	No	✓
Costa Rica	No	Electoral law	
Dominican Rep.	Yes, electoral law	No	
Ecuador	No	No	
El Salvador	No	No	✓
Guatemala	Yes, electoral law	No	
Honduras	Yes, electoral law	Electoral law	
Mexico	No	Electoral law	
Nicaragua	No	Electoral law	
Panama	No	Electoral law	
Peru	No	No	✓
Uruguay	Yes, electoral law	Electoral law	
Venezuela	No (electoral law not yet in force)	No	

Source: Manuel Alcántara, University of Salamanca.

Table 7.2. Legal Sources for the Regulation of Primary Elections

Country	Regulated by the constitution	Regulated by electoral law or political party law
Argentina	No	No
Bolivia	No	Yes
Brazil	No	No
Chile	No	No[1]
Colombia	No	Yes[2]
Costa Rica	No	Yes
Dominican Rep.	No	No
Ecuador	No	No
El Salvador	No	No
Guatemala	No	No
Honduras	No	Yes
Mexico	No	No
Nicaragua	No	No
Panama	No	Yes
Paraguay	No	Yes
Peru	No	No
Uruguay	Yes (open)	Yes
Venezuela	Yes (closed)	Pending

[1] In Chile, the political party law requires that the party leadership (Consejo General) submit its presidential candidate for ratification by party members. If the party members accept, then the candidacy is officially proclaimed.
[2] Even though internal elections are optional in Colombia, congressional law regulates the nomination procedure of party candidates by means of a primary (*consulta popular*).
Source: Manuel Alcántara, University of Salamanca.

types of internal elections are clearly different processes in terms of the sources (party law, electoral law, or the constitution) and the extent of their legal regulation (Bendel, 1998).

In fact, whereas constitutions in Latin American countries rarely stipulate how internal political party authorities should be elected, they often regulate the way parties nominate their candidates for public office. Notable examples are Uruguay and Venezuela. The rationale behind this appears to be based on the complex distinction between what is considered private and public. While the parties in terms of their internal functioning are generally considered to be subject to private law, the selection of candidates to public office is subject to public law. The trend toward the democratization of candidate selection has brought with it a greater subjection of parties to public law.

Table 7.1 shows that matters involving the selection of party officials are generally dealt with in the internal statutes of the parties themselves. In Argentina, Colombia, Chile, El Salvador and Peru, neither the constitution nor electoral or political party legislation deal with this matter in any way. The legal framework in most of the remaining countries endows political parties with the autonomy to organize themselves according to their own statutes.

Only in the Dominican Republic, Guatemala, Honduras, and Uruguay is the election of internal officials regulated by law.

Types of Internal Elections for Presidential Candidates

Internal elections for presidential candidates can be classified according to the scope of participants the method uses. The first classification involves determining whether the presidential candidates are elected strictly by the members of the respective political party, or elected in open primaries that allow for participation of citizens who are not party members. Classification by method requires determining whether the party uses primaries, conventions, party leadership nomination, nomination by party leadership and then internal primaries, or primaries subject to ratification by national party conventions (Freidenberg and López Sánchez, 2001).

Table 7.3 shows the systems used for nominating presidential candidates for 55 political parties in 18 Latin American countries.

Primary Election Experiences in Latin America

Since the most prevalent trend in the region is toward the use of primaries, more emphasis will be put on analyzing this mechanism. Countries in the region can be divided into three main groups according to their current situation with respect to primaries (Table 7.4): (i) countries whose primary elections are mandated and regulated by law; (ii) countries without laws governing primaries, but which do hold them; (iii) countries with no regulations or practice of holding primary elections.

A more detailed classification of primaries (Figure 7.1) can be made based on the following criteria:

- Open (all citizens may participate) or closed (only party members may participate);
- Separate (each party holds its elections on different days) or simultaneous (all are held the same day);
- With or without oversight by the electoral management body;
- With or without public funding.

Countries with Legally Recognized Primary Elections

This first category includes eight Latin American countries that have established stipulations regarding the use of primaries in their constitution, political party regulations or electoral laws that must be adhered to by all political groups in the selection of candidates for public office. Costa Rica was the first to adopt such regulations, followed by Uruguay and Paraguay (each in 1996), and, more recently, Bolivia, Panama, Honduras and Venezuela. In these seven countries the law regulates and requires the use of primaries by political parties. In the last case, Colombia, the law does not require primaries but regulates their use if parties choose to hold them.

Table 7.3. Nomination Mechanisms of Political Parties for Presidential Candidates

	Open primaries	Closed primaries	Conventions	Party leadership	Party directorate proposes candidates; internal primaries are then held	Primaries subject to ratification by national party leadership
Argentina	FREPASO (1994) FREPASO-UCR (1999)	PJ (1988)[1]	PJ (1982, 94, 99)[1] UCR (1982, 89, 94)			
Bolivia	MNR (1999), MIR (1999)		UCS,[2] MNR,[2] MIR,[2] ADN[2]			
Brazil			PDT, PMDB, PSDB, PT, PFL			
Chile	Concertación (1993, 99)	PS	PPD		PDC, RN, UDI	
Colombia	PLC (1990, 94)[1]	PCC (1998)	PCC, PLC (1998)[1]			
Costa Rica	PLN, PUSC[1,4]					
Dominican Rep.		PRD, PRSC (1996)	PRSC[2]		PLD[3]	
Ecuador		ID (1984)	PSC, DP, ID, PRE	PRE		
El Salvador		FMLN	ARENA			
Guatemala			FRG, PAN			
Honduras		PLH, PNH (1989-2001)				
Mexico	PRI (1999)	PRD, PRI (since 2001)[5]	PAN, PRD	PRI (until 1999)		
Nicaragua			PLC (1996, 2001)	PLC		FSLN (1996, 2001)
Panama		PA (1998), PRD (1998)	PA,[2] PRD[2]			
Paraguay		ANR-PC, PLRA				
Peru			PAP			
Uruguay	EP-FA (1999) PC (1999) PN (1999)		EP-FA,[2] PC,[2] PN[2]			
Venezuela			AD, COPEI, Ind. MAS	MVR, PPT, PV		

Note: For a list of the full names of the parties that correspond to these acronyms, see Appendix 7.1 at the end of this chapter.
[1] More than one actor participates in the process.
[2] The mechanism was used until electoral reforms were implemented and electoral norms modified.
[3] The national party conventions qualify the candidates and later they compete among themselves.
[4] According to the party statutes, the leadership has the right to ratify the results of the primaries (party conventions) in which party members choose the presidential nominee for the party. In practical terms, the primaries are open, since electors only declare their affiliation to a party at the polling place for the primary election.
[5] No election has been held under the new party statute.
Source: Freidenburg and Sánchez López (2001).

Table 7.4. Primary Elections in Latin America

Country	Regulated by the constitution or political/electoral legislation	Observed in practice
Bolivia	Yes	Yes
Costa Rica	Yes	Yes
Honduras	Yes	Yes
Panama	Yes	Yes
Paraguay	Yes	Yes
Uruguay	Yes	Yes
Venezuela	Yes	Yes (sometimes)
Colombia	Yes (not mandatory)	Yes (sometimes)
Argentina	No	Yes (sometimes)
Chile	No	Yes (sometimes)
Mexico	No	Yes (sometimes)
Nicaragua	No	Yes (sometimes)
Dominican Rep.	No	Yes (sometimes)
El Salvador	No	Yes (sometimes)
Ecuador	No	Yes (one time by one party)
Brazil	No	No
Guatemala	No	No
Peru	No	No

Note: The dark shaded countries are those where primaries are required and regulated by law. The lightly shaded countries are those where primaries are not required by law but in practice have been held. The un-shaded countries are those where primaries are neither required nor have been held.
Source: Manuel Alcántara, University of Salamanca.

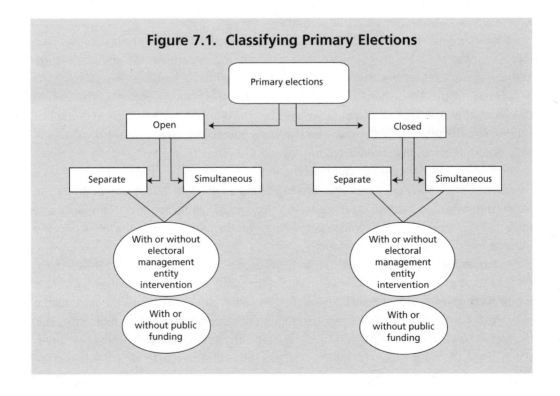

Figure 7.1. Classifying Primary Elections

For years in **Costa Rica,** electoral legislation has enforced the system of internal primaries (known there as "national conventions") as a free, universal, direct, secret electoral polling mechanism for nominating presidential candidates. Similarly, in some electoral jurisdictions, popular elections are also held for other representative offices. Political parties decide whether these will be open or closed as well as when to schedule them. Formally, the results of the primaries are subject to ratification by the party directorate, but it is doubtful that the results would in fact be overturned. The two main political parties—the Partido Liberación Nacional (PLN) and the Partido Unidad Social Cristiana (PUSC)—hold open primaries on different days. No public funding is provided specifically for this activity. The national electoral registry is used and the role of the electoral management body is limited to resolving any conflicts that may arise.

In **Uruguay**, the 1996 constitutional reform replaced the double simultaneous voting system with an open primary procedure for all political parties. These elections are held for all parties on the last Sunday in April, several months before the general election in October. The 1998 Internal Elections Law for Political Parties stipulated that the Electoral Court shall hear all cases dealing with electoral activity and procedures involving the internal elections of political parties. Enforcement of this procedure began in April 1999.

The reform required that primary elections be held simultaneously for nominating presidential candidates. Since no party membership registries exist, the primary election for all political parties begins and ends on the same day and voting for a political party is tantamount to affiliation with it. Although voting is not mandatory, primary elections are backed by all the guarantees and requirements characteristic of any national electoral process. Any candidate obtaining one vote over 50 percent of the total vote is automatically nominated as the party's presidential candidate for the general election. If this requirement is not met, the candidate must be elected by political party convention, with no restrictions with respect to who are the potential candidates.

Since the return to democracy in 1989, political parties in **Paraguay** have regularly held internal closed elections to nominate their national and departmental party assemblies. These assemblies then elect the party's executive authorities: The Governing Board (*Junta de Gobierno*) for the Asociación Nacional Republicana (ANR), widely known as the Partido Colorado; the Board of Directors (*Directorio*) for the Partido Liberal Radical Auténtico (PLRA); and the Directorate (*Dirección*) for the Partido Encuentro Nacional (PEN). The April 1996 reform requires that candidates for any elected office be elected by party members through a free, fair, direct and secret closed primary.

Each political party organizes elections to be held on the date it deems appropriate and has its own rules and supervisory mechanisms. No specific public funding is available, and there is little electoral management body oversight. To participate in the elections one must be registered in the respective party.

In **Panama**, closed primary elections were adopted as a result of reforms to the Electoral Code enacted in 1997. These reforms introduced the nomination of presidential candidates for the party whose member heads the ticket. Thus, allied parties endorsing the presidential candidate of another party are not required to hold primary elections. According to this law, in order to be eligible to vote, voters must register with the political party under the supervision of the Electoral Tribunal. Moreover, an electoral subsidy using public funds was approved to defray expenses involved in holding primary elections. It should be pointed out that the Electoral Tribunal has no jurisdiction and wields no influence whatsoever over the internal processes of political parties, aside from the duty to send delegates as mediators for conflicts that may arise, at the express invitation of the political parties themselves. In 1998, the first primary elections were held to elect presidential and vice presidential candidates within the Partido Arnulfista, the Partido Revolucionario Democrático (PRD), and the Partido Democrático Cristiano (PDC), currently the Partido Popular (PP). The rest of the parties allied with one of these three parties rather than putting forth their own candidates.

Bolivia introduced primary elections in 1999 through changes in legislation. The political party law stipulates that any party, when formed, must be officially recognized and adopt rules and procedures ensuring fully democratic internal operation by means of free, direct and secret voting, and that the National Electoral Court and the Department of Electoral Courts are to conduct these internal processes. This same law reinforces the institutionalization of the process by stipulating that under no circumstances may compliance with internal election and candidate nomination regulations be waived, making null and void any regulation or agreement establishing extraordinary procedures or conferring powers of exemption upon one or more individuals or party entities. In short, the new legislation has made the election of leaders at all levels mandatory, including candidates for all elected posts in the country. Furthermore, the National Electoral Court enacted the regulations governing the internal electoral processes of political parties in January 2001.

Electoral legislation in **Honduras** requires that political parties hold primary elections among their members if there are at least two different groups competing to nominate candidates. Political parties with only one internal movement may choose to hold an internal process to ratify one single slate of candidates.

In **Venezuela**, the 1999 constitution requires political parties to hold primary elections. Nevertheless, in the 2000 elections not one political party held them, allegedly due to a lack of specific regulations addressing this requirement. It should be pointed out, however, that in the past, even though the previous constitution did not stipulate any requirement for political parties to hold internal elections, Acción Democrática (AD) and the Comité de Organización Político Electoral Independiente (COPEI) did use them on occasion.

The case of **Colombia** is interesting because even though the election laws do not require political parties to hold primary elections, primaries have been held on two different occasions to select the presidential candidate of the Partido Liberal (PL). Though they are not required, when primaries are held they must follow the stipulations of a special law related to internal popular consultation in political parties. Following these stipulations, the Partido Liberal held open primaries in 1990 and 1994. In 1998, however, it returned to using the closed convention system.

Countries without Regulations that Hold Primaries

In a second category of countries, political parties hold primary elections at least sporadically (that is, some parties hold them some of the time) without regulation by electoral legislation or formal commitments in this regard.

The first method in this category is to hold internal elections within the framework of electoral coalitions. In **Chile,** the binominal electoral system[1] and the political division centered around support for and opposition to Pinochet has kept most of the center-left coalition united since the "no" vote group was successfully organized for the 1988 plebiscite. The need to hold together the heterogeneous Concertación coalition led to the adoption of primaries as the means to select the presidential candidate in 1993 and 1999.

Argentina also has experience in the use of primary elections, even though neither the constitution nor its electoral or party legislation requires them. Primaries in 1999 served as the foundation for setting up the coalition (Alianza) between the Unión Cívica Radical (UCR) and the Frente del País Solidario (FrePaSo). However, in 1988 closed primaries had already been held within the Partido Justicialista (PJ) between Carlos Menem and Antonio Cafiero. Open primaries were held within the Frente del País Solidario (FrePaSo) in 1995 between José Octavio Bordón and Carlos Álvarez. These were the second open primaries held in the country after those of the Izquierda Unida in 1989 between Luis Zamora and Néstor Vicente. In both cases, the organizations holding the primaries were arrays of political forces (frentes) rather than single parties.

Unlike this model for selecting the leadership of electoral coalitions, in **Mexico** a primary election was held in 1999 within the Partido Revolucionario Institucional (PRI) to choose its presidential candidate. This involved two important issues: first, the elimination of the unpopular historical practice of handpicking the candidate, which was in clear contradiction to democratic principles; and second, the need to boost the legitimacy of a political party whose democratic credibility had been seriously damaged and was being blamed for the country's political situation. The call that was made for the most open elections possible to pick the candidate for president was regarded as the best way to make up for the PRI's past and to project the party into the future. However, according to some analysts and certain groups within the party, while this election did constitute clear progress from past practices, it was not a thoroughly open process. The Partido Acción Nacional (PAN) used a closed primary while the Partido de la Revolución Democrática (PRD) used a party convention to choose their candidates for the 2000 elections.

Primary elections (called *consultas populares*) were also held in **Nicaragua** within the Frente Sandinista de Liberación Nacional (FSLN) in 1996. These elections were open to all citizens so that they could select party candidates to run in that year's general elections. Yet, after the fact, the winners of the primary elections had to be ratified by the FSLN Council before the general elections. This authority had the potential to change the outcome of the elections, which it indeed did for the office of vice-president. For the November 2000 municipal elections, the FSLN returned to the practice of selecting its candidates through primaries that were restricted to party members.

Though electoral legislation has not regulated primary elections in the **Dominican Republic**, the various parties have been holding them sporadically since 1982. These elections have traditionally been characterized by low levels of participation. In addition, they

---

[1] In the binominal system, legislators are elected from two-member districts, with the two seats being awarded to the two party lists obtaining the most votes, unless the victorious party lists doubles the vote of the second. In the latter case, the winning party list obtains both of the seats.

have often been managed by the political elite in order to avoid the threat of party division. For the 2000 election, the Partido de la Revolución Dominicana (PRD) used closed primaries, while the Partido de la Liberación Dominicana (PLD) and the Partido Reformista Social Cristiana (PRSC) used party conventions. However, in the latter, the influence of the *caudillo* Joaquín Balaguer was evident.

Finally there is the case of **El Salvador**, where primaries are not regulated by law but are regulated in the statutes of some parties, and have been held occasionally during the period. Otherwise, party conventions have been used. The statutes of the Frente Farabundo Martí para la Liberación Nacional (FMLN) require the use of closed primaries, while the statutes of the Alianza Republicana Nacional's (ARENA) stipulate the use of party conventions.

Countries without Primary Election Regulations or Traditions

In **Brazil, Ecuador,**[2] **Guatemala and Peru,** primary elections are not regulated by law and have not been held to elect presidential candidates. In the first two of these countries, factors that might have impeded the adoption of primaries include the elitist nature of the political parties and the fear that politics might become more highly regionalized. In Guatemala, the weakness of the political party system and the high level of personalization of political parties have impeded consideration of the issue. Finally, in Peru, the disintegration of the political party system in the 1990s precluded progress on the issue of primaries.

Summary of Primary Election Experiences

This preliminary review of the experiences of the region in the use of primary elections shows that there are a variety of possible approaches. These include passing national legislation to decide whether primaries are to be used, or allowing each political party to decide for itself whether and how to implement primary elections. Even through the second approach, it could happen that primaries become general practice, yet not legislated.

Primaries are adopted in various manners in different circumstances because of the strategic considerations of political parties, both internal and external, and only secondarily because of a desire to improve the quality of democracy. To date, the most favorable scenario for the introduction of primaries has been where the formation of party alliances or the management of internal party conflict makes them useful. With regard to the former scenario, primaries may be perceived as the best solution for settling potential disputes among the leadership of the parties in the coalition, and represents a way to gather popular support for the coalition prior to the general presidential election. Such was the case in Chile in 1993 and 1999, and in Argentina in 1999, in the selection of presidential candidates for the Concertación and Alianza parties, respectively.

---

[2] Ecuador is placed in this category because there was only one instance when a political party (Izquierda Democrática in 1984) used a closed primary to nominate its presidential candidate.

It should also be kept in mind that in Chile, Argentina, Mexico, Nicaragua and Colombia, the opening up to new democratic ways to nominate presidential candidates was due to internal circumstantial reasons specific to the political parties calling for primary elections, and had little to do with the other opposing forces. Therefore, national election management bodies did not involve themselves in terms of the organization, administration, supervision or funding of the primaries, except in the case of Colombia.

Conversely, as discussed above, Costa Rica, Uruguay, Paraguay, Bolivia, Panama, Honduras and Venezuela have adopted a different approach in which primaries have been institutionalized and placed under the supervision of electoral management bodies, though regulated to varying extents in each case.

Systems that Regulate the Financing of Elections and Political Parties

The relationship between money and politics is crucial to the health and quality of democracy. Contrary to democratic ideals, monetary assets—not just individual votes and political activity—are in practice important tools for exerting influence on elected officials.

The relevance of this issue goes hand in hand with its complexity. In terms of democratic theory, regulating the use of money in politics gives rise to a conflict between the principle of freedom of expression and those of impartiality and fairness in electoral competition. Whether centered on principles or on the protection of status and privileges, the issue prompts heated debate, not to mention efforts to circumvent whatever rules are created. Even highly developed democracies have yet to satisfactorily solve this dilemma. Nor have they avoided the inevitable scandals that result, as illustrated by several cases in the United States, Japan, France, Spain, England and Germany, just to name a few (Nassmacher, 1992).

This subject is nothing new, since the money/politics connection has been associated with political parties practically since their very inception. Nonetheless, the issue has increasing salience today as compared with the past due to the increasing cost of electoral campaigns resulting from increased reliance on television marketing, consultants, opinion polls and focus groups.

In Latin America, the issue of political financing is closely related to the current disenchantment with politics. The continuous scandals involving corruption, bribery, influence peddling, and in some cases narco-trafficking reinforce the aversion many citizens feel towards politics and politicians. In addition, political parties and candidates themselves accuse one another of obtaining funds from questionable sources or handling them in improper fashion. As was shown in Chapter Two, public opinion polls confirm the poor image that the public has of political parties and their leaders, who are perceived as corrupt, lacking transparency, oriented primarily towards promoting their own interests, and reneging on their campaign promises.

To address these problems, the legal concept of using public resources to help political parties carry out campaigns, and in certain cases their day-to-day operations, has been introduced over the past few decades. Other laws have also been devised to regulate activities involving private contributions and to exercise greater public control over the financial transactions of political parties. Despite these measures, the political independence of parties remains in jeopardy because of the never-ending need to obtain ever-larger sums of money. Thus, the issue of "political funding" policy—*governing the revenues and expenditures of political parties with respect to election campaigns and day-to-day activities*—has become increasingly important in Latin America, as it has in other parts of the world. A balanced and equitable system of party funding is an indispensable requirement for truly competitive and fair elections (Njaim, 2000; González-Varas, 1995).

Nevertheless, despite being recognized today as critical, public funding was not assigned high priority during the initial stage of political transition. Once elections began to gain credibility, the political agenda started to include new issues tied in with the quality and enhancement of democracy, among them funding. Table 7.5 shows that over the past two decades, several countries have introduced laws related to the financing of political parties and electoral campaigns.

Increasing attention in Latin America is being given to this issue, to the extent that it has become a serious point of contention in several countries because of its critical role in: (i) guaranteeing fairness during electoral contests; (ii) ensuring certain levels of transparency and accountability with regard to the origin and assigned use of public and private funds; (iii) preventing influence peddling and opportunities for political corruption; and (iv)

Table 7.5. Year When Regulation of Public Political Funding Was Introduced

Country	Year
Uruguay	1928
Costa Rica	1949
Argentina	1961
Venezuela	Established in 1973, eliminated in 1999
Nicaragua	1974
Mexico	1977
Ecuador	1978
Honduras	1981
El Salvador	1983
Guatemala	1985
Colombia	1985
Chile	1988 (indirect funding)
Paraguay	1990
Peru	1991 (indirect funding)
Brazil	1995
Bolivia	1997
Panama	1997
Dominican Rep.	1997

preventing the influx of money from organized crime, particularly drug money, into the political arena.

Critical Political Financing Issues

The consolidation of democracy in Latin America has helped political parties reassume their role as main actors on the political scene, affording them constitutional legitimacy as autonomous entities with full legal status and general and collective functions. In this context, political party and electoral expenditures have grown exponentially, due mainly to the escalating costs of electoral campaigns. Such campaigns increasingly require large expenditures on television advertising, marketing, consultants, opinion surveys and the use of focus groups.

The need to run increasingly more expensive electoral campaigns and to keep political party mechanisms in permanent operation has gone hand in hand with a decline in the collection of party membership fees. This combination of factors has placed many political parties in the quandary of having to raise such large sums of money that they are ever tempted not to pay much attention to where the money comes from, thus opening the door to illegal funding.

The debate over political financing in Latin America centers on four main topics. The first has to do with whether to regulate party financing, and, if so, to what extent. There is no consistent pattern in this area among the countries of the region. Some, such as Mexico, have a detailed regulatory framework, while others, such as Uruguay and Chile, have very few regulations. The issue is complex, since there are clear limits as to what can be done. While there is a need to establish clear rules of the game to achieve greater public control over the financial operations of political parties, there is also a risk of over-regulation that could lead to more elaborate schemes to obscure party finances and evade the law.

The second key issue is the mode of financing. This involves the questions of whether to use private, public or mixed systems, and, in the case of mixed funding systems, what the proper balance should be between public and private funds. Discussion of this issue has been driven partly by various political and social sectors challenging the appropriateness of the state investing large amounts of public funds in political parties, especially in the context of the fiscal crises afflicting many Latin American governments. Opinion against high levels of public financial support is gaining strength due to the widespread credibility crisis confronting political parties and politicians.

The third issue revolves around whether to adopt mechanisms to lower the demand for money in electoral activity and ensure a more sound use of public funding. Proponents of curbs on escalating campaign costs contend that the infusion of money on such a large scale undermines the fairness of electoral competition, raises the risk of the use of illegal forms of funding, and increases the prevalence of corruption and influence peddling.

Finally, there is the matter of establishing or strengthening control mechanisms and entities, as well as a system of sanctions, in order to improve transparency, accountability and compliance with political finance legislation.

Figure 7.2. Classification of Funding according to Origin and Use

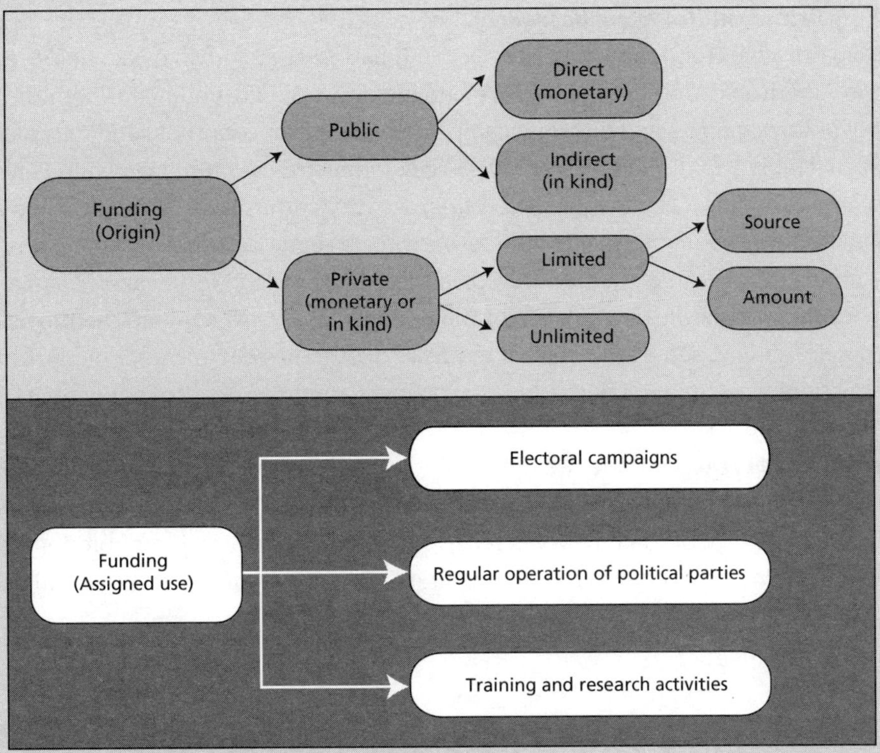

Key Features of Political Finance Systems

The major variables in terms of political finance include funding systems, activities entitled to public funding, legal barriers, allocation criteria, prohibitions against contributions with particular origins, limits on private contributions, disbursement scheduling, access of parties to the media, enforcement, and sanctions (Figure 7.2). A comparative examination of electoral legislation in Latin America with respect to these 10 variables yields the following conclusions:

1) Funding systems. Of the three basic modes of funding—public, private and mixed—all Latin American countries except for Venezuela[3] use a mixed system in which political parties receive public as well as private funds to finance their electoral campaigns or meet their day-to-day operating expenditures. Nevertheless, there are a great variety of mixed systems, ranging from those with a striking predominance of public funds (e.g., Mexico) to those with limited amounts of public funding (e.g., Chile). Countries in the region (again, except for Venezuela) use a variety of types of public financing, including direct

---

[3] In Venezuela, the constitution approved by referendum in December 1999 eliminated public funding to political parties for both electoral purposes and day-to-day operations.

funding (cash or bonds), indirect subsidies (services, tax breaks, media access, etc.), or a combination of the two (Zovatto, 1998).

2) ***Activities entitled to public funding.*** These include the day-to-day operations of the political parties, electoral campaigns, and a combination of these two categories. Eleven of the Latin American countries studied here provide direct public funding for both the operations of political parties and electoral campaigns, while four countries fund only electoral campaigns (Table 7.6). Chile and Peru have only indirect public funding, while Venezuela has no public funding. Over the past two years, some countries have been assigning a percentage of public funding to pay for the research or training activities of political parties. The countries include Argentina, Brazil, Costa Rica, El Salvador, Mexico and Panama.

3) ***Legal barriers.*** In 12 countries of the region whose laws regulate the provision of direct public funding, some type of legal requisite determines eligibility for public funding, such as obtaining a minimum percentage of votes or a minimum level of parliamentary representation (Table 7.7).

4) ***Allocation criteria.*** There are four main criteria for allocating funds to political parties: a) equal shares for each party; b) proportional to votes received; c) a combination of equal shares and proportional to votes received; and d) a combination of proportional to votes received and proportional to parliamentary representation. Among these allocation

Table 7.6. Activities Entitled to Public Funds

Country	Electoral and partisan	Only electoral
Argentina	X	
Bolivia		X
Brazil	X	
Chile	Only indirect public funding	
Colombia	X	
Costa Rica	X	
Dominican Republic	X	
Ecuador		X
El Salvador	X	
Guatemala	X	
Honduras		X
Mexico	X	
Nicaragua		X
Panama	X	
Paraguay	X	
Peru	Only indirect public funding	
Uruguay		X
Venezuela	None	

Table 7.7. Legal Barriers and Allocation Criteria

Country	Legal barrier	Allocation criteria
Argentina	Officially recognized parties must have participated in the preceding elections for national deputies.	By votes received
Bolivia	Parties must attain a minimum of 3% of the total valid votes cast nationwide in the preceding general elections (or municipal elections, accordingly).	By votes received
Brazil	Proportionate to the number of votes obtained in the last election for representatives to the Chamber of Deputies.	By votes received
Colombia	Above 5% of all votes cast. For reimbursement of expenditures for parliamentary elections, parties must obtain at least one-third of the votes received by the list that received the lower of the remainders.	By votes received
Costa Rica	Parties must obtain at least 4% of the votes validly cast nationally, or parties registered at the provincial level must attain at least 4% of the votes validly cast in their respective provinces or succeed in electing at least one deputy.	By votes received
Chile	Indirect public funding only.	
Dom. Rep.	Only those having participated in the last two general elections and those who have approved independent candidates may receive funding.	Combined (By votes received/equally)
Ecuador	Parties must have received the minimum quotient of 0.04 of the votes cast in pluripersonal elections.	Combined (By votes received/equally)
El Salvador	No legal barrier.	By votes received
Guatemala	Parties must obtain at least 4% of all votes validly cast in the general elections.	By votes received
Honduras	No legal barrier.	By votes received
Mexico	2% of all votes validly cast.	Combined (By votes received/equally)
Nicaragua	4% of all votes validly cast.	By votes received
Panama	5% of the votes validly cast in any of the three different types of elections: presidential, legislative or for the *corregidor*.	Combined (By votes received/legislative representation)
Paraguay	No legal barrier	Combined (By votes received/legislative representation)
Peru	Indirect public funding only.	By votes received
Uruguay	Participation in the internal and primary elections is required and attainment of over 500 votes (the minimum needed to cover the representation quotient).	
Venezuela	No public funding.	

modes, the one that predominates (used in ten countries) distributes funding based on the percentage of votes received (Table 7.7) (Navas, 1998).

5) *Prohibitions against contributions of certain origins.* Almost all of the countries in the region prohibit various types of contributions. Most common are the restrictions on donations by foreign governments, institutions or individuals (Table 7.8). Only slightly less common are bans on donations by particular social organizations (unions, associations, special interest groups, religious groups, etc.). Donations from government contractors and anonymous sources (except collections taken up in public) are banned in slightly less than half of the countries.

6) *Limits on private contributions (ceilings).* Bolivia, Brazil, Colombia, Costa Rica, Chile, Mexico and Paraguay set ceilings or upper limits on amounts allowed for private contributions, particularly for individuals, and to a lesser degree on contributions originating from private or public organizations.

7) *Disbursement scheduling.* There is no uniform pattern for this practice, since in some countries disbursement occurs after elections have taken place (Colombia, Costa Rica, Ecuador, Nicaragua, Paraguay and Uruguay), while in another it occurs beforehand (Argentina). In still others, the public subsidy is divided into a portion provided before or after the election (Bolivia, Dominican Republic, El Salvador, Guatemala, Honduras and Panama) (Table 7.9). Very few countries currently provide for public funding to political

Table 7.8. Prohibitions against Contributions of Certain Origins

Country	Foreign	Social or political organizations	Government contractors	Anonymous
Argentina	X	X	X	X
Bolivia	X	X		X
Brazil	X	X	X	X
Chile	X			
Colombia	X			X
Costa Rica	X			
Dominican Rep.	X	X	X	
Ecuador	X		X	
El Salvador				
Guatemala				
Honduras	X	X	X	X
Mexico	X	X	X	X
Nicaragua		X	X	X
Panama				
Paraguay	X	X	X	
Peru				
Uruguay				
Venezuela	X	X	X	X

Table 7.9. Disbursement Scheduling for Direct Public Funds for Electoral Purposes

Country	Before	After	Before and after	Other	Facilities for new political parties
Argentina	X				X
Bolivia			X		
Brazil				X[1]	
Colombia		X			
Costa Rica		X			X[2]
Chile	No direct public funding				
Dom. Rep.			X		X
Ecuador		X			
El Salvador			X		
Guatemala			X		
Honduras			X		
Mexico				X[3]	X
Nicaragua		X			
Panama			X		
Paraguay		X			
Peru	No direct public funding				
Uruguay		X			
Venezuela	No public funding				

[1] In Brazil, the national treasury distributes one-twelfth of a special fund in the Banco do Brazil on a monthly basis.

[2] Under discussion.

[3] Electoral legislation in Mexico does not expressly establish a date for the distribution of public funds for electoral campaigns, as it does for day-to-day operational expenditures. For elections held on July 2, 2000, the Federal Electoral Institute distributed the funds allocated for campaign expenditures in six monthly installments during the first six months of 2000.

groups participating in elections for the first time (Argentina, Mexico), albeit under varying conditions. Other countries such as Costa Rica are considering proposals for reform that go in this direction (Navas, 1998).

8) Political party access to the media. A distinction must be made here between television, radio and the written press media. In the case of television, there are five main categories: a) free daily time slot (*franja*), as in Brazil and Chile; b) mixed system, with public access but with a system predominated by unlimited paid advertising in privately owned media, as in Argentina; c) permanent multiparty access to the media for electoral purposes and the dissemination of ideological programs, which is a mixture of free and paid access, but limited, as in Colombia and Mexico; d) unlimited private paid access, as in Guatemala, Honduras and Venezuela; and e) private paid access with ceilings, as in Costa Rica, Ecuador and Bolivia (Navas, 1998).

Although most countries grant free media airtime to political parties, this applies mostly to public television and is limited in most cases to the electoral campaign period. Brazil and Chile forbid paid electoral announcements, but political parties are guaranteed a daily time slot of free political advertising during the electoral campaign. As for radio, most countries in the region employ a system similar to that used for television media. All countries permit parties and candidates to pay for access to the written press, and in most cases there are no limits on the publishing of paid electoral announcements, with some exceptions, including Costa Rica, Bolivia, Ecuador and Nicaragua.

9) Enforcement. Electoral legislation specifies an entity responsible for the monitoring or oversight of political party and election campaign funding in all countries except Uruguay. In most cases, the organization responsible for controlling or overseeing political party funding is the electoral management body (Table 7.10).

10) Systems of sanctions. Pecuniary sanctions are the predominant form of sanctions, followed by penalties such as the cancellation of party registration or the reduction or suspension of government funding to political parties. Costa Rica, Mexico, Paraguay and Venezuela have introduced jail terms for certain violations of electoral legislation governing funding.

Trends in Political Financing Reform

Preserving the Mixed System

The mixed funding system is used in all countries with the exception of Venezuela, where no public funding is provided. There is no clear trend in the region favoring either public or private funding. In fact, the focus of the 1996 Mexican reform stressing public funding has been emulated in proposals for electoral reform in Argentina, Brazil and Colombia. Venezuela, however, has gone against this trend by eliminating public funding, while Chile and Peru have maintained their systems of only indirect public funding.

Moving from Electoral Expenditures to Electoral Investment

Two trends that are emerging in terms of spending on elections are toward restricting political advertising expenditures, and increasing public outlays to strengthen, modernize and train political parties and politicians. Along these lines, electoral reforms in the region that have been proposed or approved have opened up a third window for public funding designed to fortify the political culture, along with research and training for political parties.

Limiting Private Contributions

Scandals involving corruption and the connections of political parties and their candidates with money made through illicit activities, particularly drug trafficking, have led to limitations on or prohibitions against private contributions of certain origins and amounts. Another reason for these measures is to avoid great disparities or unevenness among the

Table 7.10. Enforcement Agencies

Argentina	Federal judges with electoral jurisdiction
Bolivia	Electoral management body
Brazil	Electoral management body
Chile	Electoral management body
Colombia	Electoral management body
Costa Rica	Electoral management body/General Comptroller's Office
Dominican Rep.	Electoral management body/General Comptroller's Office
Ecuador	Electoral management body
El Salvador	General Comptroller's Office
Guatemala	Electoral management body
Honduras	Electoral management body
Mexico	Electoral management body
Nicaragua	General Comptroller's Office, electoral management body and the Ministry of Treasury and Credit[1]
Panama	Electoral management body/General Comptroller's Office
Paraguay	Electoral management body
Peru	Electoral management body
Uruguay	
Venezuela	Electoral management body

[1] The Electoral Attorney's Office is formed within the Attorney General Justice's Office six months before each presidential election, and enforces laws involving political party funding in Nicaragua.

coffers of political parties and to reduce the influence of plutocratic contributions and the consequent influence of fat cat donors.

Two main trends prevail among funding prohibitions. The first is increased efforts to prevent donations from abroad (from foreign governments, institutions or individuals), even for donations earmarked for the instruction, training or education of political parties. Experience suggests that allowing such contributions opens a dangerous loophole, hindering adequate control over their actual use. The second trend entails efforts to forbid contributions made anonymously, except for those obtained through collections taken up in public.

Equitable Media Access

One incipient yet growing trend is toward facilitating more equitable access to the media, and particularly television because of the key role it currently plays in electoral campaigns. Most recent legislation has included regulations aimed at ensuring free access to the media, chiefly that run by the state. This television or radio airtime is known as "antenna rights" or "antenna time."

Despite this trend, most countries in the region still have a long way to go to counteract the inequitable environment in which political forces compete. These circumstances are chiefly attributable to the following:

- The predominance of a system that combines free media access with the possibility of purchasing additional airtime in the private media, which by and large is not regulated very much and proves hard to control.
- Owners and administrators of the media frequently associate with powerful economic and political groups. Commonly, even among the collectively owned media, those who hold a controlling interest in these firms have interests that motivate them to favor political groups or to offer them better or longer time slots that openly or covertly benefit them.
- The small viewing/listening audience of state-funded television and radio stations forces even small parties to purchase airtime from private media concerns.
- Swift changes in communications technology (e.g., satellite and cable television) are giving rise to gaps in regulations related to the promotion of more equal media access among political parties.
- Even though regulations establish free time slots in many countries, very few provide support for the production of advertising, an undertaking normally requiring large sums of money.
- Sometimes biased treatment is given in the news in favor of or against certain parties or candidates.
- National bulletins or nationwide simulcasts broadcast by the state convey the tangible achievements and outcomes of its policies, giving unfair advantages in electoral campaigns to governments in power.
- Lack of legislation governing rates hinders media access and control over what the different political parties are charged.

Another still incipient trend in this area in some Latin American countries is toward greater involvement of electoral management bodies in the follow-up and enforcement of provisions dealing with equitable media access for political parties. Nevertheless, these bodies usually have insufficient capacity or resources to effectively handle the issue of political advertising and the media. Perhaps the country where the most progress has been made in this area is Mexico, where the powers of the Broadcasting Commission (*Comisión de Radiodifusión*) of the Federal Electoral Institute (IFE) were considerably broadened by the 1996 electoral reforms. One of the main responsibilities of this commission is to monitor, but not enforce, the fairness of campaign broadcasting time slots and the equal treatment of newscasts, and to widely publish reports of its findings.

Improved Accountability and Transparency in Management of Resources

A growing trend has been to require political parties to make publicly available budgetary accounts showing their administration and use of public as well as private resources. Nevertheless, this trend is just beginning in terms of the total number of countries, and, in most cases, is limited to the publication by political parties of their financial statements in bulletins, official gazettes and registers, which few citizens read.

Strengthening Enforcement Mechanisms and Entities

As shown in Table 7.10, even though electoral management bodies in most countries have the authority to supervise and control financial acts of political parties, their ability to carry out their responsibilities is severely limited. Therefore, there is a trend toward reinforcing their authority and their economic, technical and human resources relating to the ability to audit the reports submitted by political parties, as well as their powers to investigate the origin, management and actual use of resources. Moreover, in some countries other types of control entities have been utilized, such as General Comptroller's Offices (Nicaragua and El Salvador), or a combination of both electoral management bodies and Comptroller's Offices, as in Costa Rica, the Dominican Republic and Panama.

As for strengthening control mechanisms, the chief reform measures adopted in recent years have been to (i) make the supervision of political parties an ongoing rather than a temporary activity; (ii) regulate the duty of political parties to submit reports on their revenues and expenditures; (iii) establish the obligation to conduct bona fide audits to verify and supervise financial resources, with all the technical rigor that this requires; (iv) require standardized procedures and the regular submission of the reports; (v) make audits a constant practice as a means of preventive intervention; (vi) call for the widespread dissemination of the results of audits as well as of reports submitted by political parties (preferably before elections); (vii) improve the quality of donor records, making them clearer; (viii) establish ethics control councils within political parties; (ix) require that resources pass through the financial system rather than be carried out by cash transactions; and (x) establish the position of sole financial executive as the single authority over the management of party funds.

Toughening Sanctions Systems

In some countries in the region, a trend has emerged toward strengthening sanctions. Along these lines, the legal concept of illicit funding has been identified as a type of crime (*delito autónomo*), and administrative and judicial procedures have been established to punish it. In addition, candidates and donors have been assigned greater legal responsibility, since the increasingly personalized nature of politics has meant that a large portion of the private contributions go directly to the candidates (or their closest associates), and are not reported to the treasuries or controlling entities within the political parties.

Conclusions

During the period of this study, substantial progress has been made in terms of the internal democratization of political parties and reforming systems for financing political parties and electoral campaigns. After not having been in the forefront of the region's reform agendas, these issues have received increasing attention over the past 10 years. However, despite this progress, much remains to be done to strengthen the credibility of political parties and the fairness of electoral competition.

Ten Commandments of Political Financing

1. There shall be transparency regarding both income and expenditures for political parties and electoral campaigns. All party accounts shall be public.

2. There shall be a reasonable amount of public financing. This financing shall be devoted to fomenting greater equity in political contests, lessening the economic dependence of political parties on economic groups, and strengthening the political party system and political culture.

3. Preventing the influence wielded by privileged groups over elected governments shall be pursued to the furthest extent possible. Hence, it is essential to reasonably lower the demand for money by controlling the key factors that make electoral expenditures skyrocket.

4. No foreign contributions shall be allowed.

5. No anonymous contributions shall be allowed.

6. No contributions shall be made from sources linked to organized crime or other illicit activities.

7. Equitable access to the public as well as private media shall be guaranteed, particularly with regard to television.

8. All regulations shall at all times endeavor to fully prevent the violation of freedom of expression.

9. There shall be competent, efficient authorities devoted to enforcing these regulations.

10. Violators shall be punished.

Source: Humberto de la Calle (2001).

With respect to the internal democratization of political parties, the process has developed slowly, gradually and unevenly in the region. Despite this slow progress, the process appears headed in the right direction in that it holds the potential to strengthen the quality of democratic political representation.

After being on the sidelines in the 1980s, the internal democratization of political parties has since emerged in some cases as a response to growing social demands for broader participation in political parties and more transparency in their activities. In other cases, democratization has emerged as a strategy by political parties to either build coalitions or rejuvenate their bases of electoral support. Before this process got underway, most countries had very closed political parties, usually organized around exclusive forms of leadership such as *caudillos* or traditional leaders.

Despite progress, particularly with respect to primary elections that have been implemented at least partially in 14 of the countries in the region, regional experiences to date allow for only a preliminary evaluation. Thus, 20 years after the "third wave" reached the shores of Latin America, primary elections are legally regulated for nominating presidential candidates in seven of the 18 countries in this study. The countries are Bolivia, Costa Rica, Honduras, Panama, Paraguay, Uruguay and Venezuela. In Colombia, the law regulates primaries when and if political parties decide to use this procedure. In six countries (Argentina, Chile, the Dominican Republic, El Salvador, Mexico and Nicaragua), primaries are not regulated, but political parties have occasionally adopted them in different forms anyway. And finally, in Brazil, Ecuador, Guatemala and Peru, primaries are neither held nor regulated by law.

The most substantial progress in the internal democratization of parties has been made in terms of nominating candidates for popularly elected public office, rather than in electing internal party officials. This situation appears to be rooted in the resistance of traditional leadership structures to change, and in the ongoing tendency to treat political parties in some circumstances still as private entities.

Comparative analysis suggests a growing consensus in Latin America regarding the benefits of using primary elections for selecting presidential candidates. Even from the narrow vantage point of party electoral strategies, primaries appear valuable in strengthening public backing for candidates in the general election. More importantly for democracy as a whole, primaries enhance the legitimacy of those elected to the presidency, broaden the circle of potential party leaders, and provide voters with a greater range of choices, hopefully leading to the selection of more competent and responsive leaders.

However, as with all institutional reforms, the introduction of primaries may not always produce only positive effects. In some cases, it may contribute to governability problems due to the tension that can be created within political parties when party officials are in conflict with the candidates selected for public office. Thus, in the short term there is a risk that parties may become less cohesive, more fragmented, and weakened. If the adoption of internal elections fragments the leadership of the party, this may make it more difficult for the president to manage his relations with the party leadership and with the party representation in the legislature.

Thus, primaries should be adopted in a manner that contributes to the strengthening of political parties and not merely to further personalize the presidential election process. Given this danger and given the risk of potential party disunity, the process of democratizing parties is a difficult one.

This is a central challenge given citizens' marked indifference and profound mistrust of political parties across much of the region (Chapter Two). This political malaise may be alleviated to the extent that the population considers politicians and the party itself necessary for the country to function. The solution to this problem may lie in part in professionalizing the parties and strengthening the institutions that oversee their activities.

Finally, improving the functions of political parties clearly requires them to open further to society. This means responding to the demands of citizens as well as incorporating the participation of a broader segment of the electorate. The internal democratization of political parties is one means of furthering this objective, but it is not a panacea.

With respect to systems for financing political parties and electoral campaigns, a regional assessment shows the following:

- Formally, the mixed system is used throughout the region (except Venezuela), and there is no clear trend in favor of or against public funding. There is also a tendency to reinforce legal limits on private contributions both with respect to their origin (who can contribute) and their limits (ceilings on contributions). These formal features contrast, however, with the widespread perception in most Latin American countries that private funds, whose true totals are not entirely known, exceed public funds. This premise is lent support by frequent scandals involving corruption, unlawful funding, drug money, etc.

- This dark side to political funding has been inspiring reforms aimed at increasing transparency and enhancing accountability. Unfortunately, this process is not advancing as quickly or as thoroughly as is needed.

- Due to a combination of several factors (inadequate regulation, inefficient enforcement mechanisms, ineffective systems of sanctions, and political practices favorable to abuse), public funding has served to supplement private funding rather than substitute for it. Its impact has been limited, though it varies from country to country.

- Another emerging but limited and uneven trend across the region has been to establish expenditure ceilings and limits for campaigns. This entails a reorientation in the use of public resources for politics, allocating them more toward strengthening political parties by supporting research and training activities.

- Whereas some issues verge on being over-regulated, others such as fair access to the media—especially television—are somewhat under-regulated or not regulated at all. This is one of the greatest gaps in the region today, except in a few countries (Brazil, Chile and Mexico), since this is where the largest disbursements are made (in many countries, between 40 and 70 percent of all expenditures).

- The Achilles' heel of the current system, and of the vast majority of recent legal reforms, is the failure to provide effective enforcement mechanisms and an efficient system of sanctions. In many cases, these mechanisms usually end up just performing autopsies on illicit acts that have already been committed. In other words, they operate in ex post facto and ineffectual fashion vis-à-vis the results of the electoral process in question.

- Finally, the media as well as civil society has been playing a progressive, encouraging (albeit incipient) role in surveillance and monitoring of the origin and use of the resources managed by political parties.

In short, there is an uneven trend in Latin America toward achieving the following six main objectives:

1. Reducing the influence of money by diminishing its impact and controlling the factors that trigger the rapid rise of electoral expenditures;
2. Promoting fairer conditions for electoral competition;
3. Making wiser use of public money by investing in activities that are more productive for democracy and that contribute to strengthening political parties;
4. Promoting greater transparency and improved accountability in relation to both the origin and the use of public and private funds;
5. Strengthening mechanisms of control and oversight as well as the independence, efficacy and professional performance of enforcement agencies; and
6. Toughening current systems of sanctions.

During the period of this study, substantial progress has been made in reforming the process of political financing in the region. Despite these gains, much remains to be done. Consequently, this is a continually developing, dynamic issue and, as such, is likely to require a succession of sequential legal reforms adapted to the specific needs of the respective countries at any given moment. It is no wonder that in Germany, where this issue has been dealt with repeatedly over the past 40 years, political financing has been called the "never-ending legislation."

Despite the important influence that the internal democratization of parties and the reform of campaign and party financing can exert on the quality of democratic governance, it is indispensable to keep in mind that such changes are not sufficient by themselves. These reforms will be ineffective unless the political process as well is also changed; that is, the attitudes, values and behavior of politicians also need to change. In fact, democratization of political parties and the transparency and ethics of political financing depend on both the behavior of leaders and the active scrutiny of citizens, civil society organizations and the media.

Bibliography

Bendel, Petra. 2000. Los partidos políticos: condiciones de inscripción y reconocimiento legal, democracia interna, etc. In Dieter Nohlen, Sonia Picado and Daniel Zovatto (eds.), *Tratado de derecho electoral comparado de América Latina*. Mexico City: Fondo de Cultura Económica.

De La Calle, Humberto. 2001. La perspectiva desde los partidos políticos. El caso de Latinoamérica. Report presented to the first special session of the Congreso sobre Dinero y Política. December.

Freidenberg, Flavia, and Francisco López Sánchez. 2001. Partidos y métodos de selección de candidatos en América Latina: una discusión sobre reglas y prácticas. Paper presented at the XXIII International Meeting of the Latin American Studies Association, Washington, DC, 6–8 September.

González-Varas, Santiago. 1995. *La financiación de los partidos políticos*. Dyckinson.

Navas, Xiomara. 1998. La financiación electoral: Subvenciones y gastos. In Dieter Nohlen, Sonia Picado, and Daniel Zovatto (eds.), *Tratado de derecho electoral comparado de América Latina*. Mexico City: Fondo de Cultura Económica.

Njaim, Humberto. 2000. La financiación de la política. In *Diccionario Electoral*, Second Edition. San José, Costa Rica: IIDH/CAPEL.

Zovatto, Daniel. 1998. La financiación política en Iberoamérica: una visión preliminar comparada. In Daniel Zovatto and Pilar del Castillo (eds.), *La financiación de la política en Iberoamérica*. San José, Costa Rica: IIDH/CAPEL.

Appendix 7.1. Acronyms of Political Parties in Latin America

Argentina

FREPASO	Frente del País Solidario
PJ	P. Justicialista
UCR	Unión Cívica Radical

Bolivia

ADN	Alianza Democrática Nacionalista
MIR	Mov. de Izquierda Revolucionaria
MNR	Mov. Nacionalista Revolucionario
UCS	Unión Cívica Solidaridad

Brazil

PDT	P. Democrático Trabalhista
PMDB	P. Movimento Democrático Brasileiro
PSDB	P. de Social Democracia Brasileira
PT	P. dos Trabalhadores
PFL	P. de Frente Liberal

Chile

PDC	P. de la Democracia Cristiana
PPD	P. por la Democracia
PS	P. Socialista
RN	Renovación Nacional
UDI	Unión Demócrata Independiente

Colombia

PC	P. Conservador
PL	P. Liberal

Costa Rica

PLN	P. Liberación Nacional
PUSC	P. Unidad Social Cristiana

Dominican Rep.

PLD	P. de Liberación Dominicano
PRD	P. Revolucionario Democrático
PRSC	P. Rev. Social Cristiano

Ecuador

DP	Democracia Popular
ID	Izquierda Democrática
PRE	P. Roldosista Ecuatoriano
PSC	P. Social Cristiano

El Salvador

ARENA	Alianza Republicana Nacionalista
FMLN	Frente Farabundo Martí para la Liberación Nacional

Guatemala

FRG	Frente Republicano Guatemalteco
PAN	P. de Avanzada Nacional

Honduras

PL	P. Liberal de Honduras
PN	P. Nacional de Honduras

Mexico

PAN	P. de Acción Nacional
PRI	P. Revolucionario Institucional
PRD	P. Revolucionario Democrático

Nicaragua

FSLN	Frente Sandinista de Liberación Nacional
PLC	P. Liberal Constitucionalista

Paraguay

ANR	Asociación Nacional Republicana
PLRA	P. Liberal Radical Auténtico

Panama

PA	P. Arnulfista
PRD	P. Revolucionario Democrático

Peru

PAP	P. Aprista Peruano

Uruguay

FA	Frente Amplio
PC	P. Colorado
PN	P. Nacional

Venezuela

AD	Acción Democrática
COPEI	Comité de Org. Político Electoral
MAS	Movimiento al Socialismo
MVR	Movimiento V República
PPT	Patria Para Todos
PV	Proyecto Venezuela

Balancing Executive and Legislative Prerogatives: The Role of Constitutional and Party-based Factors

At the onset of the "third wave" of democratization in Latin America, a debate over the fundamental structure of the political regime hung over the political landscape. Diverse academic studies asserted that among the reasons for the previous collapse of Latin American democracies in the 1960s and 1970s were the inherent deficiencies of presidentialism,[1] the form of democracy of all 18 Latin American countries in this study. This conclusion was shared by a narrow band of scholars and political elites in some countries of the region, who argued that a "second transition" to a parliamentary system of government was necessary if the new and restored Latin American democracies were to survive.

Pessimism about the viability of presidentialism was rooted in three broad concerns (Shugart and Mainwaring, 1997). The first concern was that the separate election of the president and the legislature (and consequent "dual legitimacy") often results in political stalemate. Especially in the case of relatively fragmented party systems, it is common for the president's party to lack a majority in the legislature. This outcome is even more likely if there are bicameral legislatures, whose lower and upper houses often elect members through different rules, out of different geographical constituencies, and at different moments in time. In the context of presidentialism, governing can be quite difficult when the president's party lacks a majority, since opposition parties have relatively weak incentives to cooperate. Opposition parties are not disposed to helping the executive given that they are unlikely to receive much of the credit for policy successes, while they are likely to absorb a good share of the blame for policy failures. At the same time, refusing to support the government does not jeopardize legislators' tenure in office as it might in a parliamentary system. As a consequence, presidents may even face difficulty in rallying support from members of their own party.

---

[1] See Linz (1978 and 1990); Valenzuela (1994); Di Palma (1990); Suárez (1982); Mainwaring (1990 and 1993).

The second concern about presidentialism was that the fixed terms of office of the president and legislators can contribute to instability, since this means that the system can be politically paralyzed for an intolerable period or stuck with an incompetent or unpopular president. The very stability of the constitutional order could be threatened by various scenarios, including the objectives of extending the term of office of a successful and admired president, overcoming political paralysis, or ousting a lame duck and ineffective president. By contrast, parliamentary systems are viewed to be more flexible, since unpopular governments can be removed by votes of no confidence, while popular and effective ones can be reaffirmed and strengthened through the calling of new elections.

Finally, critics lambaste the winner-take-all nature of presidential elections. Though presidents rarely are elected with the support of more than a bare majority of the electorate (and often considerably less), they gain sole possession of the most prestigious and powerful single political office for a defined period of time. Their direct popular election from a national constituency is nevertheless likely to give them a sense of broader legitimacy and dissuade them from engaging in the painstaking and degrading task of negotiation and coalition-building with the opposition (Linz, 1994). By contrast, the norm in European parliamentary systems is coalition government founded on the support of two or more parties, which together represent a majority or more of the electorate.

More balanced political observers, however, pointed out that presidential regimes also have several advantages, and parliamentary systems are not without their own flaws (Shugart and Carey, 1992; Nohlen and Fernández, 1991; Mainwaring and Shugart, 1997). First, presidential regimes provide voters with more electoral choices, allowing them to choose a head of government and representatives who can more closely reflect their specific preferences.

Second, presidential regimes provide citizens with a more direct mechanism to hold the government accountable and to indicate their preferences in terms of government policy. While in multi-party parliamentary contexts citizens often cannot know the implications of their vote for the partisan composition of government, in presidential systems they can reward or punish the incumbent president and governing party with their votes and directly signal a preference for a given governing agenda.

Third, presidential regimes give legislators more freedom to debate alternative policy options, since opposition to the government does not endanger the survival of the government or risk the calling of new elections. Open debate in the legislature can promote the building of a broader consensus behind laws, avoid the enactment of poorly considered legislation, permit constituent-centered political representation, and enhance oversight of the executive branch. But the cost of the checks and balances revered by the founding fathers of the United States is the potential for the very type of political stalemate derided by critics of presidentialism.

The fourth argument in favor of presidential systems is that the fixed terms of presidents may provide more stability than parliamentary systems, in which it may be difficult at times to sustain viable coalition governments. The possibility in parliamentary systems of recomposing the government or calling new elections is a potentially beneficial escape valve that allows a way out of a crisis or stalemate short of a coup. But if in the context of weak, fragmented or polarized party systems it is difficult to sustain a viable coalition government, then the consequence could be a high level of cabinet instability, which would impair government performance and possibly destabilize the political system.

Finally, presidentialism can be viewed as no more disposed to encouraging winner-take-all attitudes than parliamentary systems. The balance of power design of presidentialism should impede the possibility that the winner of the presidential election, in fact, assumes all power. By contrast, in parliamentary systems with single party majorities, it is more likely for the winner of the election to assume a dominant status with few restraints on the exercise of public authority.

Thus, in the abstract realm of ideas, it is difficult to sustain the notion that parliamentary systems are in some way unequivocally superior. Parliamentarism also failed in practice to gain enough support among elites and the broader populations of Latin American countries to be chosen as a system of government. Despite the sympathy among certain elite elements for parliamentary government, only in a couple of countries were proposals to change the design of the democratic regime seriously considered by politicians and the broader public. In each of these cases, parliamentarism was rejected. Given that a massive shift of political regimes in the region is highly unlikely, attention has focused on considering the impact that more specific types of political institutional reforms can have on the performance of democratic systems (Mainwaring and Shugart, 1997; Shugart and Carey, 1992; Nohlen and Fernández, 1991; Chasquetti, 2001; Lanzaro, 2001).

The efficiency and stability of presidential democracies is greatly influenced by the manner in which the inherent tension between the executive and the legislature is resolved. This tension is muted in the case of parliamentary systems since the government is elected by the legislature and must maintain its confidence. If the governing cabinet loses the support of the legislature, either the partisan composition of the cabinet is reshuffled or the parliament is dissolved and new elections are held. But given the separate election of the executive and legislature—usually through different electoral procedures and out of different constituencies (and sometimes at distinct moments in time)—and (consequently) their separate bases of legitimacy, conflict between the two branches is more out in the open and pervasive in presidential systems.

Two caricatures of executive-legislative relations in Latin America are common in academic studies. In the first, the executive is perceived as the dominant actor, with the legislature serving as little more than a rubber stamp on the president's policy agenda. If the legislature balks at any presidential proposals, then the president resorts to decree and other powers to railroad them through. From this perspective, the legislature is also weak in monitoring and controlling the activities of the executive administration, which opens the way for corruption and the mismanagement of public funds.

The second caricature is of an executive lacking in partisan support whose plans are constantly thwarted by an obstructionist congress. The president alleviates or overcomes this situation only by abusing his decree and emergency powers or by dispensing large amounts of patronage to the constituencies of wavering legislators, concessions on legislation, or by outright bribes. Sometimes the onset of severe crisis is what is needed for the congress to finally cede its veto power over the president's agenda.

Even if these caricatures are taken to have some validity, they are at least partially contradictory. Is the primary difficulty in the operation of presidentialism in Latin America one of legislative gridlock or one of executive domination and submission by the legislature? Or can both of these imbalances be seen at different places and moments in the countries of the region?

There is one common feature of these stereotypes: the relative lack of a capacity for (positive) collective action by the legislature in the law-making and oversight process. The legislature is portrayed in both caricatures as an agent that mainly reacts to the initiatives and agendas of the executive, rather than one that also directs and steers the legislative process or engineers an oversight process. The relative weakness of legislatures in acting collectively in pursuit of policy goals or in carrying out oversight responsibilities, if true, could be due to a number of different factors. These include the fragmented character of the party and broader representation system (multiple parties or regionalization of representation), the nature of electoral system incentives (see Chapter Five), the institutional weakness of political parties (see Chapter Six), the alignment of partisan political forces, constitutional powers of presidents, the weak institutional capacity of legislatures, or cultural traditions. Given the incentives flowing from these and other sources, legislators may find it more rewarding to orient themselves toward the delivery of goods to their constituents or to court the favor of party leaders than to pursue broader national policy goals.[2]

To the extent that congress refrains from positive engagement in national policy matters, it might be responsible for the particular difficulties encountered in the event that the opposition party or parties control the congress. It also may account for the failure of congress to develop a capacity for effective oversight of the executive branch. If congress is accustomed to merely reacting to the president's initiative, then a non-majority situation for the president is more likely to result in gridlock. But if congress traditionally has a more proactive role, then policy stalemate in such circumstances might be alleviated by shifting the responsibility for pushing forward a legislative agenda to the congress.

These caricatures are obviously too simplistic to capture the full reality of the dynamic between executives and legislatures in Latin America. There is a tremendous diversity in the political makeup and social and cultural contexts in the 18 countries considered in this study. Certainly there is also a great range in the assertiveness of Latin American congresses in amending or blocking executive proposals, initiating legislation and overseeing the execution of government programs (Cox and Morgenstern, 1998; Morgenstern and Nacif, 2002).

Besides, generalizations about Latin American legislatures have typically been based on casual observation rather than in-depth studies of specific countries. Actions of legislators in modifying or lobbying for executive proposals are usually not in plain view. This is especially the case in those systems where roll call votes are normally not published and debates are not recorded—a matter that itself is likely to undermine the representative function of the congress and the disposition of legislators to concern themselves with their record on policy issues. But even when the proceedings and votes are fully on the public record, the true role of congress is obscured by the fact that much of the deal making be-

---

[2] See Shugart (1999) and Carey and Shugart (1995) for a discussion of the role of the electoral system in influencing legislators to focus on national policy matters.

tween the executive and legislators (particularly those in the governing party or coalition) typically takes place behind closed doors. Thus, in some cases the real influence of legislators may be greater than what is seen on the surface.

Types of Presidential Powers

This chapter does not aim to substantiate any particular assessment of the state of executive-legislative relations in Latin America or any other region. Instead, it will concentrate on comparing the countries of the region in terms of two sets of factors that would be expected to exert a direct influence on the nature of the relations between the executive and the legislature: 1) the nature of the president's *constitutional powers*; and 2) the degree of partisan support for the president in the congress, that is, *partisan powers*.[3]

Both of these types of powers influence the extent to which a president is able to mold policy. The former powers are built into the formal design of the presidential system embodied in the constitution, and change only as a consequence of explicit reforms of constitutional norms or related laws. The president's constitutional powers can be divided into two sets—one that relates to the president's direct powers with respect to the lawmaking process (*legislative powers*), and another that relates to the president's powers to form the cabinet and appoint other governmental officials (*non-legislative powers*). Among the president's legislative powers are the power to veto bills approved by the congress, enact legislation by decree, take exclusive initiative in some policy matters, convoke referenda or plebiscites, and shape the budget law. Non-legislative powers include both powers possessed by the president as well as those powers that the congress does not explicitly control. They include the powers to exclusively appoint and dismiss members of the cabinet, and the lack of a prerogative of the congress to censure or remove cabinet ministers.

By contrast, partisan powers are derived from many different factors, some institutional (such as electoral laws and the structure of the party system), and some circumstantial (such as the outcomes of elections and the quality of presidential leadership), and thus vary over time. Partisan powers refer to the party backing that the president can count on in the congress. They depend on both the share of the seats controlled by the president's party or party coalition in the congress and the extent to which parties are disciplined—that is, the extent to which legislators tend to vote in a bloc and as instructed by the party leadership.

Neither the president's constitutional or partisan powers unto themselves are sufficient to account for the degree to which the president is able to put his or her own stamp on policy or the overall dynamic of executive-legislative relations. A president who is endowed with strong constitutional powers may nonetheless be weak in the face of a highly frag-

---

[3] These powers are delineated and assessed for Latin American countries in Shugart and Carey (1992). The categories and scoring criteria for the powers set forth by these authors are the starting point for those followed in this chapter. The assessments for some countries were based partly on this book as well as on Shugart and Mainwaring (1997). But our own research and the information provided by country experts was used to check this information, extend it to a larger set of countries, and update it to the end of 2000. Some departures from the approach of Shugart and Carey were made with respect to the conceptualization of the powers examined and the method of scoring them.

mented party system and an unreliable base of support in the congress. Similarly, a president with fairly weak constitutional powers may appear to dominate the policymaking process if his or her party controls a majority of the seats in congress and is highly disciplined (Samuels, 2000).

Even these two broad types of power may be insufficient for understanding the real nature of the relations between the executive and legislative branches, since formal constitutional rules may not in fact be followed (and in many instances are ambiguous), and since informal and cultural norms also exert considerable influence. Thus, the cross-national examination presented in this chapter is inevitably incomplete. Nonetheless, given the importance of constitutional and partisan powers of presidents to the operation of presidential systems, examining them is a valuable starting point for promoting better understanding and for educating would-be reformers.

Presidential Powers and Democratic Governability

The concept of democratic governability entails the capacity to make and implement decisions that respond adequately to a country's pressing social and economic problems. But the definition also requires that the decisions taken be democratically legitimate and sustainable; that is, adopted on the basis of an open participatory process. In addition, the government should carry out its duties efficiently and in a manner that upholds the broader public interest.

Thus, one aspect of democratic governability is policy efficiency: the capacity to adopt policy changes directed at improving social and economic conditions. But this is not sufficient, since additional essential requirements of democratic government are that the decisions respond to public preferences and interests (individually and as organized groups) and that the government executes the law and implements policies efficiently, fairly and honestly.

Gauging the optimal balance in a president's constitutional and partisan powers for democratic governability is, therefore, a complex matter. If the goal were merely policymaking efficiency, then a presidency endowed with a large amount of both types of powers would appear to be desirable. But when presidents are dominant over the congress, then there is a greater risk that decisions will be adopted that do not reflect the interests and demands of the majority of citizens (and thus will not be legitimate and sustainable), that laws and policies will not be executed fairly and efficiently, and that public funds will be mismanaged or directed to private ends.

Thus, it seems to be desirable for the functioning of presidential democracy that legislatures share power with the executive in making laws and develop the capacity to regularly oversee the implementation of government programs and the enforcement of regulations. In order for the congress to play such a role, it is necessary for individual legislators to have adequate freedom from the party hierarchy to be accountable and responsive to their constituencies and to be able to engage in real debates over policy. At the same time, the incentives emanating from the institutional environment (electoral system, party system, constitutional rules) should encourage legislators to concern themselves with national policy matters rather than merely focusing on the delivery of particularistic goods and services to constituents (Carey and Shugart; Shugart, 1999; Shugart, et al., 2000). Aside from these incentives facing individual legislators, the system of parties represented in the legislature cannot be so fragmented that the congress as a whole is unable to take collective action.[4] In order to avoid gridlock, however, the president needs to have sufficient formal power and partisan support in the congress to play a proactive role in moving the policy process forward.

Moving beyond this simple dichotomy of strong and weak presidents complicates the picture further. How much of each type of power should presidents have if democracy is to perform well and become consolidated? The next section describes in more detail each type of presidential power. By assigning numerical scores along each dimension of power, the powers of presidents in the region are compared. The subsequent section examines the variations across the region in the degree of partisan support in the congress that presidents typically enjoy. Given the importance of other contextual factors, however, the full implications of constitutional and partisan powers for the nature of executive-legislative relations and democratic governability cannot be determined without more careful studies of individual cases.

Legislative Powers of Presidents

This section describes the types of legislative powers of Latin American presidents and the criteria for scoring them. Table 8.1 summarizes the criteria used for assigning scores.

Package Veto/Override

The package veto/override is the power of the president to block the enactment of a law approved by the congress to which he objects. This and the partial veto power described next are the only formal means a president has to directly influence the legislative output of the congress. Formally, in most presidential systems, it is the congress that is responsible for enacting all of the laws of the country. In most cases this veto power is not absolute, since the congress is given the power to persist in the passage of the legislation.

The veto power is weak when the congress can override with the votes of only a simple or absolute majority. When only a simple majority is required, the veto may delay implementation of legislation, but the president is relatively defenseless in curbing the actions of a congress determined to adopt policy changes. Given that a significant number of legislators are typically absent or abstain from voting, it is more difficult to obtain an absolute majority (50 percent plus one of the total membership of the legislative body) to overturn a veto. The veto power is stronger when the votes of a qualified majority, such as two-thirds of the members, are needed to override. A veto power in which a larger majority is required for override or one that is absolute (no override) would make the president very powerful,

---

[4] For a more extensive discussion of these tradeoffs see Shugart (1999), Carey and Shugart (1995) and Shugart and Wattenberg (2001).

since this would most likely prevent the legislature from taking any action with which the chief executive disagrees.

The veto power allows presidents to protect the status quo against efforts of the legislature to change it. But this power is not so useful when the president himself wants to bring about policy changes (Shugart and Mainwaring, 1997).

The strongest veto powers in the region are found in Ecuador, where the congress cannot override and the vetoed legislation cannot be brought up again until the following year. Veto powers are also relatively strong in the Dominican Republic, El Salvador, Guatemala and Panama, where two-thirds of the full membership of the congress is needed to override. Slightly weaker but still strong veto powers are found in Argentina, Bolivia, Chile and Mexico, where a vote of two-thirds of the present members is required to override. In Uruguay, a slightly lower threshold of three-fifths of the present members is required to override. In the remaining eight cases (Costa Rica, Colombia, Uruguay, Peru, Paraguay, Brazil, Nicaragua and Venezuela), the veto power is weaker because the vote of only an absolute majority of the membership or present members is required to override the presidential veto.

Partial (Item) Veto

This is the power of the president to veto particular provisions of an approved bill to which he objects. When the partial veto power is fully in place, the effect of the president's action is the promulgation of the non-objected portion of the bill, unless the congress insists on its original version with the majority required in the constitution. Many of the Latin American constitutions specify the possibility of a president objecting to the whole bill or part of the bill. But a partial veto power in our definition does not exist unless the implication of the partial objection by the president is that the remainder of the bill is automatically promulgated absent a congressional vote insisting on the enactment of the version it originally approved (Shugart and Carey, 1992).

Though the power of partial promulgation is not explicitly provided in many of the constitutions, numerous presidents have asserted this right and courts in some instances have accepted its validity. Thus, in the scoring for this power, a partial veto will be considered to exist when the power of partial promulgation exists either explicitly in the constitution, or when the practice has occurred without legal contest or been sanctioned explicitly by the courts. Similar to the package veto, the range in the score (0 to 4) will depend on the proportion of the legislative seats required to override.

Like the package veto, the partial veto is still a power that presidents can use to block undesired changes in the status quo. But it also engages the president more closely in the lawmaking process, since it allows him to interject his views into the details of the legislation and influence its final form, rather than merely to submit a broad yes or no opinion.

The capability to object to portions of bills approved by the congress is present in all of the countries except Bolivia, Costa Rica, El Salvador, Guatemala, Honduras and Mexico. In most countries the threshold required for overriding the partial veto is the same as that for the package veto.

Decree and Agenda-Controlling Powers

A few constitutions in Latin America provide presidents with the power to directly make laws by issuing decrees, thus circumventing the congress altogether. In this case, the president participates directly in the process of lawmaking and in altering the status quo. But it is rare for presidents to be provided a decree power without limits. Sometimes the restriction is with respect to the policy areas to which the power can be applied, and in others the power only becomes effective in particularly traumatic circumstances in the life of the nation.

It is important to not confuse the power to issue decrees of a regulatory or administrative nature with the power to legislate by decree. Most presidents do enjoy the former power, as does the U.S. president, who commonly issues executive orders. Nevertheless, the scope of this regulatory power does vary substantially, with the president in some cases being given ample latitude to interpret the intentions of the legislature in its execution of the law (Carey and Shugart, 1998; Mainwaring and Shugart, 1997; Shugart and Carey, 1992).

In addition, some constitutions explicitly permit the congress to delegate the power to legislate by decree to the president. In some cases constitutions do not address the issue, but decree powers have been delegated in practice and not successfully challenged in court. Regardless, the delegation of decree power cannot be considered on par with a constitutionally embedded power to legislate by decree. Delegated powers are temporarily issued by a congressional majority and can be carefully circumscribed. The same majority can also rescind the powers. Thus, delegated powers cannot be used to enact a package of legislation contrary to the wishes of the majority in congress (Carey and Shugart, 1998). This does not necessarily mean, however, that a legislative majority could be assembled to enact the individual measures that may be implemented through the delegated decree power. One out of four points is awarded when constitutions explicitly permit the delegation of legislative powers, since such a provision still facilitates presidents greatly in putting their own stamp on policy.

In several countries, the president is granted the power to legislate by decree on particular matters in the event of exceptional circumstances or a state of emergency. Given the ambiguity inherent in interpreting what constitutes an emergency situation, such a provision potentially opens the door to a fairly extensive form of decree power. This depends in part on whether there is an independent body, such as a constitutional court, that is given the responsibility of determining whether the use of the decree power is valid. Thus, the power to issue decrees in emergency situations is scored as greater than zero, with the actual number depending upon the scope of the power (the scope of the policy areas to which it applies) and the legal limitations that may exist on its utilization.

Aside from the explicit right to legislate by decree, constitutions in some countries permit the president to declare a bill as "urgent," thus requiring congress to act on it within a specified time period. If congress does not act within the required time period, the bill automatically becomes law. This power, therefore, still gives the congress an opportunity to reject the president's proposal before it becomes law. Nonetheless, it is an important power, since practical and procedural barriers as well as problems of coordination may give the president the upper hand vis-à-vis the congress. If the president issues a series of such "urgent" measures, it would be even more difficult for congress to coordinate against particular bills. Thus, the power gives the president great capacity to shape the legislative agenda.

Some form of explicit capability to legislate by decree or otherwise control the legislative agenda is present in Argentina, Brazil, Chile, Colombia, Ecuador, Guatemala, Honduras, Peru and Uruguay. In Brazil, the 1988 constitution provides the president with the power to issue "provisional measures" in times of "relevance and urgency" that expire if they are not converted into law in 30 days. But the condition of "emergency" has not in practice prevented this power from being used in all circumstances for many different types of bills. Since the measures can be reissued before their expiration, in effect they provide an important lawmaking power for the president (Mainwaring, 1997). In Colombia, aside from an extensive power to administer the law, the president can acquire substantial lawmaking power by declaring a state of "internal commotion" or "economic emergency." The former can be declared for a period of 90 days but can be renewed once freely, and then again with the consent of the senate. The Constitutional Court may revoke decrees issued under a state of internal commotion if they violate constitutional guarantees, and the congress may revoke or amend them at any time. Under states of economic emergency, the president can issue decrees that remain in force even when the special situation expires. In practice, presidents have been able to declare such states of exception with little justification (Archer and Shugart, 1997).

The power is more restricted in Argentina, Guatemala and Honduras, where it is only supposed to be used in "exceptional" or "emergency" circumstances. Decree authority in Argentina, Guatemala, Honduras and Chile is restricted also in terms of the areas of law to which it can be applied, a limitation that is particularly constraining in Chile. Before the 1995 constitutional reform, the president in Nicaragua could adopt laws related to spending and taxation by decree, but now such powers are restricted in principle to administrative matters.[5] This reform also took away the possibility that congress could delegate decree powers to the president.

In Ecuador and Uruguay, there is not a decree power but a capability of the executive to declare items of legislation "urgent," in which case the congress must act within a certain time period or the legislation becomes law. The adoption of the 1998 constitution in Ecuador changed the time period that congress was allowed to explicitly reject the bill in order to prevent it from becoming law from 15 to 30 days. There are no restrictions on the number of bills that the executive can term "urgent." In Uruguay, the legislature has 45 days to take action on the bill and it does not have to explicitly vote it down to prevent it from becoming law. In addition, only one piece of legislation can be designated as "urgent" at a time. Along with the power to issue "provisional measures," the president in Brazil can declare matters "urgent" with the same effect as in the case of Uruguay.

---

[5] In practice, decrees have been objected to by legislators or leaders of opposition parties on occasion on the basis that they went beyond "administrative" matters related to taxation. Some have been overturned by the legislature on such grounds.

In Chile, Colombia, Mexico, Panama, Peru and Venezuela, the constitutions explicitly authorize the delegation by the legislature of decree powers to the president.

In Bolivia, Costa Rica, the Dominican Republic, El Salvador, Guatemala, Nicaragua and Paraguay, presidents do not enjoy any form of legislative decree authority, though constitutions may permit decrees to be issued for "administrative" purposes. In Panama, Mexico and Venezuela, presidents only possess decree powers if the congress delegates them.

Exclusive Initiative

Exclusive initiative relates to cases in which the constitution gives the president the exclusive right to introduce legislation in specific policy areas. It is very common in the region for the president to have the exclusive right to introduce the budget law as well as international treaty agreements and trade tariff legislation. Therefore, when such authority exists the case is still scored as "0" for this power. But when the exclusive initiative extends into other areas of policy, such as public employment, defense appropriations, and auxiliary public spending, a score between 1 and 4 is given depending upon the extensiveness of the areas subject to this provision.

Like the veto, this power enables the president to prevent congress from changing the status quo in the particular policy areas to which it applies. A president who wants to keep an opposition congress from making changes in a given area can just refrain from introducing legislation. But this power is not very effective if the president wants to change the existing policy situation, since the congress theoretically can modify any proposal as it wishes. In some cases, however, the congress is restricted in its ability to modify the budget, a matter taken up in the next section.

Exclusive initiative powers are fairly extensive in Brazil, Chile and Colombia. They extend beyond budget law and trade matters in Bolivia, Ecuador, Panama, Peru and Uruguay.

Budgetary Powers—The Power to Define

Given the importance of budget law to the working of government and to defining the nature of executive-legislative relations, presidential powers in this area are considered as a separate item. In contrast with the U. S. Congress, many Latin American legislatures are restricted in how they can modify the budget law proposed by the executive.[6] In several systems—including Brazil, Chile, Colombia, Ecuador, El Salvador and Peru since 1993—congress is not authorized to increase the amounts allocated to items in the budget submitted by the president and also cannot increase the overall level of spending.

Congress is somewhat freer to modify the budget when it is explicitly allowed to switch spending between different items, though the overall level of spending cannot be raised. This is the case in Nicaragua, Panama, Uruguay and Venezuela. A somewhat greater capacity is provided when congress can increase spending, as long as it also provides for new rev-

---

[6] Formally in the United States, the congress is exclusively responsible for initiating and enacting the budget bill, as with all other pieces of legislation. All bills, including the budget, must originate in the congress. In practice, however, representatives from the president's party submit the executive budget proposal, which serves at least as a foundation for initial discussion. Any other legislator is also free to propose an alternative budget.

enue sources to cover the expenses. This is the case in Costa Rica and the Dominican Republic, although in the latter such modifications require the vote of two-thirds of each chamber of congress.

The president is weakest with respect to the budget when the congress can modify the budget without restrictions. Argentina, Bolivia, Guatemala, Honduras, Mexico and Paraguay give congress free reign to amend the budget law. In Mexico, however, the congress cannot create new expenditures after the budget law is enacted.

Another factor that affects the president's leverage in terms of the budget is what happens if congress does not approve a budget by the required deadline or before the start of the fiscal year. In some cases, the executive's proposal automatically becomes law. This is the case in Bolivia, Chile, Colombia, Ecuador, Panama and Peru. Under this arrangement, the president can win if his legislative supporters merely succeed in postponing debate or preventing a budget in amended form from obtaining a majority. In Argentina, the Dominican Republic, El Salvador, Guatemala, Paraguay, Uruguay and Venezuela, the budget of the previous year remains in effect for the whole fiscal year or until a new budget can be approved. In the remaining cases, there is no provision for such an eventuality. The implication is that a new bill must be approved for the work of government to continue. Otherwise, stopgap measures must be adopted.

Convoking a Referendum or Plebiscite

The power to convoke a referendum or plebiscite enables the president to put up to the vote of citizens general matters of policy or particular laws, generally after they have been rejected by the congress. It is part of a larger group of direct democracy instruments that will be considered in Chapter Ten. If fairly unrestricted in its applicability, the power to convoke a referendum or plebiscite can be an important tool for presidents to apply pressure on legislators to go along with their policy proposals and to reaffirm their popular mandate and legitimacy (Shugart and Carey, 1992). In the case that this power is unrestricted, it would be scored a "4." This power is most extensive in Peru, since the congress there does not share it. If congress also has the power to call a plebiscite or referendum, as in Ecuador, Guatemala, Nicaragua and Venezuela, the power is scored "2." The symmetric power of the congress gives it the potential to avoid a presidential veto or to pressure the president to refrain from applying the veto power. If the president can convoke a plebiscite or referendum but it is non-binding, as in the case of Argentina, it is scored "1." When the president cannot convoke such a vote, the case is scored "0."

Non-Legislative Powers of Presidents

This section describes the non-legislative powers of Latin American presidents and the criteria for scoring them. Table 8.2 summarizes the criteria used for assigning scores.

The central feature of presidential systems is the separate origin and tenure of the executive relative to the legislature. Unlike in parliamentary systems, the president is separately elected by the people and appoints and dismisses cabinet ministers. These ministers

Table 8.1. Legislative Powers of the President

Package veto
4   Veto with no override.
3   Veto with override requiring majority greater than two-thirds of the quorum.
2   Veto with override requiring two-thirds vote of members present.
1   Veto with override requiring absolute majority of assembly membership or extraordinary majority less than two-thirds.
0   No veto, or veto requiring only simple majority for override.

Partial veto
4   Veto with no override.
3   Veto with override requiring majority greater than two-thirds of the quorum.
2   Veto with override requiring two-thirds of the quorum.
1   Veto with override requiring absolute majority of assembly membership.
0   No partial veto, or veto requiring only simple majority of those present for override.

Decree power
4   The president has broad decree powers (not just those delegated by congress), they cannot easily be rescinded by congress, and they can have long-term effects.
2   The president has power to issue non-delegated decrees, but decrees are in force for a limited time or can be rescinded by congress and/or can only be issued in severe emergencies.
1   Constitution expressly states that congress can delegate legislative powers to the president and restricted decree authority (exceptional circumstances/some areas of law).
0   The president lacks decree powers and the constitution either forbids or does not address delegation of decree authority from the congress to the president.

Exclusive initiative
3   Broad areas of exclusive initiative with limited ability of legislature to amend.
2   Broad areas of exclusive initiative with ability of legislature to amend.
1   Some important areas of exclusive initiative with ability of legislature to amend.
0   Areas of exclusive initiative limited to typical forms: submission of annual budget and international treaties and agreements.

Power to convoke a plebiscite or referendum
4   The president can convoke a referendum with few restrictions (congress cannot).
2   The president has restricted powers to convoke a referendum or congress can also.
1   The president can convoke a referendum but it it is not binding.
0   The president does not have powers to convoke referendum or congress must approve.

Powers to determine spending in budget
4   The president prepares the budget and no amendment by the congress is permitted.
3   The congress cannot change the amount of spending allocated to particular items or increase the total level of spending.
2   The congress can change spending for particular items but cannot increase the overall level of spending.
1   The congress can change the total of spending (without the approval of the executive) but only if it indicates the source of revenues to cover the expenditures or other restrictions such as not increasing the public debt.
0   The congress can modify the budget without limitations.

Default budget if legislature does not act
2   If the congress rejects or does not approve the budget, the budget proposed by the executive automatically becomes law.
1   If the congress rejects or does not approve the budget, the budget of the previous year goes into force.
.5   If the congress rejects or does not approve the budget, the budget of the previous year is applied until the moment that a budget is approved.
0   If the congress rejects or does not approve the budget, then either the executive cannot spend or temporary spending measures must be adopted.

Note: This table is a modified version of Table 8.1 in Shugart and Carey (1992, p. 150).

Table 8.2. Non-Legislative Powers of the President

Cabinet formation

4 President names cabinet without need for confirmation.

3 President names cabinet ministers subject to confirmation by assembly.

2 President names premier, subject to confirmation, who names other ministers.

0 President cannot name ministers except upon recommendation of assembly.

Cabinet dismissal

4 President dismisses cabinet ministers at will.

2 Restricted powers of dismissal.

1 President may dismiss only upon acceptance by assembly of alternative minister or cabinet.

0 Cabinet or ministers may be censured and removed by assembly.

Censure

4 Assembly may not censure or remove cabinet or ministers.

3 Restricted power of censure; few ministers or does not necessarily imply removal.

2 Assembly may censure, but president may respond by dissolving assembly.

1 "Constructive" vote of no confidence; assembly may censure, but president may respond by dissolving assembly.

0 Unrestricted censure.

Note: This table is a modified version of Table 8.1 in Shugart and Carey (1992, p. 150).

usually cannot be members of the legislature while they are serving, and they are appointed and dismissed by the president rather than by the legislature. In the pure presidential system, it is the prerogative of the president to put into governmental positions persons whom he can trust and to dismiss them at his own whim. Given exclusive appointment and dismissal powers, the president is dominant with respect to the cabinet. Exclusive power over the formation and tenure of the cabinet is valuable for securing the president's government against shifting political forces in the congress and provides an instrument for building political coalitions.

But the separation of the two branches is not complete in all cases. Though the Latin American cases are true to form in terms of the president's powers of appointment and dismissal, there are some cases in which congress is authorized to censure and remove cabinet ministers.

Cabinet Formation

The president has exclusive power over cabinet appointments and cabinet dismissal in all countries of the region. Unlike in the United States, Latin American presidents do not have to obtain the "advice and consent" of their legislative bodies in making cabinet appointments. Even in the United States, cabinet appointments are almost always approved, though they may be delayed for quite some time. In the few instances when appointments have been rejected, it was usually on the basis of purported personal character flaws rather than the political views of the nominee, given the broad acceptance of the president's prerogative in forming his cabinet.[7] Thus, all the countries in this study are scored a "4" with respect to cabinet appointment powers. The United States is scored "3," given this need for senate confirmation.

Cabinet Dismissal

In all the Latin American countries as well as the United States, presidents are free to dismiss their cabinet ministers at will, without providing a justification to the congress or obtaining its assent. Therefore, presidents can ensure that the making and execution of policy in all areas conforms to their wishes. Any time there is a deviation in terms of policy, a perception of policy failure, or even a problem related to personal character, the president can remove the minister.

Censure of Cabinet Ministers

An area where there are substantial differences between countries is in the ability of the legislature to take action against cabinet ministers on its own initiative. Censure and removal of ministers is the strongest form of such powers. When this is possible and regularly exercised, the separation of powers ideal of presidentialism is severely undermined. When the cabinet becomes accountable to the congress and dependent on its continued support to remain in office, the regime takes on distinctly parliamentary characteristics. A parliamentary bent is especially pronounced when accompanied by a presidential power to dissolve the congress. The latter power, however, is only present in Peru, Uruguay and Venezuela. In each of these countries, dissolution can only be exercised after a successful motion of censure against one or more governmental officials (cabinet ministers in Peru and Uruguay and the vice president in Venezuela).

The power of censure raises the potential for political stalemate and instability, given the contradiction between the popularly elected president's right to appoint his cabinet and the opposition legislature's right of censure. The legislature can censure a cabinet member because of his or her approach to policy, but then the president can turn around and appoint a replacement with the same views. Clearly, the censure power weakens the president, since it provides a tool the legislature can use to undermine and harass the executive.

---

[7] One possible explanation for the U.S. Senate's deference to the president on cabinet appointments is that this body understands the relative weakness of its position in the appointment process. Even if the senate majority risks its political capital in rejecting a nominee, the president has the prerogative to nominate another who may be equally objectionable on political grounds. And if the senate initially succeeds in gaining the appointment and confirmation of a cabinet secretary who runs the ministry in a manner that is closer to the preferences of the senate majority, the president can still dismiss him (Shugart and Carey, 1992).

In many cases the censure power is restricted, either in the sense that it does not necessarily produce the removal of the government official in question, or that it must be supported by a large congressional majority (two-thirds or three-fifths). Some form of censure power is present in Argentina, Colombia, Ecuador, Guatemala, Panama, Peru, Uruguay and Venezuela.

Under the 1994 Argentine constitution, the congress has the power to censure and remove the chief of the cabinet, but not any of the other cabinet ministers. The motion of censure and the vote to remove require the support of two-thirds of the membership of both houses of congress. Thus far, this power has not been exercised.

Under Colombia's 1991 constitution, each chamber can propose to censure ministers for matters related to their functioning in the position. The motion of censure must be proposed by at least one-tenth of the members of the respective chamber and approved by an absolute majority of the members of each chamber. The consequence of the approval of the motion of censure is the removal of the minister. Thus far, a censure motion has not been approved, given the difficulty of obtaining an absolute majority in both houses of a fairly fragmented congress.

In Ecuador, the 1998 constitution took away the ability of the legislature to oust members of the cabinet. During the 1980s and early 1990s, this weapon was used frequently. Its effect was to seriously undermine the authority of the president and foster a climate of political uncertainty and instability. Under the current constitution, cabinet ministers can be "politically judged" at the request of one-fourth of the members of the congress, but this does not imply their removal from office.

In Guatemala, the 1985 constitution establishes that after a citation of a minister a no confidence vote can be solicited by at least four deputies. The vote must be approved by an absolute majority of the members of congress. The president can accept the dismissal of the minister or can desist on the basis that the act for which the minister was censured is defensible in accordance with the national interest and the policies of the government. But in the latter case, the congress can reaffirm the censure and remove the minister with the vote of two-thirds of the members. The congress can cite and censure as many as four ministers at the same time.

In Panama, the constitution provides that the legislative assembly can censure the cabinet ministers if in its judgment they are responsible for crimes or have committed grave mistakes that have caused serious harm to the nation. The vote of censure must be proposed by at least one-half of the legislators and approved with the vote of two-thirds. Though the constitution does not spell out the effect of the censure, it has been interpreted as implying only a moral sanction, and not the removal of the minister concerned.

In Peru, the 1993 constitution maintained the provision from the previous constitution that the congress can hold the collective cabinet or individual ministers accountable through a censure vote or the rejection of a confidence measure. The censure measure needs to be presented by no less than 25 percent of the members of congress, and its approval requires the vote of an absolute majority of the members. If censured, the cabinet or the minister must resign, but the president is empowered to dissolve the congress if it has censured or declared its lack of confidence in two cabinet ministers or more. The president cannot dissolve the congress in the last year of his or her term or during a state of emergency.

In Uruguay, the 1966 constitution establishes that either chamber of the congress can judge the performance of a cabinet minister by proposing a motion of censure with the support of the majority of those present. The censure can be directed at an individual, more than one minister, or the cabinet as a whole. The censure must be approved by an absolute majority of the members of the full congress. The approval of a motion of censure calls for the resignation of the minister, group of ministers, or the cabinet as a whole. When the censure is approved by less than two-thirds of the members of the general assembly (combined assembly of both houses of congress), the president can refuse to dismiss the minister in question. In this event, the general assembly has to vote again. If less than 60 percent of the legislators uphold the censure, the president can dissolve the congress. The president can dissolve the congress only once during his term, and not during the last year of an assembly's term. In the current democratic period, no cabinet minister has been censured and the matter of dissolution has not come up.

The 1999 Venezuelan constitution provides for removal of a cabinet minister through a motion of censure supported by three-fifths of the deputies present in the national assembly. In addition, with a vote of two-thirds of the national assembly membership, the vice president can be removed from office. If the legislature approves motions of censure three times against a vice president in one presidential term, then the president can dissolve the national assembly, but not in the last year of its term.

Colombia and Peru, where the vote of an absolute majority of the members of congress can remove a minister, are scored "0" in terms of this presidential power (in this case, high powers of congress mean low powers for the president). Given that the support of three-fifths of the present members of congress is needed to approve a motion of censure in Venezuela, this case is scored "1." Guatemala is scored "2," since the removal of a cabinet minister against the president's objections requires the vote of two-thirds of the members of the legislature. Uruguay is scored similarly, given the two-thirds threshold for outright dismissal and the possibility for the congress to be dissolved if this threshold is not reached. Argentina is scored "3.5," given the fact that only the chief of the cabinet can be censured and that approving such a motion requires the support of two-thirds of the members of both houses of congress. Panama and Ecuador are scored "4," since a vote of censure does not entail the removal of the minister from his or her position. All other countries are scored "4" because there is no provision for the censure of cabinet ministers.

Comparing the Constitutional Powers of Presidents in Latin America

Legislative Powers

The constitutional power of presidents varies significantly across the region. Considering all of the formal legislative powers together (Table 8.3), the presidents in Brazil, Chile, Colombia, Ecuador, Panama, and Peru are the most powerful. The weakest presidents overall in formal terms would appear to be those in Mexico, Honduras, Costa Rica and

Table 8.3. Legislative Powers of Latin American Presidents

	Package veto	Partial veto	Decree powers	Exclusive initiative	Convoke referenda/ plebiscite	Budgetary powers Power to define	Budgetary powers Result of no legislative action	Total
Argentina	2	2	1	0	1	0	1	7
Bolivia	2	0	0	1	0	0	2	5
Brazil	1	1	4	2	0	2	1	11
Chile	2	2	1	2	0	3	2	12
Colombia	1	1	2	2	0	3	2	11
Costa Rica	1.5	0	0	0	0	1	0	2.5
Dominican Rep.	2.5	2.5	0	0	0	2	1	8
Ecuador	3	2.5	1	1	2	3	2	14.5
El Salvador	2.5	0	0	0	0	3	1	6.5
Guatemala	2.5	0	1	0	2	0	1	6.5
Honduras	1.5	0	1	0	0	0	0	2.5
Mexico	2	0	.5	0	0	0	0	2.5
Nicaragua	1	1	0	0	2	2	2	8
Panama	2.5	2.5	.5	1	0	2	2	10.5
Paraguay	1	1	0	0	0	0	1	3
Peru	1	1	2	1	3	3	2	13
Uruguay	1	1	.5	1	0	2	1	6.5
Venezuela	0.5	0.5	1	0	2	2	1	7
Average	1.7	1	.9	.6	.7	1.6	1.2	7.6
United States	2	0	0	0	0	0	0	2

Note: The format for this table is based on Table 8.2 (p. 155) in Shugart and Carey (1992). But the scoring criteria and assessments are in many cases different, partly because of reforms that have occurred in the last decade.

Democracies in Development

Paraguay. But it is misleading to simply add up the scores, since the dimensions of power do not have the same impact on the nature and extent of presidential influence.

The powers that are likely to be most important to a president's ability to put his imprint on policy are veto and decree powers. The former, "reactive" powers, shape the president's effectiveness in blocking changes in policy that the congress might choose to enact (Shugart and Mainwaring, 1997). In the United States, the package veto is the only constitutional power a president can use to shape the direction of policy. Thus, formally, the U.S. president on most occasions has the power to prevent undesired changes in the status quo, but does not have the power to positively influence the adoption of legislation he prefers. Through surrogates he can introduce any piece of legislation, but congress decides when and if it will be debated in committee or on the floor and has full freedom to modify the bill, reject it, or introduce an alternative. Therefore, the president depends on more informal and indirect approaches to influencing policy, such as the power of persuasion based on popular legitimacy, the president's leadership role in a major political party, his or her extensive appointment powers, and the information and resource advantage that comes from being the head of the executive branch of government.

In terms of reactive powers, the U.S. president is relatively strong, since the support of two-thirds of the present members of each house of congress is needed to override the package veto. Even so, most Latin American presidents are endowed with reactive powers that exceed those of the U.S. president. In some cases these powers are greater because the package veto power itself is greater. For instance, in the Dominican Republic, El Salvador, Guatemala and Panama, a larger share of congress is needed to override (two-thirds of the membership of each house of congress rather than present members), while in Ecuador a package veto means the matter cannot be taken up until the following year. In other cases, reactive powers are larger because the president can also partially veto legislation and/or has exclusive ability to initiate legislation in certain policy areas. Explicit or de facto partial veto powers are strong in Argentina, Chile, the Dominican Republic, Ecuador, and Panama. Somewhat weaker partial vetoes are present in seven other countries. Considering the powers of exclusive initiative as well overall veto power, the countries where the reactive powers of presidents are greatest are Ecuador, Chile, Panama, the Dominican Republic and Argentina. Reactive powers are weaker in the remaining countries, given that just an absolute majority or a smaller share of the congress is needed to override the president's veto. The weakest reactive powers are in Venezuela, Honduras, Nicaragua and Paraguay.

In contrast with the U.S. president, some Latin American presidents are also endowed with powers that are "proactive" in the sense that they can influence the adoption of policies that represent a change in the status quo. The most important forms of proactive powers are decree powers and the power to control the legislative agenda. By issuing decrees or declaring matters of legislation to be "urgent," the president can engage directly in the law-making process and potentially bypass the congress altogether. Another form of proactive power is to set the level of spending and revenue in the budget, or to set spending priorities without the possibility of interference by the congress. The partial veto itself might also be included as a form of proactive power, since it can be used to influence the smaller details of enacted legislation. Considering decree and budgetary powers, the proactive powers of presidents are greatest in Brazil, Colombia and Peru, with Chile close

Table 8.4. Presidential Powers in Latin American Political Systems

	Strong proactive	Moderate proactive	Weak proactive
Strong reactive		Ecuador Chile Panama Dominican Rep.	
Moderate reactive	Brazil Colombia Peru	Argentina Bolivia El Salvador Guatemala Nicaragua	Mexico Paraguay *United States*
Weak reactive		Venezuela Uruguay	Honduras Costa Rica

behind.[8] Proactive powers are weakest in Bolivia, Honduras, Mexico, Costa Rica, El Salvador, Guatemala and Argentina.

In terms of the proactive and reactive powers of presidents, Latin American political systems can be grouped in categories as shown in Table 8.4. "Strong" presidents are in the upper left-hand quadrant of the table. Ecuador's president comes the closest to being strong in both dimensions, with especially strong veto powers, but with decree powers that are not quite as strong. Presidents in Brazil, Colombia and Peru have strong proactive powers but moderate veto powers. By contrast, presidents in Chile, Panama and the Dominican Republic have strong veto powers but just moderate decree and budgetary powers.

The weakest presidents in constitutional terms are found in Costa Rica and Honduras, which are relatively weak in terms of both proactive and reactive powers. Venezuelan and Uruguayan presidents have fairly weak veto powers but are stronger in terms of their powers to define the budget, and, in the Venezuelan case, to have decree powers delegated to them by the congress. Mexico and Paraguay are similar to the United States in having presidents with relatively strong veto powers but little power to autonomously turn proposals into policy.

Argentina, Bolivia, El Salvador, Guatemala and Nicaragua are intermediate cases in terms of presidential power. The president is endowed with either some decree authority (such as the possibility that congress can delegate such authority) or has some special authority in terms of the budget. Presidents in Argentina, El Salvador and Guatemala also

---

[8] Argentina might also be included in this group, but it depends on how the decree power in the 1994 constitution is regulated and how it is applied in practice. The constitution allows the president to issue decrees of "necessity and urgency" under "exceptional circumstances" in which ordinary legislative procedures are not possible to follow. Such decrees cannot be issued on matters of taxation, penal rules or laws related to elections or political parties. It is still unclear the role that can be played by the Bicameral Permanent Commission in determining the legality of such decrees when they are issued (Jones, 1997).

have stronger veto powers than the chief executive in the United States, but not as much as those categorized in the "strong reactive power" category.

Non-Legislative Powers

As has already been mentioned, there is no significant variation across the region in the powers to appoint and dismiss cabinet ministers. In contrast with the United States, presidents have full discretion in appointing their cabinet ministers. As in the United States, they do not have to consult congress in their decisions to dismiss cabinet ministers. Thus, in terms of appointment and dismissal powers, the Latin American cases conform with the archetypal form of presidentialism in which the "origin" and "survival" of members of the two branches is fully separated.[9] Thus, in Table 8.5 they all receive a score of "4" for each dimension.

Some of the Latin American countries, however, deviate from archetypal presidentialism in giving the congress the power to remove cabinet ministers. This provision potentially could have an important effect on the dynamic of executive-legislative relations, while also setting up the possibility of a tit-for-tat conflict. Though the congress may be able to remove a cabinet minister, the president's exclusive powers of appointment mean that he or she can immediately name a person who might be equally objectionable.

Given the difficulty of obtaining the majorities required for censure or the president's countervailing power to dissolve congress, this power has not been a major factor in most countries.[10] Thus, the semi-presidential or semi-parliamentary features that have been incorporated into some of the constitutions have not been used in practice to a significant extent. The nature of executive-legislative relations would appear to be much more affected by the influence of the legislative powers described in the previous sub-section.

Impeachment of the President

Another institutional dimension relevant to executive-legislative relations is the mechanism for impeachment of the president. In keeping with the structure of a presidential regime, the intention of most constitutions in the region is that impeachment provisions be invoked only if the president is alleged to be guilty of serious common crimes, abuse of authority, or violations of the constitution or the law. In reality, however, legislators and public officials are not easily able "to detach themselves from the broader social and political context in which a presidential crisis takes place. Congress may protect the chief executive by blocking further exposure of a scandal...Or, on the other hand, it may press charges

---

[9] Another matter is the scope of a president's appointment powers. Until fairly recently, the appointment powers of Latin American presidents were vast, since they included the right to name governors, department heads and mayors in some countries, as well as the presidents of numerous public agencies, such as state enterprises and the national bank. With the political decentralization and privatization that has occurred in most countries of the region, the scope of appointment powers has been reduced over the past two decades.

[10] The case of Ecuador is one important exception since the censure and removal of cabinet ministers was common in many of the governments of the period and added to the difficulties of governing in a fragmented political system.

Table 8.5. Non-Legislative Powers of Latin American Presidents

	Cabinet formation	Cabinet dismissal	Censure
Argentina	4	4	3.5
Bolivia	4	4	4
Brazil	4	4	4
Chile	4	4	4
Colombia	4	4	0
Costa Rica	4	4	4
Dominican Rep.	4	4	4
Ecuador	4	4	4
El Salvador	4	4	4
Guatemala	4	4	2
Honduras	4	4	4
Mexico	4	4	4
Nicaragua	4	4	4
Panama	4	4	4
Paraguay	4	4	4
Peru	4	4	0
Uruguay	4	4	2
Venezuela	4	4	1
Average	4	4	3.1
United States	3	4	4

Note: The format for the table is based on Table 8.2 (p. 155) in Shugart and Carey (1992). But the scoring criteria and assessments are in many cases different, partly because of reforms that have occurred in the last decade.

against the president when there is not real proof or public sentiment in favor of impeachment" (Pérez Linan, 2000).

Some constitutions deviate somewhat from pure presidentialism by permitting legislatures to remove the president not just in the case of the commission of serious crimes but for poor performance of duties. Thus, impeachment is a potential mechanism that can be used to get around the inflexibility of presidential regimes, allowing the removal of corrupt or unpopular presidents before their term expires. If overly politicized, however, impeachment can be a source of political instability and aggravate partisan conflict.

There is a great degree of variability within the region in terms of the potential vulnerability of presidents to impeachment. As with the other dimensions, the constitution itself is not definitive, since it can be interpreted and applied in ways that might not have been intended by those writing and enacting the provision.

In Latin America, there are three main models for impeaching the president. They entail different procedures for implementation, depending on the bicameral or unicameral nature of the congress (Table 8.6) (Pérez Linan, 2000).

Democracies in Development

1. *Congressional model.* Unicameral: the legislative assembly acts as the accuser and as the jury. Bicameral: the lower house acts as the accuser and the upper house as the jury.
2. *Dual model.* Depending on the nature of the offense, the senate or the Supreme Court acts as the jury upon accusation by the lower house.
3. *Judicial model.* Unicameral: the legislative assembly acts as the accuser and the Supreme Court acts as the jury. Bicameral: one or both branches of congress make the accusation and the Supreme Court acts as the jury.

In almost all of the cases in which the bicameral congressional model of impeachment is in force, after accusation by the lower house, the senate must vote with a two-thirds majority to convict and remove the president. The only exception is the Dominican Republic, where a three-fourths majority is required for conviction. The unicameral cases are more variable. In Peru, Panama, Guatemala and Honduras, no extraordinary majority is stipulated in the constitution, while in Nicaragua and Ecuador a two-thirds majority is required. The constitutions in Guatemala and Honduras, however, are unclear about the mode of impeachment once the charges are brought by a simple majority in the national assembly.

The Brazilian and Colombian are intermediate cases, since the institutional venue for the trial depends on the nature of the crime. In both countries, common crimes are tried in the Supreme Court, while the abuse of power and failure to perform duties are tried in the senate.

Table 8.6. Models of Impeachment

	Unicameral	Bicameral
Congressional model	Ecuador	Argentina
	Guatemala[1]	Chile
	Honduras[1]	Dominican Republic
	Nicaragua[2]	Mexico
	Panama	Paraguay
	Peru	Uruguay
Dual model		Brazil[3]
		Colombia[4]
Judicial model	Costa Rica	Bolivia
	El Salvador	
	Venezuela[5]	

[1] The unicameral legislature has the power to accuse the president of wrongdoing; however, the constitutions do not explain the means by which presidents are officially impeached.
[2] The national assembly can declare the permanent incapacity of the president with a two-thirds majority.
[3] Trial is in the Supreme Court for common criminal offenses and in the senate for criminal abuse of power
[4] The lower house issues the accusation and the senate allows the trial by suspending the president from office. For common crimes, the trial is directed to the Supreme Court, but in the case of failure to perform public duties, the senate acts as the jury.
[5] Venezuela's process is a little different than other judicial models because the Supreme Court first decides if there is merit for a trial of the president. Then the national assembly must authorize such a trial by a simple majority. If so authorized, the Supreme Court can carry out the trial and make a ruling that could lead to the removal of the president.

Of the four countries where the judicial model is used, only Costa Rica requires an extraordinary majority (two-thirds) to authorize the trial in the court system. In Venezuela, the Supreme Court must first determine if the case has merit before the national assembly can authorize a trial by a simple majority vote. In Bolivia, a simple majority is sufficient to authorize a trial, but a two-thirds majority is necessary in the Supreme Court to convict. In El Salvador, only a simple majority is needed to authorize the trial, which takes place in the Court of Appeals.

In terms of the normal route of impeachment, Peru, Panama, Guatemala and Honduras would appear to be the countries where presidents are most vulnerable. But in Guatemala and Honduras, the process is left somewhat undefined in the constitution. Given the three-fourths majority required both for the accusation in the lower house and for conviction in the upper house, the Dominican Republic would appear to be the case in which the president is most secure.

Constitutions of several countries also have a provision for removal of the president in the event that he becomes physically or mentally incapacitated. The removal of President Abdalá Bucaram in Ecuador in 1997 for alleged "mental incapacity" has elevated such clauses to relevance in a discussion of impeachment. In Ecuador, only a simple majority was required to remove a president for this reason, while a two-thirds majority was needed for impeachment. This type of provision also exists in Chile, El Salvador, Guatemala and Colombia. In Chile, a prior ruling is required by the Constitutional Tribunal, while in El Salvador and Guatemala a panel of doctors must confirm the applicability of the provision before the congress can remove on this basis. In Colombia, the provision is limited to "physical" incapacity and the text implies that the president has already voluntarily taken a leave of absence.

Aside from the case of Bucaram, there have been three other cases where impeachment or imminent threat of impeachment led to the removal or resignation of the president: President Collor de Melo in Brazil (1992), President Carlos Andrés Pérez in Venezuela (1993), and President Raúl Cubas Grau in Paraguay (1999). There were unsuccessful impeachment attempts in Ecuador in 1987 (against President Febres Cordero), in Colombia in 1996-97 (against President Ernesto Samper), and in Paraguay in 1998 (against President Cubas Grau). Threats of impeachment also anticipated the self-coups of President Alberto Fujimori in Peru and President Jorge Serrano Elías in Guatemala. The first succeeded in keeping the president in office, while the latter failed and led to Serrano's resignation.

Partisan Powers of Presidents in Latin America

In addition to the constitutional powers of presidents, the nature of the party system plays an important role in shaping the operation of presidential systems. Both the number of significant parties and party cohesiveness and discipline affect the chances for a workable accommodation between the executive and the legislature.

When the party system is highly fragmented, it is unlikely that the party of the president will control more than a small share of the legislative seats. Given the incentives built into the presidential system, it is difficult in such a scenario for the president to put together and sustain a reliable governing coalition. But this does not necessarily mean that it is desirable that the president and a hierarchically organized majoritarian party control the government. In fragmented systems, governments are likely to be ineffective, which eventually may weaken the legitimacy of democratic institutions and increase the risk of democratic regime instability. Yet in cases of majoritarian party control, restraints on the abuse of authority inherent in the presidential system are substantially reduced and government may be less "representative" and more prone to mismanagement and corruption. Thus, a middle ground in which the president's party does not fully dominate or is not rigidly disciplined is more likely to permit sufficient congressional backing, while at the same time restraining the executive from the temptation to act unilaterally and abuse the public trust.

As was shown in Chapter Six (Table 6.10), the degree of party system fragmentation varies widely across the region. Given the fairly high degree of concentration in the distribution of legislative seats in Honduras, Paraguay, Mexico, Costa Rica and the Dominican Republic, majority or near-majority governments have been a common occurrence during the period of this study; however, this situation in some of the countries has changed in recent years. Put into the language of the previous section, presidents in these countries have been able to count on substantial "partisan powers." Except for the Dominican Republic, these are cases in which the president's formal powers are relatively weak.

By contrast, with five to seven significant parties competing for public offices in Ecuador, Brazil, Bolivia and Peru, single party majoritarian governments are improbable. Possibly as compensation for their weak partisan powers, presidents in Ecuador, Brazil, Peru, and, to a lesser extent, Bolivia, have been bolstered by significant legislative powers. Chile also is characterized by a fragmented party system, but the binominal election system established under the 1980 constitution has created strong incentives for consolidating the party system into two competing party blocks. As a consequence, all the elected presidents in the post-Pinochet period have been backed by a reliable majority in the fully elected lower house.

The regional average for the period of a little more than three significant parties suggests that single party majorities are fairly rare in Latin American presidential systems. The improbability of single party majorities is compounded by the bicameral character of nine of the 18 countries in the study. The problem of electing and sustaining majorities in two chambers of congress simultaneously was likely one of the principal motivations for the switch to a unicameral legislature in Peru (1993) and Venezuela (1999).

In cases where party unity and discipline is fairly weak, even a majority of the legislative seats does not guarantee reliable support for the president. Fragmented party systems in combination with undisciplined parties tend to make it especially difficult for presidents to assemble majorities behind a policy agenda.

Coalitions in presidential systems are usually not as formalized, durable or binding on legislators as they are in parliamentary systems. Sometimes parties agree to join forces before an election in order to enhance the chances of a particular presidential candidate. But support is not ensured after the president's inauguration. Post-election governing coalitions may entail the participation of members of allied parties in the cabinet or other public agencies, but this does not necessarily ensure the support of individual legislators from these parties or imply a binding commitment on the part of the whole party. Allied parties and politicians can also switch to the opposition without risking new elections or the downfall of the government. Nonetheless, coalitions do present a potential means to at least partially overcome the gridlock that otherwise might arise due to the president's weak base of partisan support in the congress.

Coalitions taking a variety of forms and with varying practical consequences for the management of executive-legislative relations became increasingly common in Latin American in the 1990s (Lanzaro, 2001; Chasquetti, 2001). To some extent, this fact contradicts the expectations of critics of presidentialism who did not foresee coalitions as a viable possibility for avoiding the "dual legitimacy" and the tendency for stalemate endemic in the separation of powers system. In contexts in which ideological and policy differences between parties are not very salient, the comparison between benefits and costs may lean more in favor of joining a coalition than anticipated by the critics of presidentialism. Refusing to join a coalition may result in marginalization for the party and its leaders, while participation gives the party more prominence and provides leaders with positions of power and prestige. When parties are elite-driven rather than mass based, then the interests of party elites in obtaining access to power may offset the potential costs in terms of compromised principles or long-term electoral strategy.

Table 8.7 summarizes the frequency with which presidents are elected with single party majorities or assemble coalitions that, at least on paper, provide legislative majorities. The unit of analysis is the period during which the balance of power resulting from the previous election remains the same. When the president and legislators are elected at the same time, the period is simply the president's and the legislators' term of office, unless the president is replaced by someone else (usually the vice president) due to death or some other form of irregular succession. When presidential and legislative elections are not concurrent, a new period commences when either a new president or new congress is elected.

During the time frame of this study, there have been a total of 111 such periods in the 18 countries examined. In 49 of these periods (44 percent), some form of inter-party coalition supported the president for a significant block of time.[11] The case was counted as a coalition government only if a formal agreement was reached between the president and the coalition partners, or when cabinet or other governmental posts were shared with the party (rather than with "independents" from parties). Ad hoc party coalitions formed to support particular legislative initiatives were not considered as constituting a coalition government. Clearly, coalitions have been a necessary and important characteristic of executive-legislative relations in Latin America over the period of the study. Given the large number of countries examined and the length of the period, however, no effort has been made to comprehensively evaluate the efficacy of the coalitions in terms of the reliability of legislative support for presidential policy initiatives.

In 30.3 percent of all of the president-congress periods, the president's own party held a majority of the seats in the lower house (or the national assembly in the case of

---

[11] In three additional cases, coalitions were formed for a short time during the presidential-legislative period but did not survive more than one year and so were not counted.

Table 8.7. Frequency of Majority Government in Latin America

Country	President-congress periods	Percent of periods when president's party has lower house majority	Percent of periods when president's party has upper house majority	Percent of periods when president's party has majority in upper and lower house	Percent of periods with govt. majority in lower house (including coalitions)	Percent of periods with govt. majority in upper houses (including coalitions)	Percent of periods with govt. majority in lower and upper houses (including coalitions)
Argentina	9	33.33	55.56	11.11	33.33	55.56	11.11
Bolivia	5	0.00	40.00	0.00	80.00	80.00	80.00
Brazil	7	14.29	14.29	14.29	57.14	57.14	57.14
Chile	4	0.00	0.00	0.00	100.00	0.00	0.00
Colombia	7	57.14	71.43	57.14	71.43	85.71	71.43
Costa Rica	6	50.00		50.00	50.00		50.00
Dominican Rep.	8	37.50	62.50	25.00	50.00	75.00	37.50
Ecuador	12	0.00		0.00	8.33		8.33
El Salvador	8	25.00		25.00	37.50		37.50
Guatemala	6	50.00		50.00	66.67		66.67
Honduras	5	80.00		80.00	100.00		100.00
Mexico	8	75.00	87.50	75.00	75.00	87.50	75.00
Nicaragua	2	0.00		0.00	50.00		50.00
Panama	3	0.00		0.00	66.67		66.67
Paraguay	4	25.00	25.00	25.00	50.00	50.00	50.00
Peru	6	50.00	0.00	0.00	66.67	33.33	50.00
Uruguay	4	0.00	0.00	0.00	50.00	50.00	50.00
Venezuela	7	14.29	16.67	14.29	28.57	16.67	28.57
Total	111	30.27	41.54	25.68	54.05	60.00	46.84

unicameral systems). The proportion for the upper house was 41.5 percent. But only in 25.7 percent of the cases did the president's party hold a majority of the seats in the whole congress.

However, when one also counts the seats of coalition partners, in the event that a coalition existed, then in 54.1 percent of the cases the government held a majority in the lower house and in 60 percent in the upper house.[12] In 46.8 percent of the 111 cases, the government held an overall majority when the seats of coalition partners were also counted.

Single party majority governments (considering the whole congress) were most common in Honduras, Mexico, Colombia, Costa Rica and Guatemala. This partisan alignment with the president contributed to fairly strong presidents in all those countries except Colombia. Given the highly factionalized and undisciplined nature of the two main parties in Colombia, partisan majorities did not necessarily imply reliable legislative support. Single party majoritarian governments did not arise in Bolivia, Chile, Ecuador, Nicaragua, Panama, Peru or Uruguay.

Even when considering the potential support of legislators from parties allied to the government, an overall majority never occurred in Chile and was quite rare in Argentina, Ecuador and Venezuela. Though obtaining a majority in the lower house, Concertación in Chile was repeatedly denied a majority in the senate because of the presence of nonelected, conservative senators.[13]

Coalitions contributed significantly to the legislative backing of presidents in Bolivia, Brazil, Chile, Nicaragua and, to a somewhat lesser extent, Paraguay and Uruguay. In these cases, inter-party agreements and power-sharing on numerous occasions allowed minority presidents to gain the support of parties that together controlled a majority or near-majority of the legislative seats. Particularly in Brazil but also to some extent in the other cases, the theoretical majority status did not mean that the president could count on the support of individual legislators from parties in the coalition. In Bolivia and Uruguay, the inter-party coalitions, when they existed, were strongest and greatly contributed to governmental action. But even in Brazil and Nicaragua, where the coalitions were weaker and had less of an influence on the positions taken by individual legislators, government effectiveness was clearly facilitated by the support of coalition partners.

Tables 8.8 and 8.9 show the shares of seats of the president's party and governmental coalition, respectively, for each country over each of the president-congress periods. The unraveling of traditional party systems is evident in Colombia, Peru and Venezuela, where the parties of presidents at one time typically controlled a substantial share of the seats, but more recently have been much less ensured of such support. Increasingly open and competitive elections have also resulted in greater party system fragmentation in Mexico and Paraguay, and the end of governments dominated by a single party and a powerful president. In Uruguay, the ascendancy of the Frente Amplio and Nuevo Espacio has resulted in

---

[12] These are percentages of the 111 cases that were considered. If a coalition was identified, then the share of the seats controlled by all of the parties in the coalition was summed in the determination of whether the government held a majority. If there was no identifiable coalition, only the seats controlled by the president's party were considered.

[13] This problem was compounded by the fact that many of the institutional reforms the Chilean government wanted to enact required extraordinary majorities.

Table 8.8. Share of Seats of President's Party in Congress by Period
(In percent)

Country		1	2	3	4	5	6	7	8	9	10	11	12	Avg.
Argentina	LH	50.79	50.79	44.49	48.03	45.53	49.03	53.08	46.30					48.51
	UH	39.13	39.13	39.13	58.70	62.50	62.50	54.17	54.17	27.78				48.58
Bolivia	LH	36.15	33.08	25.38	40.00	25.38								32.00
	UH	37.04	59.26	29.63	62.96	40.74								45.93
Brazil	LH	41.75	77.62	2.60	7.97	7.97	12.09	19.30						24.19
	UH	29.17	83.33	0.00	6.17	6.17	12.35	16.67						21.98
Chile	LH	31.67	30.83	31.67	31.67									31.46
	UH	27.66	29.79	29.79	29.79									29.26
Colombia	LH	55.78	41.21	49.25	59.80	53.70	54.66	17.40						47.40
	UH	55.36	42.98	50.88	57.89	54.90	54.90	26.47						49.05
Costa Rica			57.89	50.88	50.88	49.12	47.37							51.23
Dominican Rep.	LH	52.75	51.67	46.67	35.00	41.67	10.83	32.89	55.70					40.90
	UH	40.74	62.96	70.00	53.33	50.00	3.33	13.33	80.00					46.71
Ecuador		42.03	12.68	16.90	43.66	19.70	15.58		3.90	23.17	0.00	26.45	21.49	20.51
El Salvador		55.00	36.70	51.70	46.40	46.40	33.30	33.30	34.50					42.16
Guatemala		51.00	15.50			53.80	55.80							44.03
Honduras		53.66	34.30	55.50	55.50	52.30								50.25
Mexico	LH	74.00	74.75	72.50	52.00	64.00	60.00	47.80	43.20					61.03
	UH	100.00	98.44	98.44	93.75	95.31	66.67	60.16	35.94					81.09
Nicaragua														
Panama			43.06	25.40										34.23
Paraguay	LH	66.67	25.00	22.50	22.50									34.17
	UH	66.67	22.22	20.00	22.22									32.78
Peru	LH	54.44	59.44	17.78			34.17							41.46
	UH	43.33	49.20	22.60										38.36
Uruguay	LH	41.41	39.39	32.32	33.33									36.61
	UH	43.30	38.87	35.48	33.33									37.75
Venezuela	LH	42.20	56.50	48.26	48.26	12.80	17.24	48.48						39.11
	UH	47.70	63.64	47.83	47.83	12.00	14.81							38.97

Note: UH = Upper house; LH = lower house.

Table 8.9. Share of Seats of Governing Coalition by Period
(In percent)

Country		1	2	3	4	5	6	7	8	9	10	11	12	Avg.
Argentina	LH	50.79	50.79	44.49	48.03	45.53	49.03	53.08	46.30	**48.25**				48.48
	UH	39.13	39.13	39.13	58.70	62.50	62.50	54.17	54.17	27.78				48.58
Bolivia	LH	**36.15**	**64.62**	**54.61**	**60.76**	**73.84**								58.00
	UH	**37.04**	**96.30**	**59.26**	**66.66**	**81.48**								68.15
Brazil	LH	**41.75**	**77.62**	2.60	**24.50**	**52.58**	**58.87**	**64.32**						46.03
	UH	**29.17**	**83.33**	0.00	**37.04**	**66.66**	**70.37**	**77.77**						52.05
Chile	LH	**57.50**	**58.33**	**58.34**	**58.34**									58.13
	UH	**46.81**	**44.68**	**42.55**	**42.55**									44.15
Colombia	LH	**97.49**	41.21	49.25	59.80	53.70	54.66	69.60						60.82
	UH	**99.11**	42.98	50.88	57.89	54.90	54.90	78.40						62.72
Costa Rica	LH	**47.37**	57.89	50.88	50.88	49.12	47.37							50.59
Dominican Rep.	LH	52.75	51.67	46.67	35.00	41.67	52.50	44.30	55.70					47.53
	UH	40.74	62.96	70.00	53.33	50.00	53.33	20.00	80.00					53.80
Ecuador	LH	**42.03**	**22.50**	**22.50**	**22.50**	**50.70**	**22.50**	**23.38**	**11.69**	**25.61**	0.00	26.45	47.94	26.85
El Salvador	LH	55.00	36.70	51.70	46.40	**52.40**	33.30	33.30	34.50					42.91
Guatemala	LH	51.00	**74.10**	0.00	0.00	53.80	55.80							39.12
Honduras	LH	53.66	**81.30**	55.50	55.50	52.30								59.65
Mexico	LH	74.00	74.75	72.50	52.00	64.00	60.00	47.80	**44.60**					61.21
	UH	100.00	98.44	98.44	93.75	95.31	66.67	60.16	**39.85**					81.58
Nicaragua	LH	**55.40**	**45.20**	**33.80**										50.30
Panama	LH	**82.10**	**50.00**											55.30
Paraguay	LH	66.67	**66.25**	22.50	22.50									44.48
	UH	66.67	**60.00**	20.00	22.22									42.22
Peru	LH	60.00	59.44	17.78	**55.00**	**55.83**	34.17							47.04
	UH	**53.33**	49.18	22.58										41.70
Uruguay	LH	41.41	39.39	**63.63**	**55.55**									50.00
	UH	43.30	38.87	**67.74**	**56.66**									51.64
Venezuela	LH	42.20	56.50	48.26	48.26	24.63	29.06	**61.20**						44.30
	UH	47.70	63.64	47.83	47.83	22.00	24.07							42.18

Note: UH = Upper house; LH = lower house. Bolded numbers indicate president-congress periods when governments were supported by inter-party coalitions.

a three or four-way division of the party system, making it nearly impossible for a single party to contemplate governing alone.

As a consequence of these tendencies toward increasingly dispersed party systems as well as the weakening of parties in some cases, coalitions are likely to become even more necessary in the future. Figure 8.1 shows that the steady decline in the percentage of single party majority governments has been matched with an increase in coalition-backed governments. The result of these parallel trends is a relatively modest decline in the percentage of governments with a majority in congress when the president's party's coalition partners are considered.

Throughout the whole period, the viability of governments in Bolivia, Brazil, Chile and Ecuador has depended on coalitions. Given the increased fragmentation of party systems, however, coalitions also appear to have become more necessary in Argentina, Costa Rica, Colombia, El Salvador, Mexico, Panama, Paraguay, Peru and Uruguay. The reduction in the partisan powers of presidents in Paraguay and Mexico is especially relevant given that in these cases presidents have few constitutional resources with which to move their agenda forward. The breakdown of the traditional party system in Venezuela also presents the likelihood of a more fractured division of power as the unifying influence of President Chávez fades.

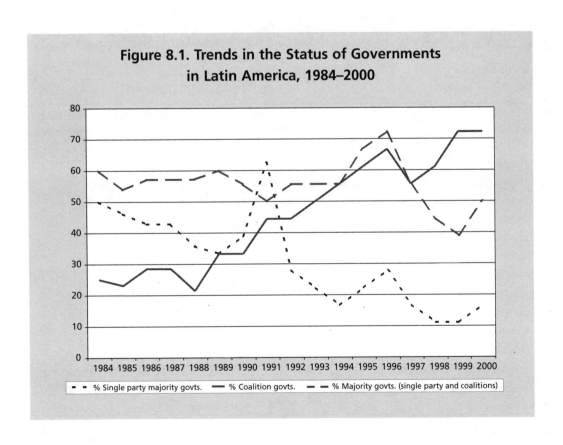

Figure 8.1. Trends in the Status of Governments in Latin America, 1984–2000

- - % Single party majority govts.   — % Coalition govts.   — — % Majority govts. (single party and coalitions)

Comparing Constitutional and Partisan Powers of Presidents

In countries with fragmented party systems, presidents generally have been granted fairly deep constitutional powers, especially in terms of proactive powers (decree, budget powers) (Table 8.10) (Shugart and Carey, 1992). All countries with low partisan powers have at least moderate proactive powers. Given their need to deliver goods (the benefits of a growing economy, jobs, budgetary resources, etc.) to their constituents and clients, legislators may be willing to grant presidents considerable power when they know that they are unable to get things done themselves (Archer and Shugart, 1997). Some countries such as Bolivia, El Salvador and Uruguay, where presidents typically are relatively weak in partisan terms, nonetheless are also fairly weak in constitutional terms.

By contrast, countries with relatively concentrated party systems tend to be those in which the president's legislative powers are weaker. Partial exceptions to this rule are Panama, the Dominican Republic and, to some extent, Argentina.

Compensating for a fragmented party system with a president endowed with proactive legislative powers, however, may not be the best scenario for building a strong system of checks and balances and a legitimate system of representation. For this objective, there is no substitute for a congress that has a capacity for collective action and that develops the professional capabilities to coparticipate in the policymaking process and oversee the executive branch. Thus, even in this case, constitutional powers may be useful in extreme

Table 8.10. Legislative vs. Partisan Powers

Constitutional legislative powers	President's partisan powers			
	Very low	Medium low	Medium high	Very high
High proactive/high reactive	Ecuador, Chile			
High proactive/moderate reactive	Brazil	Peru, Colombia		
Moderate proactive/high reactive			Panama, Dominican Republic	
Moderate proactive/ moderate reactive		Bolivia, El Salvador	Argentina, Guatemala Nicaragua	
Moderate proactive/weak reactive		Uruguay	Venezuela	
Weak proactive/moderate reactive			Mexico, United States	Paraguay
Weak			Costa Rica	Honduras

moments of crisis, but it is valuable for the institutionalization of the checks and balances system that presidents develop policies through consensus among parties in the legislature, no matter how difficult this may sometimes be.

Conclusions

The governability of presidential democracies is closely connected to how the inherent tensions and competing responsibilities between the executive and legislative branches are sorted out. On the one hand, governments need to be able to act. They need to respond efficiently and effectively to pressing social and economic problems and to adopt policies that will promote improvements in the well being of society over the long term. Presidents, in particular, are elected with this broad mandate to manage these national problems. Thus, the president and the executive need to have sufficient constitutional powers and partisan support in order to permit effective government.

On the other hand, intrinsic to the idea of democracy is that government policies should be responsive to the views and interests of citizens, and that elected officials should be held accountable for how they exercise public authority and use public funds. Thus, the effective execution of the representative and oversight responsibilities of the legislative branch is also essential to democratic governability. Carrying out these functions is clearly at odds with an imperial presidency, but not in contradiction with the implementation of effective governmental responses to social problems.

For the congress to develop its representation and oversight capacities, presidents must not be endowed with such a high degree of proactive legislative powers that they can develop policies, including the budget, in relative isolation and at times bypass the congress altogether. In addition, opposition forces must have a voice in the congress and pro-government legislators need sufficient independence from the party hierarchy and the proper electoral incentives to play a role in shaping policy choices and take part in the legislative oversight function.

Developing legislative policymaking and oversight capacities is impaired if there is an overly fragmented division of seats among political parties. A legislature strongly divided along partisan lines—especially if that partisanship is exacerbated by regional and ethnic divisions—may block positive policy actions proposed by the executive. At the same time, the legislature may be unable to act collectively to develop alternative approaches or to effectively monitor the executive.

Thus, the evidence discussed in this chapter suggests that democratic governability is complicated in several countries by an excessively fragmented party system. This may be rooted at least in part, as we saw in Chapter Five, in characteristics of the electoral system. Moreover the extent of party system fragmentation has been growing over the last two decades. This could complicate effective policymaking and increase the incentive of presidents to take advantage of their proactive lawmaking powers and reduce the role of legislatures.

This is precisely the dangerous scenario that critics of presidentialism warned would limit its effectiveness and stability. Despite this growing tendency toward multiple parties, however, no country has changed the fundamental structure of its political regime from presidentialism to parliamentarism or semi-presidentialism. Nevertheless, a few countries have incorporated some semi-parliamentary or semi-presidential features that had existed beforehand in other countries of the region. These have included providing congress with the power to censure and remove cabinet ministers; providing the president with the power, in highly specified circumstances, to dissolve the legislature; and in one case, establishing the position of a chief of the cabinet partly accountable to the legislature. But these features, whether adopted prior to or during the region's recent democratization period, did not significantly affect how the systems functioned in practice, except in a couple of cases. Another incipient though still fairly weak trend has been to attempt to control or limit presidential decree powers and strengthen the capacity of the legislature by modernizing information systems and increasing staff support for legislators and legislative committees.

A clear reaction to the fragmentation of party systems has been a growing tendency for elected presidents to forge coalitions with other parties in order to govern more effectively. As a consequence of the increased dispersion of party systems and in some cases the weakening of parties, coalitions are likely to become even more necessary in the future. Figure 8.1 showed that the steady decline in the percentage of single party majority governments has been matched with an increasing number of coalition-backed governments. The result of these parallel trends is a relatively modest decline in the percentage of governments with a majority in congress when the president's party's coalition partners are considered.

Clearly, government effectiveness has been facilitated by resorting to this somewhat parliamentary form of governance within presidentialism. Maintaining coalitions has been facilitated in two particular cases (Bolivia and Chile) by features of the electoral system that provide fairly powerful incentives for parties to form alliances. But determining the general viability of coalitions for alleviating governability problems in multi-party presidential systems is a matter that demands more detailed study.

The endowment of presidents with inordinate legislative powers has also in some cases impaired developing the capacity of the legislature to engage itself effectively in policymaking and executive oversight. Of course, the development of such capacities has also been limited in some cases by electoral system features, such as the lack of democratic procedures within political parties and the excessive degree of control exerted by leaders in the selection of candidates. The high rate of turnover of legislators—whether because of mandated term limits, party nominating procedures, or the lack of prestige and rewards of a legislative career—has also in some cases deterred strengthening the legislative branch. If legislators have little desire or ability to build a career in the legislature and remain in office, they also have little incentive to be responsive to their constituents or to invest in developing the knowledge and capacities necessary to perform a more proactive policymaking and oversight role.

To a great extent, the circumstances in which Latin American democracies operated during the 1980s and early 1990s also influenced the approach to policymaking. Economic crises and growing problems of public safety provided the incentive and a justification for centralized policymaking structures and a relatively minimal role for congress.

Bibliography

Archer, Ronald P., and Matthew Soberg Shugart. 1997. The Unrealized Potential of Presidential Dominance in Colombia. In Scott Mainwaring and Matthew Soberg Shugart (eds.), *Presidentialism and Democracy in Latin America*. New York: Cambridge University Press.

Carey, John M., and Matthew Soberg Shugart. 1995. Incentives to Cultivate Personal Vote: A Rank Ordering of Electoral Formulas. *Electoral Studies* 14.

——— (eds.). 1998. *Executive Decree Authority*. Cambridge: Cambridge University Press.

Chasquetti, Daniel. 2001. Democracia, multipartidismo y coaliciones en América Latina: evaluando la difícil combinación. In Jorge Lanzaro (ed.), *Tipos de presidencialismo y coaliciones políticas en América Latina*. Buenos Aires: Consejo Latinoamericano de Ciencias Sociales.

Cox, Gary, and Scott Morgenstern. 1998. Reactive Assemblies and Proactive Presidents: A Typology of Latin American Presidents and Legislatures. Paper presented at the 21st International Congress of the Latin American Studies Association, Chicago, 24–26 September.

Di Palma, Giuseppe. 1990. *To Craft Democracies: An Essay on Democratic Transitions*. Berkeley: University of California Press.

Jones, Mark P. 1996. *Electoral Laws and the Survival of Presidential Democracies*. Notre Dame: University of Notre Dame Press.

Lanzaro, Jorge. 2001. Tipos de presidencialismo y modos de gobierno en América Latina. In Jorge Lanzaro (ed.), *Tipos de presidencialismo y coaliciones políticas en América Latina*. Buenos Aires: Consejo Latinoamericano de Ciencias Sociales.

Lijphart, Arend. 1990. Presidencialismo y democracia de mayoría. In Oscar Godoy Arcaya (ed.), *Hacia una democracia moderna: la opción parlamentaria*. Santiago: Ediciones Universidad Católica de Chile.

Linz, Juan J. 1978. Crisis, Breakdown and Reequilibration. In Juan J. Linz and Alfred Stephan (eds.), *The Breakdown of Democratic Regimes*, Vol. 1. Baltimore: The Johns Hopkins University Press.

———. 1990. The Perils of Presidentialism. *Journal of Democracy* 1(4). Fall.

———. 1994. Presidential or Parliamentary Democracy: Does It Make a Difference? In Juan J. Linz and Arturo Valenzuela (eds.), *The Failure of Presidential Democracy: The Case of Latin America*, Vol. 2. Baltimore: The Johns Hopkins University Press.

Mainwaring, Scott. 1990. Presidentialism in Latin America. *Latin American Research Review* 25(1).

———. 1993. Presidentialism, Multipartism and Democracy: The Difficult Combination. *Comparative Political Studies* 2(26).

———. 1997. Multipartism, Robust Federalism, and Presidentialism in Brazil. In Scott Mainwaring and Matthew Soberg Shugart (eds.), *Presidentialism and Democracy in Latin America*. New York: Cambridge University Press.

Mainwaring, Scott, and Matthew Soberg Shugart. 1997. Presidentialism and the Party System. In Scott Mainwaring and Matthew Soberg Shugart (eds.), *Presidentialism and Democracy in Latin America*. New York: Cambridge University Press.

Morgenstern, Scott, and Benito Nacif (eds.). 2002. *Legislatures and Democracy in Latin America*. New York: Cambridge University Press.

Nohlen, Dieter, and Mario Fernández (eds.). 1991. *Presidencialismo versus parlamentarismo, América Latina*. Caracas: Editorial Nueva Sociedad.

Perez Linan, Anibal. 2000. The Institutional Determinants of Impeachment. Paper presented at 23rd International Congress of the Latin American Studies Association, Miami, 16–18 March.

Samuels, David. 2000. Fiscal Horizontal Accountability? Toward a Theory of Budgetary "Checks and Balances" in Presidential Systems. Paper presented at the conference on Institutions, Accountability and Democratic Governance in Latin America, University of Notre Dame Kellogg Institute, 8–9 May.

Shugart, Matthew Soberg. 1999. Efficiency and Reform: A New Index of Government Responsiveness and the Conjunction of Electoral and Economic Reforms. Mimeo.

Shugart, Matthew Soberg, and John M. Carey. 1992. *Presidents and Assemblies: Constitutional Design and Electoral Dynamics*. Cambridge: Cambridge University Press.

Shugart, Matthew Soberg, and Scott Mainwaring. 1997. Presidentialism and Democracy in Latin America: Rethinking the Terms of the Debate. In Scott Mainwaring and Matthew Soberg Shugart (eds.), *Presidentialism and Democracy in Latin America*. New York: Cambridge University Press.

Shugart, Matthew Soberg, Erika Morena, and Brian F. Crisp. 2000. The Accountability Deficit in Latin America. Paper presented at the conference on Institutions, Accountability and Democratic Governance in Latin America, University of Notre Dame Kellogg Institute, 8–9 May.

Shugart, Matthew Soberg, and Martin P. Wattenberg (eds.). 2001. *Mixed-Member Electoral Systems: The Best of Both Worlds?* New York: Oxford University Press.

Suárez, Waldino. 1982. El poder ejecutivo en América Latina: Su capacidad operativa bajo regímes presidencialistas de gobierno. *Revista de Estudios Políticos* 29. Instituto de Estudios Políticos, Madrid.

Valenzuela, Arturo. 1978. *The Breakdown of Democratic Regimes: Chile*. Baltimore: The Johns Hopkins University Press.

———. 1994. Party Politics and the Crisis of Presidentialism in Chile: A Proposal for a Parliamentary Form of Government. In Juan J. Linz and Arturo Valenzuela (eds.), *The Failure of Presidential Democracy: The Case of Latin America*, Vol. 2. Baltimore: The Johns Hopkins University Press.

CHAPTER NINE

Democratic Accountability Institutions in Latin America: Legal Design vs. Actual Performance

While the question of how to hold public officials accountable in a democracy has long been debated, the issue has been subject to renewed scrutiny in Latin America's "third wave" democracies.[1] The democratic transitions have seen efforts to constitutionalize agencies responsible for controlling the exercise of public authority—an objective that runs against once prevalent approaches to governing in the region, and which is somewhat foreign to the classical concept of three separate and counterbalancing branches of power. The idea was for these agencies to be independent of the traditional branches of government. Until recently, governmental institutions, particularly those pertaining to the executive, have been scarcely controlled, either by their own monitoring systems or by other branches of government.

The traditional concept of democratic accountability emphasizes the supervision and control of public authorities by citizens through elections, and by the other branches of government. Elections, however, have long been recognized to be insufficient, though still important, in terms of full accountability.[2] Where representative institutions are deficiently developed and legislator accountability mechanisms poorly configured, there is a particular need for additional layers of protection against the abuse of public authority (O'Donnell, 1994). Over the past two decades, countries in the region have adopted constitutional and other institutional reforms—both with respect to these traditional instruments and to innovative institutions—aimed at enhancing the accountability of governmental institutions.

---

[1] See O'Donnell (1994, 1999 and 2000); Schedler, Diamond and Plattner (1999); Centro Latinoamericano de Administración para el Desarrollo (CLAD) (2000); Fox (2000); Smulovitz and Peruzotti (2000); Shugart, Moreno and Crisp (2000).

[2] The limits and possibilities of elections and representative institutions serving as a basis for ensuring accountability are examined in Przeworski, Stokes and Manin (1999), Lupia and McCubbins (1998), and Shugart, Moreno and Crisp (2000).

This chapter examines the creation, development, and reform of these semi-autonomous agencies for accountability.

Other types of reforms have also had the potential to enhance accountability, even if this was not their sole or principal aim. Many countries have introduced mechanisms for direct citizen participation, thus providing opportunities for the public to have input into decision-making and, in limited cases, to revoke the mandate of public officials (see Chapter Ten).

In addition, a far-reaching process of judicial reform has been taking place in the region that has helped redefine the role of the justice system itself. Though the process is ongoing and the changes required are profound, rules and codes as well as the administration and management of the justice system itself have been reformed in many countries. Such reforms have been necessary to respond more adequately to the consensus for more secure and legally predictable property rights, greater citizen access to and trust in the justice system, and improved efficiency and quality of judicial decisions. Legal system reform has been viewed as an essential part of the broader processes of democratic consolidation and economic reform (Hammergren, 1998).

An important objective of judicial reform in some cases has been to establish a more independent judiciary that can more effectively exercise legal accountability and ensure adherence to constitutional precepts and universal protection of civil rights. An independent and effective judiciary is necessary to protect against infringements of the constitution and other laws by public authorities, provide for even-handed interpretation and enforcement of laws, and administer criminal justice in an unbiased fashion. Clearly, this is an area where ongoing long-term efforts are needed to help create a judiciary that can fully perform its necessary role in establishing the democratic rule of law (Domingo, 1999).

The reconceptualization of the state as being created by and serving citizens has contributed markedly to the recognition of the importance of holding public officials accountable and of ensuring transparency in the management of public funds. The redefinition of the public domain as an area of citizen responsibility and ownership has gone together with the elevation of the "participative" concept of democracy in democratic theory. In this perspective, public accountability and transparency are irreplaceable elements of good governance and good policy (Avritzer, 2000; Cohen, 2000; Bohman, 2000).

Over the past decade, accountability and governability have been prominent in academic analyses of the new Latin American democracies. These studies have focused attention on the potential tension that exists between the need to exercise control over political power and the need for effective government. On the one hand, for government to adequately respond to pressing social problems and citizen demands, power must be sufficiently concentrated to enable the making of sound and timely decisions. On the other, it is dangerous to confer vast power upon particular individuals or institutions, since doing so runs the risk that such authority will be abused. The logical conclusion is that the use of power should be effectively monitored and controlled, but in a way that is not detrimental to the efficacy of the decision-making process.

Many Latin American countries have developed and strengthened their institutions for overseeing the exercise of public authority and have reformed their judicial systems. Particularly important to reduce governmental corruption is to introduce or strengthen merit systems in public administration and internal mechanisms for monitoring and controlling the actions of officials within public agencies. Such reforms have been beneficial where they have been successfully implemented, but much work remains to be done. But these mechanisms for building accountability are themselves insufficient.

The concept of accountability can also be expressed by the word "answerability," since it implies the ability to ensure that officials in government are answerable for their actions. Making public officials answerable entails the use of three different mechanisms. First, officials must be obligated to inform citizens and public agencies about their decisions, knowing that their conduct is monitored externally. Second, those who wield power must explain or justify their decisions and actions if so demanded by citizens or other public officials or institutions. Third, holding public officials accountable for evident abuses of power or the public trust requires that such conduct be subject to negative sanctions (Schedler, 1999). Though the public documentation of abuses of authority is indispensable, it is not a sufficient basis for accountability, since effective deterrence requires that there be predictable negative consequences for those who commit such violations (Fox, 2000). The three aspects of accountability—transparency and monitoring, justification, and enforcement—are all needed to manage the diverse forms that the abuse of authority might take.

Ensuring accountability in practice requires attention to a wide range of capabilities and structures in an array of organizations and legal and procedural areas. Not only must public officials and agencies be compelled to fully and accurately disclose their decisions and budgetary accounts, but there must also be a range of independent, motivated and capable bodies to monitor the information provided, detect improprieties, determine legal responsibility, and impose sanctions when appropriate. At the same time, a participatory citizenry, a vibrant and well-organized civil society, and a pluralistic and independent media are essential to monitor government activities, expose abuses of power and violations of civil rights, raise public expectations of state performance, and bring political pressure to bear so that the oversight institutions can and do take the appropriate remedial actions.

There are several types of mechanisms to enforce accountability within the Latin American legal tradition, depending on the nature of the transgression of authority. Sometimes there are several enforcement mechanisms operating at the same time (Groisman and Lerner, 2000). The first type of enforcement mechanism inherent in a democratic system is *political sanction*, through which a public official can be removed by defeat in a competitive election or, in the context of some constitutions or particular circumstances, through the revocation of the mandate by vote of the citizens (recall) or the congress (censure or political judgment). The exercise of political accountability does not necessarily result from a violation of the law, but may result merely from perceptions that the official performed unsatisfactorily or was insufficiently responsive to his or her constituents. The second type of enforcement, *administrative sanction*, comes into play when rules, procedures or ethical norms within an organization are breached. The third, *civil sanction*, consists of the obligation to repair damages caused by an action that constitute a violation of the law. Finally, *criminal sanction* is used when a crime or misdemeanor is committed. There is also *fiscal sanction*, which implies, in addition to criminal liability, the need to remedy monetary or proprietary harm to the state or groups of citizens.

Accountability promoted through actions and institutions within the state can be referred to as "horizontal accountability," while that which is promoted through the actions of individual citizens, civil society organizations or other non-state actors is "vertical accountability." The effectiveness of accountability depends on the positive interaction between these two dimensions (Figure 9.1). Proper mechanisms for electoral accountability and strong civil society organizations are needed to generate the constant pressure to uncover and punish abuses of authority, and to develop and sustain accountability agencies with sufficient authority, capability and political independence. But without the existence of independent and properly authorized state agencies, vertical accountability mechanisms will not result in the sanctioning of officials who abuse their powers, and instead will likely fuel citizen frustration, cynicism and apathy (O'Donnell, 1999; Fox, 2000; Shugart, Moreno and Crisp, 2000). Horizontal agencies such as independent and effective electoral management bodies and courts are also necessary to allow the vertical electoral mechanisms to function credibly, fairly and without corruption.

Recently, there has been particular emphasis on establishing horizontal accountability agencies to fight corruption and promote transparency in Latin America. Anti-corruption initiatives have focused on creating national entities solely devoted to fighting corrupt practices. As is the case for other semi-autonomous accountability agencies, to be effective these entities must enjoy broad public respect, be credible, operate transparently, and be subject to the scrutiny of the press and civil society (Pope and Vogl, 2000). Nonetheless, they must also be afforded considerable political autonomy to avoid being undermined, ignored or manipulated by the political elite.

Guillermo O'Donnell (1999) has defined horizontal accountability as ". . . the existence of state agencies that are legally enabled and empowered, and factually willing and able, to take actions that span from routine oversight to criminal sanctions or impeachment in relation to actions or omissions by other agents or agencies of the state that may be qualified as unlawful." This definition not only takes into account endogenous factors, such as the legal authority and the institutional design of the agencies responsible for enforcing the controls, but also exogenous factors that enable these agencies to take the actions that they are legally authorized to carry out.

Horizontal accountability is practiced by two types of institutions (O'Donnell, 2000):

1. Balance institutions. These are the traditional institutions that exercise horizontal balance accountability, or control by means of a balancing between separate branches of authority with somewhat distinct but also overlapping responsibilities and powers. The separate origin and distinct missions of these institutions gives incumbents in each an incentive to prevent infringements on the jurisdiction and authority of the others and check against large-scale abuses of constitutional power. This involves reactive and relatively sporadic control, since, in theory, it is only wielded when a branch of government senses that its authority has been infringed upon by other institutions, or when constitutional rights or important laws have been violated.

2. Mandated agencies. These are public institutions (many of them recently created or institutionalized) that practice horizontal mandated accountability, since they were not established so much for the purpose of regulating the overall balance between the main branches of government but to curb more specific, though still fairly undefined, risks of infringement on the use of power. Agencies with similar names and purposes differ greatly across countries in terms of their institutional origins, the nature of their relationship with the three traditional branches of authority, the procedures through which their top officials are appointed, the range of their authority, and the source of their financing (Table 9.1). As a consequence, the nature and degree of their political autonomy and their capacity to monitor, investigate and punish abuses of power or violations of citizen rights vary greatly. Since their function is precisely to exercise control, they are proactive in their job of monitoring transgressions of authority or corruption. The result of the efforts to complement traditional accountability institutions are complex and sometimes overlapping agencies (including auditor generals, courts of accounts, attorney general's offices, public prosecutor offices, offices of the public or human rights ombudsman), which perform their assigned tasks with varying degrees of effectiveness and political independence.

The actual outcome in terms of democratic accountability is quite difficult to determine, given the diverse institutions involved and the wide variation across countries in the nature of their responsibilities and powers and the extent to which they exercise them in practice. Within the limitations imposed by the relative novelty of the institutions and the

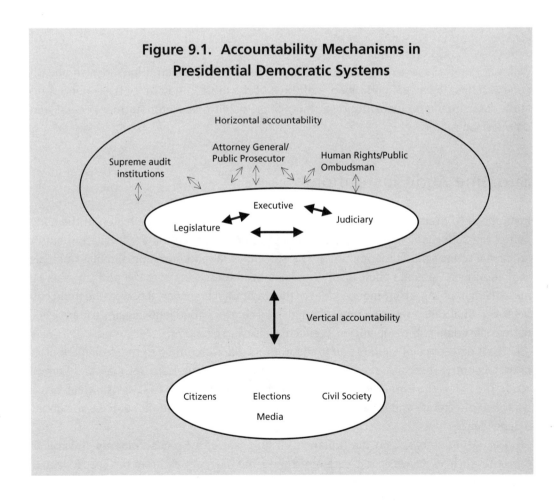

Figure 9.1. Accountability Mechanisms in Presidential Democratic Systems

Table 9.1. English and Spanish Names for Horizontal Accountability Agencies

Supreme audit institutions

Comptroller's Office	Contraloría General
General Accounting Office	Tribunal de Cuentas
Auditor General's Office	Auditoría General
Court of Accounts	Fiscalización Superior
Inspectors-General	Corte de Cuentas

Prosecutorial/Investigative agencies

Public Prosecutor	Procuraduría General
Prosecutor General	Ministerio Público
Special Prosecutor	Fiscalía General
Attorney General's Office	

Agencies defending rights of citizens

Human Rights Ombudsman	Defensoría del Pueblo
Public Ombudsman	Procuraduría para la Defensa de los Derechos Humanos
Civil Rights Commission	Comisión Nacional de Derechos Humanos

deficiency of available information, this chapter examines the institutional design and, in general terms, the actual performance of three of the most important of these control institutions: supreme audit institutions, offices of the public prosecutor/attorney general, and ombudsman offices.

Supreme Audit Institutions

Institutions to oversee budgeting were created in the countries of the region in the early part of the 20th century. Most were established to be dependent on the legislature but in functional terms semi-autonomous. The most significant modernization and institutionalization of these supreme audit institutions has been the efforts over the past 20 years to make them in practice truly independent of the traditional branches of power. The trend has been a gradual shift away from purely formal legal control of budgetary figures toward evaluations based on criteria of efficiency, effectiveness and economy.

The jurisdictions of supreme audit institutions differ according to the design adopted in each country. There are three models relevant to Latin America (Groisman and Lerner, 2000). The first is the **French model** of the court of accounts (*Cour des Comptes*), which has a collegiate directorate and is part of the national public administration, but has substantial independence.

The second is based on the **Italian** (*Corte dei Conti*) **and Spanish models** (*Tribunal de Cuentas*), which also have a collegiate directorate, are independent from the executive and legislative branches, and have the power to enforce the laws governing the administration of the budget and to sanction abuses of authority (judicial powers). This model was adopted by Guatemala, Brazil and El Salvador. It was also used in Argentina until 1993 when the *Auditoria General*, which lacks judicial powers, replaced the *Tribunal de Cuentas*.

The third is the **Anglo-American model** of the unipersonal comptroller's or accounting office. This office originates in and reports to the legislative branch and possesses no judicial powers, although it does monitor execution of the budget to confirm compliance with the budget law. This model has been adopted by most of the countries in the region. However, in Nicaragua, the comptroller's office was replaced by a court of accounts because the executive believed that the former institution had too much power.

The court of accounts aims to ensure formal and legal conformity of budgetary execution with the budget law, rather than considering efficiency criteria (Groisman and Lerner, 2000). Courts of accounts with judicial enforcement powers may establish administrative legal responsibility for the misuse of public funds or violations of the law. This procedure is followed in Brazil, Chile, El Salvador, Guatemala and Panama. Some institutions that do not have judicial powers, however, may urge other public institutions to prepare the legal case and procedures to be followed in order to determine responsibility. This is the procedure established in Uruguay, Paraguay, Costa Rica and Nicaragua.

Regardless of whether institutions have judicial functions, some have prior or ex ante powers of control. The purpose of this control is to verify the legality or appropriateness of administrative actions before their implementation, authorizing them or suspending their effects. This is the procedure followed in the Dominican Republic, El Salvador, Panama, Peru and Uruguay, although some of these countries are considering moving to a results-based approach (Table 9.2).

Although supreme audit institutions (mainly *contralorías*) that follow the Anglo-American model have no judicial functions, they nonetheless have instruments of control that can be very effective in certain cases. The recommendations and findings made in their reports are not binding, but these agencies generally use follow-up mechanisms that serve as deterrents. In these cases, the controls seek to correct rather than to penalize. This approach has been used in Argentina (since 1993), Bolivia, Colombia, Ecuador and Venezuela.

Regarding the institutional relationship of Latin America's supreme audit institutions, most pertain to the legislative branch, are independent, or are tied to the executive. In Argentina, Brazil, Costa Rica, Guatemala, Honduras, Mexico,[3] Nicaragua, Paraguay and Uruguay, audit institutions are dependent on the legislature. In Chile, Colombia, Ecuador, Panama and Peru, they are independent. And in Bolivia and the Dominican Republic,[4] they are tied to the executive branch. The court of accounts in El Salvador is not associated with the legislative branch, but does submit an annual report to that branch of government. A noteworthy case is Venezuela, where the comptroller's office is connected with *poder*

---

[3] Mexico has two audit agencies: the supreme audit institution of the federation and the secretary of comptrollership and administrative development. The former is tied to the legislature and the latter to the executive branch.

[4] The Dominican Republic also has the *Camara de Cuentas*, which is tied to the legislature. But this agency has few resources and little power.

Table 9.2 Supreme Audit Institutions

Country	Control ex ante	Institution tied to the executive	Institution tied to the legislature	Independent institutions	Indictments it can issue: juicio de cuentas and violations of law[1]
Argentina Auditoría Gral. de la Nación			✓	Financial and functional independence	
Bolivia Contraloría Gral. de la República		✓			
Brazil Tribunal de Cuentas de la Unión			✓	Financial and functional independence	✓ (juicio de cuentas)
Chile Contraloría Gral. de la República				✓	✓ (both)
Colombia Contraloría Gral. de la República				✓	✓ (juicio de cuentas)
Costa Rica Contraloría Gral. de la República	✓		✓	Financial and functional independence	
Dominican Rep. Contraloría General Camara de Cuentas	✓	✓			
Ecuador Contraloría Gral. del Estado				Administrative, budgetary and financial autonomy	
El Salvador Corte de Cuentas de la República	✓	(Submits report to Congress)		✓	✓ (juicio de cuentas)
Guatemala Contraloria de Cuentas de la República			✓	Functional independence	✓ (juicio de cuentas)
Honduras Contraloría Gral. de la República			✓	Functional and administrative independence	
Mexico Entidad de Fiscalización Superior de la Federación			✓	Technical and managerial autonomy	

Table 9.2 (continued)

Country	Control ex ante	Institution tied to the executive	Institution tied to the legislature	Independent institutions	Indictments it can issue: juicio de cuentas and violations of law[1]
Nicaragua Contraloría Gral. de la República			✓	Functional and administrative autonomy	
Panama Contraloría Gral. de la República	✓			✓	✓ (juicio de cuentas)
Paraguay Contraloría Gral. de la República Tribunal de Cuentas			✓		
Peru Contraloría Gral. de la República	✓			✓	
Uruguay Tribunal de Cuentas de la República	✓		✓	(Functional autonomy)	
Venezuela Contraloría Gral. de la República				Citizen power (functional, administrative and organizational autonomy)	

[1] *Juicio de cuentas* normally implies the finding of legal responsibility by the audit institution and the initiation and execution of the judicial process. A violation of law requires the involvement of another judicial authority.

ciudadano (defined in the constitution as a separate branch of government), thus affording it, in theory, extensive independence from the three traditional branches of government. For all of these institutions, however, the real litmus test for their independence is the extent to which they are autonomous in budgetary and functional terms. This quality, which varies from country to country, does not emerge merely as a result of a constitutional stipulation.

There is a greater variety in the design of supreme audit institutions in terms of the nature of their directorships (Table 9.3). Four countries appoint directors for five-year terms (Honduras, Panama, Paraguay and Uruguay); three for four years (Colombia, Ecuador and Guatemala); two for eight years (Argentina and Costa Rica); two for seven years (Peru and Venezuela); one for 10 years (Bolivia); one for six years (Nicaragua); one for three years (El Salvador); one for one year (Brazil), although members of the directorate in that country

Table 9.3. Supreme Audit Institution Directors

Country	Nomination of director/directorate	Term of office	Removal of director/directorate
Argentina Presidente de la Auditoría	Legislature	8 years (reelectable)	
Bolivia Contralor Gral. de la República	Executive (at proposal of senate)	10 years	Legislature through a judgment of responsibilities by the Supreme Court
Brazil Ministro–Presidente de la Tribunal de Cuentas de la Unión	*President* – By collegial Tribunal de Cuentas *Minister* – ⅓ by the president with senate confirmation; ⅔ by the congress	1 year Until 70 years old	Supreme federal tribunal
Chile Contralor Gral. de la República	Designated by president subject to agreement of senate majority	Indefinite until 75 years old	Chamber of deputies carries out accusation and the senate removes
Colombia Contralor Gral. de la República	Legislature (from list presented by constitutional court, Supreme Court and state council)	4 years	Supreme Court, after previous accusation of national prosecuting attorney
Costa Rica Contraloría Gral. de la República	Legislature	8 years and reelectable	Legislature
Dominican Rep. Contraloría Gral. de la República Camara de Cuentas	Executive	Indefinite	
Ecuador Contralor Gral. del Estado	President (from list presented by congress)	4 years	Legislature (after impeachment)
El Salvador Presidente de la Corte de Cuentas de la República	Legislature	3 years and reelectable	Legislature
Guatemala Contralor Gral. de Cuentas	Legislature	4 years and not reelectable	Legislature
Honduras Contralor Gral. de la República	Legislature	5 years	Legislature
Mexico Titular de la Entidad de Fiscalización Superior de la Federación	Legislature	8 years	Legislature; also by impeachment
Secretario de Contraloría y Desarrollo Administrativo	Executive	Indefinite	Executive, freely; plus by impeachment

Democracies in Development

Table 9.3. (continued)

Country	Nomination of director/directorate	Term of office	Removal of director/directorate
Nicaragua Contralor Gral. de la República	Legislature (from list proposed by the president and members of the legislative assembly)	5 years	Legislature
Panama Contralor Gral. de la República	Legislature	5 years and reelectable	Supreme Court
Paraguay Contralor Gral. de la República Tribunal de Cuentas	Legislature	5 years	Executive, after agreement of senate
Peru Contralor Gral. de la República	By legislature (proposed by the president)	7 years	Legislature
Uruguay Presidente del Tribunal de Cuentas	Legislature	5 years	Legislature after definite sentence of court of justice or competent court
Venezuela Contralor Gral. de la República	Legislature (from list presented by citizen committee)	7 years (reelectable)	Legislature after pronouncement of supreme tribunal of justice

stay indefinitely until the age of 70); and one that is appointed and removed at the whim of the president (the Dominican Republic). In Mexico, the director of the supreme audit institution is appointed for eight years, while the director of the secretary of comptrollership and administrative development is appointed for an indefinite period by the president.

Directors are generally designated by the legislative branch in Argentina, Colombia, Costa Rica, El Salvador, Guatemala, Honduras, Mexico (the federation audit institution), Nicaragua, Panama, Paraguay, Peru, Uruguay and Venezuela. In Brazil, the president of the *Tribunal de Cuentas* is appointed by the members of the tribunal. Two-thirds of tribunal members are appointed by the congress and the remainder by the president, subject to senate confirmation. In the other countries, the executive appoints the directors. In Chile, however, the president designates the controller general subject to approval of a majority in the senate.

Institutional design varies even more concerning removal from office. In 11 countries, the comptroller can be removed by the same power through which he or she is appointed. In Brazil, Colombia and Panama, the judiciary issues the order for removal from office. In Colombia, Ecuador, Nicaragua, Paraguay and Venezuela, candidates for comptroller are presented in groups of three to be selected by another branch of government. Only the secretary of comptrollership and administrative development in Mexico and the comptroller in the Dominican Republic are freely appointed and removed by the president.

Performance of Supreme Audit Institutions

In the process of formulating, enacting and executing the budget, the separation of powers of the executive and legislative branches is the chief source of public accountability. As pointed out in Chapter Eight, the budgetary powers divided between the two branches include the power to propose or initiate the budget law (formally conferred upon the president throughout the region); the power of the legislative branch to modify the budget proposed by the president; and the power of the president to veto the budget or to modify it after it has been approved by the legislature. Aside from these constitutionally embedded powers, the balance of partisan forces in the congress can also significantly influence the roles performed by the two branches of government in the budgetary process.

In Latin American presidential systems, the executive tends to dominate this process throughout its various stages. This does not necessarily mean that the executive per se infringes upon the powers of the legislative branch, but rather that its formal authority is broad in this area. Nevertheless, the excessive power of the executive with respect to the budget has been viewed as impeding the establishment of horizontal and vertical accountability, leading some critics to allege that Latin American presidents are virtual budgetary dictators. Thus, the process of establishing compliance with the budget law depends not only on the existence of independent audit institutions with considerable capability and authority, but on a minimum balance of power in budgetary matters between the legislative and executive branches.

Some recommendations appear in the specialized literature concerning the ideal design for supreme audit institutions. These recommendations point to the need for institutions with highly professional members, functional and administrative autonomy, and, to the extent possible, budgetary autonomy. Autonomy and independence may be advantageous and necessary, but sometimes they are not exclusively dependent upon institutional design. For example, while financial autonomy may be called for in the constitution, the actual means for establishing this in practical terms, such as guaranteeing a fixed share of the budget, requires additional steps. In theory, the former courts of accounts in some countries were independent. But despite wielding broad powers and judicial authority, their actions were limited to reporting excesses, and perpetrators were seldom prosecuted. When work of the court of accounts caused trouble for the ruling government, members would typically be removed from office illegally by the president and replaced with presidential allies. This was possible because of the control wielded by the president over the legislative branch and the court system. In Nicaragua, reports submitted by the comptroller's office led to such an intense clash that an immediate consequence was adoption of a reform that gave rise to the current collegial directorate.

There are factors beyond institutional design that support the effectiveness of agencies responsible for horizontal accountability. These agencies need access to reliable information in a timely fashion, and require ongoing support of and participation by civil society and external actors (O'Donnell, 1999).

Thus, a mutually reinforcing and positive interaction between the elements of horizontal and vertical accountability is essential. In fact, a good proportion of the success enjoyed by supreme audit institutions in Latin America has resulted from citizen cooperation either in reporting to or working with the control authorities to assist in exposing violations of laws by public authorities. The organization of forces in the political system also affects the development of effective accountability with respect to public finances. Divided government, for example, can contribute to the development of such capacity. However, divided government also increases the potential for conflict between the legislative and executive branches and for governmental ineffectiveness, which under certain circumstances can endanger the stability of the democratic regime. Thus, the short- and long-term development of an effective oversight capability may conflict with the need for effective decision-making (Kenney, 2000).

General comptroller offices were the most common form of supreme audit institution to be adopted in Latin America in the 20th century, due partly to the influence of the Kemmerer mission. But this type of audit institution encounters some difficulties because of the different legal functions divided in overlapping fashion between diverse public institutions involved in enforcing and administering the law.

Attorney General/Prosecutor General Office

The role of initiating the process of determining legal and criminal responsibility has been constitutionally assigned to different entities, including the Ministerio Público, Procuraduría General, and more recently, Fiscalía General. Given the diverse institutional natures and functions of these distinct law enforcement entities, it is not possible to develop a consistent classification for describing them in the region. Nor is it easy to link the common Anglo-American names for the entities (such as the public prosecutor, solicitor general or attorney general) with Spanish language equivalents in the Latin American political systems. At the risk of conceptual imprecision the word "attorney general" is used to refer to the Latin American institution "Ministerio Público," although its functions are not always the same as that of the Anglo-American institution.

The duties of the attorney general vary from country to country. They include issuing indictments and carrying out the accusatory function and criminal proceedings; directing and promoting procedural and criminal procedural investigations; defending the legal authority and the interests of the state; and defending the civil and human rights of citizens. The most important actions against corruption over the past decade have been headed by the offices of the attorney general or prosecutor general. Thus, the independence and competence of these agencies is critical to democratic governability in the region.

In some countries, more than one institution performs the most important function of the attorney general. In Colombia, the attorney general's office oversees, and initiates legal proceedings against, top-level public officials, protects civil rights guarantees, and defends the legal authority of the state. But the accusatory function is carried out by the general prosecutor's office, which pertains to the judiciary rather that the attorney general's office. In Ecuador, within a single ministry (Ministerio Público), the functions of criminal prosecution and representation of the state's interests in legal matters are divided into two agencies—the attorney general's office (Procuraduría) and the prosecuting attorney's office (Fiscalía General).

During the 1990s, most countries of the region began to introduce major reforms to their criminal justice systems. These included Colombia (1991), Argentina (1992), Guatemala (1994), Costa Rica (1998), El Salvador (1998), Paraguay (1999), Venezuela (1999), and Bolivia, Chile, Ecuador and Honduras (2000). These reforms have been described as a change from inquisitorial or quasi-inquisitorial systems to accusatorial or more accusatorial systems. This entails the introduction of oral and public trials instead of written proceedings and the creation of a sharp distinction between the investigating and the prosecutorial role, on the one hand, and the adjudicating role, on the other. In addition, this reform involves introducing some degree of prosecutorial discretion and alternative dispute resolution mechanisms to simplify the criminal process.

One of the important matters of debate with respect to the institutional design of attorney general offices concerns their institutional position. There is an ongoing discussion regarding the advantages and disadvantages of linking the attorney general's office with the executive branch or the judiciary, or establishing it as an entity independent of the other branches of government (as expressed in Spanish, an *extrapoder*) (Duce, 1999). With respect to this relationship, Table 9.4 shows that in six countries (Brazil, Costa Rica, Mexico, Panama, Paraguay and Dominican Republic), the attorney general's office is linked with the judiciary, while only in Uruguay is it linked with the executive branch. Even though formally belonging to the judicial branch, the attorney general in Mexico is appointed by the president, and performance of his duties are under the jurisdiction of the executive branch.[5] Thus, the formal connection to a given branch of government such as the judiciary is not always an indicator of the real functional relationship.

Attorney general offices in other countries of the region are independent from the traditional branches of government. Colombia is atypical, since its attorney general's office is autonomous. However, its prosecutor general's office, which carries out accusatory duties, is formally part of the judiciary but is functionally autonomous. In Venezuela, the attorney general's office is linked with *Poder Ciudadano*. Starting with the 1988 constitutional reform in Brazil, true independence from the other branches of government was conferred upon the attorney general. The office was given broader jurisdiction, new powers of control over the abuse of power, and the defense of social and collective rights by means of public actions. Thus, the predominant option in the region is independence from the executive, meaning either operational autonomy—the creation of an *extrapoder* separate from any branch of the government—or the establishment of links with the judiciary.

Despite the importance of the debate over the institutional position of the attorney general's office, in many cases the discussion has been overly theoretical, limiting attention to the problems these institutions confront in practice.

A second matter of debate with respect to attorney general offices involves their function in the new criminal procedure model. Under this new approach, the prosecuting function of the attorney general's office is responsible for preliminary investigation and accusation, whereas under the previous approach the facts were brought by other criminal investigation entities. The new approach has been instituted in most Latin American countries, though the previous system was retained in specific cases, such as under the reform of the Argentine federal system in 1992. The attorney general's specific role in the new con-

---

[5] Nevertheless, the administration of President Fox has announced a reform bill that would create a general prosecuting attorney's office that is independent of the executive branch.

Table 9.4. Attorney General Offices (Ministerio Público)

Country	Name of the office	Institution tied to the judiciary[1]	Independent institution or *extrapoder*	Institution tied to other institutions
Argentina	Ministerio Público Fiscal and Ministerio Público de la Defensa		✓	
Bolivia	Fiscalía General de la República		✓	
Brazil	Ministerio Público de la Unión/de los Estados	✓	Functional and administrative autonomy	
Chile	Ministerio Público		✓	
Colombia	Procuraduría General de la Nación		✓	
Costa Rica	Fiscalía General de la República	✓	Complete functional independence	
Dominican Rep.	Ministerio Público	✓		
Ecuador	Ministerio Público		✓	
El Salvador	Procuraduría General de la República		✓	
Guatemala	Fiscalía General and Procuraduría General de la Nación		✓	
Honduras	Ministerio Público		✓	
Mexico	Ministerio Público Federal	✓		
Nicaragua	Ministerio Público		✓	
Panama	Ministerio Público	✓		
Paraguay	Ministerio Público	✓	Functional and administrative autonomy	
Peru	Ministerio Público		✓	
Uruguay	Ministerio Público		Technical independence	✓ Executive
Venezuela	Ministerio Público			✓ Civic power

[1] In Mexico and the Dominican Republic, the attorney general is appointed by the president but according to the constitution is tied to judicial branch.

text of the accusatory system of criminal procedure varies from one country to another, but it is a central figure in the new criminal prosecution process.

With respect to mechanisms for appointing and removing the public prosecutor, there is a clear role in most countries for the executive and judicial branches. Appointment of the attorney general is made primarily by the executive in nine countries, although in several of these the consent of a branch of the legislature (usually the senate) is needed, or the executive selects from a list of candidates prepared by either the legislature or part of the judiciary (Table 9.5). In Chile, the Supreme Court recommends candidates and the president

Table 9.5. Appointment and Tenure of the Attorney General

Country	Term of office	Reappointment	Institution(s) that appoint the director	Institution that removes the director
Argentina	Not defined in the constitution	Not defined in the constitution	Executive (with the agreement of ⅔ of the senate)	Not defined in the constitution
Bolivia	10 years	Yes (after one term has passed)	National congress	Chamber of deputies
Brazil	2 years	Yes (one time)	President (with the approval of the absolute majority in senate)	President (after the authorization of absolute majority of senate)
Chile	10 years	Yes (not immediately)	President (proposed by the Supreme Court and with the agreement of the senate)	Supreme Court (requested by the president or the chamber of deputies)
Colombia	4 years	Yes	Senate (from a list of candidates proposed by the president, the Supreme Court and the Consejo de Estado)	Supreme Court (previous accusation of the Fiscal General de la Nación)
Costa Rica	Not defined?	Not defined?	Supreme Court	Not defined
Dominican Rep.	Not limited	Yes	President	President (freely)
Ecuador	6 years	No	National congress (from a list of candidates presented by the Consejo Nacional de la Judicatura)	National congress
El Salvador	3 years	Yes	Legislative assembly	Legislative sssembly
Guatemala	5 years	Yes	President	President
Honduras	5 years	Yes (one time)	National congress	National congress
Mexico	Not limited	Yes	President (ratified by the senate or the permanent commission of the congress of the union)	President (freely or by political or legal trial)
Nicaragua	5 years	Yes	National assembly (from a list of candidates presented by the president and the deputies)	President
Panama	10 years	Yes	Cabinet and the president (with the approval of the legislative assembly)	Supreme Court

Table 9.5. *(continued)*

Country	Term of office	Reappointment	Institution(s) that appoint the director	Institution that removes the director
Paraguay	5 years	Yes	Executive (with the approval of the senate and from a list of candidates proposed by the Consejo de la Magistratura)	Chamber of senators (in political trial accused by the chamber of deputies)
Peru	3 years	Yes (only for 2 years more)	Junta de Fiscales Supremos	Congress
Uruguay	Indefinite		Executive (with the consent of the chamber of senators or its permanent commission)	Executive (with the agreement of the chamber of senators or its permanent commission)
Venezuela	7 years	Yes	National assembly (from a list of candidates presented by the civic power. If no agreement in 30 days, the list is submitted to a popular vote)	National assembly (with the previous pronouncement of the Supreme Court)

appoints from among this list with the assent of two-thirds of the senate. The Supreme Court also has the power to remove the incumbent from office. In Brazil, the president appoints the attorney general from among those in the career civil service after the candidate has been designated by an absolute majority of the senate. Only in Colombia (since 1991) are the three branches of government involved in appointing and dismissing the attorney general. The senate appoints from a short list of candidates presented by the president, the Supreme Court and the council of state.

The term of office of attorney generals varies widely. The term is indefinite in Mexico and the Dominican Republic; 10 years in Bolivia, Chile, and Panama; seven years in Venezuela; six years in Ecuador; five years in Guatemala, Honduras, Nicaragua and Paraguay; four years in Colombia; three years in El Salvador and Peru; and two years in Brazil.

Reelection of attorney generals is explicitly permitted in most countries, although in a restricted manner in several. In Brazil, the incumbent may be reelected only once. In Bolivia and Chile, the attorney general may be reelected only after the lapse of the 10-year term of his or her successor. In Honduras, the incumbent can be reelected for only one additional term, while in Peru the term can be extended two years through reelection. Where the term of office is indefinite (Mexico and the Dominican Republic), continuation depends on reappointment by the president. In other countries, such as Colombia, El Salvador, Guatemala, Nicaragua, Panama, Paraguay and Venezuela, the attorney general can be reelected indefinitely.

Performance of the Attorney General's Office

The undue emphasis on issues such as the optimal institutional design or procedural model for attorney general offices has led analysts to overlook other problems not directly related to these particular features. Problems associated with implementing reforms or the relationship between the attorney general's office and other state entities, for example, have been virtually ignored.

The issue of autonomy and independence, as indicated earlier, does not depend solely on institutional design, but on other factors as well. What is important is whether the organization has sufficient operational autonomy to function properly, not so much whether it operates from an institutional position formally independent from the branches of government. This is somewhat similar to the chief problem facing many judicial systems in the region.

The risk involved in linking the attorney general's office with the executive branch is the potential for it to become politicized. One of the most serious problems currently facing the attorney general's office in some Latin American countries is "the intervention of the executive branch in determining its policies" (Duce, 1999). This not only leads to possible politicization of criminal prosecution, but also to impunity in cases of political or administrative corruption, or even in cases of human rights violations.

The chief risk involved in judicial intervention in the public prosecutor's office is the potential for what might be called "judicialization." In many countries, judges have had to assume the responsibility of leading investigations. The judiciary has had to perform the functions of the public prosecutor by directing criminal prosecutions. In such cases, the role of the courts as an independent and fair adjudicator of the legal process is likely to be compromised.

These problems of politicization and judicialization have led to the conclusion that the formal institutional design of the attorney general's office as an independent agency was insufficient to make it function in a truly autonomous fashion. Thus, the issue of independence from the standpoint of the relationship between the attorney general's office and the traditional branches of power should be re-examined in a way that takes into account the more practical aspects of autonomy.

There has been little discussion, on the other hand, of the negative consequences that might result from an attorney general's office being afforded too much autonomy. The experience of the office in Brazil shows that undue autonomy can be detrimental in terms of internal control. The autonomy conferred by the 1988 constitution on the new Brazilian attorney general's office, together with its low level of institutionalization "gives its members a great deal of freedom, leaving the identity of the institution open and reliant upon the individual characteristics of its members" (Sadek and Cavalcanti, 2000). Institutional credibility is a factor in legitimizing public decisions, especially in cases when officials have not been elected by popular vote. The attorney general's office in Brazil has been described by the media in terms ranging from "true defender of human rights" to "irresponsible exhibitionist." Settling the issue of who controls the controller is definitive in putting in place a true rule of law.

A second problem facing attorney general offices throughout the region is the lack of coordination between this institution and other organizations related to the criminal justice system, particularly the executive and judicial branches and police forces. Because of this lack of coordination, a certain level of institutional isolation constrains the efficiency of the attorney general's office. Problems related to criminal investigation are largely due to the lack of coordination between judges, prosecuting attorneys and the police.

A third problem has been that, in most cases, the organizational capacity of attorney general offices has not been sufficient to cope with the overload of work. Managing the workload is critical both to efficiency and legitimacy. The legal instruments of attorney general offices have been insufficient for developing an effective policy to streamline the workload. Such inefficiency carries with it the potential negative consequence of a loss of the institution's legitimacy, thus possibly giving rise to a private system of justice fraught with abuses and inequities. The loss of legitimacy also may undermine vertical accountability mechanisms necessary to strengthen the potential of the attorney general's office to enforce horizontal accountability. This is especially true in cases where the citizenry has placed great hope in the capability of these new institutions to alleviate many of the problems they perceive in the operation of democracy in their countries.

A fourth potential problem with attorney general offices is associated with the implementation of reforms, the success of which depends not only on well-conceived institutional designs but also on the way in which proposed changes are implemented. In some countries, a lack of implementation has been one of the chief problems of the reform process. Reforms need to be carried out in such a way that the interests of the other traditional actors in the justice system are taken into account.

A final factor to keep in mind is the need for these agencies and their staff to be professionalized. There is a clear shortage of professionals in charge of managing the offices of attorney generals across the region. Poor or inefficient career or civil service systems have weakened or failed to develop the pool of human resources that serves as the hiring base for management.

The Ombudsman's Office

By current definition, an ombudsman is generally an independent investigator authorized to receive complaints from citizens, make the state answerable for its shortcomings, and provide compensation to victims for damages caused by ineffective or unfair governmental actions or human rights violations.

The concept of the ombudsman's office has its roots in the 19th century in Scandinavia, where the institution of a parliamentary commissioner was created to monitor public administration and provide citizens with an instrument to defend their rights. By the second half of the 20th century, the concept of the ombudsman had spread to other European countries and, through the influence of Great Britain, to its commonwealth. France and

Spain exported the concept to some African and Latin American countries. Finally, with the fall of the Berlin Wall, this concept has recently reached countries in Central and Eastern Europe.

Over the past two decades, ombudsman's offices have been established throughout Latin America in the context of the transition from authoritarianism to democracy. Guatemala was first to adopt the institution in 1985, followed after 1990 by Mexico, El Salvador, Colombia, Costa Rica, Paraguay, Honduras, Peru, Argentina, Bolivia, Nicaragua, Panama, Ecuador, and in some states in Brazil and Venezuela. The establishment of an ombudsman's office is currently on the political agenda in Chile and Uruguay.

While the first ombudsman models in Scandinavia and Europe were limited to cases of poor administration or governmental negligence, the influence of the 1978 Spanish constitution has extended the jurisdiction of such offices in modern Latin America to accountability for human rights violations. More recently, some cases also included environmental protection, freedom of the press, and the supervision of elections.

As in Spain, ombudsman's offices in much of Latin America formed part of efforts to overcome legacies of violations associated with past authoritarian regimes. Within this context of support for democratic transition, ombudsman's offices were granted a high level of legitimacy by society.

Moreover, the institutional design and mechanisms of these offices developed according to the specific needs and demands of citizens of each country. In Colombia, the ombudsman's office has become involved in peace efforts; in El Salvador and Guatemala, in monitoring human rights in the context of the peace accords; in Bolivia, in narcotics elimination programs; in Costa Rica, in some sensitive privatization processes involving state-owned businesses; and in Peru, in the monitoring of electoral processes.

The basic characteristics of this institution are the non-binding nature of its decisions or recommendations, its investigative powers for supervising the actions of public officials, its full autonomy from the government and the courts; and its obligation to report to the congress.

Ombudsman's offices are generally associated with the legislative branch, although most are operationally, administratively, and, in some cases financially, autonomous (Table 9.6). Thus, in most countries ombudsman's offices report to congress, though they may be otherwise autonomous or linked with other institutions. In Honduras and Nicaragua, the ombudsman's office is an autonomous, independent entity with its own legal status, but it submits a report annually to the national assembly. In Colombia, the office is linked with the attorney general's office, while in Venezuela, it is linked with *Poder Ciudadano*, though it still reports to the legislative branch.

Even though their decisions or recommendations are non-binding, rulings of these agencies can include effective instruments of accountability. In Argentina, the ombudsman's office can perform an active role in the legal process. In Bolivia, it can file for the reversal of judgments on grounds of their unconstitutionality, file direct appeals to reverse verdicts, or apply for a writ of habeas corpus without having to make a ruling. In Colombia, it can lodge protective legal actions, while in Guatemala it can denounce administrative behavior injurious to the interests of individuals, and condemn an act by the executive. These

Table 9.6. Ombudsman's Offices

Country	Year of creation	Institution tied to the legislature	Formally autonomous type	Tied to others institutions
Argentina Defensoría del Pueblo	1993	✓	Operational and financial independence	
Bolivia Defensor del Pueblo	1994		Functional autonomy	
Colombia Defensor del Pueblo	1991			✓ (Attorney General)
Costa Rica Defensoría de los Habitantes de la República	1992	✓	Operational and discretionary independence	
Dominican Rep. Defensor del Pueblo	2001			
Ecuador Defensoría del Pueblo	1998	✓	Operational and financial independence	
El Salvador Procuraduría para la Defensa de los Derechos Humanos	1993	✓		
Guatemala Comisión de Derechos Humanos	1985	✓		
Honduras Comisionado Nacional de los Derechos Humanos	1992		Operational and financial independence	
Mexico Comisión Nacional de Derechos Humanos	1990	✓		
Nicaragua Procuraduría para la Defensa de los Derechos Humanos	1995		✓	
Panama Defensoría del Pueblo	1997		✓	
Paraguay Defensoría del Pueblo	1992	✓	Functional autonomy	
Peru Defensoría del Pueblo	1993		✓	
Venezuela Defensoría del Pueblo	1999		Operational and financial independence	✓ Citizen branch of government

actions, if they also receive the support of other players or control agencies, can contribute to the process of enforcing accountability.

Ombudsman's offices also carry out other functions that help create a bridge between society and the government. They may have the authority to undertake and initiate lawsuits, receive and act on complaints from citizens, provide assistance to victims of certain offenses, or instruct citizens on how to defend their rights.

In almost all of the Latin American countries, the legislative branch has the authority to appoint the ombudsman (Table 9.7). Such appointments generally require a qualified majority, usually two-thirds of the votes cast by members of the institution in charge. Panama is distinct in that the president appoints the ombudsman, albeit on the basis of a motion by the legislature.

In some countries, selection of the ombudsman involves mechanisms for including participants from civil society. Such is the case in Ecuador, where the congress elects the ombudsman after conferring with legally recognized human rights organizations, and in Nicaragua, where legislative deputies propose a list of candidates after consulting with major civil society organizations.

Most ombudsmen in Latin America are permitted reelection, except in the case of Venezuela. In some countries, the legislature is authorized to remove the ombudsman from office, while in others, such as Bolivia, Colombia, Panama and the Dominican Republic, the Supreme Court wields this authority.

Performance of Ombudsman's Offices

As already pointed out with respect to supreme audit institutions and attorney general offices, autonomy may be constructive and necessary, but it does not depend solely on institutional design. According to most constitutional and legal provisions in the region, the ombudsman's office is typically part of the legislative branch, functionally and administratively autonomous, and reports to the legislative branch, and thus indirectly to the citizens.

In such a design, the autonomy of the ombudsman's office can depend on the division of political forces in power. In divided governments, political incentives may be such that the actions of the ombudsman's office elicit the support and follow-up of the legislature, thus making it more effective. But this can increase the probability of conflict between the executive and legislative branches, thus having a potentially negative effect on democratic governance.

If the president commands a majority in the legislature, any initiative of the ombudsman aimed at sanctioning irregularities committed by the executive branch may be blocked. This was the case in Peru, where President Fujimori's control over the legislature blocked action on the ombudsman's initiatives to punish abuses committed by the armed forces and intelligence organizations.

Establishing an appointment process, requiring a qualified majority of legislators and providing for input from civil society organizations may be constructive from the standpoint of democracy. Such arrangements have caused problems in some countries, however, when political agreement could not be reached on appointment of the ombudsman. For example, as of the end of 2000, the first ombudsman in Paraguay had not been appointed because

Table 9.7. Appointment and Tenure of the Ombudsman

Country	Term of office	Reappointment	Institution that appoints the director	Institution that removes the director from office
Argentina	5 years	Yes (one time)	Congress	Congress
Bolivia	5 years	Yes (one time)	Congress	Supreme Court
Colombia	4 years	Yes	Chamber of representatives (from a list of three candidates presented by the president)	Supreme Court (previous accusation by the national prosecuting attorney)
Costa Rica	4 years	Yes (one time)	Legislative assembly	Legislative assembly
Dominican Rep.	6 years	Yes (one time)	Senate	Supreme Court
Ecuador	5 years	Yes (one time)	Congress (with the recommendations of recognized human rights organizations)	Congress
El Salvador	3 years	Yes	Legislative assembly	Legislative assembly
Guatemala	5 years	No	Congress (from a list of three candidates presented by the human rights commission)	Congress
Honduras	6 years	Yes	Congress	Not defined
Mexico	5 years	Yes (one time)	Senate	Senate (by political trial) or the chamber of deputies (by "declaración de procedencia en materia penal")
Nicaragua	5 years	Yes	National assembly (from a list reviewed with the pertinent civil associations)	National assembly (previous audience of the attorney general)
Panama	5 years	Yes (one time)	President (candidates are chosen by the commission of human rights of the legislative assembly between the people who freely postulate themselves)	Supreme Court
Paraguay	5 years	Yes	Chamber of deputies	Chamber of senators (accusation by the chamber of deputies)
Peru	5 years	Yes (one time)	Congress	Congress
Venezuela	7 years	No	National assembly (from a list of three candidates presented by the evaluation committee of postulations of citizen power). If no agreement in 30 days, the list is submitted to a popular vote.	National assembly (previous pronouncement of the Supreme Court of Justice)

the required majority vote could not be reached in the chamber of deputies, despite repeated attempts. The same thing happened in El Salvador, where no ombudsman could be appointed for several years in a row.

As pointed out with respect to the other two sets of institutions, agencies of horizontal accountability cannot function in an isolated fashion. In Peru, for example, the 1993 constitutional reform established the office of the ombudsman, formally endowing it with the authority to wield control. However, at the same time, the nucleus of power centered in the presidency, the armed forces and the intelligence agency was reinforced. Consequently, though the constitution authorized and legally empowered the ombudsman's office to wield control within its jurisdiction, the concentration of power reinforced by the *autogolpe* (self-coup) did not allow this agency in practice to take actions to protect citizens from violations of their civil rights.

This factor is even more important if the agencies responsible for enforcing accountability are not authorized to make binding decisions. If no support is available from other state agencies, particularly from the courts, accusations made by institutions such as ombudsman's offices may have the effect of building the hostility of public opinion without actually sanctioning the culprits, in some cases threatening the governance of democratic regimes.

The level of legitimacy of a control official or a control agency can be very important to the practice of horizontal accountability. The Peruvian ombudsman's office, for example, achieved a high level of legitimacy, largely due to the leadership wielded by its director. This is another factor that can work in favor of accountability in cases in which other state agencies are not willing to cooperate with the control efforts of ombudsman's offices. For there to be strong leadership, however, there must be a complementary relationship between horizontal accountability enforced through the ombudsman's office and vertical accountability stemming from public opinion. Since the decisions handed down by ombudsman's offices are non-binding, they must persuade and mobilize society to demand respect for citizen rights. Thus, positive interaction between the ombudsman's office and civil society organizations is essential.

Conclusions

Clearly, there have been constitutional breakthroughs in Latin America in terms of establishing semi-autonomous organizations to control the exercise of public authority. More than ever, the health of democracy today depends on their performance. The need to protect and guarantee fundamental citizen rights and promote civic participation has contributed to the most recent constitutional developments. Consequently, the institutionalization of horizontal accountability agencies aims to strengthen the rule of law and enhance the performance, transparency and integrity of the actions of the state.

Over the past two decades, constitutional and legal reforms have led to the creation of ombudsman's offices and public prosecutor's offices in many countries. During this period, reforms have also sought to more firmly root these institutions in the democratic system and develop their independence and capabilities. Such efforts at institutionalization have also been directed toward supreme audit institutions. Most of these were created in the first half of the 20th century, but they generally did not function as independent agencies.

With respect to Latin America, it has been suggested that the creation of horizontal accountability agencies should consider how they would react in given situations, such as if the head of the executive branch were to be accused of serious abuses of authority. In fact, such an eventuality has already been faced by the presidential regimes that predominate in the region. Public prosecutors, attorney generals, comptrollers and ombudsmen have exercised legal authority in many cases over the past decade in the hemisphere, with mixed results. Such experiences have corroborated the need to endow these entities with sufficient constitutional and legal authority to deal with cases of nonfulfillment of duties of office or abuses of power. The cases involving the comptroller's office in Nicaragua, the general prosecuting attorneys' offices in Venezuela and Colombia, the public prosecutor's office in Brazil, and the ombudsman's office in Peru have served as strong tests of the role and authority of these types of agencies relative to the executive branch.

In order for democracy and the horizontal accountability agencies to gain legitimacy, the public must see that investigations eventually lead to effective trials, judgments and sanctions that are consistent with ethical and legal standards. In each case, the agency must possess and be capable of exercising the political autonomy required to earn the respect of the citizenry.

One factor essential for effective work by horizontal accountability agencies is that they not work separately, but rather in the context of a "network of relatively autonomous powers" supported by an active civil society and a favorable climate of public opinion (O'Donnell, 2000). In cases of control agencies working in relative institutional isolation, positive feedback between vertical and horizontal accountability is even more important, since the backing of public opinion may encourage and mobilize other state institutions to support initiatives taken by a given control entity seeking to hold public officials accountable.

Overlapping and redundant forms of control have been proposed as a way to enhance the ethics of public decision-making, but this can lead to stalemate and less effective public policy. Thus, there needs to be clearer specification of the responsibilities and authorities of the different horizontal accountability agencies in order for them to efficiently carry out their monitoring and controlling tasks while also permitting the government to perform effectively.

Another problem facing accountability agencies in the region is the lack of institutional coordination between these organizations and others that participate in or form part of the criminal justice system. The result is a certain institutional isolation that endangers the efficiency and effectiveness of these agencies. The growth of impunity, for instance, is at least partly attributable to the lack of coordination between judges, prosecuting attorneys, ombudsmen, comptrollers, attorney generals and the police.

The public legitimacy of an agency and its director is also likely to influence its effectiveness. Prosecuting attorney's offices, ombudsman's offices and comptrollers' offices have at times come to enjoy considerable credibility and legitimacy, largely due to the tenure of particular leaders. Nevertheless, there remains the danger that some of these officials will be installed without the institutionalization of the offices that they command, as has occurred in some countries.

Essential to establishing an autonomous accountability agency is guaranteeing that it will act responsibly. Several different mechanisms may be established to ensure public participation in policy formulation and supervision in order to further transparency. (Clearly, this may not be advisable when carrying out criminal and disciplinary proceedings, where secrecy is essential to the success of investigations.) Citizen participation also mobilizes the support of other public and private institutions and constitutes a proper response to the classic question: "Who controls the controller?" Without significant public participation, the legitimacy and effectiveness of these institutions may well be undermined by public opinion, and they may face challenges to their power on many fronts.

Similarly, any type of analysis of these agencies must start with acknowledging the wide gap in the region between formal legal authority and the real world performance, independence and authority of these institutions and individuals.

Finally, while it is true that these horizontal accountability agencies can help surmount the deficit of democracy in the region, the very institutional and cultural context may contribute to their failure. When operating in unfavorable national and cultural contexts, institutions that are "sophisticated" from the standpoint of democratic development will have a limited impact if not accompanied by systematic civic education and public campaigns against governmental corruption and mismanagement. It must not be forgotten that the importance of accountability institutions lies as much in their contribution to overall democratic development and civic education as the particular legal outcomes they might achieve.

Bibliography

Avritzer, Leonardo. 2000. Teoría democrática, esfera pública y deliberación. *Revista Metapolítica* 4(14). April–June.

Bohman, James. 2000. La democracia deliberativa y sus críticos. *Revista Metapolítica* 4(14). April–June.

Centro Latinoamericano de Administración para el Desarrollo (CLAD). 2000. *Responsabilización en la nueva gestión pública Latinoamericana*. Buenos Aires: CLAD – Inter-American Development Bank.

Cohen, Joshua. 2000. Procedimiento y sustancia en la democracia deliberativa. *Revista Metapolítica* 4(14). April–June.

Cox, Gary, and Scott Morgenstern. 2002. Conclusion. In Scott Morgenstern and Benito Nacif (eds.), *Legislatures and Democracy in Latin America*. New York: Cambridge University Press.

Domingo, Pilar. 1999. Judicial Independence and Judicial Reform in Latin America. In Andreas Schedler, Larry Diamond, and Marc Plattner (eds.), *The Self-Restraining State: Power and Accountability in New Democracies*. Boulder, CO: Lynne Rienner Publishers.

Duce, Mauricio. 1999. Problemas en torno a la reconfiguración del public prosecutor en América Latina. Translation of Chapter III of Criminal Justice System in Latin America. Masters' thesis, International Legal Studies Program, Stanford University Law School. May.

Fox, Jonathan. 2000. Civil Society and Political Accountability: Propositions for Discussion. Paper presented at the conference on Political Institutions, Accountability and Democratic Governance in Latin America, University of Notre Dame Kellogg Institute, 8–9 May.

Groisman, Enrique, and Emilia Lerner. 2000. Responzabilización por los controles clásicos. In Centro Latinoamericano de Administración para el Desarrollo (CLAD), *La responsabilización en la nueva gestión pública Latinoamericana*. Buenos Aires: CLAD – Inter-American Development Bank.

Hammergren, Linn. 1998. Institutional Strengthening and Justice Reform. USAID Center for Democracy and Governance.

Kenney, Charles D. 2000. Reflections on Horizontal Accountability: Democratic Legitimacy, Majority Parties and Democratic Stability in Latin America. Paper presented at the conference on Political Institutions, Accountability and Democratic Governance in Latin America, University of Notre Dame Kellogg Institute, 8–9 May.

Lupia, Arthur, and Mathew D. McCubbins. 1998. *The Democratic Dilemma: Can Citizens Learn What They Need to Know?* Cambridge: Cambridge University Press.

O'Donnell, Guillermo. 1994. Delegative Democracy. *Journal of Democracy* 5(1). January.

———. 1999. Horizontal Accountability in New Democracies. In Andreas Schedler, Larry Diamond and Marc Plattner (eds.), *The Self-Restraining State: Power and Accountability in New Democracies*. Boulder, CO: Lynne Rienner Publishers.

———. 2000. Further Thoughts on Horizontal Accountability. Paper prepared for the conference on Political Institutions, Accountability and Democratic Governance in Latin America, University of Notre Dame Kellogg Institute, 8–9 May.

Pope, Jeremy, and Frank Vogl. 2000. Making Anticorruption Agencies More Effective. *Finance and Development* 37(2). June.

Przeworski, Adam, Susan C. Stokes, and Bernard Manin (eds.). 1999. *Democracy, Accountability and Representation*. Cambridge: Cambridge University Press.

Sadek, Maria Tereza, and Rosalgela Batista Cavalcanti. 2000. The New Public Prosecution and the Efficiency of Accountability Mechanisms. Paper prepared for the conference on Political Institutions, Accountability and Democratic Governance in Latin America, University of Notre Dame Kellogg Institute, 8–9 May.

Schedler, Andreas. 1999. Conceptualizing Accountability. In Andreas Schedler, Larry Diamond and Marc Plattner (eds.), *The Self-Restraining State: Power and Accountability in New Democracies*. Boulder, CO: Lynne Rienner Publishers.

Schedler, Andreas, Larry Diamond, and Marc Plattner (eds.). 1999. *The Self-Restraining State: Power and Accountability in New Democracies*. Boulder. CO: Lynne Rienner Publishers.

Shugart, Matthew Soberg, Erika Moreno, and Brian F. Crisp. 2000. The Accountability Deficit in Latin America. Paper prepared for the conference on Institutions, Accountability and Democratic Governance in Latin America, University of Notre Dame Kellogg Institute, 8–9 May.

Smulovitz, Catalina, and Enrique Peruzotti. 2000. Societal and Horizontal Controls: Two Cases about a Fruitful Relationship. Paper presented at the conference on Institutions, Accountability and Democratic Governance in Latin America, University of Notre Dame Kellogg Institute, 8–9 May.

CHAPTER TEN

Direct Democracy Institutions in Latin America

Even though all Latin American political regimes are representative democracies, a growing number of countries during the period of this study introduced or adopted procedures and mechanisms for direct citizen participation in decision-making. These mechanisms, also known as direct democracy institutions, are a means of political participation through direct and universal suffrage.[1] Their aim is to collectively involve citizens directly in the decision-making process rather than to elect representatives to make decisions for them.

What can be gained for democracy, however, if direct democracy mechanisms cannot be made to function? History shows that Greek democracy—more specifically the type practiced in Athens and in some medieval urban communes—was short-lived or incomplete, and that any concrete achievements in terms of the ideal of "pure" democracy were rather limited.

However, experiences in Liechtenstein, Italy, at the subnational level in the United States, and particularly in Switzerland, demonstrate the potential of direct democracy as a mechanism for giving expression to the popular will. Even these experiences, however, do not necessarily provide insights into how these institutions operate in Latin America.

Given the generally low levels of public trust in legislative bodies and political parties (see Chapter Two), direct democracy mechanisms are viewed by certain sectors as valid options to improve the quality and depth of political representation, boost participation, and strengthen the legitimacy of democratic institutions. Thus, a debate has been opened in the region with respect to the potential benefits and risks of these institutions.

Critics suggest that direct democracy mechanisms may undermine institutions of representative democracy, and that there is a risk that they will be used for demagogic pur-

---

[1] Given the focus of this book on political institutions at the national level, analysis of direct democracy mechanisms in this chapter will also be limited to this level.

poses. Defenders of such mechanisms contend, however, that this supposed contradiction between direct democracy and representative democracy is an anachronism, since comparative experience shows that direct democratic institutions can complement representative democratic processes rather than supplant or weaken them.

Types of Direct Democracy Institutions

There are a number of direct democracy institutions in Latin America and a variety of ways to describe them. Constitutions refer to similar institutions using different terminology. These terms and mechanisms include popular legislative initiative (*iniciativa legislativa popular*), referendum or plebiscite, or the more direct translation "popular consultation" (*consulta popular*), recall (*revocatoria de mandato*), and open town meeting (*cabildo abierto*). Thus, it is not feasible to identify a common terminology for the purpose of cross-country comparison that is faithful to the diverse notions of these concepts in the countries of the region.

This chapter classifies direct democracy mechanisms into the first three groups above: *popular consultations* (by far the most frequently used); *popular legislative initiatives*; and *recall votes*. Given that these mechanisms are interconnected (for instance, a legislative initiative can lead to the calling of a popular consultation), the classification is somewhat loose and is intended merely to enhance the clarity of the description of the various mechanisms in the region.

Popular consultation embraces both plebiscites and referenda. Though some experts distinguish between plebiscite (direct vote of the people on important political matters), and referendum (direct popular vote on the approval of laws or constitutional texts), this chapter will use the term popular consultation indistinctly to refer to both of these mechanisms. In general, popular consultations refer to votes by citizens to decide or express opinions on matters that are constitutional in nature or relating to legislative proposals or issues of national importance.

The second direct democracy mechanism, legislative popular initiative, entails the right of citizens, through the gathering of sufficient signatures, to introduce bills to make partial or complete reforms to laws or the constitution.

The third mechanism, recall votes, gives citizens the capacity to vote to remove an elected official from office.

A more comprehensive classification of the array of direct democracy mechanisms first distinguishes according to their area of application and origin (Figure 10.1). This involves distinguishing between mechanisms targeted at individual elected officials and those with a substantive, law-making purpose, as well as between mechanisms triggered from the bottom up, from the top down, and those that occur as a result of an institutional requirement.

The mechanism of popular consultation may be either compulsory or optional. Compulsory mechanisms can be subdivided into two categories: (a) consultations called for in relation to predetermined issues specifically ordained in the constitution, and (b) consultations established for predetermined situations, which are only set in motion when a predefined circumstance arises (such as a dispute between the executive branch and the congress that is irresolvable within the framework of the representative system).

Figure 10.1. Classification of Direct Democracy Mechanisms

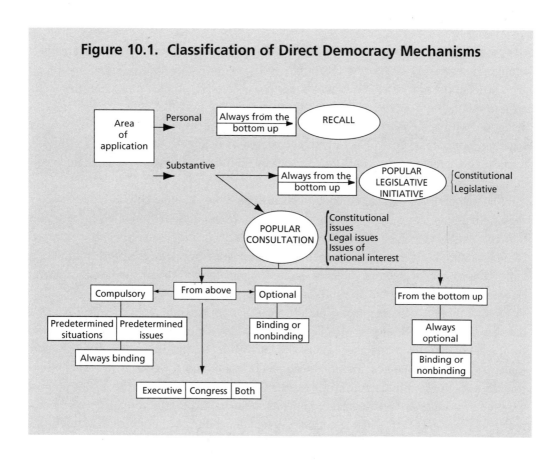

Popular consultations that are compulsory for predetermined issues are provided for in El Salvador, Panama and Guatemala, which require that certain decisions affecting national sovereignty be put up to the vote of citizens. In El Salvador, these consultations are called for to make decisions regarding the political unification of Central American countries; in Panama, for deciding the future of the Panama Canal; and in Guatemala, for establishing laws related to the border dispute with Belize.

The constitutions in Chile and Peru mandate compulsory popular consultations for predetermined situations. Peru requires that constitutional reforms be put to a popular vote when they are backed by an absolute majority in congress, but support falls short of the two-thirds majority required for their enactment. Constitutional reforms are put to a popular vote in Chile only if the executive branch and the legislature cannot reach an agreement.

Optional popular consultation mechanisms may be further divided into two categories: (a) when the call for a popular vote is imposed from the top down (that is, the branches of government have the exclusive right to implement the mechanism), and (b) when the initiative behind the consultation comes from the bottom up, that is, from the citizenry itself. Popular consultations coming from the top down may originate from either the executive branch or the congress, or from both in a coordinated fashion. Popular consultations driven from the bottom up result from citizen initiatives that must pass some kind of threshold for the process to go forward, such as obtaining the signatures of a minimum percentage or number of registered voters or citizens.

Optional popular consultations have been legislated in at least nine countries in the region. In Argentina, Brazil, Nicaragua and Paraguay, the initiative either chiefly or exclusively lies with the congress. In Guatemala, both the executive branch and the congress have the authority. In Colombia, only the legislature may initiate a referendum for the sole purpose of convening a constitutional convention. In the remaining countries, popular consultations are an option reserved for the executive branch.

The outcomes of popular consultations may be either binding or non-binding, and if they are binding, they may or may not require a minimum quorum. In Latin America, popular consultation mechanisms established to ratify constitutional reforms are in all cases binding. It should be noted, however, that except in Uruguay, where the participation of at least 35 percent of registered voters is required, no country in the region requires a given quorum to validate a popular consultation.

In Colombia, Ecuador, Uruguay and Venezuela, popular consultations with respect to laws are binding. In Nicaragua, popular consultations are binding when they are proposed by at least 60 percent of the members of the legislature. In Argentina, the congress determines when the popular consultation is binding or non-binding. However, the outcomes of popular consultations initiated by the president are non-binding, as are the results of those initiated by congress when a law has not been passed calling for the vote. In Colombia, the results of popular consultations are binding when derived from a proposal initiated by the president and approved by the congress.

A noteworthy characteristic is that, in many countries such as Colombia, Uruguay, Paraguay and Peru, restrictions are placed on the issues that may be considered in popular consultations, while in other countries, such as Argentina, Brazil and Nicaragua, there are no stated limits.

Finally, only in Colombia and Uruguay can popular consultation be used to abrogate as well as ratify laws. However, in both these countries, certain types of legislation (such as tax policy) may not be put to a popular consultation.

Popular legislative initiatives are mandated in the constitutions of almost half of the countries in Latin America, but their use has been rather limited, with the exception of Uruguay. This mechanism is usually ad parlamentum, meaning that the proposals presented through a citizen-driven initiative are studied by the legislature, which reaches a decision on them without consulting with the electorate again. However, a few countries provide for a legislative initiative mechanism that results in a popular vote by citizens to decide the matter without the need for consideration by the legislature. In Uruguay, constitutional reform or other legal initiatives originating from the citizenry with the backing of at least 10 percent of the eligible electorate must be put to a popular consultation. In Colombia, when a bill introduced by popular initiative has been rejected by parliament, it must be put to a vote in a "referendum for approval" if 10 percent of the registered voters so request.

Recall votes are in most cases limited to the subnational area, but in Colombia, Panama and Venezuela they can be applied at the national level. In Venezuela, this option has been established for the offices of all popularly elected public servants, including the president. Nevertheless, to date this mechanism has not been used at the national level in any country in the region. At the subnational level, the mechanism has been established and used in numerous countries (for example, Argentina, Ecuador, Peru, Bolivia and Colombia).

Table 10.1 classifies countries into three categories according to whether direct democracy mechanisms are in the constitution and whether they have been used. In the first group of ten countries (dark shading), at least one of these mechanisms exists and one or more has been applied. The three countries in the second group (light shading) have some type of direct democracy mechanism in the constitution, but none has been used to date. Finally, in the third group of five countries (no shading), no provision has been made for these kinds of mechanisms at the national level.

At the outset of the 1990s, there was a proliferation of direct democracy mechanisms throughout Latin America. This trend reflected the desire to broaden public participation in order to remedy the crisis of representation and fight the pervasive corruption in the political system. However, these mechanisms did not play an important role in the first phase of the transition to democracy, since neither the democratic transition processes in South America nor the peace accords that ended the armed conflicts in Central America envisioned these institutions.

Table 10.1
Direct Democracy Mechanisms at National Levels in Latin America

Country	Popular legislative initiative		Plebiscite/ Referendum		Recall	
	Exists	Used	Exists	Used	Exists	Used
Argentina	Yes	No	Yes	Yes	No	No
Brazil	Yes	No	Yes	Yes	No	No
Chile	No	No	Yes	Yes	No	No
Colombia	Yes	Yes	Yes	No	Yes	No
Ecuador	Yes	No	Yes	Yes	No	No
Guatemala	Yes	No	Yes	Yes	No	No
Panama	No	No	Yes	Yes	Yes	No
Peru	Yes	No	Yes	Yes	No	No
Uruguay	Yes	Yes	Yes	Yes	No	No
Venezuela	Yes	No	Yes	Yes	Yes	No
El Salvador	No	No	Yes	No	No	No
Nicaragua	Yes	No	Yes	No	No	No
Paraguay	Yes	No	Yes	No	No	No
Bolivia	No	No	No	No	No	No
Costa Rica	No	No	No	No	No	No
Honduras	No	No	No	No	No	No
Mexico	No	No	No	No	No	No
Dominican Rep.	No	No	No	No	No	No

As a consequence of Latin America's constitutional reforms in the 1980s and particularly the 1990s, 13 countries now provide for direct democracy mechanisms in their national constitutions. Nevertheless, to date only Uruguay and, to a lesser extent, Ecuador, have made frequent use of these mechanisms. Despite the wide variety of direct democracy mechanisms provided for in its 1991 constitution, Colombia has used this formal mechanism only once at the national level. (The 1990 popular consultation that led to the drafting of the 1991 constitution did not follow formal constitutional procedures.) In three of the 13 countries where such mechanisms are in the constitution—El Salvador, Nicaragua and Paraguay—they have not been used to date. Finally, five countries (Bolivia, Costa Rica, Dominican Republic, Honduras and Mexico) make no provision in their constitutions for these mechanisms at the national level.[2]

All of the new constitutions adopted in Latin America during the 1980s and 1990s included direct democracy mechanisms. The reasons behind their introduction were different across the region, but two conditions have been influential in several of the cases. First was the rise in influence of "outsider" political interests, including neopopulist presidents or previously excluded parties who came to dominate constituent assemblies; and second, when rule by traditional political interests has come under strong pressure to democratize political institutions (Barczak, 2001). (Uruguay is an exception, since direct democracy institutions were introduced back in 1919.) The consequences of these conditions is that direct democracy mechanisms have been little used and therefore have had relatively little effect in terms of enhancing democratic representation and legitimacy.

Use of Direct Democracy Institutions

Table 10.2 presents a summary of the use of direct democracy mechanisms in countries throughout the region during the period of this study. Between 1978 and 2000, 31 popular consultations were held in 10 countries. Significantly, five were held during authoritarian government regimes: in Panama in 1983, Uruguay in 1980, and Chile in 1980, 1988 and 1989. In Panama, the plebiscite approved in 1983 was aimed at reforming the constitution in order to strengthen the authoritarian regime of General Noriega. The results of the 1980 plebiscite in Uruguay were unfavorable to the military, thus opening the way to four years of negotiations culminating in the reinstatement of democracy. Conversely, General Pinochet's regime prevailed in Chile in 1980 and imposed its own constitution. In the 1988 consultation—envisioned in the 1980 constitution as an instrument to validate the continuation of President Pinochet—the outcome was unfavorable. The purpose of the 1989 popular consultation, which was approved, was to change the constitution to promote the withdrawal of Pinochet from power and to facilitate the democratic transition.

The remaining 26 cases present a great variety of issues and results. Popular consultations were not binding in Argentina in 1984, Colombia in 1990 and 1997, and Ecuador in

---

[2] Costa Rica provides for the use of referenda in its constitution, but only at the subnational level. Several efforts have been made to extend these mechanisms to the national level, and the legislative assembly has recently been studying the issue.

Table 10.2. Direct Democracy Mechanisms Used from 1978 to 2000

Country	Date	Mechanism	Issue	Outcome	Effect
Argentina	Nov. 1984	Popular consultation	The Beagle decision	Passed	Legitimizing, non-binding. Support for the administration of President Alfonsín, author of the proposal.
Brazil	April 1993	Plebiscite	Monarchy vs. republic	Republic	Legitimization of the prevailing regime, binding.
	April 1993	Plebiscite	Parliamentarianism vs. presidentialism	Presidentialism	Legitimization of the prevailing regime and the presidential system.
Colombia	March 1990	Informal popular consultation	Possibility of reforming the constitution by extra-parliamentarian means. Direct popular vote advanced by students [7th ballot]	Affirmative	Because of this informal popular consultation, a constituent assembly was convened and its members were elected in December 1990.
	Oct. 1997	Popular consultation	Support for pacification	Approved	Irrelevant. Attempted legitimization of the peace process by the president's office.
Chile	Sep. 1980	Plebiscite	New constitution establishing the new regime.	Approved	New constitution and new electoral system.
	Oct. 1988	Plebiscite	According to the 1980 constitution, whether to extend President Pinochet's term of office	Rejected	The rejection of the military proposal made by means of direct popular vote, as anticipated since 1980. This subsequently allowed the acceleration of the democratic process.
	June 1989	Plebiscite	Constitutional reform	Approved	Confirmation of the negotiations for transition toward democracy.
Ecuador	Jan. 1978	Plebiscite	Constitution	Approved	Legitimization of the transition.
	June 1986	Popular consultation	Candidacies independent of the political parties	Rejected	Non-binding, irrelevant.
	Aug. 1994	Consulta-encuesta containing seven questions[1]	Provide legitimacy to the president	Most approved except for the one on the budget of the parliament	Non-binding. Mere display of support for President Sixto Durán, who initiated the process. Items not implemented.

Table 10.2. *(continued)*

Country	Date	Mechanism	Issue	Outcome	Effect
Ecuador	Nov. 1995	Consulta-encuesta	Authority of the president to dissolve parliament one time during his term of office; also, change the term for legislators elected at provincial level from two to four years	All points rejected	Non-binding. Became a plebiscite to oppose the administration of President Sixto Durán, the initiator of the process.
	May 1997	Consulta-encuesta containing 11 questions	Support for removal of President Bucarám from office and his replacement by Alarcón	Approved	Legitimized the downfall of the president and the confirmation of his replacement. Because of the popular consultation, a constitutional convention was convened, which approved a new constitution, including some of the measures put to popular consultation.
Guatemala	Jan. 1994	Referendum	Constitutional reform	Approved	Approval of constitutional reforms needed because of adjustments made to the system of institutions in the wake of the unsuccessful self-coup by President Jorge Serrano.
	May 1999	Referendum	Constitutional reforms made to implement the peace accords	Rejected	Became a plebiscite hostile to the government instead of focusing on the constitutional issue under discussion.
Panama	April 1983	Referendum	Constitutional reform	Approved	Strengthening the authoritarian regime of President Noriega.
	Nov. 1992	Referendum	A 58-point constitutional reform	Rejected	Attempted legitimization of the reforms introduced by the democratic regime.
	Aug. 1998	Plebiscite	Constitutional reform, instant re-election of the president, and other points	Rejected	The administration of President Pérez Balladares was voted down.
Peru	Oct. 1993	Plebiscite	New constitution	Approved	Legitimization of President Fujimori's new regime.

Table 10.2. *(continued)*

Country	Date	Mechanism	Issue	Outcome	Effect
Uruguay	Nov. 1980	Plebiscite	New constitution proposed by military government	Rejected	Rejection brought pressure on military to start process of liberalizing regime.
	April 1989	Referendum	General amnesty law for the military and police	Approved	Lent popular backing to a very controversial decision.
	Nov. 1989	Plebiscite	Constitutional reform	Approved	Approval of agreements reached previously by political party leaders.
	Dec. 1992	Referendum	Proposal to revoke law partially privatizing the state-owned telephone company	Approved	Expressed the continued statist sentiments of the electorate.
	Aug. 1994	Plebiscite	Constitutional reform separating municipal and national elections on the ballot	Rejected	
	Nov. 1994	Plebiscite	Constitutional reform to establish regulations to protect retired persons and those receiving pensions	Approved	Reformed constitution to add protections for an important group of citizens.
	Nov. 1994	Plebiscite	Constitutional reform reserving 27% of the budget for education	Rejected	
	Dec. 1996	Plebiscite	Constitutional reform to modify the electoral system	Approved	Brought about important reform of electoral system, eliminating double simultaneous vote and replacing it with primaries and general elections.
	Oct. 1999	Plebiscite	Two constitutional reforms: prohibition of candidacy for members of state enterprises, and fixed percentage of the budget set aside for the judicial branch	Rejected	
Venezuela	April 1999	Referendum	Agreement with executive resolution to elect a constituent assembly and how it should be formed	Approved	Process that formed part of the initiative of President Chávez to reform the political system.

Table 10.2. *(continued)*

Country	Date	Mechanism	Issue	Outcome	Effect
Venezuela	Dec. 1999	Plebiscite	Constitutional reform	Approved	Endorsement of reform enacted by the constituent assembly.
	Dec. 2000	Plebiscite	Calling of legislative elections	Rejected	Rejected calling of labor union elections within 180-day period.

Note: In five of the cases of direct democracy in this table—Chile (1980, 1988, 1989), Panama (1983) and Uruguay (1980)—the mechanisms were used in the context of authoritarian regimes. Thus, the use of direct democracy mechanisms for purposes related to democratic governance has been even scarcer than indicated by the list in this table.
[1] The term *consulta-encuesta* was used in Ecuador because the format of the ballot for the direct popular vote was similar to that of questionnaires used in public opinion polls.

1986 and 1997 for the *consultas-encuestas*. This last vote led to the calling of a constituent assembly, which incorporated in the proposed constitutional reform a good portion of what had been previously approved in the popular consultation.

The other cases of popular consultation were binding. Of these, 17 were held to approve or reject constitutional reforms: six in Uruguay, with three approved and three rejected; two in Chile, both approved; one in Brazil, which was rejected; three in Panama, with one approved and two rejected; two in Guatemala, with one approved and one rejected; and one each in Ecuador, Peru and Venezuela, all approved. Two of the popular consultations, both in Uruguay, were aimed at overturning legislation. The popular consultation in Colombia in 1990 legitimized and formed a constituent assembly on the very same day. The same procedure was followed in Venezuela in April 1999. In December 2000, another referendum was called by President Chávez's government to test support for calling labor union elections within a 180-day period. Calling a referendum on this matter conflicted with the regulations of the International Labour Organization. The citizenry responded to the petition of labor unions not to participate and the initiative was rejected, with a turnout of only 20 percent.

The self-coups of President Fujimori in Peru, which succeeded, and President Serrano Elías in Guatemala, which failed, led to popular consultations in both countries in 1993. Each resulted in the formation of constituent assemblies, and the establishment of a new constitution in Peru and reforms to the constitution in Guatemala. The profound political crisis in Venezuela that led to the erosion of the political party system that had been in existence since the 1961 *Punto Fijo* pact resulted in popular consultations in 1999 that established a constituent assembly and ratified the constitution enacted by it.

The only popular consultation carried out in the context of a peace process was in Guatemala in 1999, which was broadly rejected by the citizens. These mechanisms were not used in the peace processes in Nicaragua or in El Salvador.

In terms of the origins of the popular consultations during the 1978–2000 period, the vast majority originated with initiatives from the top down. The executive branch convoked the 1984 popular consultation in Argentina, the 1997 popular consultation in Colombia, and the four *consultas-encuestas* in Ecuador in 1997. Regarding the approved constitutional reforms, it should be emphasized that although legislative bodies or constitutional conventions officially encouraged them in seven of the 16 cases, the executive branch initiated the process. The seven cases were Guatemala (1994), Panama (1998), Peru (1993), Venezuela (1999 and 2000), and, under military regimes, Chile (1980) and Uruguay (1980).

In summary, the executive initiated 13 of the 31 popular consultations that were held. Another 11 were the result of agreements among politicians that resulted in constitutional reform proposals either approved or rejected, or constitutional provisions agreed on beforehand, such as the aforementioned 1993 popular consultation in Brazil and the one in Chile in 1988. Altogether, 24 of the 31 popular consultations held arose from initiatives coming from the top down.

The last seven cases were due to initiatives coming from the bottom up. Six took place in Uruguay: two approved constitutional reforms (1989, 1994), two rejected constitutional reforms (1994, 1999) and two referenda to repeal laws. The seventh case, as indicated above, was that of Colombia in 1990, which was extra-constitutional in nature and led to the drafting and adoption of the 1991 constitution.

Assessment of Direct Democracy Institutions

Frequency of Use

Only modest use has been made over the past two decades of mechanisms for direct citizen participation at the national level. In fact, direct democracy institutions have been used in only 10 of the 13 countries where they figure in the constitution. In Chile, the mechanisms were used only under the previous authoritarian regime, as they were under nondemocratic regimes in Uruguay in 1980 and Panama in 1983. Overall, institutions for direct democracy were used by far most often during the period in Uruguay, followed by Ecuador and, more recently, Venezuela.

Though these mechanisms have not often been used, there has been an increase in their use over the period. Nine popular consultations (five under authoritarian regimes) took place during the 1980s, while 22 took place during the 1990s.

No general rule explains why some countries have used these mechanisms at the national level more than others. The prevailing circumstances in the two countries in which they have been most used could scarcely be more different. In Uruguay, these mechanisms had been in existence long before the restoration of democracy, and the party system is relatively institutionalized.[3] In Ecuador, the weak and fragmented party system sometimes prompted presidents to use popular consultations in defensive fashion in a vain attempt to fend off harassment by the legislature and bolster declining public support.

---

[3] The possibility to use referenda to repeal laws was an innovation that occurred after the democratic transition.

Direct democracy mechanisms have been scarcely used in the region's three largest countries. Argentina and Brazil have each used them only once, and the Mexican constitution does not even provide for them.

Origins of Use

This chapter has pointed out that 24 of the 31 popular consultations during the period of the study originated from the top down and only seven from the bottom up (with six of those in just one country, Uruguay). This experience is consistent with the historical tendency for direct democracy institutions to be used by those in positions of power.

The top down approach to using direct democracy mechanisms has been pursued across the region with mixed results for those in power. In Panama, former President Pérez Balladares failed in his attempt to modify the constitution to permit his re-election. In Ecuador, President Sixto Durán got a favorable response in the first popular consultation during his administration, but lost the second one, resulting in the weakening of his government. The Uruguayan government suffered a defeat in 1994 when it attempted to impose a constitutional reform to separate municipal and national voting lists, a reform that had already been approved by two-thirds of the members of parliament. (The same reform was subsequently approved in 1996.) President Fujimori in Peru and President Chávez in Venezuela successfully used direct democracy mechanisms to reform their respective national constitutions in ways consistent with their political goals.

The Role of Civil Society

The constitutions of several countries allow for constitutional reforms to be initiated by citizens, thus providing them with a greater decision-making role. Each country requires a certain percentage of registered voters to sign a petition for such a process to take place. However, to date, only Uruguay has used this mechanism, with the initiatives ending successfully two of the three times. Reform initiatives launched by civil society organizations in 1989, 1994 and 1999 were aimed at increasing the budget or benefits for workers in the retirement system, education sector and the judiciary, respectively. Only the initiatives of 1989 and 1994 were approved.

Referenda held to overturn laws in Uruguay were also the result of popular initiatives. A coalition of left and center-left parties and an ad hoc civil society movement sponsored the 1989 referendum aimed at revoking the amnesty law. This referendum was defeated. The 1992 referendum that overturned a law that would have partially privatized the state-owned telephone enterprise was spearheaded by a similar coalition of partisan forces, together with a group of labor unions representing the telephone workers. Clearly, the participation of Uruguayan civil society organizations was limited, since in both cases an alliance was needed between these ad hoc social movements and political party forces. In Colombia, the seventh ballot student movement (*movimiento estudiantil de la 7ª papeleta*) exerted pressures that led to the 1991 constitutional reform. In the remainder of the cases, initiatives came mainly from the president or the legislature.

Several countries provide for legislative initiatives from citizens, imposing the requirement that a given percentage of the population sign a petition. The constitutions of some countries (e.g., Brazil and Venezuela) also stipulate that if the legislature rejects a bill introduced by popular initiative, a certain percentage of the citizens may request that it be put to a referendum. Paraguay, Peru and Uruguay also provide for this mechanism in their constitutions, but as has been the case with the other countries mentioned earlier, the laws needed to implement the mechanism have yet to be enacted.

The use of these mechanisms at the national level generally has not increased the influence of civil society in public decision-making. Greater citizen control over the government and other representative institutions has resulted in only a very few cases. The only clear examples were the popular consultations used in Uruguay to attempt to repeal laws.

In short, aside from the 1990 informal popular consultation in Colombia and the attempted constitutional reform efforts in Uruguay, civil society has assumed a more prominent role in controlling and restraining than in creating and innovating. Furthermore, despite constitutional provisions for implementing these mechanisms, civil society initiatives are not easy to carry out. They require the convergence of political will around a relevant, motivating issue and the development of a social movement to carry the process forward. Formally, there are no other examples to date beyond Uruguay's attempts to repeal laws and approval in Colombia of an anti-kidnapping law. Even in Uruguay, the last two attempts to repeal laws through popular consultations failed because the minimum requirement for signatures on the petition (25 percent of the legally registered electorate) was not met.

The Behavior of the Citizenry

The actions and behavior of citizens in terms of participating in direct democracy institutions have varied. No overall trend has emerged in the region in this regard. What has been clear is that citizens often do not vote in a manner that focuses on the particular issue put before them; rather, they vent their frustration at the poor performance of the government in power. Therefore, popular consultations in some countries have served as a means of expressing overall disenchantment with politics and politicians.

One example is the unequivocal rejection by Uruguayan citizens of the 1994 mini-constitutional reform, which was backed by all the major political parties. Apparently, the outcome had little to do with the specific content of the issues before the public. Another example was the popular consultation in Guatemala in 1999. The reforms designed to ratify the peace accords that ended the 26-year long civil war were of little interest to the public, which on the whole did not participate in the process. A high percentage of those who did participate voted "no" as a means of expressing dissatisfaction with the government in power.

There is also no clear tendency for either preserving the status quo or bringing about significant change. While the rejection of parliamentary reforms in Brazil's 1993 referendum preserved the status quo, the seventh ballot student movement initiative in Colombia promoted political change.

As a result of such unpredictability, elected officials may be becoming more cautious about using direct democracy mechanisms, resorting to them only when they feel fairly confident that the outcome will be favorable, or applying them only when obliged to do so, as in the case of constitutional reforms.

Low levels of electoral participation in popular consultations reflect considerable apathy on the part of voters. The Guatemalan and Colombian examples were particularly noteworthy for poor levels of participation, although this is consistent with high levels of abstention typical of these countries in regular elections. Some popular consultations have been approved or rejected with less than 50 percent of registered voters participating. Nonetheless, even in these cases the results were accepted, even by those whose position on the matter at hand was defeated.

Consequences for the Political System

There is not clear evidence that the use of direct democracy mechanisms at the national level has significantly improved or worsened the performance of political systems across the world. With a few exceptions, the democracies of Europe and North America either do not provide for national popular consultations, or rarely invoke them. Experience to date in Latin America indicates that at the national level these mechanisms, in the way that they have been used, have generally not had the desired impact in improving representation or participation.

Neither have direct democracy mechanisms substantially affected democratic political stability. Just as with any other electoral engineering mechanism, their functioning must be analyzed in relation to the broader institutional framework. In general, these mechanisms have not been used to resolve disputes between the legislature and the executive branch. One of the few examples of their use in this way was when Ecuadorian Presidents Sixto Durán and Fabián Alarcón unsuccessfully resorted to popular consultations to enhance the popular legitimacy and legislative backing of their weakened administrations.

In some countries or at particular moments, the use of these mechanisms could even be considered to have been counterproductive to political stability. Ecuador once again serves as an example. Non-binding popular consultations without subsequent implementation have actually exacerbated that country's problems of democratic governability.

The complexity of economic and financial issues at the national level makes it difficult to try to solve them through citizen participation through direct democracy institutions. Therefore, constitutions in most Latin American countries have expressly excluded such matters from being considered in popular consultations.

However, these mechanisms were used by civil society organizations tied to center-left parties to try to impose limits on economic reforms in Uruguay and Ecuador. The paradigmatic case was the 1992 repeal of the law enacted by the Uruguayan government to partially privatize the state-owned telephone enterprise. However, a similar attempt several years later to hold a plebiscite in order to oppose a law regulating the distribution of electricity and gas failed, as did a challenge to the private retirement and pension system.

In Ecuador, attempts by civil society groups to call a popular consultation to counter the economic plan and the dollarization policy of President Gustavo Noboa failed because, according to the electoral management body, the required number of signatures were not obtained.

Conclusions

In general, the use as well as the impact of direct democracy mechanisms at the national level in most Latin American countries has been limited.

These mechanisms have been used for different intentions and have had mixed and even unexpected results. Their purposes have ranged from demagogic manipulation to the defense of conservative or traditionalistic positions, and to popular initiatives to bring about change. Two extreme cases where prevailing authoritarian regimes resorted to these mechanisms to keep themselves in power (Chile in 1988 and Uruguay in 1980) ended up backfiring.

Thus, in view of the Latin American experiences considered in this chapter, several matters should be considered when assessing the impact that direct democracy mechanisms have had in the region. First, the mechanisms have been fairly recently adopted and applied. With the exception of Uruguay, direct democracy mechanisms are a relatively new feature of democracy in Latin America. Hence, more time is needed to evaluate their effects and their scope of application. Second a proper legal framework should be established to improve the functioning of these mechanisms. For example, the law must address the different options available to activate such mechanisms. Experience has shown that during the period covered by this study, these mechanisms were primarily initiated from the top down. As has already been mentioned, legal norms should also clearly specify the situations and issues that may be dealt with through the application of the various direct democracy mechanisms.

In general terms, democracy will be strengthened to the extent that the use of direct democracy mechanisms is rooted in and contributes to strengthening citizenship. This goal can be supported through civic education that promotes the development of values associated with the exercise of political participation that goes beyond just electoral participation. As things now stand (see Chapter Two), levels of interpersonal trust and faith in political institutions in Latin America are very low. This makes it difficult to mobilize and coordinate civil society and improve or broaden political participation.

In societies such as those in Latin America, where there are persistently high levels of poverty and inequality, direct democracy mechanisms, if wisely used, may help offset the trend toward delegitimatizing the political system. Direct democracy institutions can provide an additional means for political expression, which at times may be a valuable way for people to signal their frustrations to those in positions of power. But it is important in this context to avoid the danger that these same mechanisms might be used for demagogic purposes. Thus, distinct limits to the types of issues that may be dealt with through direct democracy mechanisms should be established.

It is also important that direct democracy mechanisms be viewed as instruments for strengthening democracy that complement rather than substitute for representative democratic institutions. It is true the direct democracy mechanisms can strengthen political legitimacy and open channels of participation for reconciliation between citizens and their representatives. But the central institutions to articulate and aggregate citizen preferences remain political parties and the legislature. These must be strengthened if the quality and legitimacy of democratic representation is to be improved.

Finally, the fact that direct democracy mechanisms have been scarcely used and have had little impact at the national level—not only in Latin America but in other democracies in the world—suggests that they may be more suitable and beneficial at the subnational level. This notion finds some support in instances when such mechanisms have been used at subnational levels in European and North American democracies, as well as in some Latin American countries.

Beyond the assessment of the results of using direct democracy mechanisms comes the acknowledgment that they are likely here to stay. The main concern, therefore, is how to use them properly and, more importantly, when to use them and with regard to what issues.

Bibliography

Aguilar de Luque, Luis. 1986. Participación política y reforma. Aspectos teóricos y constitucionales. *Revista de Derecho Público* no.102, Madrid.

Barczak, Monica. 2001. Representation by Consultation? The Rise of Direct Democracy in Latin America. *Latin American Politics and Society* 43(3). Fall.

Bogdanor, Vernon. 1994. Western Europe. In David Butler and Austin Ranney (eds.), *Referendums around the World: The Growing Use of Direct Democracy*. Washington, DC: AEI Press.

Cronin, Thomas E. 1998. *Direct Democracy: The Politics of Initiative, Referendum and Recall*. Cambridge: Harvard University Press.

Thibaut, Bernhard. 1998. Instituciones de democracia directa. In Dieter Nohlen, Sonia Picado, and Daniel Zovatto (eds.), *Tratado de derecho electoral comparado de América Latina*. Mexico: Fondo de Cultura Económica.

CHAPTER ELEVEN

Main Trends in Democratic Reform

Latin America's experience with democracy over the past two decades has been the broadest and the most lasting in its history. This trend has persisted despite the fact that many of these democratic systems emerged under difficult socioeconomic conditions or in the midst of serious social conflicts.

The extension of democracy has increased the freedom of citizens across the region to express their views, choose their leaders, organize themselves politically, and gain access to information about their government. It has also meant greater protection of their basic rights to due process and to be free from unjust forms of punishment and unwarranted intrusions by the state in their private affairs.

Democratization has also prompted an ongoing process of change in the relationship between citizens and the state. While citizens previously took a more passive stance toward the state, they now increasingly expect public officials and the government to be accountable to them, and they demand a voice in the decision-making process. As a consequence, citizens are organizing themselves into a growing number and a wide range of civil society organizations so as to increase their involvement in public decisions and enhance governmental accountability. In addition, there is a more free and diverse media that can inform citizens about the problems facing society and the actions of public officials and the government as a whole.

Thus, just as democracy has raised expectations for better living standards, improved public services and more responsive, efficient and honest government, it has also enhanced the proclivity and capacity of the public to examine whether those expectations are being addressed in practice. To some extent, then, it is neither unexpected nor necessarily unhealthy that citizens in new democratic systems with unfavorable socioeconomic conditions tend to be unhappy with the regime's performance. Higher expectations, increased scrutiny and demands for change fuel efforts for improved government and better performance in the long term. In most of Latin America—where incomes and educational levels are low and poverty and inequality are widespread—it is to be expected that the actual delivery of better employment opportunities and living standards is the key benchmark of success for democracy.

Nonetheless, recent surveys of public attitudes towards democracy, particularly in some countries, are cause for some concern. Surveys conducted over 1996–2000 showed relatively healthy levels of support for democracy as a system of government. On average, about 61 percent of citizens interviewed expressed a preference for democracy, while only 18 percent were open to authoritarian alternatives. But in the 2001 survey the percentage of respondents indicating a clear preference for democracy fell to 48 percent. The encouraging news was that those who became more suspicious of democracy at least did not become more sanguine about prospects for improvement under authoritarianism. Nevertheless, if these recent survey trends continue, the region's democracies may become more prone to backsliding in terms of institutionalization, and may even become destabilized.

In addition, continued low levels of public satisfaction with the performance of democracy could eventually weaken support for democratic values and increase the appeal of alternative forms of government. Average levels of satisfaction with democracy in countries of the region fell to about 25 percent in 2001, after having hovered around 35 percent in prior years. Similarly, with just a couple of exceptions, citizen confidence in political parties and the legislature is low across the region. Aside from representing a potential threat to the long-term stability of democracy, low citizen respect for elected politicians and political parties may undermine the ability of the executive and congress to make and implement policies that are socially legitimate and sustainable.

Clearly, one of the factors that accounts for growing public disenchantment with democracy has been the relatively disappointing pace and unequal distribution of economic growth, which has hindered progress in reducing poverty and in increasing employment opportunities. The inability of governments to control crime, coupled with ongoing deficiencies in the quality of public services, have also contributed to public discontent with democracy.

Aside from the results of democracy, citizens also appear to be dissatisfied with the way democratic politics operate in their countries. Though a certain level of cynicism is common in all democratic systems, the perception that politicians and political parties are primarily concerned about gaining and keeping power and enriching themselves, rather than pursuing the public interest, is particularly pervasive in most of Latin America. Cynicism about politics and political institutions also reflects, and may be reinforced by, the unusually low degree of trust between individuals in society.

While dissatisfaction with democracy has eroded confidence in democratic institutions and, in some cases, contributed to support for political "outsiders" or anti-party politicians, this has not implied a substantial increase in support for authoritarian government. Despite having a fair amount of confidence in the armed forces as an institution, Latin Americans are generally not nostalgic about a return of military rule. Thus, most of the region's citizens are disillusioned democrats but are not yet authoritarians.[1]

---

[1] See *The Economist*, July 28, 2001.

Trends in electoral participation are another potential barometer of the public mood with respect to democratic government. Though the percentage of citizens abstaining from voting has increased, and in a few cases there has been a larger share of protest or "null" votes, turnout in Latin America remained about average relative to other world regions. The 7 percent decline in turnout over the study period points neither to a crisis of representation nor to growing legitimization of democracy. The absence of a more dramatic decline in electoral turnout might be attributed to the obligatory nature of voting in most countries. Increased integrity of the electoral process, on the other hand, could be a countervailing factor that has sustained average voting levels in the region.

At the level of individual countries, however, trends in electoral participation do in some cases more clearly reveal a growing disenchantment with democratic politics. In such cases, sharp reductions in citizen electoral participation reflect a broader disillusionment with democratic politics that has gone hand in hand with the breakdown of the traditional party system and a loss in the credibility of the legislature.

Disenchantment with the processes and results of democracy has been one of the factors behind frequent democratic political reforms across the region. Each of the 18 countries examined in this study has reformed or replaced the constitution that it brought into the study period. Nearly all of the countries have also reformed laws governing elections and political parties, as well as other laws regulating the operation and structure of the justice system and semi-autonomous accountability agencies.

Despite the busy agenda of political reform, no country went so far as to change the basic structure of the political regime. Contrary to the line of academic thought warning that presidentialism was not viable in conflict-torn and multi-party countries typical of Latin America, no country abandoned this regime type in favor of parliamentarism or semi-presidentialism. Especially during the period of economic crisis management and structural adjustment in the 1980s and early 1990s, presidentialism in Latin America was characterized by a strong executive that dominated congress in the policy-making process.

Despite this common trend and the uniformity of their formal presidential designs, political systems in the region varied considerably with respect to other institutional features, which were subject to many reforms during the period. In fact, partly as a response to the perceived imbalance in executive and legislative power, a few countries joined others before them in incorporating some semi-parliamentary or semi-presidential features. These included providing congress with the power to censure and remove cabinet ministers, providing the president with the power in highly specified circumstances to dissolve the legislature, and in one case establishing a chief of the cabinet position partly accountable to the legislature. Whether adopted prior to or during the region's recent democratization period, these features did not generally have a significant effect on how the systems functioned in practice, with a couple of exceptions. Another incipient though still fairly weak trend was to control or limit presidential decree powers and to strengthen the capacity of the legislature by modernizing information systems and increasing staff support for legislators and legislative committees.

On the whole, presidents remained relatively powerful in terms of the powers granted them by the constitution. Some systems in the region continue to grant presidents the power to legislate by decree or otherwise control the legislative agenda, while others at least provide for the possibility that the legislature can delegate such powers to the president. Presidents also retained the upper hand in terms of the budget, in part due to formal restrictions in most countries on congressional power to make amendments, but also due to the executive's considerable advantages with respect to staff and resources. Partial veto powers and exclusive powers to initiate legislation in some policy areas also bolstered the strength of presidents relative to the congress. The endowment of presidents with substantial formal powers can impede the development of proactive policy-making and oversight capacity by the congress. On the other hand, of course, if presidents are too weak governmental effectiveness may be undermined.

Constitutional rules, however, only go so far in accounting for the balance of power between the executive and legislative branches. On the one hand, rules are often subject to various interpretations and can be bent in the executive's favor if it is influential in the congress or the Supreme Court or Constitutional Court. On the other hand, there are several other factors that shape the character of executive-legislative relations, including the degree of fragmentation of the party system, the extent of partisan support for the president in congress, and socioeconomic conditions. Fragmented party systems can deprive presidents of workable majorities in the congress while also weakening the collective action capability of the congress. Concentrated party systems make single party governmental majorities more likely, thus potentially strengthening presidents relative to the congress. Economic or social crises can also be used to legitimize the usurpation of decision-making authority by the president, or the delegation of that authority by the congress to the executive branch.

The alignment of partisan forces between the two branches and the fragmentation of the party system are influenced by the electoral system used for the president and the legislature. With respect to presidential election, there was a clear trend in the region away from the plurality system toward a majority runoff or a runoff with a reduced threshold system. Five countries changed in this direction, while only one moved in the opposite direction (even then, in only limited fashion).

The shift away from the plurality system was motivated either by the aim of amplifying the mandate of the winner or by partisan power strategies (such as preventing a third, minority party from obtaining the presidency). Given the recent nature of the reforms and the limited number of cases, it is difficult to rigorously judge the outcome of such reforms. But experience to date suggests that the goal of strengthening mandates has not been fulfilled. Governability may have even been undermined in the cases in which the winner of the second round was not the same candidate who won the first round. In addition, the move to the majority runoff system would be expected over time to contribute to the fragmentation of the party system, which is likely to reduce the share of the vote the elected president obtains in the first round and his party's share of the legislative seats. The negative indirect effects of a runoff system would be expected to be less significant, however, in cases where a lower threshold, such as 40 percent, was adopted as the minimum needed to elect a winner in the first round.

The timing of presidential and legislative elections also affects the partisan alignment between the executive and the legislature. When the terms of presidents and legislators are the same length and elections for the two offices are held simultaneously, fewer parties would be expected to obtain significant representation in the congress and the president's party (or coalition) is more likely to obtain and sustain a majority. A concentrating effect on the party system of simultaneous elections is particularly expected when the president is elected by plurality. Cases where legislative elections are held in the middle of the president's term (as well as simultaneous with the presidential election) also can weaken the executive vis-à-vis the congress.

In terms of the timing of presidential and mid-term elections, the six reforms across the region split evenly in each of the two directions. Three countries separated the cycles of the elections for the two branches, while three others either merged the cycles or eliminated or reduced the frequency of mid-term legislative elections. Corroborating the downside of nonconcurrent elections, two of the countries that moved toward fully simultaneous elections were among those with the most fragmented party systems and clear governability problems.

Presidential reelection was another area of significant reform, but again there was no clear trend. Five countries lowered restrictions on reelection, while four tightened them. Given that the history of many countries in the region is marked by long periods of rule by *caudillos*, this matter is particularly contentious. Critics see reelection as exposing the political system to this risk of democratic dictatorship and as reinforcing the tendency inherent in presidentialism toward personalistic and hegemonic leadership. But proponents view reelection as a more democratic approach, since it allows citizens to more freely choose who should be their president and permits them to hold the incumbent accountable for his or her performance. Though the record is somewhat mixed, there are at least three cases (Fujimori, Balaguer, Menem) that critics could point to as backing up the dangers of permitting immediate reelection.

The system used for electing legislators is another institutional feature which, through its impact on party system fragmentation and legislator incentives, influences the balance of executive and legislative powers and policy-making roles. Legislative election systems were reformed in various and sometimes significant ways across the region during the period, but in only one case was the proportional or majoritarian character of the system changed. Thus, the Latin American experience in recent years is consistent with the scholarly view, based on a longer and more global perspective, that political economy factors weigh against the probability of profound electoral system reforms.

In systems for the lower house (or national assembly in the case of unicameral systems), the principle of proportional representation continues to predominate (15 of 18 countries). But given the preponderance of small to medium-sized electoral districts and the use in about half of the cases of the d'Hondt formula, most of the systems are only moderately proportional. Thus, while these systems tend to permit some legislative representation for relatively small parties, that representation usually falls short of the parties' vote share. Nevertheless, on balance the systems tend to favor the function of representation, and consequently moderate party system fragmentation, and disfavor the function of effectiveness.

Due to constitutional reforms, two fewer countries (nine instead of 11) have bicameral legislatures. Some form of a majoritarian election system is used in five of the systems with an upper house, one is segmented, and three use pure proportional representation. Aside from the instances where the upper house bodies were closed down, one system was changed from moderate to pure proportional representation, one went from indirect to direct election of members (and from a plurality to plurality with representation of the minority system), and another changed from a plurality to a mixed plurality and proportional representation system.

Just by its existence, the upper house tends to make governing more difficult, since it requires forming governing majorities in two chambers simultaneously instead of just one. Proportional representation systems in the upper house tend to exacerbate this tendency. Depending upon the nature of the election system, though, upper houses can contribute to the representativeness of the system by facilitating regional based representation or by enhancing the proportionality of representation at the national level.

While generally subtle in nature, the election system reforms in the lower house have generally tipped the scales slightly more in favor of representation. The most common reform to have this effect was expanding the size of the congress and, consequently, the size of electoral districts. Other reforms achieved the same by changing the electoral formula. In the upper house, the record is more mixed. The closure of two upper houses in the region clearly favored the value of effectiveness, while the other three cases of reform favored representativeness to varying degrees.

The prevalence of proportional representation systems in the lower house has likely contributed, along with other factors, to the significant increase in the number of parties obtaining representation in legislatures across the region. The two-party systems present in several countries at the beginning of the study period have largely given way to two-and-a-half or three-party systems. In other countries, party systems that were already moderately fragmented became more highly fragmented. As a consequence, single party majority governments have become considerably less common in the region. While the president's party held a majority in the legislature in nine countries at the beginning of the period, this had fallen to just two countries by the end. The fragmentation of party systems could complicate the effectiveness of policy-making and increase the incentive of the president to take full advantage of his proactive lawmaking powers and potentially bend the rules to circumvent the legislature. It also may hinder the ability of congress to act collectively and proactively in the policy-making process and in overseeing the executive.

With more fragmented party systems, the governability of presidential democracies in the region increasingly hinges on building inter-party coalition governments, sometimes formalized in what are called governability pacts. Coalitions contributed significantly to the legislative backing of presidents in several countries where without them effective government would not have been possible. The governing coalition and its theoretical majority status did not always mean that the president could count on the support of individual legislators from parties in the coalition. Nor did such support always hold up over the length of the president's term. But clearly, government effectiveness has been facilitated by the resort to this somewhat parliamentary form of governance within presidentialism. The maintenance of coalitions has been facilitated in two particular cases (Bolivia and Chile) by features of the electoral system that provide fairly powerful incentives for parties to form alliances. However, determining the general viability of coalitions for alleviating governability problems in multi-party presidential systems is a matter that demands more detailed study.

Legislative election systems also affect the nature of representation, particularly whether it is party or constituency based. Legislators are elected from closed and blocked party lists in most lower houses (10 of 18 cases) and upper houses (six of nine cases) in the region. Such systems discourage development of close ties between legislators and their constituents—the election system attribute designated as participation. Given that the party determines which candidates appear on the list and in what order, candidates and incumbents do not have a strong incentive to concern themselves with the views and demands of their constituents. Voters, in turn, are discouraged from learning the identities of individual candidates or tracking the conduct of those who get elected. While in such a system the electors can potentially hold the party accountable, it is not generally feasible for them to hold legislators individually accountable.

Election system reforms over the period of the study have favored participation, although they have not brought about a substantial change across the region. The clearest changes in favor of participation were the adoption of personalized proportional representation systems in Bolivia and Venezuela. In these systems, electors are given two votes, one for a closed and blocked party list for the proportional representation portion of the system, and one for a candidate(s) in the personalized portion of the system. If the process for selecting the candidate(s) in the personalized contest is open to party members or the electorate as a whole, then the ties between legislators and their constituents are likely to be stronger than if the candidates are selected more exclusively by the core party leadership or at a party convention.

In a few other cases, reforms have encouraged participation by giving electors the option of selecting individuals within the party list, thus determining which specific candidates are elected. While preference votes do tend to democratize the candidate selection process, it is not clear that they effectively increase the accountability of individual incumbents to constituents or encourage effective representation with respect to national policy matters. The complexity and high information costs entailed by list systems with preference votes in multi-member constituencies limits the accountability of representatives to their constituents. At the same time, preference votes risk weakening parties, since they encourage competition between candidates within the same party rather than just competition between parties. Competition within the party skews the incentives of elected representatives toward differentiating themselves from competitors through the delivery of particularistic goods and services to the portion of the constituency that elected them, rather than working on behalf of a broader (often party-centered) program of policies that address national problems.

Another type of reform that clearly favors participation has been the separation of the ballots for different elected offices so that electors are not forced to vote along party lines. In many cases, the ballots for national offices have been separated from those for subnational offices. In others, the ballots for president have been separated from those for congress, and those for the lower house separated from those for the upper house. When such reforms have been carried out without changing the timing of presidential and legislative elections, they have clearly favored the value of participation without posing too great a risk in terms of effectiveness.

Aside from their effect on the number of parties that obtain representation and the nature of the links between representatives and constituents, electoral rules also affect the credibility and institutional strength of political parties and party systems. Closed and blocked lists and other forms of party control over candidate nominations have, in some cases, facilitated the formation of parties that are strong in the limited sense of having relatively centralized and continuous leadership structures and disciplined party blocks in the legislature. But as evidenced from public opinion data, the high volatility of electoral outcomes, and the relatively short period of vitality of many parties, hierarchically structured parties have in most cases not contributed to the creation of parties that earn the deep respect and loyalty of citizens. Clearly, however, many nonelectoral system factors, such as the poor performance of democratic governments, have also affected the decline in public esteem for political parties.

Party systems in the region vary considerably in terms of their degree of institutionalization. While in some countries basically the same group of parties has anchored the field of democratic competition over the period, in others, few parties have been able to hold onto public support, party organizations are weak, and legislators exhibit scarce loyalty to the party through which they are elected. Though there appears to have been a general loss of confidence in political parties and politicians in the region during the period, the trend was particularly sharp in a few countries. In these cases, electoral volatility has clearly increased, parties' bases of social support have become more diffuse, and the central parties at the beginning of the period have been partially or largely eclipsed. In a couple of other cases, however, some progress may have been made in institutionalizing a party system in a competitive, democratic context.

Partly in response to public disaffection regarding political parties, a process of internal democratization of political parties gradually developed over the period. Several countries adopted laws regulating the use of primaries for the nomination of presidential candidates, while individual parties in other countries cases used primaries on a voluntary basis. At this point, primaries are regulated and mandatory in seven of the 18 countries. The use of primaries for selecting candidates has the potential to enhance the legitimacy of political parties and make the party leadership more diverse, fluid and responsive to members. But care must be taken in the adoption of primaries so that they do not further personalize the presidential election process and weaken the party leadership, thus complicating internal relations between party officials and the presidential candidate. To yield its full potential, internal democratization of political parties needs to be extended to more countries in the region and used in the candidate selection processes for other elected offices as well as for internal party officials.

Another area of reform crucial to strengthening the image and credibility of political parties and the broader process of democratic representation relates to electoral campaign and party finance systems. During the period of the study, significant reforms were carried out in many countries, but as in most democracies in the world, much more remains to be done. Several important reform trends have included preserving the mixed public and private funding system; taking incipient steps toward funding the operations of political parties rather than purely campaign expenditures; limiting private contributions; improving the equity of access to the media; improving accountability and transparency in the origin and use of resources; strengthening enforcement mechanisms and agencies; and toughening sanctions. Despite the reforms, however, deficiencies remain in many countries of the region in such areas as controls on the level of campaign spending, ensuring equal access to the media (especially television), and weak enforcement of mechanisms and sanctions.

The transparency and ethics of public and private funding depend on both the behavior of leaders and scrutiny by citizens, civil society organizations and the media. In this respect, there has certainly been incipient progress. The media and civil society now play a larger role in monitoring the origin and use of the resources managed by political parties.

The introduction of direct democracy mechanisms has been seen by some as another means to strengthen the legitimacy of democratic processes and to broaden citizen participation. Partly as a consequence of constitutional reforms adopted during the study period, 13 countries now provide for some form of direct democracy at the national level. But very few countries have made frequent use of these mechanisms. By far the most common instrument has been the *consulta popular* (referendum or plebiscite). Popular legislative initiatives have been used rarely, and recall not at all at the national level. With a few important exceptions, the mechanisms have been used by the executive or the legislature to legitimize their proposals, rather than by citizens or civil society organizations to spur action by decision-makers in a given area.

For direct democracy mechanisms to enhance the quality of democracy, they should be developed and used in such a way that they complement rather than substitute for representative mechanisms of democracy. The limited extent to which these national forms of direct democracy have been used to date in the region is consistent with international experience that suggests that such mechanisms may be more efficiently employed at the sub-national level. But given that they have only been established recently in many countries, more time is needed to evaluate the effects of these mechanisms on the operation of democracy and the potential scope of their application.

Political reform during the period has also been directed to enhancing accountability and strengthening the rule of law through the horizontal dimension. The central pillars of the horizontal dimension of accountability are the three traditional branches of government: the executive, the congress and the judiciary. The executive is generally superior in terms of formal powers and policy-making capacity. Legislative branches are weaker in part because of problems with respect to party system institutionalization, skewed electoral system incentives, party system fragmentation, and insufficient organizational and technical resources. The lack of independence of the judiciary often compromises this branch's ability to check abuses of power by the other branches and uphold the constitution.

There have been a variety of reforms—including those related to the electoral system, the president's constitutional powers, and the judicial system—aimed at reducing this imbalance of power and capability between the three traditional branches. But the risk of political bias and the complexity involved in guaranteeing respect for civil liberties, checking abuses of power by public officials, and verifying the effectiveness and integrity of governmental accounts have justified efforts to create quasi-independent agencies to supplement the checks and balances provided by the three main branches. Especially where representative institutions are deficiently developed and judicial bodies not fully independent, there is a clear need for overlapping layers of protection against the abuse of public authority and violations of citizens' rights.

Thus, over the past two decades most countries of the region have established or further institutionalized other "mandated" agencies of horizontal accountability that are institutionally linked with one of the traditional branches, but usually intended to be functionally and administratively autonomous (O'Donnell, 2000). Along these lines, Ombudsman's Offices have been created in many countries to receive and respond to complaints brought by citizens about unfair or ineffective governmental actions or violations of civil rights. Reforms have also strengthened the independence of public prosecutor's offices so that criminal prosecution can be more free from political influence, human rights better protected, and political and administrative corruption more effectively controlled and punished. In addition, supreme audit institutions, which were generally created in the first half of the 20th century, have been reformed to make them more accountable to the legislature, as well as more autonomous and effective in terms of their operations and financing.

Reforms of accountability agencies have generally been beneficial for promoting more fair and effective government. But in some cases, the functional and administrative autonomy guaranteed by law does not exist in practice. In addition, there is often a lack of institutional coordination between these organizations and others that participate in or form part of the criminal justice system. Ultimately, unless their financial and operational independence is firmly guaranteed, such entities are prone to manipulation by the executive or the other two branches of government. That is why the effectiveness of these institutions depends on the existence of a network of counter-balancing powers, especially a capable legislature and independent judiciary, as well as an active civil society, independent media, and favorable climate of public opinion.

This book has provided a broad overview of the political reform trends in Latin America since the third wave of transitions to democracy. Due to obvious limits of time and resources, the book did not consider such critical areas as political decentralization, justice system reforms, and the reform of electoral management procedures and institutions. The regional scope of the study allowed for describing the extent of institutional arrangements, identifying general reform trends, and undertaking a preliminary and mostly theoretical consideration of the potential implications of reform trends for democratic governability. But this broad perspective did not permit the more detailed examination of country experiences necessary to draw more firm conclusions about the actual impact of particular reforms. Clearly, a better understanding of the impact of different designs on the performance of particular institutions and democracy as a whole will depend on additional research focused more closely on the experiences of a smaller group of countries.

What is clear from this examination of the Latin American experience over the past two decades is that democratic institutions have profound effects on the functioning of democratic government. For a number of important reasons, therefore, the matter of how democratic politics is structured and how it operates should be at the forefront of the development agenda.

First, it is clear that economic development policies can only succeed over time if their design and implementation take into account underlying political conditions and the capacities of state institutions. Thus, consideration of how to make democracy function better should not be treated as something subordinate or subsequent to economic policy reform. Rather, the ultimate success of such efforts profoundly depends on developing legitimate democratic institutions that adequately represent citizens, hold public officials accountable, enforce efficiency, and uphold the rule of law.

Second, the broader effort to modernize the state and its institutions, which is key to the region's social and economic development, cannot be successful without concomitant progress in ensuring the quality of democratic governance. Sustained investment and balanced development depend critically on a predictable and sound regulatory and policy framework, property rights, the fair enforcement of contracts, and effective and equitable government investments in health and education. But creating this environment for growth also depends fundamentally on establishing legitimate democratic institutions that adequately represent citizens, hold public officials accountable, enforce efficiency, and uphold the rule of law.

Finally, freedom to participate in public decision-making as well as guarantees of civil liberties associated with a strong democratic system are intrinsic to the broader concept of development, defined as the expansion of human choices to live secure, healthy and fulfilling lives (UNDP, 2001; Sen, 1999). Thus, aside from contributing indirectly to development through its role in creating and maintaining market institutions and equitably developing human potential, democracy also can be considered to be part and parcel of the development process.

Bibliography

Sen, Amartya Kumar. 1999. *Development as Freedom*. New York: Knopf.

O'Donnell, Guillermo. 2000. Further Thoughts on Horizontal Accountability. Paper presented at the conference on Political Institutions, Accountability and Democratic Governance in Latin America, University of Notre Dame Kellogg Institute, 8-9 May.

United Nations Development Program. 2001. *Human Development Report*. New York: United Nations.

Summary of Selected Political Institutional Rules by Country

Argentina

Electoral Systems

Presidential election system: Runoff with reduced threshold. A runoff is required between the top two finishers unless a candidate receives more than 45 percent of the valid affirmative votes or 40 percent with a margin of at least 10 percent of the valid affirmative votes over the second place candidate.

Presidential term and reelection: Four years; immediate reelection after which one presidential term must pass to seek another reelection.

Timing of presidential and legislative elections: Partially simultaneous. Presidential election coincides with the election of half the members of the chamber of deputies and one-third of the senate; at halfway point in presidential term, one-half of the chamber and one-third of the senate is elected.

Unicameral/Bicameral legislature: Bicameral

Legislative terms: Lower house: four years with half renewed every two years; Upper house: six years with one-third renewed every two years.

Legislative election system: Lower house: Proportional representation in medium-sized districts; upper house: plurality with representation of minority (two seats for plurality, one seat for first minority).

Size of legislative bodies: Lower house: 257; Upper house: 72

Number of electoral districts: Lower house: 24; Upper house: 24

Ballot form: Lower house: closed and blocked lists; Upper house: closed and blocked lists.

Average district magnitude: Lower house: 5.4; Upper house: 3.0

Seat allocation formula: Lower house: d'Hondt, with barrier of 3 percent of the registered voters at district level; Upper house: plurality and representation of minority.

Effective number of parties (start, end, average) (by lower house seats): 2.2, 2.6, 2.7

Primaries for selecting presidential candidates: Not regulated but held by some parties in particular circumstances.

Funding of political parties and electoral campaigns: Mixed public and private; direct and indirect public funding both for day-to-day activities and for electoral campaigns.

Electoral management body: Cámara Nacional Electoral. Part of the judiciary. Three members are judges appointed by the president with the agreement of the senate.

Constitutional Powers of the President and Legislature

Package veto: Yes. Congress can override with a two-thirds majority vote of members present in each chamber.

Partial veto: Yes, if removal of parts "does not alter the spirit or the unity of the bill as passed by congress." Congress can override with a two-thirds majority vote of members present in each chamber.

Decree power: Yes. Only when "exceptional circumstances" make it impossible to follow ordinary procedures for the approval of laws is it possible for the president to dictate decrees, but these cannot be issued for election laws, penal laws, tax laws, or political parties. Must be countersigned by all of the cabinet ministers and the chief of the cabinet. Within 10 days the decrees must be submitted to a bicameral commission.

Exclusive initiative: No provision

Budgetary powers: Congress can modify the budget without restrictions. If not approved by the deadline, the budget from the previous year remains in effect.

Appointment powers: The president alone appoints and removes the cabinet ministers along with the chief of the cabinet.

Dissolution of congress: No provision

Censure/Removal of ministers by legislature: Only the chief of the cabinet of ministers may be removed by the vote of an absolute majority of the members in each chamber. Other cabinet ministers cannot be removed. The chief of the cabinet and each of the cabinet ministers can be impeached through the same procedure as in the case of the president.

Impeachment of the president: The chamber of deputies, with a two-thirds majority, accuses the president of bad performance or offenses in the exercising of his/her functions or for common crimes. A two-thirds majority vote in the senate is needed to find guilt, at which point the president is removed from office and declared incapable of occupying any public position.

Supreme Court/Constitutional Court

Role/Authority: No authority over political decisions, but does have authority over any constitutional norm; a posterior form of control that can also be exercized by other judges at the level of lower courts. The Supreme Court is the highest court of appeal.

Constitutional tribunal: No

Appointment of judges: Appointed by the president with the agreement of two-thirds of the members present of the senate.

Number of judges: Not fixed by the constitution. Currently composed of nine judges.

Tenure: Indefinite provided good conduct until 75 years of age, after which time their tenure may be extended for five year periods if the executive and senate so agree.

Procedure for bringing matters before the court/tribunal: Cases may be brought by citizens, judges or the Ministerio Público.

Accountability Agencies

Supreme Audit Institution

Name: Auditoría General de la Nación

Institutional relationship: Congress; financial and operational independence.

Authority: Cannot initiate criminal proceedings or institute corrective measures. Can issue recommendations and observations and receive citizen complaints.

Appointment of director: Appointed by the opposition party with the most seats in congress

Removal from office: For serious misconduct or offenses in the exercising of his/her functions.

Term of office: Eight years (reappointment possible)

Attorney General Office/Public Prosecutor Office

Name: Ministerio Público Fiscal y Ministerio Público de la Defensa

Institutional relationship: None

Authority: Promotion of justice; investigation and prosecution; protection of human rights; assistance to and protection of the vulnerable; defense of the state/society.

Appointment of director: Appointed by the executive with the agreement of two-thirds of the members present in the senate.

Removal from office: For bad performance or offenses in the exercising of his/her functions; for common crimes.

Term of office: Indefinitely until 75 years of age.

Human Rights Ombudsman

Name: Defensoría del Pueblo

Institutional relationship: Congress; financial and operational independence.

Authority: Make recommendations; initiate and carry out investigations; receive citizen complaints; monitor and control the government to uphold human rights and other constitutional rights and guarantees.

Appointment of director: Appointed by congress with the agreement of two-thirds of the members present in each chamber.

Removal from office: Removed by congress with the agreement of two-thirds of the members present in each chamber.

Term of office: Five years (one time reappointment)

Direct Democracy Mechanisms

Popular consultation: Yes
Popular legislative initiative: Yes
Recall: No

Bolivia

Electoral Systems

Presidential election system: Majority with runoff in the congress. If no candidate receives an absolute majority, the congress elects the president among the two leading candidates.
Presidential term and reelection: Five years; One time reelection after at least one presidential term has passed.
Timing of presidential and legislative elections: Simultaneous; same ballot-one vote for president, vice president, senate and the portion of the chamber of deputies elected through closed and blocked party lists.
Unicameral/Bicameral legislature: Bicameral
Legislative terms: Lower house: five years; Upper house: five years
Legislative election system: Lower house: Personalized proportional representation; half of members of lower house elected in single member districts in a personalized vote but overall seats awarded according to party vote share: Upper house: Plurality with representation of minority—two seats for plurality party, one seat for second place party.
Size of legislative bodies: Lower house: 130; Upper house: 27
Number of electoral districts: Lower house: nine; Upper house: nine
Ballot form: Lower house: Individual candidates in single member districts and closed and blocked lists; Upper house: Closed and blocked lists
Average district magnitude: Lower house: 14.4; Upper house: 3.0
Seat allocation formula: Lower house: d'Hondt; Upper house: plurality-minority
Effective number of parties (start, end, average) (by lower house seats): 4.1, 5.4, 4.4
Primaries for selecting presidential candidates: Regulated by electoral/political party law; in practice observed.
Funding of political parties and electoral campaigns: Mixed public and private; direct and indirect public funding both for day-to-day activities and for electoral campaigns.
Electoral management body: Corte Nacional Electoral. Autonomous. Seven members. At least three must be professional lawyers; all must be private citizens to ensure autonomy and impartiality. One is appointed by the president; the other six are appointed by a two-thirds majority of congress.

Constitutional Powers of the President and Legislature

Package veto: Yes. Congress can override with a two-thirds majority vote of members present.
Partial veto: Yes. Congress can override with a two-thirds majority vote of members present.

Decree power: No provision; prohibited for congress to delegate authority to executive.

Exclusive initiative: Executive puts forth development plans, determines military expenditures and the size, attributions and salaries of the public sector.

Budgetary powers: Congress can modify the budget without limitation. The executive should present the budget within the first 30 ordinary sessions of congress. Congress can consider the budget for 60 days. If congress does not act within this timeframe, the law sent by the executive automatically becomes law.

Appointment powers: The president alone appoints and removes the cabinet ministers.

Dissolution of congress: No provision

Censure/removal of ministers by legislature: Each chamber can interpellate ministers individually or collectively and censure his/her conduct by an absolute majority of the members present. This implies the resignation of the censured ministers, which can be accepted or rejected by the president.

Impeachment of the president: Congress authorizes the trial of the president for offenses committed in the execution of his/her functions by way of a joint session of both chambers. No extraordinary majority is stipulated. The Supreme Court carries out the trial. A two-thirds majority is required for conviction/removal.

Supreme Court/Constitutional Court

Role/Authority: Supreme Court: highest court of appeal; tries public officials for crimes and misconduct; resolves lawsuits related to contracts and agreements of the government; Constitutional tribunal: Resolves constitutionality of laws and decrees; resolves conflicts between branches of power at national level and between different levels of government.

Constitutional tribunal: Yes

Appointment of judges: Supreme Court: Appointed by congress from a list of nominees from the judiciary cabinet and the agreement of two-thirds of the members; Constitutional tribunal: Appointed by congress with the agreement of two-thirds of the members present.

Number of judges: Supreme Court: 12; Constitutional Tribunal: 5

Tenure: Supreme Court: 10 years; Constitutional Tribunal: 10 years

Procedure for bringing matters before the court/tribunal: Supreme Court: matters may only be brought by the president, senators, deputies, Fiscal General de la República or the Defensor del Pueblo when the matter is abstract or remedial; otherwise, anyone may bring a matter before the tribunal; Constitutional Tribunal: same as for Supreme Court.

Effect of ruling: Supreme Court: Specific reach; Constitutional Tribunal: General reach.

Accountability Agencies

Supreme Audit Institution

Name: Contraloría General de la República

Institutional relationship: President

Authority: Can initiate criminal proceedings and institute corrective measures, issue recommendations and observations and receive citizen complaints.

Appointment of director: Appointed by the president from a list of nominations from the senate.
Removal from office: Removed by the senate by accusation by the chamber.
Term of office: 10 years (eligible for reappointment after one term has passed.)

Attorney General Office/Public Prosecutor Office

Name: Ministerio Público (Fiscalía General de la República)
Institutional relationship: Independent.
Authority: Promotion of justice and the law; investigation and prosecution; assistance to and protection of the vulnerable; defense of the state/society; direct the proceedings of the judicial police.
Appointment of director: Appointed by congress with the agreement of two-thirds of the members present.
Removal from office: Removed by the senate by reason of accusation brought before it by the chamber of deputies.
Term of office: 10 years (eligible for reappointment after one term has passed.)

Human Rights Ombudsman

Name: Defensor del Pueblo
Institutional relationship: Independent, but must give account to congress. Budget is directed by the legislative budget. Receives no instruction from public powers.
Authority: Make recommendations; initiate and carry out investigations; monitor and control the actions of the public administration; bring claims of unconstitutionality before the Constitutional Tribunal.
Appointment of director: Appointed by congress with the agreement of two-thirds of the members present.
Removal from office: Removed by the Supreme Court at the request of the attorney general for committing offenses.
Term of office: Five years (one time reappointment)

Direct Democracy Mechanisms

Popular consultation: No
Popular legislative initiative: No
Recall: No

Brazil

Electoral Systems

Presidential election system: Runoff with absolute majority. If no candidate receives an absolute majority of the valid votes (blanks and nulls excluded), a second-round runoff election is held.

Presidential term and reelection: Four years; One immediate reelection is allowed.

Timing of presidential and legislative elections: Simultaneous. Only exception is that one-third or two-thirds of senate are not subject to election at the time of the presidential election.

Unicameral/Bicameral legislature: Bicameral

Legislative terms: Lower house: four years; Upper house: eight years – one-third or two-thirds of senate alternately renewed every four years

Legislative election system: Lower house: proportional representation in large districts; Upper house: plurality in single member or two member districts, depending on portion of senate to be elected.

Size of legislative bodies: Lower house: 513; Upper house: 27

Number of electoral districts: Lower house: 27; Upper house: 27

Ballot form: Lower house: closed and unblocked lists; Upper house: open lists

Average district magnitude: Lower house: 19.0; Upper house: 1.0 and 2.0

Seat allocation formula: Lower house: Hare and largest average; Upper house: plurality

Effective number of parties (start, end, average) (by lower house seats): 2.4, 7.1, 6.7

Primaries for selecting presidential candidates: Not regulated; practiced only on a limited basis (i.e., by very few parties).

Funding of political parties and electoral campaigns: Mixed public and private; direct and indirect public funding both for day-to-day activities and for electoral campaigns.

Electoral management body: Tribunal Superior Eleitoral. Part of the judiciary. Seven members. Three judges are appointed by and from the Supremo Tribunal Federal, two judges by and from the Tribunal Superior de Justiça, and two lawyers by the president. The Tribunal Superior Eleitoral has a "temporary membership," with two-year terms, on rotation. Only a member of the Supremo Tribunal Federal can preside over the Tribunal Superior Eleitoral.

Constitutional Powers of the President and Legislature

Package veto: Yes. Congress can override with the vote of an absolute majority of jointly assembled members.

Partial veto: Yes. Congress can override with the vote of an absolute majority of jointly assembled members.

Decree power: Yes. Presidents can issue provisional measures (*medidas provisória*), but they lose effect if not converted into law within 60 days. No prohibition against reenacting decrees once they expire. (Changed in 2001 so that only one reissue of the provisional measure is permitted). The president can also declare items of legislation urgent. This blocks the legislative agenda until there is a vote on the president's urgent bill.

Exclusive initiative: The size of the armed forces; administrative and judicial organization; taxation matters; the civil service; administration of the territories; organization of the attorney general and the public prosecutor (federal and state); the federal district and territories; creation and structure of ministries and other bodies of public administration.

Budgetary powers: The president prepares the annual budget, budget guidelines, and multiyear budget plan and congress approves the budget in a joint session. Congress is not permitted to initiate programs or projects not included in the president's budget. Congress can approve amendments to the annual budget only if they are compatible with the multiyear budget of the president and are compatible with the law on budgetary guidelines. Congress may not authorize expenditures that will exceed the budgetary revenue. The budget is only an "authorization to spend." The president has the freedom to impound or spend items by his own discretion.

Appointment powers: The president alone appoints and removes the cabinet ministers.

Dissolution: No provision.

Censure/Removal of ministers by legislature: No provision for removal of ministers by congress.

Impeachment of the president: For common crimes and criminal abuse of power. If the charges are accepted by two-thirds of the chamber of deputies, the president is suspended for 120 days while submitted to trial before the Supreme Court for common criminal offenses and the senate for criminal abuse of power.

Supreme Court/Constitutional Tribunal

Role/Authority: Resolves constitutionality of laws; resolves conflicts between branches of power at national level and between different levels of government; tries public officials for common crimes; preventative and a posteriori control.

Constitutional tribunal: Supreme Court and Constitutional Tribunal are both part of the Supremo Tribunal Federal.

Appointment of judges: Appointed by the president after their nomination has been confirmed by an absolute majority of the senate.

Number of judges: 11

Tenure: Indefinite until 70 years of age. Minimum age for initial appointment, 35; maximum age, 65.

Procedure for bringing matters before the court/tribunal: Cases may be brought by organizations, but not by individuals. Cases can be brought on appeal from the Superior Tribunal de Justiça (federal appeals court).

Effect of ruling: Specific reach; attempts to make ruling binding on lower courts. However, decisions by the Supremo Tribunal Federal are not binding on lower courts and may be overturned in a different case by a lower court immediately.

Accountability Agencies

Supreme Audit Institution

Name: Tribunal de Contas da União (federal accounting court).

Institutional relationship: An auxiliary agency to congress; financial and operational independence.

Authority: The Tribunal de Contas União (TCU) can prepare briefs analyzing the accounts of public officials and agencies and can "suggest" that they be rejected or approved by the Congress. It refers cases to the federal prosecutors for possible indictment and prosecution. The TCU can apply relatively small fines for misuse of funds and suggest corrective measures.

Appointment of members: One-third appointed by the president with the prior approval of the senate; two-thirds appointed by the congress.
Removal from office: Removed by the Supreme Court.
Term of office: Until 70 years of age

Attorney General Office/Public Prosecutor Office

Name: Ministério Público da União/dos Estados
Institutional relationship: Judiciary; operational and administrative independence.
Authority: Monitor and control the actions of the public administration and government; defense of the state/society.
Appointment of director: Appointed by the president and approved by an absolute majority of the senate.
Removal from office: Removed by the president after vote of an absolute majority in the Senate
Term of office: Two years (reappointment possible); Minimum age 35; maximum age 65.

Human Rights Ombudsman

Does not exist. However there is a special secretariat for human rights within the Ministry of Justice, but this does not have the same role/functions as a "Human Rights Ombudsman;" nor does it have constitutional status. Human rights protection is the prerogative of the federal prosecutor's office.

Direct Democracy Mechanisms

Popular consultation: Yes
Popular legislative initiative: Yes
Recall: No

Chile

Electoral Systems

Presidential election system: Runoff with absolute majority. If no candidate receives an absolute majority, a second-round runoff election is held.
Presidential term and reelection: Six years; alternating reelection after one presidential period has passed
Timing of presidential and legislative elections: Not simultaneous; only simultaneous every 12 years.
Unicameral/Bicameral legislature: Bicameral
Legislative election system: Lower house: binominal; Upper house: binominal
Legislative terms: Lower house: four years; Upper house: eight years – one-half of senate renewed every four years.

Size of legislative bodies: Lower house: 120; Upper house: 48 members, with 38 elected by citizens, nine designated by state institutions and one former president (as of December 2000).

Number of electoral districts: Lower house: 60; Upper house: 19

Ballot form: Lower house: one vote for candidate; Upper house: one vote for candidate

Average district magnitude: Lower house: 2.0; Upper house: 2.0

Seat allocation formula: Lower house: seats allocated to the most voted candidates from the first and second place party lists unless the first place party list doubles the votes of the second in which case the first party list obtains both seats. Voters choose candidates within party lists but votes accrue to the party list. Upper house: same system as in lower house.

Effective number of parties (start, end, average) (by lower house seats): 5.1 (2.6), 5.1 (2.5), 5.1 (2.5). (Effective number considering coalitions instead of parties in parentheses).

Primaries for selecting presidential candidates: Not regulated but held by some parties in particular circumstances.

Funding of political parties and electoral campaigns: Mixed public and private; only indirect public funding which is only for electoral campaigns, not everyday party activities.

Electoral management body: 1) *Servicio Electoral*. Part of the Ministry of the Interior (functional autonomy). Director is appointed by the president with the agreement of the senate. Institution in charge of supervising and controlling the electoral organizations (Juntas Electorales and Juntas Inscriptoras). 2) *Tribunal Calificador de Elecciones*. Autonomous. Five members: four judges or former judges of the Supreme Court and one citizen who acted as chairman or vice-chairman of the lower or upper house for a term of not less than one year, who is appointed by the Supreme Court also by lottery.

Constitutional Powers of the President and Legislature

Package veto: Yes. Congress can override with a two-thirds majority vote of members.

Partial veto: Yes. Congress can override with a two-thirds majority vote of members.

Decree power: Yes. The president may request, and congress authorize, for up to one year, the delegation of authority to order provisions with the force of law. This authorization cannot include matters referring to nationality, citizenship, elections or referendum or to matters comprised in constitutional guarantees or requiring special quorum. With the signature of all ministers, the president may decree expenditures not authorized by law to meet urgent needs that derive from public calamities, external aggression, internal commotion, serious damage or risk to national security or from the exhaustion of resources aimed at maintaining services which cannot be stopped without causing serious harm to the country. These cannot exceed 2 percent of the annual budget.

Exclusive initiative: Legislation regarding the alteration of the political and administrative division of the country or the financial or budgetary administration of the state, including the modifications of the budget law, matters related to the sale and rent of state assets and laws dealing with the use of the armed forces abroad. The president also has the exclusive initiative to impose, eliminate or reduce any tax; create new civil service positions; contract loans to the state; change remunerations and benefits to civil servants; establish the minimum wage; establish collective bargaining procedures; and establish and modify social security system rules.

Budgetary powers: The executive presents the budget. Congress cannot increase or decrease the level of revenues; it can only reduce expenditures, but not those established by permanent laws. The determination of the level of revenues is the exclusive responsibility of the president. If not approved within 60 days, the budget of the president becomes law.

Appointment powers: The president alone appoints and removes cabinet ministers.

Dissolution: No provision

Censure/Removal of ministers by legislature: No provision for removal for political reasons. The lower house can accuse a cabinet minister which should be presented by no less than 10 nor more than 20 of its members for having gravely compromised the honor or security of the nation, for infringing the constitution, or the laws or for having left them unexecuted; or for crimes of treason, misuse of public funds. The senate acts as the jury. If found guilty, the minister is removed from office.

Impeachment of the president: The chamber of deputies decides if there is cause for accusation against the president for acts compromising the honor or security of the nation or openly infringing the constitution or the law. A majority vote is necessary to declare cause for accusation. The senate determines by a two-thirds majority the culpability of the president, at which point the president is removed from office and unable to occupy any public position for a period of five years. Also, the president can be declared unfit because of mental or physical incapacity, but this requires a prior ruling by the constitutional tribunal.

Supreme Court/Constitutional Tribunal

Role/Authority: The Supreme Court has the power to supervise all of the courts in the country (except for the constitutional tribunal, the electoral tribunal at the national and regional levels, and the military tribunals in times of peace). It also has the authority to consider disputes over jurisdiction that may arise between political or administrative authorities and the various courts that do not belong to the sphere of the senate. The Supreme Court, acting on its own or upon petition can declare as non-applicable any legal provision contrary to the constitution. The Supreme Court can also hear appeals against decisions of other court levels.

Constitutional Tribunal: No, but part of Supreme Court; obligatory, preventative and a posteriori control.

Appointment of judges: Supreme Court: appointed by the president from a list of 5 nominees from the Supreme Court; Constitutional Tribunal: three judges appointed by the Supreme Court, two by the National Security Council, one by the senate and one by the president. Those appointed by the president, National Security Council and the senate must be lawyers.

Number of judges: Supreme Court: 21; Constitutional Tribunal: 7

Tenure: Supreme Court: Indefinite until 75 years of age; Constitutional Tribunal: eight years

Procedure for bringing matters before the court/tribunal: Constitutional Tribunal: cases may be brought only by the president, the senate or the chamber of deputies, but not by individuals.

Effect of Ruling: Specific reach.

Accountability Agencies

Supreme Audit Institution

Name: Contraloría General de la República
Institutional relationship: None
Authority: Supervision of the lawfulness of the acts of the executive and of the revenues and expenditures of public resources; examination and judgement of the accounts of people managing the use of the assets of public institutions; can determine legal and fiscal responsibility without the intervention of the justice system; can issue recommendations and observations and receive citizen complaints.
Appointment of director: Appointed by the president with majority agreement of the senate.
Removal from office: Removed by the senate with the previous accusation of the chamber of deputies.
Term of office: Indefinitely until 75 years of age.

Attorney General Office/Public Prosecutor Office

Name: Ministerio Público
Institutional relationship: None
Authority: investigation and accusation; assistance to and protection of the vulnerable; demand of disciplinary action from the court.
Appointment of director: Appointed by the president at the request of the Supreme Court and with the agreement of two-thirds of the senate.
Removal from office: Removed by the Supreme Court at the request of the president, the chamber of deputies or 10 of its members for incapability, bad performance or negligence.
Term of office: 10 years (eligible for reappointment after one term has passed.)

Human Rights Ombudsman

None.

Direct Democracy Mechanisms
Popular consultation: Yes
Popular legislative initiative: No
Recall: No

Colombia

Electoral Systems

Presidential election system: Runoff with absolute majority. If no candidate receives an absolute majority, a second-round runoff election is held between the top two candidates.

Presidential term and reelection: Four years; reelection prohibited.

Timing of presidential and legislative elections: Not simultaneous; election of the president and vice-president cannot coincide with any other election. Legislative elections occur two to three months in advance of presidential elections.

Unicameral/Bicameral legislature: Bicameral

Legislative terms: Lower house: four years: Upper house: four years

Legislative election system: Lower house: proportional representation in medium sized districts; Upper house: proportional representation in one large national district.

Size of legislative bodies: Lower house: 160 (1998); Upper house: 102

Number of electoral districts: Lower house: 33; Upper house: 1

Ballot form: Lower house: closed and blocked lists; Upper house: closed and blocked lists

Average district magnitude: Lower house: 4.9; Upper house: 102

Seat allocation formula: Lower house: Hare and greatest remainder; Upper house: Hare and greatest remainder

Effective number of parties (start, end, average) (by lower house seats): 2.0, 3.2, 2.5

Primaries for selecting presidential candidates: Regulated by electoral/political party law; in practice observed.

Funding of political parties and electoral campaigns: Mixed public and private; direct and indirect public funding both for day-to-day activities and for electoral campaigns.

Electoral management body: Institution in charge of the administrative aspects of the electoral processes: Consejo Nacional Electoral. Autonomous. Seven members appointed by the Consejo de Estado (three elected by each one of the two parties that have obtained the highest number of votes in the last election, and one by the party that follows them in the number of votes). Institution in charge of the organization of electoral processes: Registraduría Nacional del Estado Civil. Autonomous. Director appointed by the Consejo Nacional Electoral.

Constitutional Powers of the President and Legislature

Package veto: Yes. Congress can override with a majority vote of all members in each house.

Partial veto: Yes. Congress can override with a majority vote of all members in each house.

Decree power: Yes. The legislature may delegate decree authority to the executive for a maximum period of six months. Authority cannot be delegated for codes, statutes, organic laws, or taxes. The president also has the power to regulate bills passed by the congress by decree. Congress may amend or revoke decrees declared in a state of economic emergency at any time. The president may issue decrees during a state of economic emergency that may remain in effect after its expiration.

Exclusive initiative: Structure of the executive ministries; salaries of public employees; norms for foreign exchange, external trade, the national debt and tariffs; granting authority to executive to negotiate contracts and loans; establishment of revenues and expenses of administration and functions of the central bank; creation or authorization of state enterprises; negotiating loans with state or selling state assets; treaties or agreements.

Budgetary powers: The submission of the budget is the exclusive authority of the executive. Congress cannot increase or include new spending items without the written permission of the treasury minister. Congress can eliminate or reduce spending items, except for expenditures for public debt servicing and contractual obligations of the state. If congress does not remit the budget, that presented by the executive goes into force.

Appointment powers: The president alone appoints and removes the cabinet ministers.

Dissolution: No provision

Censure/Removal of ministers by legislature: Each chamber can cite and require the minister to come to the sessions of congress. If the minister fails to attend, the chamber can propose a motion of censure with a vote of one-tenth of its members. The approval of the motion of censure requires the vote of an absolute majority of the members of each chamber, at which time the minister is removed from office.

Impeachment of the president: The chamber of deputies issues the accusation to the senate, which allows the trial by suspending the president from office. For common crimes, the senate directs the trial to the Supreme Court. In the case of failure to perform public duties, the senate acts as jury.

Supreme Court/Constitutional Tribunal

Role/Authority: Supreme Court: Highest court of appeals; judge president and other public officials; Constitutional Tribunal: decide on constitutionality of laws and proposals for referenda and plebiscites.

Constitutional tribunal: Yes; obligatory, preventative and a posteriori control.

Appointment of judges: Supreme Court: Appointed by the Supreme Court from a list of nominees from the Sala Administrativa del Consejo Superior de la Judicatura; Constitutional Tribunal: Appointed by the senate from a list of three nominees from the president, three from the Supreme Court and three from the Consejo del Estado.

Number of judges: Supreme Court: 23; Constitutional Tribunal: 9

Tenure: Supreme Court: eight years; Constitutional Tribunal: eight years

Procedure for bringing matters before the court/tribunal: Constitutional Tribunal: cases may be brought by citizens or the president; Supreme Court: appeal from lower courts.

Effect of ruling: Supreme Court: between parties to the case; Constitutional Tribunal: general reach.

Accountability Agencies

Supreme Audit Institution

Name: Contraloría General de la República

Institutional relationship: Constitution; administrative and financial independence.

Authority: Can institute corrective measures, issue recommendations and observations and receive citizen complaints. Can establish fiscal responsibility (*Juicio de Cuentas*).

Appointment of director: Appointed by the congress (from a list of nominees presented by the constitutional court, the Supreme Court and the *Consejo del Estado* of the judicial branch.

Removal from office: Removed by the Supreme Court with the previous accusation of the Fiscal General de la Nación.

Term of office: Four years (no immediate reappointment)

Attorney General Office/Public Prosecutor Office

Name: Ministerio Público (Procuraduría General de la Nación)
Institutional relationship: None
Authority: Promotion of justice; investigation, prosecution and discipline; protection of human rights; assistance to and protection of the vulnerable; defense of the state/society; supervision of constitutional, legal, judicial and administrative compliance.
Appointment of director: Appointed by the senate from a list of nominees from the president, the Supreme Court and the *Consejo del Estado.*
Removal from office: Removed by the Supreme Court with the previous accusation of the Fiscal General de la Nación.
Term of office: Four years (reappointment possible)

Human Rights Ombudsman

Name: Defensor del Pueblo
Institutional relationship: Ministerio Público under the direction of the Solicitor General (Procurador General de la Nación)
Authority: Make recommendations; take actions to protect human rights through legal injunction or class action; present legal reform proposals; civil rights education.
Appointment of director: Appointed by chamber of deputies based on recommendations by the President.
Removal from office: Removed by the Supreme Court with the previous accusation of the Fiscal General de la Nación.
Term of Office: Four years (reappointment possible)

Direct Democracy Mechanisms

Popular consultation: Yes
Popular legislative initiative: Yes
Recall: Yes

Costa Rica

Electoral Systems

Presidential election system: Runoff with reduced threshold. A runoff is necessary between the top two finishers if no candidate obtains at least 40 percent of the votes.
Presidential term and reelection: Four years; reelection prohibited.
Timing of presidential and legislative elections: Simultaneous
Unicameral/Bicameral legislature: Unicameral
Legislative terms: Four years

Legislative election system: Proportional representation in medium-sized districts

Size of legislative body: 57

Number of electoral districts: 7

Ballot form: Closed and blocked lists

Average district magnitude: 8.1

Seat allocation formula: Hare quotient, 50 percent subquotient and largest remainder

Effective number of parties (start, end, average) (by lower house seats): 2.4, 2.6, 2.3

Primaries for selecting presidential candidate: Regulated by electoral and/or political party law; in practice observed.

Funding of political parties and electoral campaigns: Mixed public and private; direct and indirect public funding for electoral campaigns.

Electoral management body: Tribunal Supremo de Elecciones. Autonomous (Electoral function is considered as a fourth power of government). Three judges and six substitutes appointed based on the agreement of two-thirds of the Supreme Court.

Constitutional Powers of the President and Legislature

Package veto: Yes. Congress can override with a two-thirds majority vote of members.

Partial veto: No provision

Decree Power: No provision

Exclusive initiative: No provision, except in an extraordinary sessions of congress convoked by the executive, the only matters that can be treated are those mentioned in the measure convoking the session.

Budgetary powers: The executive is responsible for submitting the budget. The president cannot veto the budget. The assembly cannot increase the expenditures budgeted by the executive without indicating the revenues that will cover them. The ordinary and extraordinary budgets can only be modified by laws initiated by the executive, as is also the case with all instances in which expenditures are increased or new expenditure items are created.

Appointment powers: The president alone appoints and removes the cabinet ministers.

Dissolution: No provision

Censure/Removal of ministers by legislature: The assembly, with two-thirds of the votes of the present members, can censure ministers when it judges them responsible for unconstitutional or illegal acts or for serious errors that have caused or can cause evident harm to the public interest. The censure does not imply the removal of the minister.

Impeachment of the president: The legislative assembly makes the accusation with the vote of two-thirds of its members. The Supreme Court carries out the trial. The president can be found responsible for acts compromising the honor, functioning or security of the nation or openly infringing on the constitution or the law, for common crimes and for criminal abuse of power.

Supreme Court/Constitutional Tribunal

Role/Authority: Highest court of appeals. Supervises and administers judicial system. Section of Supreme Court determines constitutionality of laws and resolves conflict between branches of government.

Constitutional Tribunal: No, but section of Supreme Court exercises constitutional control; obligatory, preventative and a posteriori control.

Appointment of judges: Supreme Court: appointed by the legislative assembly with the agreement of a majority of the members present; Constitutional Tribunal (section of Supreme Court): appointed by the legislative assembly with the agreement of two-thirds of the members.

Number of judges: Supreme Court: not defined; Constitutional Tribunal: seven

Tenure: Supreme Court: eight years, but are reelected for another eight years unless two-thirds of membership of congress decides that their tenure should not be continued; Constitutional Tribunal (section of Supreme Court): Eight years

Procedure for bringing matters before the court/tribunal: Constitutional Tribunal (section of Supreme Court): cases may be brought by anyone when *a posteriori*, but may only be brought by the Supreme Court, Electoral Tribunal or the Contraloría General when preventative.

Effect of ruling: Ordinary law: specific reach. Constitutional matters: general reach

Accountability Agencies

Supreme Audit Institution

Name: Contraloría General de la República

Institutional relationship: Legislative assembly; operational and financial independence.

Authority: Exercises control over the management of the budget. Can initiate investigations to ascertain administrative responsibility and institute corrective measures, issue recommendations and observations and receive citizen complaints.

Determination of responsibility: Binding recommendation. Bring determination to the attention of the tribunal or the prosecutor.

Appointment of director: Appointed by the legislative assembly.

Removal from office: Removed by the legislative assembly with a two-thirds majority vote for offenses committed in exercising of function or for inability to adequately perform duties.

Term of office: Eight years (reappointment possible)

Attorney General Office/Public Prosecutor Office

Name: Ministerio Público (Fiscalía General de la República)

Authority: Investigate and prosecute in respect to unconstitutional actions of legislative or executive branches.

Institutional relationship: Judiciary (operational independence)

Authority: Promotion of justice and application of the law by the courts; promotion of judicial efficiency and legal conformity; solicitation of accusation against government officials; initiation of proceedings of unconstitutionality of penal regulations of the legislative branch or of the executive branch.

Appointment of director: Appointed by the Supreme Court by an absolute majority.

Removal from office: Not defined

Term of office: Not defined

Human Rights Ombudsman

Name: Defensoría de los Habitantes de la República
Institutional relationship: Legislature (operational and discretionary independence)
Authority: Make recommendations; initiate and carry out investigations; receive citizen complaints; denunciation; monitor and control the actions of the public administration and government.
Appointment of director: Appointed by the legislative assembly with the agreement of an absolute majority.
Removal from office: Removed by the legislative assembly for negligence or serious violations in the exercise of duties.
Term of office: Four years (one time reappointment)

Direct Democracy Mechanisms

Popular consultation: No
Popular legislative initiative: No
Recall: No

Dominican Republic

Electoral Systems

Presidential election system: Majority runoff. Runoff between top two finishers if no candidate obtains a majority (50 percent + 1) in the first round.
Presidential term and reelection: Four years; reelection allowed after one presidential term has passed.
Timing of presidential and legislative elections: Not simultaneous. President and legislature each have four-year terms but on separate cycles. Whole congress is elected two years into the presidential term.
Unicameral/Bicameral legislature: Bicameral
Legislative terms: Lower house: four years; Upper house: four years
Legislative election system: Lower house: proportional representation in medium-sized districts; Upper house: plurality
Size of legislative bodies: Lower house: 149; Upper house: 30
Number of electoral districts: Lower house: 30; Upper house: 30
Ballot form: Lower house: closed and blocked lists; Upper house: vote for candidate
Average district magnitude: Lower house: 5.0; Upper house: 1.0
Seat allocation formula: Lower house: d'Hondt; Upper house: plurality
Effective number of parties (start, end, average) (by lower house seats): 2.0, 2.3, 2.4
Primaries for selecting presidential candidates: Not regulated but held by some parties in particular circumstances.

Funding of political parties and electoral campaigns: Mixed public and private; direct and indirect public funding both for day-to-day activities and for electoral campaigns.

Electoral management body: Junta Central Electoral. Autonomous. Five judges and five substitute judges appointed by the senate.

Constitutional Powers of the President and Legislature

Package veto: Yes. Congress can override with a two-thirds majority vote of members in each house.

Partial veto: Yes. Congress can override with a two-thirds majority vote of members in each house.

Decree power: No provision

Exclusive initiative: No provision except budget and international treaties and conventions.

Budgetary powers: The executive is responsible for submitting the budget during the second ordinary legislative session. Congress can modify the items of the budget submitted by the executive with a vote of two-thirds of the members of each chamber and by establishing the funds that will finance these expenditures. If the executive asks for modification only a simple majority is required. If the budget is not approved during this session, the budget and spending law of the previous year remains in effect.

Dissolution: No provision

Appointment powers: The president alone appoints and removes the cabinet ministers.

Censure/Removal of ministers by legislature: Congress can interpellate government ministers and directors and administrators of autonomous institutions with a vote of two-thirds of the present members of the chamber. Censure does not exist.

Impeachment of the president: The chamber of deputies makes the accusation for crimes or grave errors in the execution of his/her functions with a vote of three-quarters of its members. The senate can vote to remove the president from office with a vote of three-quarters its members.

Supreme Court/Constitutional Tribunal

Role/Authority: Has authority over constitutionality of laws and acts; a posteriori control. Judge penal accusations against public officials. Highest court of appeal.

Constitutional Tribunal: No

Appointment of judges: Appointed by the Consejo Nacional de la Magistratura.

Number of judges: 16

Tenure: Indefinite

Procedure for bringing matters before the court/tribunal: Cases may be brought by the executive, one of the presidents of congress or any interested party.

Effect of ruling: General reach.

Accountability Agencies

Supreme Audit Institution

Name: Contraloría General de la República

Institutional relationship: Tied to executive branch.

Authority: Monitor the use of public funds to check the consistency with the budget law. Approves expenditures of departments in ex ante fashion.

Appointment of director: Appointed by the senate from a list of three nominations from the president

Removal from office: Removed from office by the president without restriction

Term of office: indefinite (no reappointment)

Attorney General Office/Public Prosecutor Office

Name: Ministerio Público

Institutional relationship: Judiciary

Authority: Promotion of justice; investigation and prosecution; assistance to and protection of the vulnerable.

Appointment of director: Appointed by the president

Removal from office: Removed by the president without restriction

Term of office: Indefinite (reappointment possible)

Human Rights Ombudsman

Name: Defensor del Pueblo

Institutional Relationship: Not defined

Authority: Make recommendations; monitor and control the administration.

Appointment of director: Appointed by the senate with the agreement of two-thirds of the members from a list from the chamber of deputies.

Removal from office: Removed by the Supreme Court for negligence or serious violations in the exercising of functions

Term of office: Six years (one time reappointment)

Direct Democracy Mechanisms

Popular consultation: No

Popular legislative initiative: No

Recall: No

Ecuador

Electoral Systems

Presidential election system: Runoff with absolute majority and reduced threshold. A runoff is necessary between the top two finishers unless a candidate receives a majority (50 percent + 1) or 45 percent with a minimum of 10 percent difference with the nearest opponent.

Presidential term and reelection: Four years; Alternating reelection after one presidential term has passed.

Timing of presidential and legislative elections: Simultaneous

Unicameral/Bicameral legislature: Unicameral

Legislative terms: Four years

Legislative election system: Plurality in multi-member constituencies

Size of legislative bodies: 123

Number of electoral districts: 22

Ballot form: Open lists

Average district magnitude: 5.5

Seat allocation formula: Plurality

Effective number of parties (start, end, average) (by lower house seats): 3.9, 5.7, 5.7

Primaries for selecting presidential candidates: Not regulated; not practiced.

Funding of political parties and electoral campaigns: Mixed public and private; direct and indirect public funding both for day-to-day activities and for electoral campaigns.

Electoral management body: Tribunal Supremo Electoral. Autonomous. Seven members represent the parties that obtained the highest number of votes in the last election. Appointed by the agreement of an absolute majority of congress.

Constitutional Powers of the President and Legislature

Package veto: No. Congress cannot override. Legislature cannot revisit the legislation until one year later.

Partial veto: Yes. Congress can override with a two-thirds majority vote of members if it does so within 30 days of the partial objection by the president. Otherwise the bill as modified by the president becomes law.

Decree power: Yes. The president may declare an economic measure urgent; it becomes law after 30 days unless congress votes to reject it. In a state of emergency, the president can advance the collection of taxes or other revenues.

Exclusive initiative: Only the president can initiate legislation that eliminates, adds or changes taxes, public spending or the administrative divisions of the country.

Budgetary powers: The executive submits the budget. If it is not approved by November 30, the budget law presented by the executive becomes law. Congress cannot increase the amount of revenue and expenditures unless approved by the executive. Congress approves or modifies revenue or expenditures in one debate. Current expenditures cannot be financed by public indebtedness.

Appointment powers: The president alone appoints and removes the cabinet ministers.

Dissolution: No provision

Censure/Removal of ministers by legislature: One-quarter of the membership of congress is needed to launch a political judgement. Cabinet ministers can be prosecuted for constitutional or illegal infractions committed in the performance of their responsibilities. Congress can censure with the vote of a two-thirds majority of its members. The censure results in the immediate removal of the official, except in the case of governmental ministers whose permanence in office is the responsibility of the president. If the censure entails penal responsibility of the official, the case is transferred to a competent judge.

Impeachment of the president: Congress is in charge of the accusation and trial of the president. One-quarter of its members must ask for impeachment for the process to begin and it must be approved by two-thirds of congress. The president can only be impeached for committing offenses against the security of the state or for kickbacks, bribes or embezzlement. The president can also be removed by a simple majority of congress for mental or physical incapacity.

Supreme Court/Constitutional Tribunal

Role/Authority: Highest court of appeal (*corte de casación*).
Constitutional Tribunal: Yes; a posteriori control.
Appointment of judges: Supreme Court: Appointed by the Supreme Court with the agreement of two-thirds of its members; Constitutional Tribunal: appointed by congress.
Number of judges: Supreme Court: not defined; Constitutional Tribunal: nine
Tenure: Supreme Court: indefinite; Constitutional Tribunal: Four years.
Procedure for bringing matters before the court/tribunal: Supreme Court: through appeals from lower courts or directly; Constitutional Tribunal: cases may be brought by the president, congress, the Supreme Court, provincial or municipal councils, 1,000 civilians or any person with a favorable report from the Defensoría del Pueblo.
Effect of ruling: Constitutional Tribunal: general reach. Law repealed.

Accountability Agencies

Supreme Audit Institution

Name: Contraloría General del Estado
Institutional relationship: Autonomous (operational, financial and budgetary independence)
Authority: Exercises control over revenues, expenditures, investments, and use of public resources. Can carry out audits of management of public sector agencies and institutions and their providers. It can pronounce in regard to the legality, transparency and efficiency of the institutional results. It has the exclusive power of determining administrative and civil responsibility.
Appointment of director: Appointed by the president from a list of three candidates presented by the congress.
Removal from office: Removed by congress with the absolute majority vote of its members for constitutional or legal infractions.
Term of office: Four years (reappointment possible)

Attorney General Office/Public Prosecutor Office

Name: Ministerio Público
Institutional relationship: Independent
Authority: Promotion of justice; investigation and prosecution; assistance to and protection of the vulnerable; rehabilitation and sentencing; creation and direction of specialized police force and medical law department.
Appointment of director: Appointed by congress from a list of three candidates presented by the Consejo Nacional de la Judicatura.

Removal from office: Removed by congress with the absolute majority vote of its members for constitutional or legal infractions.
Term of office: Six years (no reappointment)

Human Rights Ombudsman

Name: Defensoría del Pueblo
Institutional relationship: Congress (operational and financial independence)
Authority: Make recommendations; monitor and control the administration; defend and protect human rights; propose laws.
Appointment of director: Appointed by congress with the agreement of two-thirds of the members (present) and recommendations of recognized human rights organizations.
Removal from office: Removed by congress with the absolute majority vote of its members for constitutional or legal infractions.
Term of office: Five years (one time reappointment)

Direct Democracy Mechanisms

Popular consultation: Yes
Popular legislative initiative: Yes
Recall: No

El Salvador

Electoral Systems

Presidential election system: Runoff with absolute majority. If no candidate receives an absolute majority, a second-round runoff election between the top two finishers is held.
Presidential term and reelection: Five years; Alternating reelection after one presidential term has passed
Timing of presidential and legislative elections: Not simultaneous. Only simultaneous every 15 years.
Legislative election system: Proportional representation in medium sized districts
Unicameral/Bicameral legislature: Unicameral
Legislative terms: Three years
Size of legislative body: 84
Number of electoral districts: 15
Ballot form: Closed and blocked lists
Average district magnitude: 5.6
Seat allocation formula: Hare and largest remainder
Effective number of parties (start, end, average) (by lower house seats): 2.6, 3.5, 3.1
Primaries for selecting presidential candidates: Not regulated but held by some parties in particular circumstances.

Funding of political parties and electoral campaigns: Mixed public and private; direct and indirect public funding both for day-to-day activities and for electoral campaigns.

Electoral management body: Tribunal Supremo Electoral. Autonomous. Five members appointed by the legislative assembly from each of the lists of candidates presented: three by the three parties that have obtained the highest number of votes in the last presidential elections and two by the Supreme Court.

Constitutional Powers of the President and Legislature

Package veto: Yes. Congress can override with a two-thirds majority vote of members.

Partial veto: Yes. Congress cannot override.

Decree power: No. The president may only authorize the disbursement of unappropriated funds to meet needs created by a state of emergency. Otherwise no other decree powers.

Exclusive initiative: No provision.

Budgetary powers: The president submits the budget through the finance minister. Congress approves the budget through open debate and a majority vote. If not approved by December 31, the budget of the previous year is put into effect until a new budget is approved. The legislative assembly can reduce or reject the credits solicited by the executive, but never can increase them. Congress must approve by a two-thirds majority international or domestic loans solicited by the executive.

Appointment powers: The president alone appoints and removes the cabinet ministers.

Dissolution: No provision

Censure/Removal of ministers by legislature: The legislative assembly can interpellate/interrogate ministers and the presidents of official autonomous institutions. After investigation by the special commissions or by interpellation the assembly, in its entirety, may vote for censure. This censure only constitutes a moral sanction and may motivate the minister to resign or the president to ask for the resignation.

Impeachment of the president: The president is accountable to the legislative assembly for official offenses and common crimes committed. The legislative assembly determines if there is cause for accusation and admits the accusation to the court of appeals (*Cámara de Segunda Instancia*) for trial. During this time the president is suspended from his/her duties. The Supreme Court can review the decision by the appeals court and can overturn it. In addition, the legislative assembly can remove the president for reason of mental or physical incapacity by a two-thirds vote after a prior unanimous ruling by a five-member commission of doctors named by the legislative assembly.

Supreme Court/Constitutional Tribunal

Role/Authority: Has authority over constitutional, civil, penal and administrative matters.

Constitutional Tribunal: Section of the Supreme Court; preventative and a posteriori control.

Appointment of judges: Appointed by legislative assembly from two lists, one from the *Consejo Nacional de la Judicatura* and the other from the direct vote of lawyers in elections organized by the *Federación de Asociaciones de Abogados*.

Number of judges: Supreme Court: 15; Constitutional bench: 5

Tenure: Nine years
Procedure for bringing matters before the court/tribunal: Cases may be brought by citizens or the Fiscal General de la República.
Effect of ruling: General reach

Accountability Agencies

Supreme Audit Institution

Name: Corte de Cuentas de la República
Institutional relationship: None; must give reports to congress
Authority: Cannot initiate criminal proceedings or institute corrective measures. Can issue recommendations and observations and receive citizen complaints.
Appointment of director: Appointed by the legislative assembly with a two-thirds majority vote of its members
Removal from office: Removed by the legislative assembly.
Term of office: Three years (reappointment possible).

Attorney General Office/Public Prosecutor Office

Name: Procuraduría General de la República
Institutional relationship: Independent
Authority: Protection of human rights; assistance to and protection of the vulnerable in criminal proceedings; legal assistance to the poor; name, remove and give license to all prosecutors, officials and other employees of the office.
Appointment of director: Appointed by legislative assembly with the agreement of two-thirds of the members.
Removal from office: Removed by legislative assembly with the agreement of two-thirds of the members.
Term of office: Three years (reappointment possible)

Human Rights Ombudsman

Name: Procuraduría para la Defensa de los Derechos Humanos
Institutional relationship: Independent
Authority: Make recommendations; initiate and carry out investigation; monitor and control the administration; assistance to and protection of victims; promotion of judicial and administrative resources.
Appointment of director: Appointed by legislative assembly with the agreement of two-thirds of the members.
Removal from office: Removed by legislative assembly with the agreement of two-thirds of the members.
Term of office: Three years (reappointment possible)

Direct Democracy Mechanisms

Popular consultation: No. Only for the reunification of the Federal Republic of Central America.
Popular legislative initiative: Yes
Recall: No

Guatemala

Electoral Systems

Presidential election system: Majority runoff. If no candidate receives an absolute majority, a second-round runoff election is held.
Presidential term and reelection: Four years; reelection prohibited.
Timing of presidential and legislative elections: Simultaneous
Unicameral/Bicameral legislature: Unicameral
Legislative terms: Four years
Legislative election system: Proportional representation in medium sized districts
Size of legislative body: 113
Number of electoral districts: 24
Ballot form: Closed and blocked lists
Average district magnitude: 4.7
Seat allocation formula: d'Hondt
Effective number of parties (start, end, average) (by lower house seats): 3.0, 2.4, 3.2
Primaries for selecting presidential candidates: Not regulated; not practiced.
Funding of political parties and electoral campaigns: Mixed public and private; direct and indirect public funding both for day-to-day activities and for electoral campaigns.
Electoral management body: Tribunal Supremo Electoral. Autonomous. Five judges and five substitutes are appointed by an agreement of two-thirds of congress from a list of nominations by the postulation committee.

Constitutional Powers of the President and Legislature

Package veto: Yes. Congress can override with a two-thirds majority vote of members.
Partial veto: No. Congress cannot override.
Decree power: The executive can dictate provisions that are necessary in the case of grave emergencies or public calamities. Need to give account to congress in the following sessions. Otherwise no decree provisions.
Exclusive initiative: No provision.
Budgetary powers: The executive is responsible for submitting the budget 120 days prior to the beginning of the fiscal year. If the budget is not approved by the beginning of the fiscal year, the budget of the previous year will go into effect. There are no restrictions on the ability of congress to amend the budget.
Appointment powers: The president alone appoints and removes the cabinet ministers.

Dissolution: No provision.

Censure/Removal of ministers by legislature: Congress has the power to interpellate government ministers. Government ministers are obligated to present themselves before congress to be interrogated. This may lead to a vote of no confidence that must be solicited by at least four deputies. If an absolute majority of all of congress returns a vote of no confidence, the minister must resign immediately. But if the president and the cabinet consider the censurable acts consistent with the public interest and government policy, the minister must return before congress within eight days. If the minister does not return, he is removed from his position and is unable to hold the position of minister for at least 6 months. If congress returns an affirmative vote of two-thirds of all its members, it ratifies the vote of no confidence and the minister is removed from office. Congress can vote to remove as many as four ministers at one time.

Impeachment of the president: The legislature can accuse the president of common crimes or misconduct with a two-thirds majority. In addition, the legislature can declare the physical or mental incapacity of the president with a two-thirds majority vote. The declaration must be based on the opinion of a five-member commission of doctors named by the executive board of the medical association following the request of the legislature.

Supreme Court/Constitutional Tribunal

Role/Authority: Highest court of appeals.

Constitutional Tribunal: Yes; preventative and a posteriori control.

Appointment of judges: Supreme Court: Appointed by congress from lists of 26 nominees from the faculties of law of each university, the general assembly of the College of Lawyers and Notaries and the Court of Appeals; Constitutional Tribunal: one member each from the Supreme Court, congress, the president, the University of San Carlos and the general assembly of the College of Lawyers.

Number of judges: Supreme Court: 13; Constitutional Tribunal; 5

Tenure: Supreme Court: Five years; Constitutional Tribunal: Five years

Procedure for bringing matters before the court/tribunal: Through appeal from cases tried in the lower courts.

Effect of ruling: Specific reach for disputes related to ordinary law and general reach for constitutional matters.

Accountability Agencies

Supreme Audit Institution

Name: Contraloría General de Cuentas

Institutional relationship: None

Authority: Can issue recommendations, make observations, and receive citizen complaints. Can establish fiscal responsibility.

Appointment of director: Appointed by congress with an absolute majority

Removal from office: Removed by congress for negligence or lack of suitability.

Term of office: Four years (reappointment possible)

Attorney General Office/Public Prosecutor Office

Name: Ministerio Público (Fiscal General y Procuraduría General de la Nación)
Institutional relationship: None
Authority: Promotion of justice; investigation and prosecution.
Appointment of director: Appointed by the president from a list of 6 nominees from the postulation committee.
Removal from office: Removed by the president with just cause or by congress with the agreement of two-thirds of all members.
Term of office: Five years (reappointment possible)

Human Rights Ombudsman

Name: Procurador de Derechos Humanos
Institutional relationship: Congress
Authority: Can make recommendations, initiate and carry out investigations, receive citizen complaints, monitor and control the executive, censure and make denunciations.
Appointment of director: Appointed by congress from a list of three nominations from the commission.
Removal from office: Removed by congress with the agreement of two-thirds of all members.
Term of office: Five years

Direct Democracy Mechanisms

Popular consultation: Yes
Popular legislative initiative: Yes
Recall: No

Honduras

Electoral Systems

Presidential election system: Plurality
Presidential term and reelection: Four years; reelection prohibited
Timing of presidential and legislative elections: Simultaneous.
Unicameral/Bicameral legislature: Unicameral
Legislative terms: Four years
Legislative election system: Proportional representation in medium-sized districts
Size of legislative body: 128
Number of electoral districts: 18
Ballot form: Closed and blocked lists

Average district magnitude: 7.1

Seat allocation formula: Hare and largest remainder

Effective number of parties (start, end, average) (by lower house seats): 2.2, 2.2, 2.1

Primaries for selecting presidential candidates: Regulated by electoral/political party law; in practice observed.

Funding of political parties and electoral campaigns: Mixed public and private; direct and indirect public funding only for electoral campaigns.

Electoral management body: Tribunal Nacional de Elecciones. Autonomous. The number of members varies depending on the number of parties legally registered (each party appoints one member and the Supreme Court appoints one member or two if the parties appoint an even number of members).

Constitutional Powers of the President and Legislature

Package veto: Yes. Congress can override with a two-thirds majority vote of members.

Partial veto: No. Congress cannot override.

Decree power: The executive can dictate extraordinary measures in economic and financial matters when the national interest requires, with the requirement of giving account to congress.

Exclusive initiative: The president introduces trade policies, tariffs etc.

Budgetary powers: The executive submits the budget and congress approves a budget taking this as the base. The executive cannot veto the budget bill approved by congress. The budget is to be submitted within the first 15 days of September. There are no restrictions on the ability of congress to amend the budget.

Appointment powers: The president alone appoints and removes the cabinet ministers.

Dissolution: No provision

Censure/Removal of ministers by legislature: Congress can interpellate cabinet ministers, but this does not have an effect on their tenure in office.

Impeachment of the president: Congress declares if there is cause for accusation against the president. No extraordinary majority is stipulated.

Supreme Court/Constitutional Tribunal

Role/Authority: Highest court of appeals

Constitutional Tribunal: Section of the Supreme Court

Appointment of judges: Appointed by majority in legislature (after 2001 reform, two-thirds majority required for appointment of judges from list proposed by legislative commission)

Number of judges: Nine (after 2001 reform, 15 judges)

Tenure: Four years (after 2001 reform, seven years)

Procedure for bringing matters before the court/tribunal: Appeal from the lower courts.

Effect of ruling: For ordinary law, specific reach. For constitutional issues, general reach.

Accountability Agencies

Supreme Audit Institution

Name: Contraloría General de la República
Institutional relationship: Congress (operational and administrative independence)
Authority: Can initiate criminal proceedings and institute corrective measures, issue recommendations and observations and receive citizen complaints.
Appointment of director: Appointed by the congress.
Removal from office: Removed by the congress for omission or irregularity.
Term of office: Five years (eligible for reappointment after one term has passed.)

Attorney General Office/Public Prosecutor Office

Name: Procuraduría General de la República
Institutional relationship: None
Authority: Promotion of justice; investigation and prosecution; protection of constitutional rights; assistance to and protection of the vulnerable; defense of the state/society; monitor and control the administration; and combat corruption and drug-trafficking.
Appointment of director: Appointed by congress with the agreement of two-thirds of the members from a list of five nominees.
Removal from office: Removed by congress with the agreement of a majority of the members.
Term of office: Five years (eligible for reappointment after one term has passed.)

Human Rights Ombudsman

Name: Comisionado Nacional de los Derechos Humanos
Institutional relationship: Autonomous in functional, administrative and technical terms.
Authority: Guard the fulfillment of the rights and guarantees established in the constitution; Initiate and carry out investigations; inform about the state of human rights in the country; receive and investigate citizen complaints of rights violations; recommend remedial actions by authorities responsible for abuses.
Appointment of director: Appointed by the congress.
Removal from office: Immune from legal prosecution. Can only be removed for notorious negligence in performance of duties.
Term of office: Six years; can be renewed by congress with majority vote.

Direct Democracy Mechanisms

Popular consultation: No
Popular legislative initiative: No
Recall: No

Mexico

Electoral Systems

Presidential election system: Plurality.

Presidential term and reelection: Six years; reelection prohibited.

Timing of presidential and legislative elections: Simultaneous, but the entire lower house is elected every three years. The entire senate is elected every six years, simultaneous with the presidential election.

Unicameral/Bicameral legislature: Bicameral.

Legislative terms: Lower house: three years; Upper house: six years; reelection prohibited.

Legislative election system: Lower house: segmented – 200 by proportional representation in five multi-member districts and 300 by plurality in single member districts; Upper house: segmented plurality with representation of minority and proportional representation in 32 member national district.

Size of legislative bodies: Lower house: 500; Upper house: 128

Number of electoral districts: Lower house: 300 single member districts, five multi-member districts; Upper house: 32 three-member districts (states), one national district.

Ballot form: Lower house: candidate in single member districts and closed and blocked lists; Upper house: two votes for separate closed and blocked lists.

Average district magnitude: Lower house: single-member districts: 1, proportional representation: 40; Upper house: plurality: 3, proportional representation: 32

Seat allocation formula: Lower house: single-member districts: plurality, proportional representation: corrected Hare with greatest remainder (2 percent of national vote required to obtain seats in multiple-member districts; to participate in multiple-member district multiple member district parties must present candidates in at least 200 single member districts; no party can obtain a percentage of total seats which exceeds by more than 8 percent its share of the national vote; no party can obtain more than 300 seats in the lower house); Upper house: plurality with representation of the minority; proportional representation: corrected Hare with greatest remainder (2 percent of national vote required to obtain seats in national district)

Effective number of parties (start, end, average) (by lower house seats): 1.8, 2.6, 2.3

Primaries for selecting presidential candidates: Not regulated but held by some parties in particular circumstances.

Funding of political parties and electoral campaigns: Mixed public and private; direct and indirect public funding both for day-to-day activities and for electoral campaigns.

Electoral management body: Electoral organization: 1) Instituto Federal Electoral (IFE). Autonomous and composed of the general council, which has one president and eight council members plus 14 members without a vote. Elected by two-thirds of the present members of the lower house. 2) Tribunal Electoral del Poder Judicial de la Federación (TRIFE). Autonomous and integrated by seven electoral lawyers appointed by the senate by two-thirds of the present members on the basis of nominations from the Supreme Court. Part of the judiciary branch.

Constitutional Powers of the President and Legislature

Package veto: Yes. Congress can override with a two-thirds majority vote of members in each house.

Partial veto: No. Congress cannot override.

Decree power: No. In the event of an invasion, serious disturbance of the public peace, or any other event that may place society in great danger or conflict, the president may suspend constitutional guarantees with consent of congress or its permanent committee. Congress shall delegate authority it deems necessary to the presidency.

Exclusive initiative: No provision.

Budgetary powers: Executive submits budget by November 15, except in year in which it assumes office. Congress can act without restrictions in modifying the budget. It cannot approve new expenditures that are not called for in the budget that it approves.

Appointment powers: The president alone appoints and removes the cabinet ministers.

Dissolution: No provision

Censure/Removal of ministers by legislature: Censure does not exist.

Impeachment of the president: The president can only be accused by congress of treason and grave common crimes. The senate decides the course of action based on the applicable penal legislation. A two-thirds majority is required.

Supreme Court/Constitutional Tribunal

Role/Authority: Has authority over any constitutional norm; a posteriori control.

Constitutional Tribunal: No

Appointment of judges: Appointed by the senate with the agreement of two-thirds of the members present on the basis of a list of three proposed by the president.

Number of judges: 11

Tenure: 15 years; reelection prohibited.

Procedure for bringing matters before the court/tribunal: Cases may be brought by citizens whose rights have been affected by an "act of authority;" state bodies for conflicts over jurisdiction; one-third of the chamber of deputies for federal laws expedited by congress; one- third of the senate for federal laws expedited through congress or international agreements; the Procurador General de la República for federal and state laws or international agreements; one-third of the local legislators for laws expedited through their respective legislatures; one-third of the members of the assembly of representatives of the Distrito Federal for laws expedited through the assembly; official political parties for federal and local electoral law; and state political parties for electoral laws expedited through their state legislature.

Effect of ruling: Specific reach for matters of ordinary law; specific reach for disputes regarding constitutionality of laws unless resolution by Supreme Court of unconstitutionality approved by eight votes.

Accountability Agencies

Supreme Audit Institution

Name: Entidad de Fiscalización Superior de la Federación
Institutional relationship: Lower house (technical and managerial autonomy)
Authority: Can initiate criminal proceedings and institute corrective measures, issue recommendations and observations and receive citizen complaints.
Appointment of director: Appointed by the lower house with the agreement of two-thirds of the members present.
Removal from office: Removed by the lower house with the agreement of two-thirds of the members present, or by political trial or for criminal charges
Term of office: Eight years (one time reappointment)

Attorney General Office/Public Prosecutor Office

Name: Ministerio Público Federal
Institutional relationship: Judiciary
Authority: Promotion of justice; investigation and prosecution; protection of constitutional rights; ensure judicial compliance and application of penalties.
Appointment of director: Appointed by the president and ratified by the senate or the permanent commission of congress.
Removal from office: Removed freely by the president, by political trial in the congress or criminally prosecuted in the courts.
Term of office: Indefinite

Human Rights Ombudsman

Name: Comisión Nacional de Derechos Humanos
Institutional relationship: Senate
Authority: Make recommendations; receive citizen complaints; promote human rights and guarantees.
Appointment of director: Appointed by the senate with the agreement of two-thirds of the members present or the permanent commission of congress.
Removal from office: Removed by political trial in the congress or criminally prosecuted in the courts.
Term of office: Five years (one time reappointment)

Direct Democracy Mechanisms

Popular consultation: No
Popular legislative initiative: No
Recall: No

Nicaragua

Electoral Systems

Presidential election system: Runoff with reduced threshold. A runoff is necessary between the top two finishers unless a candidate receives 40 percent of the valid votes or 35 percent and an advantage of 5 percent over the nearest competitor.

Presidential term and reelection: Five years; alternating one-time reelection after at least one presidential term has passed

Timing of presidential and legislative elections: Simultaneous

Unicameral/Bicameral legislature: Unicameral

Legislative terms: Five years

Legislative election system: Proportional representation in medium-sized districts

Size of legislative body: 90

Number of electoral districts: 18

Ballot form: Closed and blocked lists

Average district magnitude: 5.0

Seat allocation formula: Hare and remainder quotient

Effective number of parties (start, end, average) (by lower house seats): 2.1, 2.8, 2.4

Primaries for selecting presidential candidates: Not regulated but held by some parties in particular circumstances.

Funding of political parties and electoral campaigns: Mixed public and private; direct and indirect public funding only for electoral campaigns.

Electoral management body: Consejo Supremo Electoral. Autonomous. Seven judges and three substitutes appointed by the national assembly based on nominations by the president and deputies and the agreement of 70 percent of the national assembly.

Constitutional Powers of the President and Legislature

Package veto: Yes. Congress can override with a two-thirds majority vote of members.

Partial veto: Yes. Congress can override with a two-thirds majority vote of members.

Decree power: Yes. The president is authorized to dictate executive decrees in administrative matters. During a state of emergency, the president is authorized to approve the general budget and forward it to the national assembly for review.

Exclusive initiative: The president has exclusive initiative for treaties and international agreements.

Budgetary powers: The executive is responsible for formulating and submitting the budget. If it is not approved by December 15, the budget submitted by the executive enters into effect provisionally for the first quarter. The national assembly cannot increase spending. It can only move spending between budgetary items. No extraordinary spending measures can be created except by law and by providing resources to finance them. The constitution expressly indicates that the annual budget law cannot create taxes.

Appointment powers: The president alone appoints and removes the cabinet ministers.

Dissolution: No provision

Censure/Removal of ministers by legislature: The national assembly has the power to require the obligatory appearance of governmental ministers and vice ministers. The commissions of congress can solicit information and documentation and the presence of ministers to provide information on the performance of their functions. The national assembly can require the interpellation of governmental ministers and vice ministers. By a majority of its members, the national assembly can consider whether the case has a legal basis and the interpellated official is stripped of immunity from prosecution. The national assembly will send to the president a report in which it will express its opinion on the performance of the corresponding official and can recommend his removal from office.

Impeachment of the president: The legislative assembly can declare the permanent incapacity of the president with a two-thirds majority.

Supreme Court/Constitutional Tribunal

Role/Authority: Has authority over constitutionality of the law, acts, regulations and constitutional conflicts among the state powers; a posteriori control.

Constitutional Tribunal: No

Appointment of judges: Appointed by the national assembly with the agreement of 60 percent of the members and the recommendation of pertinent civil associations

Number of judges: 16

Tenure: Five years

Procedure for bringing matters before the court/tribunal: Cases may be brought by any citizens in respect to matters of constitutionality.

Effect of ruling: General and specific reach.

Accountability Agencies

Supreme Audit Institution

Name: Contraloría General de la República

Institutional relationship: Legislative assembly

Authority: Can establish legal and fiscal responsibility for improper management of public funds, issue recommendations and observations and receive citizen complaints.

Appointment of director: Appointed by the national assembly from a list of three candidates presented by the president and members of the national assembly.

Removal from office: Removed by the national assembly for justified cause.

Term of office: Five years

Attorney General Office/Public Prosecutor Office

Name: Ministerio Público

Institutional relationship: None

Authority: Investigation and prosecution; defense of the state/society

Appointment of director: Appointed by the national assembly with the agreement of 60 percent of the members and the recommendation of the president.

Removal from office: Removed by the president, for common crimes, incompetence, negligence, abuse of power.

Term of office: Five years (reappointment possible)

Human Rights Ombudsman

Name: Procuraduría para la Defensa de los Derechos Humanos
Institutional relationship: None
Authority: Make recommendations; promote human rights and guarantees; monitor and control the administration.

Appointment of director: Appointed by the national assembly with the agreement of 60 percent of the members and the recommendation of pertinent civil associations

Removal from office: Removed by the national assembly with the agreement of 60 percent of the members and by way of debate and prior appearance by the Procurador.

Term of office: Five years (reappointment possible)

Direct Democracy Mechanisms

Popular consultation: Yes
Popular legislative initiative: Yes
Recall: No

Panama

Electoral Systems

Presidential election system: Plurality
Presidential term and reelection: Five years; Alternating reelection after two presidential terms (10 years) have passed
Timing of presidential and legislative elections: Simultaneous
Unicameral/Bicameral legislature: Unicameral
Legislative terms: 5 years
Legislative election system: Proportional representation in small districts
Size of legislative body: 72
Number of electoral districts: 40
Ballot form: Closed and unblocked lists
Average district magnitude: 1.8
Seat allocation formula: Single member districts; plurality; multiple-member districts; Hare
Effective number of parties (start, end, average) (by lower house seats): 3.7, 3.3, 3.8
Primaries for selecting presidential candidates: Regulated by electoral/political party law; in practice observed.

Funding of political parties and electoral campaigns: Mixed public and private; direct and indirect public funding both for day-to-day activities and for electoral campaigns.

Electoral management body: Tribunal Electoral. Autonomous. Three judges are appointed by each of the public powers (legislature, executive and Supreme Court).

Constitutional Powers of the President and Legislature

Package veto: Yes. Congress can override with a two-thirds majority vote of members.

Partial veto: Yes. Congress can override with a two-thirds majority vote of its members.

Decree power: Yes. The legislative assembly can concede to the executive, when solicited and when necessity demands them, extraordinary powers to be exercised during the recess of the legislative assembly. Authority cannot be delegated with respect to international treaties, the budget, or taxes.

Exclusive initiative: No provision.

Budgetary powers: The executive formulates and submits the budget. The legislative assembly can eliminate or reduce expenditures, except those for debt servicing, contractual obligations of the state and the financing of previously authorized public investments. The assembly cannot increase expenditures or include new expenditures without cabinet approval, nor increase revenues without the permission of the Contralor General. If revenues are changed or if expenditures are reduced or eliminated in some items, the legislative assembly can apply the quantities available to other expenditures or investments with cabinet approval. If not voted on by the first day of the corresponding fiscal year, the budget proposed by the executive is adopted with the decision of the cabinet. If rejected, the budget of the previous fiscal year is extended until a new budget is approved. The items in the current budget dealing with debt servicing, contractual obligations of the state and the financing of previously authorized investments are automatically approved. The legislative assembly cannot pass laws that abolish or modify those related to revenue sources without establishing new substituting revenues or increasing revenues from existing sources and without obtaining a report from the Contraloría General regarding their fiscal effectiveness.

Appointment powers: The president alone appoints and removes the cabinet ministers.

Dissolution: No provision

Censure/Removal of ministers by legislature: The legislative assembly, by simple majority, can summon any minister or director of any autonomous agency to provide verbal or written reports. The legislative assembly can censure ministers judged responsible for crimes or grave errors causing harm to the interests of the state. The vote must be proposed by at least half of the legislators and approved with the vote of two-thirds of the assembly. It is a moral sanction and does not entail removal of minister.

Impeachment of the president: The president can be held accountable for: exceeding his constitutional authority; acts of violence or coercion in the electoral process, for impeding the meeting of the legislative assembly or other public agencies; and for crimes against the international persona of the state or against the public administration. For the first two, the penalty is removal and prevention from assuming another public position for a period of time defined by law. For the third, common law applies.

Supreme Court/Constitutional Tribunal

Role/Authority: Determines the constitutionality of laws, decrees, agreements, resolutions and other acts and resolves cases involving the national government; preventative and a posteriori control.

Constitutional Tribunal: No

Appointment of judges: Appointed by the cabinet, subject to the approval of the legislative assembly.

Number of judges: Nine

Tenure: 10 years

Procedure for bringing matters before the court/tribunal: Cases may be brought by the President when preventative and any citizen when a posteriori.

Effect of ruling: General reach

Accountability Agencies

Supreme Audit Institution

Name: Contraloría General de la República

Institutional relationship: None

Authority: Can establish fiscal responsibility for improper management of public funds (*juicio de cuentas*)

Appointment of director: Appointed by the legislative assembly.

Removal from office: Removed by the Supreme Court for reasons defined by the law.

Term of office: Equal to that of the president (reappointment possible).

Attorney General Office/Public Prosecutor Office

Name: Ministerio Público

Institutional relationship: Judiciary

Authority: Promotion of justice; investigation and prosecution; defense of the state/society; protection of constitutional rights; monitor and control the administration; provision of legal counsel to administrative officials; accusation of public officials.

Appointment of director: Appointed by the cabinet, subject to the approval of the legislative assembly.

Removal from office: Removed by the Supreme Court for common crimes.

Term of office: 10 years (reappointment possible)

Human Rights Ombudsman

Name: Defensoría del Pueblo

Institutional relationship: None

Authority: Make recommendations; initiate and carry out investigations; receive citizen complaints; promote human rights and guarantees.

Appointment of director: Appointed by the president on the recommendation of the legislative assembly; candidates selected by a human rights commission.

Removal from office: Removed by the Supreme Court for physical or mental incapacity, negligence or common crimes.

Term of office: Five years (one time reappointment)

Direct Democracy Mechanisms

Popular consultation: No

Popular legislative initiative: Yes

Recall: Yes

Paraguay

Electoral Systems

Presidential election system: Plurality

Presidential term and reelection: Five years; reelection prohibited.

Timing of presidential and legislative elections: Simultaneous

Unicameral/Bicameral legislature: Bicameral

Legislative terms: Lower house: five years; Upper house: five years

Legislative election system: Lower house: proportional representation in medium sized districts; Upper house: proportional representation in large national district.

Size of legislative bodies: Lower house: 80; Upper house: 45

Number of electoral districts: Lower house: 18; Upper house: 18

Ballot form: Lower house: closed and blocked lists; Upper house: closed and blocked lists

Average district magnitude: Lower house: 4.4; Upper house: 45

Seat allocation formula: Lower house: d'Hondt; Upper house: d'Hondt

Effective number of parties (start, end, average) (by lower house seats): 1.9, 2.3, 2.2

Primaries for selecting presidential candidates: Regulated by electoral and/or political party law; in practice observed.

Funding of political parties and electoral campaigns: Mixed public and private; direct and indirect public funding both for day-to-day activities and for electoral campaigns.

Electoral management body: Tribunal Superior de Justicia Electoral. Autonomous. Three members appointed by the senate based on a list of nominees from the magistrate council (Consejo de la magistratura) and the agreement of the executive.

Constitutional Powers of the President and Legislature

Package veto: Yes. Congress can override with an absolute majority vote in each house.

Partial veto: Yes. Congress can override with an absolute majority vote in each house.

Decree power: Yes. The president may issue a decree which, in order to be valid, must be countersigned by the respective minister.

Exclusive initiative: No provision.

Budgetary powers: The executive is responsible for submitting the budget. The congress acts without constitutional restrictions in modifying the budget. If the legislature rejects the budget proposal the budget of the previous year remains in effect until a new budget is presented and approved.

Popular consultation/Popular legislative initiative: Legislative referenda do not have to be binding. Congress decides if the referendum is merely consultative or if it will be binding. The initiative for bringing a proposal to call a referendum can be taken by the executive, five senators or 10 deputies. The procedure followed is the constitutional procedure for the formation and approval of laws. The following cannot be matters of referendum: international relations issues, international treaties or agreements, expropriations, national defense, limitation of real estate property, tax, monetary or banking issues, contracting of loans by the state, the budget, elections. Constitutional amendments must be approved by both chambers of Congress and later by a popular referendum.

Appointment powers: The president alone appoints and removes the cabinet ministers.

Dissolution: No provision

Censure/Removal of ministers by legislature: Each chamber by an absolute majority of their members can summon and interpellate ministers. If the minister does not appear before the chamber or if the chamber considers his declarations to be unsatisfactory, they can censure with two-thirds of the total membership of the chamber and recommend his removal from office. The censure does not bring the immediate removal of the minister. The president must accept the recommendation for removal.

Impeachment of the president: The president is subject to political judgement for bad performance of his functions, offenses committed in the execution of duties or for common crimes. The accusation is made by the chamber of deputies by a two-thirds majority and passed for judgment to the senate. To find the president guilty the senate must accept the accusation with a two-thirds majority. In the case of supposed commission of offenses, it is passed on to ordinary justice.

Supreme Court/Constitutional Tribunal

Role/Authority: Has constitutional authority over laws, executive decrees, regulations, administrative resolutions, judicial resolutions and sentences and others normative provisions; *a posteriori* control.

Constitutional Tribunal: No

Appointment of judges: Appointed by the senate with agreement of the executive based on a list of nominees from the Consejo de la Magistratura.

Number of judges: Nine

Tenure: Indefinite until 75 years of age.

Procedure for bringing matters before the court/tribunal: Cases may be brought by any citizen.

Effect of ruling: Specific reach.

Accountability Agencies

Supreme Audit Institution

Name: Contraloría General de la República
Institutional relationship: Congress
Authority: Monitors and reports on the execution of the national budget, the budget of state agencies and departments and other public entities; can issue recommendations and observations, receive citizen complaints, and denounce misconduct.
Appointment of director: Appointed by the chamber of deputies with an absolute majority, from a list of three candidates proposed by the senate.
Removal from office: Removed by the senate based on the accusation of the chamber of deputies and the agreement of two-thirds of the members for bad performance, offenses in the exercising of functions or common crimes.
Term of office: Five years (one time reappointment)

Attorney General Office/Public Prosecutor Office

Name: Ministerio Público
Institutional relationship: Judiciary (operational independence)
Authority: Promotion of public and social justice; prosecution; defense of the state/society; protection of constitutional rights.
Appointment of director: Appointed by the executive, with the agreement of the senate on the basis of a list proposed by the Consejo de la Magistratura.
Removal from office: Removed by the senate based on the accusation of the chamber of deputies and the agreement of two-thirds of the members for bad performance, offenses in the exercising of functions or common crimes.
Term of office: Five years (reappointment possible)

Human Rights Ombudsman

Name: Defensoría del Pueblo
Institutional relationship: Parliamentary commission; autonomous.
Authority: Make recommendations; initiate and carry out investigations; receive citizen complaints; promote human rights; public censure.
Appointment of director: Appointed by the chamber of deputies with the agreement of two-thirds of the members and recommendation of the senate.
Removal from office: Removed by the senate based on the accusation of the chamber of deputies and the agreement of two-thirds of the members for bad performance, offenses in the exercising of functions or common crimes.
Term of office: Five years (reappointment possible)

Direct Democracy Mechanisms

Popular consultation: Yes
Popular legislative initiative: Yes
Recall: No

Peru

Electoral Systems

Presidential election system: Majority runoff. If no candidate receives an absolute majority (50 percent + 1), a second-round runoff election is held.
Presidential term and reelection: Five years; one immediate reelection after which one presidential term must pass before the individual can be reelected again.
Timing of presidential and legislative elections: Simultaneous
Unicameral/Bicameral legislature: Unicameral
Legislative terms: Five years
Legislative election system: Proportional representation in large districts
Size of legislative bodies: 120
Number of electoral districts: 25
Ballot form: Closed and unblocked lists; two preference votes
Average district magnitude: 4.8
Seat allocation formula: d'Hondt
Effective number of parties (start, end, average) (by lower house seats): 2.5, 4.0, 3.5
Primaries for selecting presidential candidates: Not regulated; not practiced.
Funding of political parties and electoral campaigns: Mixed public and private; only indirect public funding only for electoral campaigns.
Electoral management body: Electoral organization: Oficina Nacional de Procesos Electorales; autonomous; director appointed by the Consejo Nacional de la Magistratura. Jurisdictional aspects of the electoral processes: Jurado Nacional de Elecciones; autonomous; five members (one appointed by the Supreme Court, one by the Junta de Fiscales Supremo, one by the Colegio de Abogados de Lima, one by the deans of the law faculties of the public universities and one by the deans of the law faculties of the private universities. Electoral registrar: Registro Nacional de Identificación y Estado Civil; autonomous; director appointed by the Consejo Nacional de la Magistratura.

Constitutional Powers of the President and Legislature

Package veto: Yes. Congress can override with an absolute majority of congress membership.
Partial veto: Yes. Congress can override with an absolute majority of congress membership.
Decree power: Yes. The president may dictate extraordinary measures through urgency decrees with the force of law regarding economic and financial matters when required by national interest. Congress may delegate authority to the president to issue decrees with the force of law. All decrees are subject to approval by a majority vote in the council of minis-

ters. If Congress does not pass the budget bill by November 30, the president promulgates the budget by decree.

Exclusive initiative: The executive is responsible exclusively for treaties and agreements and the Cuenta General.

Budgetary powers: The executive is responsible for submitting the budget. If not approved by November 30, the executive's budget proposal enters into effect. Congress cannot create or increase public spending with respect to its own budget.

Appointment powers: The president alone appoints and removes the cabinet ministers.

Dissolution: The president can dissolve the congress if it has censured or denied confidence in two or more cabinet ministers. Congress cannot be dissolved during the last year of the president's mandate or during a state of emergency.

Censure/Removal of ministers by legislature: Any congressional representative can request in writing that ministers provide reports that are thought to be necessary. The motion of censure against the cabinet or any minister must be presented by at least 25 percent of the members of congress. An absolute majority vote by congress is required. The cabinet minister should resign and the president accept the resignation within 72 hours.

Impeachment of the president: The permanent commission of congress makes the accusation against the president and congress can suspend or disqualify him from exercising a public position for up to 10 years or remove him from his position without prejudice to any other responsibility. The president can only be accused of treason, impeding presidential, parliamentary, regional or municipal elections, dissolving congress (except in the cases foreseen in Article 134 of the constitution) and impeding the meeting or functioning of congress, the national elections body or other electoral system organizations.

Supreme Court/Constitutional Tribunal

Role/Authority: Exercises authority over constitutional rights through protective action, habeas corpus and popular actions; highest court of appeals; a posteriori control.

Constitutional tribunal: Yes; a posteriori control.

Appointment of judges: Supreme Court: appointed by the Consejo de la Magistratura; Constitutional Tribunal: appointed by congress with the agreement of two-thirds of the members.

Number of judges: Supreme Court: 18; Constitutional Tribunal: 7

Tenure: Supreme Court: seven years with possibility of reelection; Constitutional Tribunal: five years

Procedure for bringing matters before the court/tribunal: Supreme Court: cases may be brought by the individual in question or his/her representative; Constitutional Tribunal: cases may be brought by the president, the Fiscal de la Nación, the Defensor del Pueblo; 25 percent of congress, 5,000 citizens, the president of the region or specialists

Effect of ruling: Supreme Court: specific reach; Constitutional Tribunal: general reach.

Accountability Agencies

Supreme Audit Institution

Name: Contraloría General de la República

Institutional relationship: Decentralized entity; constitutionally autonomous.
Authority: Can establish legal and administrative responsibility for improper management of public funds, issue recommendations and observations and receive citizen complaints.
Appointment of director: Appointed by congress at the recommendation of the president.
Removal from office: Removed by the congress for constitutional infractions or offenses committed in the exercising of functions
Term of office: Seven years (reappointment possible).

Attorney General Office/Public Prosecutor Office

Name: Ministerio Público
Institutional Relationship: None
Authority: Promotion of justice and morality; investigation and prosecution; defense of the state/society; protection of rights; assistance to and protection of the vulnerable; monitor and control the judiciary; provision of legal counsel to administrative officials; accusation of public officials.
Appointment of director: Appointed by the Junta de Fiscales Supremos.
Removal from office: Removed by the congress for constitutional infractions or offenses committed in the exercising of functions
Term of office: Three years (extendable for two years)

Human Rights Ombudsman

Name: Defensoría del Pueblo
Institutional relationship: None; must present budget to the executive.
Authority: Make recommendations; propose measures and reforms.
Appointment of director: Appointed by congress with the agreement of two-thirds of the members.
Removal from office: Removed by the congress for a constitutional infractions or offenses committed in the exercising of functions
Term of office: Five years (one time reappointment)

Direct Democracy Mechanisms

Popular consultation: Yes
Popular legislative initiative: Yes
Recall: No

Uruguay

Electoral Systems

Presidential election system: Majority runoff. If no candidate receives an absolute majority, a second-round runoff election is held.

Presidential term and reelection: Five years; alternating reelection after at least five years has passed.

Timing of presidential and legislative elections: Simultaneous

Unicameral/Bicameral legislature: Bicameral

Legislative terms: Lower house: five years; Upper house: five years

Legislative election system: Lower house: proportional representation at national level, but legislators are elected from districts; upper house: Proportional representation in large national district.

Size of legislative bodies: Lower house: 99; Upper house: 30

Number of electoral districts: Lower house: 19; Upper house: 1

Ballot form: Lower house: closed and blocked lists; Upper house: closed and blocked subparty lists

Average district magnitude: Lower house: seats allocated according to national vote totals; Upper House: 30

Seat allocation formula: Lower house: modified d'Hondt; Upper house: d'Hondt

Effective number of parties (start, end, average) (by lower house seats): 2.9, 3.1, 3.2

Primaries for selecting presidential candidates: Mandated by the constitution; in practice observed.

Funding of political parties and electoral campaigns: Mixed public and private; direct and indirect public funding only for electoral campaigns.

Electoral management body: Corte Electoral. Autonomous. Nine members (five "neutrals" appointed by a two-thirds majority of a joint session of the general assembly (house and senate) and four party representatives, according to electoral results.

Constitutional Powers of the President and Legislature

Package veto: Yes. Congress can override with a vote of three-fifths of members present in each house.

Partial veto: Yes. Congress can override with a vote of three-fifths of members present in each house.

Decree power: No. The president may declare legislation introduced by the executive as urgent. If no vote has been taken by congress within 45 days, it becomes law; if one chamber approves the bill in a different form the time period is extended by 20 days and the modified version becomes law if the other chamber does not act. The president may not send more than one "urgent" measure at a time or send additional urgent measures while one is still under consideration.

Exclusive initiative: Bills that create or eliminate taxes or fix minimum wages or prices are the exclusive responsibility of the executive.

Budgetary powers: The legislature cannot increase spending, but can only change it between budgetary items. The legislature can only make decisions with regard to the overall expenditures per item, program, salary scale, number of officials and resources, but cannot increase spending over the levels proposed. The executive formulates and submits the budget within the first six months of its mandate. It is in effect for the government's entire mandate. If it is modified in the second chamber, it returns to the first. If the modifications are rejected, it passes to the general assembly. If time periods are not met, the budget is considered rejected and the previous budget remains in effect.

Appointment powers: The president alone appoints and removes the cabinet ministers.

Dissolution: The president can dissolve the congress if less than 60 percent of legislators upheld the censure of a cabinet minister(s).

Censure/Removal of ministers by legislature: Either chamber can propose a censure motion with the absolute majority support of those present. The motion must be approved by an absolute majority. If approved by less than a two-thirds majority, the president can refuse to dismiss the minister in question. The vote has to be repeated and the president can dissolve congress if less than 60 percent of legislators upheld the censure.

Impeachment of the president: The chamber of representatives, by majority vote can accuse the president before the senate of violating the constitution or other serious offenses. The senate holds a public trial and must produce a two-thirds majority vote to find responsibility and to remove from the president from office.

Supreme Court/Constitutional Tribunal

Role/Authority: Has jurisdictional control over all national laws and departmental decrees; a posteriori control.

Constitutional Tribunal: No

Appointment of judges: Appointed by the general assembly with a two-thirds majority vote of all members.

Number of judges: Five

Tenure: 10 years or until 70 years of age, whichever comes first.

Procedure for bringing matters before the court/tribunal: Cases may be brought by any individual affected, including judges.

Effect of ruling: Specific reach to the parties to the case.

Accountability Agencies

Supreme Audit Institution

Name: Tribunal de Cuentas de la República

Institutional relationship: Legislature, but with functional autonomy.

Authority: Can intervene preventatively in ensuring the conformity with the law of expenditures and payments. Can issue recommendations and observations and denounce cases of irregularity or mismanagement of funds.

Appointment of members: Seven members appointed by the two houses of congress in joint session with a two-thirds majority vote of the members.

Removal from office: Accused by the lower house before the upper house, where a two-thirds majority is necessary for removal.

Term of office: Five years (reappointment possible).

Attorney General Office/Public Prosecutor Office

Name: Ministerio Público y Fiscal

Institutional relationship: Executive (technical independence)

Authority: Promotion of justice; defense of the state/society; protection of rights and liberties; provision of legal counsel to the executive and the Junta Asesora Anticorrupción.

Appointment of director: Appointed by the executive with the consent of three-fifths of the senate or permanent commission.

Removal from office: Removed by the executive with the agreement of the senate or the permanent commission, for ineptitude, negligence or common crimes

Term of office: Indefinite

Human Rights Ombudsman

None.

Direct Democracy Mechanisms

Popular consultation: Yes
Popular legislative initiative: Yes
Recall: No

Venezuela

Electoral Systems

Presidential election system: Plurality

Presidential term and reelection: Six years; immediate one-time reelection

Timing of presidential and legislative elections: Not simultaneous. Legislative elections every five years and presidential elections every six years.

Unicameral/Bicameral legislature: Unicameral

Legislative terms: Five years

Legislative election system: Personalized proportional representation

Size of legislative bodies: 165

Number of electoral districts: 24

Ballot form: Candidate in single member districts and closed and blocked lists

Average district magnitude: 6.1

Seat allocation formula: d'Hondt

Effective number of parties (start, end, average) (by lower house seats): 2.6, 3.4, 3.7

Primaries for selecting presidential candidates: Regulated by constitutional law; electoral/political party law regulation pending; not yet practiced. The prevailing interpretation has been that the constitution does not require primaries.

Funding of political parties and electoral campaigns: Only private funding.

Electoral management body: Consejo Nacional Electoral. Autonomous. Five members not involved with political organizations. Three are elected by civil society, one by the political science and law faculties of the national universities, and one by the civic power. As of the end of the period of the study, this procedure had yet to be put into operation. The current Consejo Nacional Electoral was appointed by a provisional legislative body in June 2000.

Constitutional Powers of the President and Legislature

Package veto: Yes. Congress can override with an absolute majority of members present.
Partial veto: Yes. Congress can override with an absolute majority of members present.
Decree power: Yes. The president is empowered to dictate, upon authorization by an enabling law, decrees with the force of law.
Exclusive initiative: The executive is responsible for submitting the law on public indebtedness.
Budgetary powers: The national assembly can alter budget items but cannot authorize measures that lead to the reduction of public revenues or to expenditures that exceed the revenue estimates of the budget proposal. There can be no expenditure that has not been foreseen in the budget law. Additional credits can only be allowed for necessary expenditures not foreseen and only if the treasury has the necessary resources to cover the expenditure. The cabinet must vote in favor of the expenditure, which must then be approved by the national assembly.
Appointment powers: The president alone appoints and removes the cabinet ministers.
Dissolution: The president can dissolve congress if it has censured or denied confidence in the vice president three times.
Censure/Removal of ministers by legislature: The national assembly can exercise its control function through the following: interpellations, investigations, questions, authorizations, and parliamentary approvals. The assembly or its commissions can carry out investigations deemed relevant to matters of their competence. Public officials are obligated to appear before the commission if summoned and provide the requested information. The national assembly can vote by special majorities to censure the vice president (two-thirds) and government ministers (three-fifths). If so voted, the minister should resign.
Impeachment of the president: The Supreme Court decides if there is merit for a trial/prosecution of the president. The national assembly must authorize such a trial by a simple majority. If authorized, the Supreme Court continues until it makes a definitive ruling. It can call for the removal of the president.

Supreme Court/Constitutional Tribunal

Role/Authority: Has constitutional authority over laws, acts, executive decrees, regulations, state laws and municipal ordinances, international treaties; a posteriori control.
Constitutional Tribunal: No (Sala Constitutional within the Supreme Court)
Appointment of judges: Appointed by the national assembly from a list of three candidates presented by a judicial candidate committee.
Number of judges: 20
Tenure: 12 years
Procedure for bringing matters before the court/tribunal: Not defined.
Effect of ruling: General reach

Accountability Agencies

Supreme Audit Institution

Name: Contraloría General de la República
Institutional relationship: Civic power (operational and organizational independence)
Authority: Monitors and controls revenues, expenditures, assets as well as management of public funds. Can initiate investigations of irregularities in relation to use of public property and can dictate measures, impose reparations, and apply administrative sanctions. Brings to the attention of prosecuting authorities any crimes committed in the use of public resources. Issues recommendations and observations and receive citizen complaints.
Appointment of director: Appointed by the national assembly from a list of three candidates presented by a candidate evaluation committee of the civic power and with the agreement of two-thirds of its members. If no decision is made after 30 days, the decision will be put to a referendum.
Removal from office: Removed by the national assembly with the prior decision of the Supreme Court.
Term of office: Seven years (no reappointment)

Attorney General Office/Public Prosecutor Office

Name: Ministerio Público
Institutional relationship: Civic power
Authority: Promotion of justice and morality; investigation, prosecution and sentencing; defense of the State/society; protection of rights; assistance to and protection of the vulnerable; monitor and control the judiciary; supervision of public officials.
Appointment of director: Appointed by the national assembly from a list of three candidates presented by a candidate evaluation committee of the civic power and with the agreement of two-thirds of its members. If no decision is made after 30 days, the decision will be put to a referendum.
Removal from office: Removed by the national assembly with the prior decision of the Supreme Court
Term of office: Seven years (reappointment possible)

Human Rights Ombudsman

Name: Defensoría del Pueblo
Institutional relationship: Civic power (operational and financial independence)
Authority: Make recommendations and observations· initiate and carry out investigations; receive citizen complaints; defend and promote human rights and guarantees; propose laws; discipline public officials.
Appointment of director: Appointed by the national assembly from a list of three candidates presented by a candidate evaluation committee of the civic power and with the agreement

of two-thirds of its members. If no decision is made after 30 days, the decision will be put to a referendum.

Removal from office: Removed by the national assembly with the prior decision of the Supreme Court.

Term of office: Seven years (no reappointment).

Direct Democracy Mechanisms

Popular consultation: Yes
Popular legislative initiative: Yes
Recall: Yes

Electoral Turnout in Latin America, 1978–2000

Argentina					
Year	Election	Registered voters	Total votes	Total votes/ Registered	Total votes/VAP	Blank and invalid votes/ Total votes
1983	Presidential	17,809,598	15,324,251	86.04	81.18	3.70
1983	Legislative	17,809,598	15,305,795	85.94	81.08	2.97
1985	Legislative	18,460,189	15,793,050	85.55	81.17	2.97
1987	Legislative	19,112,829	16,455,912	86.10	82.02	2.54
1989	Presidential	20,258,136	17,086,704	84.34	82.55	2.72
1989	Legislative	20,258,136	17,086,704	84.34	82.55	2.60
1991	Legislative	20,767,707	17,046,386	82.08	79.80	9.31
1993	Legislative	21,457,238	17,323,981	80.74	78.56	5.56
1995	Presidential	22,160,325	18,168,999	81.99	79.79	8.14
1995	Legislative	22,160,325	18,203,452	82.14	79.94	6.86
1997	Legislative	23,174,271	18,467,794	79.69	78.53	7.90
1999	Presidential	24,109,306	19,755,024	81.94	81.32	5.64
1999	Legislative	24,109,306	18,953,456	78.61	78.02	3.80

Bolivia

Year	Election	Registered voters	Total votes	Total votes/ Registered	Total votes/VAP	Blank and invalid votes/ Total votes
1980	Presidential	2,004,284	1,489,484	74.32	55.85	12.11
1980	Legislative	2,004,284	1,489,484	74.32	55.85	12.11
1985	Presidential	2,108,458	1,728,365	81.97	57.00	12.98
1985	Legislative	2,108,458	1,728,365	81.97	57.00	12.98
1989	Presidential	2,136,587	1,573,790	73.66	46.50	10.03
1989	Legislative	2,136,587	1,573,790	73.66	46.50	10.03
1993	Presidential	2,399,197	1,731,309	72.16	45.69	4.83
1993	Legislative	2,399,197	1,731,309	72.16	45.69	4.83
1997	Presidential	3,252,501	2,321,117	71.36	54.63	6.20
1997	Legislative	3,252,501	2,316,198	71.21	54.52	10.88

Brazil

Year	Election	Registered voters	Total votes	Total votes/ Registered	Total votes/VAP	Blank and invalid votes/ Total votes
1986	Legislative	68,576,451	65,133,227	94.98	76.66	28.27
1989	Presidential I	82,056,226	72,277,408	88.08	78.88	6.45
1989	Presidential II	82,056,226	70,250,194	85.61	76.66	5.83
1990	Legislative	83,820,556	71,940,913	85.83	76.61	43.71
1994	Presidential	94,743,043	77,920,633	82.24	75.47	18.78
1994	Legislative	94,743,043	77,660,795	81.97	75.21	41.16
1998	Presidential	106,101,067	83,290,705	78.50	73.71	18.70
1998	Legislative	106,101,067	83,282,476	78.49	73.70	20.03

Chile

Year	Election	Registered voters	Total votes	Total votes/ Registered	Total votes/VAP	Blank and invalid votes/ Total votes
1989	Presidential	7,557,537	7,158,727	94.72	87.25	2.50
1989	Legislative	7,557,537	7,158,646	94.72	87.25	5.05
1993	Presidential	8,085,439	7,383,286	91.32	82.95	5.61
1993	Legislative	8,085,439	7,385,016	91.34	82.97	8.75
1997	Legislative	8,069,624	7,046,351	87.32	73.29	17.75
1999	Presidential I	8,084,476	7,271,572	89.94	72.87	2.98
1999	Presidential II	8,084,476	7,326,753	90.63	73.43	2.16

Colombia

Year	Election	Registered voters	Total votes	Total votes/ Registered	Total votes/VAP	Blank and invalid votes/ Total votes
1978	Presidential	12,580,851	5,075,719	40.34	36.18	.35
1978	Legislative	12,580,851	4,180,121	33.23	29.80	.22
1982	Presidential	13,734,093	6,840,362	49.81	43.00	.36
1982	Legislative	13,734,093	5,584,037	40.66	35.10	.19
1986	Presidential	15,839,754	7,229,937	45.64	40.34	.70
1986	Legislative	15,839,754	6,909,838	43.62	38.56	.36
1990	Presidential	13,903,324	6,035,039	43.41	30.08	1.83
1990	Legislative	13,779,188	7,631,691	55.39	38.03	.38
1991	Legislative	15,037,528	5,486,540	36.49	26.60	12.75
1994	Presidential I	17,147,023	5,821,331	33.95	26.05	1.16
1994	Presidential II	17,147,023	7,427,742	43.32	33.24	1.58
1994	Legislative	17,028,961	5,576,174	32.75	24.96	16.34
1998	Presidential I	20,857,801	10,751,465	51.55	43.43	2.28
1998	Presidential II	20,857,801	12,310,107	59.02	49.73	4.36
1998	Legislative	20,767,388	9,471,113	45.61	38.26	10.77

Costa Rica

Year	Election	Registered voters	Total votes	Total votes/ Registered	Total votes/VAP	Blank and invalid votes/ Total votes
1978	Presidential	1,058,455	860,206	81.27	76.00	3.38
1978	Legislative	1,058,455	859,888	81.24	75.97	4.57
1982	Presidential	1,261,127	991,679	78.63	74.91	2.53
1982	Legislative	1,261,127	991,545	78.62	74.90	3.59
1986	Presidential	1,486,474	1,261,300	84.85	81.94	6.03
1986	Legislative	1,486,474	1,216,051	81.81	79.00	3.61
1990	Presidential	1,692,050	1,384,326	81.81	77.85	2.55
1990	Legislative	1,692,050	1,383,956	81.79	77.83	3.45
1994	Presidential	1,881,348	1,525,979	81.11	74.78	2.35
1994	Legislative	1,881,348	1,525,624	81.09	74.77	2.53
1998	Presidential	2,045,980	1,431,913	69.99	61.55	3.02
1998	Legislative	2,045,980	1,430,579	69.92	61.50	3.29

Dominican Republic

Year	Election	Registered voters	Total[1] votes	Total votes/ Registered	Total votes/VAP	Blank and invalid votes/ Total votes
1978	Presidential	2,283,784	1,655,807	72.50	60.81	na
1978	Legislative	2,283,784	1,645,565	72.05	60.44	na
1982	Presidential	2,601,684	1,922,367	73.89	61.73	3.72
1982	Legislative	2,601,684	1,807,094	69.46	58.03	na
1986	Presidential	3,039,347	2,111,938	69.49	59.78	na
1986	Legislative	3,039,347	2,112,101	69.49	59.78	na
1990	Presidential	3,275,570	1,958,509	59.79	49.22	1.22
1990	Legislative	3,275,570	1,840,553	56.19	46.26	3.00
1994	Presidential	3,598,328	3,015,750	83.81	67.73	na
1994	Legislative	3,598,328	3,015,750	83.81	67.73	na
1996	Presidential I	3,750,502	2,903,859	77.43	61.80	na
1996	Presidential II	3,750,502	2,880,425	76.80	61.30	.67
1998	Legislative	4,129,564	2,093,686	50.70	42.27	.59
2000	Presidential	4,251,218	3,236,906	76.14	62.09	1.30

[1]Valid votes in 1986, 1994, and 1996 for presidential legislative elections. In 1996, valid votes are used for the first round of the presidential elections, while total votes are used for the second round.

Ecuador

Year	Election	Registered voters	Total votes	Total votes/ Registered	Total votes/VAP	Blank and invalid votes/ Total votes
1978	Presidential I	2,088,874	1,700,175	81.39	44.85	19.04
1979	Presidential II	2,088,874	1,691,274	80.97	44.61	11.50
1979	Legislative (provincial)	2,088,874	1,678,924	80.37	44.29	14.62
1979	Legislative (national)	2,088,874	1,675,195	80.20	44.19	14.11
1984	Presidential I	3,590,729	2,646,844	73.71	57.37	16.59
1984	Presidential II	3,590,729	2,964,298	82.55	64.25	9.56
1984	Legislative (national)	3,590,729	2,636,656	73.43	57.15	na
1984	Legislative (provincial)	3,590,729	2,656,884	73.99	57.59	na
1986	Legislative (provincial)	4,255,346	3,149,690	74.02	63.98	na
1988	Presidential I	4,673,980	3,630,615	77.68	69.17	16.25
1988	Presidential II	4,673,980	3,611,074	77.26	68.79	12.82
1988	Legislative (national)	4,673,980	3,601,990	77.06	68.62	na
1988	Legislative (provincial)	4,673,980	3,607,581	77.18	68.73	na
1990	Legislative (provincial)	5,259,114	3,561,081	67.71	63.67	na
1992	Presidential I	5,710,363	4,090,643	71.64	68.70	16.47
1992	Presidential II	5,710,363	4,174,097	73.10	70.10	10.27
1992	Legislative (national)	5,710,363	4,057,116	71.05	68.13	20.60
1992	Legislative (provincial)	5,710,363	4,056,337	71.03	68.12	21.04
1994	Legislative (provincial)	6,175,991	4,044,433	65.49	63.86	23.94
1996	Presidential I	6,662,003	4,525,881	67.94	67.25	15.82
1996	Presidential II	6,662,003	4,777,547	71.71	70.99	12.17
1996	Legislative (national)	6,662,003	4,521,207	67.87	67.18	22.06
1996	Legislative (provincial)	6,662,003	4,516,197	67.79	67.11	21.88
1998	Presidential I	7,072,496	4,537,822	64.16	63.52	15.29
1998	Presidential II	7,072,496	4,960,075	70.13	69.43	11.62
1998	Legislative (provincial)	7,072,496	3,341,902	47.25	46.78	na

El Salvador

Year	Election	Registered voters	Total votes	Total votes/ Registered	Total votes/VAP	Blank and invalid votes/ Total votes
1984	Presidential I	na	1,419,503	na	60.45	10.79
1984	Presidential II	na	1,524,079	na	64.90	7.85
1985	Legislative	na	1,101,606	na	45.74	12.38
1988	Legislative	1,600,000	1,083,812	67.74	41.62	14.12
1989	Presidential	1,834,000	1,003,153	54.70	37.52	6.39
1991	Legislative	2,180,000	1,153,013	52.89	40.87	8.81
1994	Presidential I	2,821,002	1,411,320	50.03	46.11	7.35
1994	Presidential II	2,821,002	1,246,220	44.18	40.71	3.93
1994	Legislative	2,821,002	1,453,299	51.52	47.48	7.43
1997	Legislative	3,004,174	1,162,126	38.68	34.98	3.66
1999	Presidential	3,171,224	1,223,215	38.57	34.85	3.35
2000	Legislative	3,264,724	1,242,842	38.07	34.46	4.85

Guatemala

Year	Election	Registered voters	Total votes	Total votes/ Registered	Total votes/VAP	Blank and invalid votes/ Total votes
1985	Presidential I	2,753,572	1,907,771	69.28	52.17	11.99
1985	Presidential II	2,753,572	1,800,324	65.38	49.23	7.92
1985	Legislative	2,753,572	1,904,236	69.16	52.07	12.58
1990	Legislative	3,204,955	1,801,596	56.21	42.79	10.92
1990	Presidential I	3,204,955	1,808,718	56.44	42.96	14.07
1991	Presidential II	3,204,955	1,450,603	45.26	34.45	5.18
1994	Legislative	3,480,196	730,724	21.00	15.48	11.20
1995	Legislative	3,711,589	1,666,328	44.90	34.31	12.69
1995	Presidential I	3,711,589	1,737,033	46.80	35.77	10.83
1996	Presidential II	3,711,589	1,368,830	36.88	28.19	4.24
1999	Presidential I	4,458,744	2,397,212	53.76	44.07	8.58
1999	Presidential II	4,458,744	1,800,676	40.39	33.10	3.64
1999	Legislative	4,458,744	2,395,627	53.73	44.04	11.20

Honduras

Year	Election	Registered voters	Total votes	Total votes/ Registered	Total votes/VAP	Blank and invalid votes/ Total votes
1981	Presidential	1,588,316	1,214,735	76.48	72.21	2.85
1981	Legislative	1,588,316	1,214,735	76.48	72.21	2.85
1985	Presidential	1,901,757	1,598,247	84.04	81.99	3.50
1985	Legislative	1,901,757	1,598,247	84.04	81.99	3.50
1989	Presidential	2,368,293	1,799,146	75.97	79.57	2.53
1989	Legislative	2,368,293	1,799,146	75.97	79.57	2.53
1993	Presidential	2,734,121	1,776,204	64.96	67.85	3.69
1993	Legislative	2,734,121	1,776,204	64.96	67.85	3.69
1997	Presidential	2,901,743	2,091,733	72.09	69.27	5.48
1997	Legislative	2,901,743	2,084,411	71.83	69.03	8.92

Mexico

Year	Election	Registered voters	Total votes	Total votes/ Registered	Total votes/VAP	Blank and invalid votes/ Total votes
1979	Legislative (PR)	27,912,053	23,726,319	85.00	74.71	na
1979	Legislative (plurality)	27,937,237	23,782,382	85.13	74.89	na
1982	Presidential	31,526,386	23,592,888	74.84	67.45	4.47
1982	Legislative (PR)	31,516,370	22,866,719	72.56	65.38	4.90
1982	Legislative (plurality)	31,520,884	20,919,880	66.37	59.81	na
1985	Legislative (PR)	35,278,369	18,281,851	51.82	47.51	5.09
1985	Legislative (plurality)	35,278,369	17,879,924	50.68	46.46	4.70
1988	Presidential	38,074,926	19,106,176	50.18	45.20	na
1988	Legislative (PR)	38,074,926	18,820,415	49.43	44.52	3.30
1988	Legislative (plurality)	38,074,926	18,109,221	47.56	42.84	na
1991	Legislative (PR)	36,676,167	24,149,001	65.84	52.10	4.18
1991	Legislative (plurality)	36,676,167	24,032,482	65.53	51.85	4.36
1994	Presidential	45,729,057	35,285,291	77.16	69.58	2.86
1994	Legislative (PR)	45,729,057	34,811,903	76.13	68.64	3.66
1994	Legislative (plurality)	45,729,057	34,686,916	75.85	68.40	3.66
1997	Legislative (PR)	52,208,966	30,120,221	57.69	54.41	2.84
1997	Legislative (plurality)	52,208,966	29,771,911	57.02	53.78	2.84
2000	Presidential	58,782,737	37,601,618	63.97	62.36	2.09
2000	Legislative (PR)	58,782,737	37,407,935	63.64	62.04	2.32
2000	Legislative (plurality)	58,782,737	37,165,393	63.23	61.64	2.32

Nicaragua

Year	Election	Registered voters	Total votes	Total votes/ Registered	Total votes/VAP	Blank and invalid votes/ Total votes
1990	Presidential	1,752,088	1,510,838	86.23	75.36	5.98
1990	Legislative	1,752,088	1,512,107	86.30	75.42	6.13
1996	Presidential	2,421,067	1,849,362	76.39	75.95	4.95
1996	Legislative	2,421,067	1,865,833	77.07	76.62	7.49

Panama

Year	Election	Registered voters	Total votes	Total votes/ Registered	Total votes/VAP	Blank and invalid votes/ Total votes
1989	Presidential	1,186,754	911,885	76.84	67.43	na
1994	Presidential	1,499,451	1,104,578	73.67	71.29	3.42
1994	Legislative	1,499,451	1,091,756	72.81	70.47	5.33
1999	Presidential	1,746,989	1,330,730	76.17	75.54	4.23
1999	Legislative	1,746,989	1,306,390	74.78	74.16	5.89

Paraguay

Year	Election	Registered voters	Total votes	Total votes/ Registered	Total votes/VAP	Blank and invalid votes/ Total votes
1989	Presidential	2,226,061	1,202,826	54.03	56.88	2.01
1989	Legislative	2,226,061	1,157,781	52.01	54.75	1.90
1993	Presidential	1,698,984	1,180,082	69.46	49.23	4.70
1993	Legislative	1,698,984	1,148,408	67.59	47.91	4.08
1998	Presidential	2,049,449	1,650,725	80.54	59.23	2.90
1998	Legislative	2,049,449	1,649,419	80.48	59.18	3.33

Peru

Year	Election	Registered voters	Total votes	Total votes/ Registered	Total votes/VAP	Blank and invalid votes/ Total votes
1980	Presidential	6,471,101	5,121,328	79.14	57.33	24.69
1980	Legislative	6,471,101	4,573,141	71.10	51.19	20.59
1985	Presidential	8,333,433	7,544,836	90.54	72.96	13.84
1985	Legislative	8,333,433	6,608,533	79.79	63.91	11.77
1990	Presidential I	10,013,225	7,837,116	78.27	65.88	15.25
1990	Presidential II	10,007,614	7,958,232	79.52	66.90	9.55
1990	Legislative	10,007,614	6,818,536	68.10	57.32	27.24
1995	Presidential	11,974,396	8,803,049	73.52	64.74	15.39
1995	Legislative	11,974,396	7,961,114	66.48	58.55	45.10
2000	Presidential I	14,567,468	11,816,708	81.12	76.50	8.29
2000	Presidential II	14,567,468	11,800,310	81.00	76.39	31.12
2000	Legislative	14,567,468	11,942,810	81.98	77.31	16.81

Uruguay

Year	Election	Registered voters	Total votes	Total votes/ Registered	Total votes/VAP	Blank and invalid votes/ Total votes
1984	Presidential	2,197,503	1,930,931	87.87	94.78	2.29
1984	Legislative	2,197,503	1,930,931	87.87	94.78	2.29
1989	Presidential	2,319,022	2,056,355	88.67	96.91	4.17
1989	Legislative	2,319,022	2,056,355	88.67	96.91	4.17
1994	Presidential	2,330,154	2,130,618	91.44	95.90	4.76
1994	Legislative	2,330,154	2,130,618	91.44	95.90	4.76
1999	Presidential I	2,402,160	2,192,044	91.25	93.84	2.05
1999	Presidential II	2,402,160	2,206,112	91.84	94.44	2.97
1999	Legislative	2,402,160	2,192,044	91.25	93.84	2.05

Venezuela

Year	Election	Registered voters	Total votes	Total votes/ Registered	Total votes/VAP	Blank and invalid votes/ Total votes
1978	Presidential	6,223,903	5,448,801	87.55	75.13	2.13
1978	Legislative	6,223,903	5,449,790	87.56	75.15	3.06
1983	Presidential	7,777,892	6,792,208	87.33	78.05	4.88
1983	Legislative	7,777,892	6,825,180	87.75	78.43	3.58
1988	Presidential	9,185,647	7,518,663	81.85	73.29	2.49
1988	Legislative	9,185,647	7,500,085	81.65	73.11	3.78
1993	Presidential	9,668,795	5,829,216	60.29	48.89	3.63
1993	Legislative	9,668,795	5,829,216	60.29	48.89	19.18
1998	Presidential	10,991,482	6,988,291	63.58	51.04	6.45
1998	Legislative	10,991,482	5,764,091	52.44	42.10	14.47
2000	Presidential	11,681,645	6,600,196	56.50	45.74	4.72
2000	Legislative	11,623,547	6,573,663	56.55	45.56	31.89

Results of Presidential and Legislative Elections (CD-ROM)

This CD-ROM contains national election data for the 18 Latin American countries covered in *Democracies in Development: Politics and Reform in Latin America*. Results are provided for the elections within the time period of the study, which covers 1978-2000. However, the specific period for certain countries begins at the point of the first reasonably free and fair elections following 1978.

The main file in the CD-ROM contains tables for each country showing the distribution of votes by political party for presidential elections, the distribution of votes by political party for congressional elections (lower house and upper house in the case of bicameral systems), and the distribution of legislative seats by political party. Some parties that obtained relatively few votes are excluded from the tables in the main file in order to make those tables more legible. However, a link to more detailed data tables in Microsoft Excel workbook files is provided above each of the tables in the main file. The election data in the Microsoft Excel files served as the basis for the analysis of the trends in electoral participation in Chapter Three, the properties of election systems in Chapters Four and Five, the characteristics of party systems in Chapter Six, and the partisan support for presidents in Chapter Eight.

The election data was compiled from reports or Web sites of the official electoral bodies where possible, but was also taken from secondary sources. While elections would seem to avail themselves of quantitative precision, in fact the precise vote counts are subject to revision weeks and even months after the election. This is one of the bases for variations found in the results reported in different secondary sources and even between different reports published by the official electoral bodies. As a consequence, the authors cannot guarantee the complete accuracy of the data, especially in cases where it was derived from secondary sources.